D0228799

A Moral Reckoning

The Role of the Catholic Church in the Holocaust
and Its Unfulfilled Duty of Repair

DANIEL JONAH GOLDHAGEN

LITTLE, BROWN

A *Little, Brown* Book

First published in the United States of America in 2002 by
Alfred A. Knopf
First published in Great Britain in 2002 by Little, Brown

Copyright © 2002 by Daniel Jonah Goldhagen

The moral right of the author has been asserted.

"What Would Jesus Have Done?" was originally published
in *The New Republic.*

A CIP catalogue record for this book
is available from the British Library.

ISBN 0 316 72446 7

Printed and bound in Great Britain
by Clays Ltd, St Ives plc

Little, Brown
An imprint of
Time Warner Books UK
Brettenham House
Lancaster Place
London WC2E 7EN

www.TimeWarnerBooks.co.uk

We feel We owe no greater debt to Our office and to Our time than to testify to the truth with Apostolic Firmness: "to give testimony to the truth." . . . In the fulfillment of this, Our duty, we shall not let Ourselves be influenced by earthly considerations . . .

Pius XII, Summi Pontificatus (October 20, 1939)

CONTENTS

INTRODUCTION

FRAMING
the Problem

The *Shoah* was the work of a thoroughly modern neopagan regime. Its antisemitism had its roots outside of Christianity . . .

> Holy See's Commission for Religious Relations with
> the Jews, "We Remember: A Reflection on the Shoah"
> (March 1998)

Christian anti-Judaism did lay the groundwork for racial, genocidal anti-semitism by stigmatizing not only Judaism but Jews themselves for oppro-brium and contempt. So the Nazi theories tragically found fertile soil in which to plant the horror of an unprecedented attempt at genocide.

> United States Catholic Conference, *Catholic Teaching
> on the* Shoah: *Implementing the Holy See's* We Remem-
> ber (2001)

CHRISTIANITY IS A RELIGION of love that teaches its members the highest moral principles for acting well. Love your neighbor. Seek peace. Help those in need. Sympathize with and raise up the oppressed. Do to others as you would have them do to you.

Christianity is a religion that consecrated at its core and historically, spread throughout its domain a megatherian hatred of one group of people: the Jews. It libelously deemed them, sometimes in its sacred texts and doctrine, to be Christ-killers, children of the devil, desecrators and defilers of all goodness, responsible for an enormous range of human calamities and suffering. This hatred—Christianity's betrayal of its own essential and good moral principles—led Christians, over the course of almost two millennia, to commit many grave crimes and other injuries against Jews, including mass murder. The best-known and largest of these mass murders is the Holocaust.

The question for Christians, especially for the Catholic Church, is, What must a religion of love and goodness do to confront its history of hatred and harm, to make amends with its victims, and to right itself so that it is no longer the source of a hatred and harm that, whatever its past, it would no longer endorse? This is the question also of this book.

WHO DID WHAT? Why did they do it? In what ways are they culpable? These are the three big questions of the Holocaust. In *Hitler's Willing Executioners: Ordinary Germans and the Holocaust,* I tackled the first two questions, focusing on the ordinary Germans who were the principal perpetrators of the Holocaust and showing that they slaughtered Jews because, moved by antisemitism, they believed that killing them was just, right, and necessary.[1] This was also generally true of those Lithuanians, Poles, Ukrainians, and others who participated in the mass murder. Because the book's purpose was to explain the perpetration of the Holocaust, not to judge the perpetrators, in it I stated openly that it "is a work of historical explanation, not of moral evaluation."[2] For this reason the book left untouched the third, equally explosive subject of moral culpability. It also did not take up the principal post-Holocaust questions: Who is responsible for making amends with the victims, and what must they do?

In *Hitler's Willing Executioners* I presented no explicit moral judgments about culpability and no program of repair. It was, of course, obvious that I condemn the Germans' and their helpers' eliminationist persecution and mass murder of the Jews and their persecution and slaughter of other victim groups, including the mentally ill, Roma and Sinti (commonly called Gypsies), homosexuals, "asocials," Poles, Russians. When the book appeared at the end of March 1996, those, especially in Germany, who abhorred the airing of the obscured facts and unwelcome truths that it contained attacked the book and me personally, including by leveling the fictitious charge that I was explicitly passing the moral judgment of collective guilt.[3] These attacks, many manifestly disreputable, did, however, indicate something fundamental that lay behind the large furor around the book, something that deserves our attention.

Hitler's Willing Executioners unwittingly provoked a moral uproar, and a moral subtext continually enveloped—and partly derailed—the extensive written and verbal discussion around the book. The book sought to restore to Germans their humanity, which had heretofore generally been denied them by the standard dehumanizing characterization of them as thoughtless, automatonlike cogs in a machine. It therefore challenged the existing conventional view, and pointedly insisted that Germans be seen and treated for what they were: individual moral agents. It investigated their views of Jews, and of the justness of the eliminationist persecution, including physical annihilation. It brought forth and emphasized critical information that had for long been denied, obscured, and covered up—even though some of the information had for decades been available—that so many of the perpetrators knew that they could avoid killing but chose to torture and to kill their victims, and were often demonstrably gleeful about it. It showed that the conventional notion that the German people in general were terrorized is a myth and that, exceptions notwithstanding, Germans essentially assented to the violent eliminationist persecution of the Jews. All of this, however implicitly, forcefully made unavoidable the previously widely avoided moral question: Who is culpable, in what way, and for what?

Germans and people in other countries were suddenly grappling with the problems of moral judgment in a way that many of them never had; human beings had replaced abstract structures and impersonal forces as actors, and they, Germans and others, were shown to have been animated by views that most people today abhor, and, in substantial numbers, to have willfully done terrible, criminal things. The facile moral excuses and rationalizations— that Germans had been terrorized, had not known about the crimes, and so on—that had exculpated so many people and comforted so many more were, however implicitly, exposed as hollow. Moral charges were in the morally charged air.

Because of the barrage of false views imputed to me, I wrote a foreword to the German edition of the book (since reprinted in other editions, including the English-language paperbacks) that contained the following: "Because the analysis of this book emphasizes that every individual made choices about how to treat Jews, its entire mode of analysis runs contrary to, and provides powerful argument against, any notion of collective guilt." [4] I clarified, if briefly, my views about "collective guilt," which I have always emphatically rejected, but the question of how we might judge the perpetrators and other involved people for their actions during this period—the moral issues—I left aside, so in the discussion about my book they remained mainly subterranean.

It is true that in answering the first two principal questions of the Holocaust—who did what, and why did they do it?—the book provided the necessary foundation for answering the third question: In what ways are they culpable? It also makes it possible to move to the next stage of investigation—the post-Holocaust stage—which is to ask: Based on the answers to these three principal questions, what social, political, and moral responses and measures should we conclude are desirable or even necessary? That *Hitler's Willing Executioners* implied and set the stage for such a further investigation was recognized by Jürgen Habermas. In his speech "Goldhagen and the Public Use of History" Habermas explained:

Goldhagen's investigations are tailored to address precisely those questions that have polarized our public and private discussions for the past half century. . . . The truly fundamental question at issue [is]: What does it mean to assign the responsibility for historical crimes retrospectively—if it is just this reckoning that we are now undertaking with the goal of generating an ethical-political process of public self-understanding? Goldhagen provides a new stimulus to a reflection about the proper public use of history.[5]

With this book, I take up the moral issues and their social and political implications that remained unaddressed though immanent in the first book, exploring them in a general way while focusing empirically on the Catholic Church and the Holocaust. It is precisely my hope to further generate a general ethical-political process of public understanding and self-understanding, which in the particular instances of the Church and other relevant institutions also includes institutional self-understanding. What *Hitler's Willing Executioners* did for explaining the contours and causes of the Holocaust, for restoring the human beings to the center of our understanding of its perpetration, this book is intended to do for clarifying moral culpability, for judging the actors, and for thinking about how they and others might best right their wrongs.

LIFT THE MORAL BLACKOUT

In the vast realm between the sound bite of media talk shows and op-ed pages on the one hand and the technical discourses of philosophical and theological tracts on the other, the serious investigation of issues of morality and judgment is rarely to be found. Sustained, accessible moral argument and evaluation—especially when it is sustained moral judgment—is not in vogue. It is fine to judge maleficent or lascivious politicians in moralizing, snap, and flip ways. It is fine to judge the perpetrators of spectacular domestic and other crimes who provide the daily theater of pathology that spices up the personal and social lives of our voyeuristic societies. These are sport, big-game hunting, where the hunters risk nothing and gain satisfaction and glory.

But it seems to be decidedly not fine to discuss seriously in public how to judge the people with whom so many feel affinity, who have or may have committed grievous offenses such as ordinary Germans and the ordinary citizens of other countries during the Holocaust. Serious moral inquiry cuts close to the bone of the investigator. It leads to where our principles, once we establish them, and logic lead us. It is a journey, once embarked upon, over which we have little control, and which sometimes, often, touches down along the way, or even terminates in unpleasant places with disturbing views of others and ourselves, and disquieting conclusions about what others or we must do.

Our moral culture is degraded partly by the flipness of our public culture, partly by the abdication of many people in the academy of their obligation to engage moral issues, or engage them in a way that both meets a high standard and is accessible to those who are not professional philosophers. One does not have to be a cultural conservative—I am not—to recognize and criticize all this. Our moral culture is also degraded because in our pluralistic world—a world generally to be celebrated—the genuine difficulties of confronting value pluralism, especially the problem of people not wanting to seem to be imposing their values on others, have made many people skittish about applying serious moral discussion to the public sphere. People who are not guided by religious values often seem reluctant to enter this realm, the realm of religion par excellence. Whether out of distaste for engaging religion or out of a belief that, without a religious grounding, they are at a serious disadvantage, those who could talk the talk have left much of the turf of serious moral discussion to the religious.

It is precisely votaries of various religions who are willing, even eager, to take on the task. As the most populous and centralized religion, Catholicism, under the aegis of the Roman Catholic Church and its various national churches, is around the world the most prominent participant in, and exemplar of, sustained moral discussion directed at the broad interested public. Through the frequent encyclicals, declarations, and letters of Popes, the pronouncements of national churches and their bishops, the homilies of priests, and the individual statements of many Church intellectuals, the Church and its clergy are active moral commentators on a wide range of matters, both public and personal. Latin American bishops in the 1970s propounded liberation theology, a moral argument grounded in theology in favor of antiestablishment politics for the poor to bring about social justice and an end to oppression. After 1979 they were silenced by the newly ascended Pope John Paul II, whose politics clashed with theirs. In the 1980s American bishops published a treatise arguing for the immorality of nuclear weapons, and another against the economic inequality produced by the American economy. John Paul II has made considered public pronouncements on a large array of moral and political issues, ranging from personal conduct to our duties to one another, to the necessity of including moral considerations in our economic systems, to issues of war and peace. National Catholic churches regularly address political issues relevant to their countries.[6] These and other interventions in the public sphere have been morally forceful because of the Catholic Church's traditions of culti-vated intellection and of intimate engagement with public life.

Although serious moral discussion of many important aspects of West-ern public life, particularly politics, was never much in vogue except among the rebellious, it flagged significantly in the West during the cold war. To be sure, the 1960s saw an upsurge in moral condemnation by the young of per-ceived injustices of their societies and especially of the Vietnam War. In Germany the generation known as sixty-eighters took their parents to task for what they did or failed to do during the Nazi period. But in general dur-ing the postwar decades the security concerns of the cold war seemed to trump many important moral concerns or at least to shunt them to a lesser status in both international and domestic affairs. If morality conflicted with reasons of state, as it so frequently does, then the acute danger seen to be posed by the Soviet Union made it for the West an unaffordable luxury, seemingly not worth seeking out in the first place. This, of course, was never the right position to take. In today's post–cold war world, it is even less justifiable. Considered moral investigation, the foundation for virtuous action, must reclaim its central place in public life.

The moral blackout has been deep in the discussion of the Nazi period. For a long time people failed to investigate and publicly discuss, sloganeer-ing aside, the relevant moral issues intensively, if at all.[7] West Germany had to be rehabilitated. It was better not to shine upon it the withering light of moral scrutiny. Without the cessation of public inquiry soon after the Nuremberg trials, the Germans would have been difficult to enlist in the struggle against communism, which at the time was seen to override all other considerations. Investigating the widespread criminality of large seg-ments of the Western populace and their institutions, especially in Ger-many, would have created for the Soviets a devastating propaganda and moral bonanza. And after all, within Germany and many other countries whose populations participated to some significant degree in the persecu-tion and the mass murder, such investigations would have tarnished (fur-ther) the national self-image and led to the condemnation of many of their citizens for having persecuted or killed members of a people, the Jews, who were still widely demonized and hated. For this there was little appetite. Looking forward rather than backward was the safe and chosen path.

The unwillingness to undertake genuine public moral investigation in discussing the Nazi period, particularly the Holocaust, went one step fur-ther with the removal of the actual, involved human beings from considera-tion as attention and conceptual primacy were focused on structures, collectivities, and irresistible forces. Two tacks, their seeming differences notwithstanding, were complementary in producing this mind-set that prevented genuine moral inquiry.

The first is the collective-guilt charge that was really shorthand for a series of related notions that Germans' guilt resided in their national character—in something that was a common property of theirs, essential and unchanging; their guilt was therefore deemed collective and intergenerational. During World War II and in its immediate aftermath such charges were frequently heard; prior to the cold war, they were a kind of common sense. Since then such notions, although held by many people, even in Germany, have been by and large delegitimized in public discussion, uttered publicly only by the insistent few.[8] Complementing the collective-guilt charge itself have been all those, especially in Germany, who attack people by claiming that they are falsely charging Germans with collective guilt. Someone who refuses to toe the exculpatory line—that ordinary Germans were more or less blameless for all the horrors of the Nazi period—can be saddled with the charge of advocating collective guilt.

The charge of collective guilt hinders moral inquiry. When it is asserted as a moral fact—that collective guilt exists—it focuses attention on the collectivity, which divests the individual of his individuality, of his moral agency, and his individual moral responsibility. When it is used as a cudgel, it intimidates those who might wish to undertake genuine moral inquiry, which could lead to the conclusion of widespread, though not collective, moral culpability among Germans or others.

The second morally stupefying tack had an even more deleterious effect on inquiry. Academics elided almost all the human beings from the investigation of the Holocaust's perpetration, both empirically and conceptually. A few superhuman monsters—Adolf Hitler, Heinrich Himmler, Adolf Eichmann—were left in focus. They garnered almost all the attention, diverting our gaze from the tens of millions of Germans who, in some way, willingly supported and embraced Nazism, Hitler, and the country's other leaders. The ordinary Germans who made this regime and its crimes possible were, after the war, miraculously transubstantiated overnight into beings who had been terrorized and coerced, and were unknowing. "*Der Terrorapparat*" (the terror apparatus) and "*Wir haben nichts gewusst*" (we knew nothing) became the paradigmatic linguistic tropes of a mythologized and morally neutered public history. Germans were retroactively divested of their agency—many Germans themselves, in agentic acts of false self-representation and re-creation, willingly worked to bring this about. Germans were divested of moral responsibility, preemptively exculpated because little or nothing was left to investigate morally.[9]

The perpetrators of the crimes were robbed even more thoroughly of their agency. Those intellectuals who had the most influence on academics' and the public's thinking at once expressed the whitewashing spirit of their times and powerfully reinforced its tendencies. Most notable were the avatars of the theory of totalitarianism, particularly Hannah Arendt, who by decree divested the perpetrators of their antisemitism, turning them into role-fulfilling petty bureaucrats and their deeds into nothing more than the expression of the "banality of evil." Stanley Milgram, with his obedience experiments at Yale University, asserted the compatible notion that the perpetrators were like robots whose buttons could be pushed by any authority. These and other views, different as they in some ways are, nevertheless dovetailed with the endlessly intoned notion that the perpetrators, like other Germans, had been terrorized and coerced. That Arendt and Milgram had done no research worth speaking of about the perpetrators seemed irrelevant to many academics and nonacademics alike who latched on to their politically expedient and morally numbing—and therefore, for many people, comforting—claims.[10]

The consequence of these and other political and intellectual distortions was a field of inquiry into the Holocaust and the Nazi period that, though heavily worked, was in many respects in need of fundamental rethinking. Until recently, it contained virtually nothing about the central actors, the perpetrators of the mass murders. Who they were, how they became perpetrators, what their lives were like in killing institutions, what choices they had, the details of their treatment of their victims were all but unknown. Conceptually, the perpetration of the Holocaust—its killing and seemingly endless personalized degrading, mocking, and torturing of Jews—was erroneously written off to impersonal social psychological forces, authority structures and authoritarian personalities, coercion, bureaucratic mindsets, abstract structures and institutions, like the SS, the Nazi Party, and totalitarian terror apparatus—almost anything but a recognition of what is as obvious for the perpetrators of the Holocaust as it is for the perpetrators of other mass murders, in Cambodia, Rwanda, Turkey, or the former Yugoslavia: The human beings who slaughtered the victims had views about what they were doing, and these views substantially informed their choices to act in the ways that they did.

Going against this grain was one group of people who did investigate the perpetrators intensively, developed in-depth knowledge of them, and did conclude again and again that the mass murderers of the Jews were not coerced, knew what they were doing, and were motivated by racism and antisemitism. They were the German judges who, after the war, sat in judgment of the mass murderers. Again and again, the German courts judged the perpetrators guilty for having killed Jews. They judged the perpetrators guilty, according to the most stringent rules of evidence, for having killed because of their "base motive" of "race-hatred."[11]

Among the German public, the courts' frequent proceedings from the late 1950s through the 1980s were never broadly supported, and their findings were poorly publicized. The academics working on these themes, with virtually no exceptions, systematically ignored the critical, readily available data that the legal investigations were unearthing. This included the fact, known but all but ignored by now for over thirty years, that no German perpetrator was ever killed, sent to a concentration camp, or severely punished for refusing to kill Jews, and that though many of the perpetrators knew explicitly that they could exempt themselves from killing, only a few of them chose not to be willing executioners.

The interpreters of this period also ignored the trenchant conclusions that the evidence compelled the judges to draw: that the perpetrators were vicious antisemites who made choices about how to act, and that typically those choices were, systematically, to mock, beat, degrade, torture, and kill their victims. Instead, these same academics put forward almost any explanation of the German perpetrators' conduct other than one that recognizes human agency, namely, that people, informed by their moral understanding of the world, have the capacity to say no—and often regarding the persecution of the Jews, many Germans and many others chose to say yes.

It has become obvious in the last few years that a wide-ranging reinvestigation of many received notions about the Holocaust and the Nazi period is necessary. It has been necessary because many of these notions, including those that have attained the status of unquestioned conventional wisdom, have been exposed as myths. For Germany, the myth of totalitarian terror, the myth of utter coercion, the myth of ignorance of the concentration camps and of the slaughter of the Jews. Beyond Germany, the myth of the helpless coerced Swiss, the myth of the wholly dragooned peoples of German-occupied Europe who resisted as best they could all the Germans' criminal policies. At the center of this by now widespread rejection of the dominant paradigm of external coercion is a recognition of human agency, which necessitates the end of the caricature of Germans and others, whether perpetrators or bystanders, as unknowing, unthinking automatons or as herdlike, simply frightened, optionless people. This recent development is critical because only with this recognition is moral responsibility restored and genuine moral inquiry possible. The central premise underlying the reinvestigation of the Holocaust and the Nazi period that is finally under way has been the need to shift the focus of inquiry to the events' actors and to treat them as moral agents.[12]

It is time for the Catholic Church to be similarly reexamined. The countries allied with Germany aside, the Church was the most powerful institution remaining intact and independent in German-occupied and
-dominated Europe. Its national churches across the continent, including
in Germany, were immensely influential, and Pope Pius XII in Rome was
the de facto moral voice of Europe, of a civilization under assault. Despite
the tens of thousands of books written about this period, the Church has
escaped full scrutiny.

Public controversy over Pius XII's conduct regarding the Holocaust first
erupted in 1963 with Rolf Hochhuth's play *The Deputy*, which shocked
many around the world by daring to condemn the Pope's silence. Earlier
much had been published on the Pope, the Church, and Christian theology
before, during, and after the Holocaust, but there was little public criticism
of the Pope's conduct. Indeed, he had received considerable praise, even
from Jews who were more concerned with contemporary politics, with
inhibiting the expression of more antisemitism, and with trying, in vain, to
get the powerful Church to take a more favorable position on Israel.[13]
Hochhuth's damning play provoked a flood of publications, including the
Church's own eleven-volume edition of wartime diplomatic documents
with commentary, *Actes et documents du Saint Siège relatifs à la seconde guerre
mondiale*, a collection carefully selected by the Church's custodians of the
Pope's reputation to respond to Hochhuth's charge.[14] A large specialized literature has since been produced on the story of Pius XII and the Holocaust,
most of which has escaped the broader public's attention.

In particular, over the last few years, considerable new scholarship has
been published on Pius XII and the Holocaust, and with the Church having
pushed forward the process of Pius XII's beatification, which may lead to
him being anointed a saint, renewed public attention has been focused on
his conduct regarding the Jews. The new books have punctured central
myths about the Pope and the Church. They have made critical contributions to our understanding of different aspects of the Church's actions
leading up to, during, and after the Holocaust. This work, especially books
by James Carroll, David Kertzer, Michael Phayer, Garry Wills, and Susan
Zuccotti, on which I often draw for the new evidence they have unearthed
and new perspectives they have introduced,[15] makes it possible to develop
a broader and deeper understanding of the Church's stance toward Jews
and other critical issues during the Nazi period and in the subsequent
half century, and to conduct an inquiry into relevant aspects of the
Church's and its clergy's moral character then, and of its stances and practices today.[16]

THE RELUCTANCE TO ENGAGE in sustained moral inquiry into, and to render moral judgment on, people's conduct during the Holocaust no doubt at least partly results from a reluctance to offend powerful institutions and people and, therefore, to bring public censure, however unjust, on oneself. People who speak simple truths about ordinary Germans' participation in the Holocaust, about the Germans' use of Jews and non-Jews as slave labor, about the existence of widespread antisemitism in Germany during the Nazi period, about Swiss banks having stolen money from victims of the Holocaust or their heirs, about some leading German historians having been devoted Nazis serving the regime in its racist murderous policies and subsequently training influential members of the postwar generation of German historians, about the Catholic Church or Pius XII not being guiltless, get personally attacked with charges of prejudice and of persecuting the innocent. They get censured with fabricated motives attributed to them, for supposedly being anti-German, anti-Swiss, or anti-Catholic. They get censured for daring to pass judgment on others, for imputed arrogance. No matter that the alternative to passing judgment is to say that we should let mass murderers and those who aided them in various ways, and those who criminally profited from the mass murder, escape without censure. These charges are transparently disingenuous, hypocritical assaults to fend off scrutiny of the factually and morally indefensible, scrutiny that is seen as threatening to contemporary moral and political standing, economic interests, and academic careers.

The facts: During the Nazi period, many ordinary Germans were antisemites, did support the eliminationist persecution of the Jews, and did commit mass murder. The German government, German companies, and many ordinary Germans did enslave people on a vast scale. Swiss banks (and institutions in other countries) did steal from the victims and did help to finance the Germans' apocalyptic onslaught. Some leading German historians served the Nazi regime, justifying with their work, among other things, its policy of foreign conquest and subjugation, which they knew included mass murder—and their students, some of the most prominent historians in Germany today, kept it buried.[17] The Catholic Church was a source of an enormous amount of antisemitism and acted badly toward Jews in many ways.

To state these facts, while acknowledging that exceptions to the rule existed in each instance, and to say that we ought to judge institutions and people who held pernicious beliefs and committed grave crimes and other offenses, it need hardly be said, is different from the antisemitic charges, through the ages, against the essentially powerless and persecuted Jews, different from the fictions that Jews sought to dominate the world, sought to destroy Christianity, Germany, and all goodness. The most famous modern antisemitic tract, the *Protocols of the Elders of Zion*, was a forgery. Hitler's antisemitism, and the kindred contemporaneous views of millions more in Germany and around Europe, consisted of a highly elaborated set of fantasies. The charges of international Jewish conspiracy today coming from neo-Nazis and antisemites, and their ideological sympathizers and de facto supporters, are just the latest versions in this long history of fabricated charges and hatred.[18] That it is necessary to mention the distinction—between telling the plain, abundantly documented truth about what many individual Germans and Swiss, the Catholic Church, and others did during the Nazi period on the one hand, and on the other hand the lies that antisemites have propagated about Jews—shows, in itself, how warped the discussion of the Nazi period has become, where today politically motivated commentators routinely violate scholarly standards, distort the facts, and attack the messengers when seeking to defend their indefensible contentions.

Even though, or perhaps because, sustained moral inquiry about the Holocaust is systematically eschewed, moral discussions intrude as a subtext into discussions about explaining different aspects of the Holocaust. Just as human beings are explanation-seeking animals, they are also moral-judging animals; they try to understand and to assess right and wrong. This cannot be fully suppressed. Those who would suppress judgment about those culpable in different aspects of the persecutions of this period invent morally damaging charges against those seeking the truth, which inhibits genuine moral inquiry. So discussions about explaining why things happen, which is an analytical and not a moral undertaking, often get overlaid with, and overwhelmed by, moral defenses and attacks.[19]

Because it occurs or erupts in this ill-considered manner, moral discussion of the Holocaust, whether it be about Germans, Poles, Ukrainians, French, Dutch, the Catholic Church, or whomever, is often unsystematic, confused, and lacking in measured and sustained inquiry. Essentially, it mirrors, in hyperventilated character and mean quality, the sound-bite moralizing of political talk shows.

Judgments, moreover, are typically left to the narrow norms and codes of law or to what passes for "common sense." In a world of plural values these are all that we putatively share. Law is helpful for thinking about crimes and, perhaps, legally punishable civil offenses. However, there are other blameworthy acts, such as spreading prejudice, which has been and in many countries continues to be outside the boundaries of law but which certainly would come under the purview of any moral investigation worthy of the name. And common sense is too skimpy and often too shaky a set of moral positions on which to base a considered moral investigation.[20]

Because people do make moral judgments, and because such judgments stealthily envelop discussions of the Holocaust and the Nazi period, we should openly acknowledge several things. Moral judging—including by historians who deny passing such judgments—is already an integral part of our confrontation with this past. The problem is not that we judge but that such judging has been done spottily and on the sly. This does not mean that it has not been influential. It has been, often in fending off the truth. We might as well, we ought to turn moral inquiry into a valued activity, devote ourselves to it, even if we are not professional philosophers, undertake it as best we can in an open, concerted way.

It is our right to judge. As I discuss at greater length in part two, it is our duty to judge. If any event cries out for a concerted moral reckoning of those involved, it is the Holocaust—which is why those who even implicitly suggest as much are attacked by those who know how devastating the judgments ought to be. If there is any institution and set of people who are fit to be the subjects of such an investigation, and who themselves ought to welcome it, it is the Catholic Church and its clergy. This is so mainly because of the Church's self-understanding as a moral institution and its prominent contemporary role as a forceful moral voice in public discourse. The Church itself, Catholics, the victims, and those who care about each of them, all stand in need of a moral reckoning with the Catholic Church. This appears obvious. Yet when it comes to the Holocaust people are skittish about judging the Church and its members.[21] Why?

MORAL INQUIRY AND THE CATHOLIC CHURCH

With the Catholic Church, as with other institutions and people, three related moral reckonings are at issue. The Church, Pius XII, and bishops and priests across Europe reckoned morally during the Nazi period and, by and large, decided that allowing or abetting the Germans' and their helpers' persecution of the Jews and even letting the Jews die was preferable to intervening on their behalf. The postwar Church, including and perhaps especially the contemporary Church, has reckoned morally and sees little, if any, fault with its and its clergy's moral reckonings before and during the Holocaust. The third moral reckoning, our own, always necessary, is here made more urgent by the failure of the first and the insufficiency of the second. We need to reckon morally, among other reasons to assess and, when necessary, to take issue with the Church's moral reckonings.

A moral reckoning with the Catholic Church must proceed by keeping distinct things that are routinely and wrongly jumbled together: the discrete analytical tasks of describing, of explaining, of judging, and of proposing remedies. Each is important, requires its own distinct methods and procedures, and is, in principle, different from the others, even if the various tasks build upon one another. Explaining something requires having a proper description, namely, an accurate understanding of what it is that needs to be explained and of those factors that possibly could explain it; judging culpability requires having a correct explanation of the actors' actions, including their motives; and proposing remedies requires a proper understanding of what needs to be remedied. A great deal of attention has been given to the methods and procedures underlying description and, within the social sciences, to those underlying explanation. But relatively little attention has been paid, outside of academic philosophy and theology and the narrow confines of law, to the methods and procedures for judging culpability and for proposing remedies or, put differently, undertaking moral repair.

It also behooves us to emphasize the need for sobriety when approaching the Holocaust. Much nonsense has been written about it that denies basic facts, that contravenes everything we know about mass murder, or that violates basic research methods and even the elementary rules of logic and inference.[22] The same has been true when people have rendered moral judgments. We need to be clear about our assumptions and framework of analysis, present our reasoning and how we arrive at conclusions openly, follow the well-established rules of inference, and always investigate the topics comparatively, thinking—even if not always writing about it—whether our positions would make sense, be justified, be correct, if we were discussing other, analogous instances, or if the identities of the actors and the victims were different.

Even in the rare, more serious attempts to engage in moral discussion over *Hitler's Willing Executioners*, several odd notions about morality were offered that are worth discussing, because they are common and bear on the analysis in this book.

By showing that Germans grew up in an antisemitic culture, which had antisemitism as its common sense—akin to whites growing up in the racist antebellum American South—and that therefore most Germans in the nineteenth and first part of the twentieth centuries became antisemites, I supposedly rob Germans of their agency, in religious terms of their free will. This is asserted even though my book's overall approach argued strenuously—and its specific arguments repeatedly showed—that the Germans were agents, and even though it argued this against the then-existing conventional views that vigorously denied their agency.

For anyone who believes that human agency or free will exists, the assumption or claim that Germans were not agents, did not have free will, because the views that they held they had learned from their culture is philosophically bizarre. All people have views imparted to them by their societies, including foundational models of thought about which they are not even aware.[23] If this claim nullifying agency is correct about Germans before or during the Nazi period, then it would also be true for all people at all times, and therefore we could never speak of agency because there would be none.

Philosophically or theologically, Germans in the first half of the twentieth century were no less agents and no less morally responsible than were American whites who were prejudiced against or enslaved blacks in the 1850s or who were prejudiced against blacks and enforced Jim Crow in the 1950s, or than Americans or Germans today who have been taught and have never doubted all kinds of matters that we may endorse or criticize, including, among so many other notions, that freedom and democracy are good things, that people have greater obligations to citizens of their own countries than they do to citizens of other countries, that the state is obliged to provide extensive social security to all citizens (in Germany) or that it is not (in the United States). That we do not like what many Germans believed about Jews and many other matters during the Nazi period, or did as a consequence of their beliefs, does not render the people nonagents, creatures lacking free will, any more than are people of other societies who act upon socially received notions that we do not find objectionable. This appears to be another instance where strange assertions are made regarding aspects of the Holocaust that are not made about similar features of other historical or contemporary events—indeed that would look silly, if they were.

Additionally, this claim that my view admits no agency suffers from two fatal empirical problems. First, as I repeatedly acknowledged and pointed out, some Germans did develop views of Jews that were at odds with the dominant antisemitic one of their culture. This shows that the possibility existed for others to do so. They did so because of the second problem for this view. Even in Germany before and during the Nazi period there were resources to contest the dominant view of Jews or the rightness of the eliminationist persecution. Christian morality, for example, does maintain that all people are deserving of moral respect and "You shall not kill." Moreover, Germans knew that many people around the world thought that their views of Jews were wrong and evil, and objected to the eliminationist persecution, especially the mass annihilation, of Jews that flowed from these views. This is why the Germans made some attempts to conceal their mass murdering from the rest of the world. This knowledge in itself should have led every German to reconsider his view of Jews and the rightness of such a radical persecution. Just this fact belies any empirical claim that Germans did not have access to some of the kind of information that this philosophical view of agency—wrongheaded and undefended as it is—deems necessary for someone to be classified as an agent.

A second objection to the alleged moral implications of the findings and explanations in *Hitler's Willing Executioners* is that they are unappealing. Held up against the book's imputed moral implications—that such critics have wrongly characterized these implications can for now be ignored—is the alleged superiority of Hannah Arendt's view in *Eichmann in Jerusalem: A Report on the Banality of Evil* or Jean-Paul Sartre's view in *Anti-Semite and Jew*. Arendt's view is said to be superior because it "allows her to preserve, in a far more convincing manner than Goldhagen, the idea of moral and criminal responsibility for the Holocaust." Sartre's view is deemed preferable because it "preserves moral culpability."[24] There are two disqualifying flaws with this objection to my views.

The greater interest or appeal of one moral question over another has no bearing on whether an explanation is correct. Because we may not like the moral implications of why a certain man today commits murder, we do not proclaim that he must have done it for a reason other than the one that actually led him to kill. We might wish that the moral question that emerges from a person's reason for acting, either today or in 1942, were different from the one that does emerge, but that does not give us permission to declare that the person's real reason for acting was not his and then to invent a reason more compatible with our philosophical interests. Arendt's and Sartre's acolytes do precisely this, which should be no surprise because this is the problem plaguing Arendt's and Sartre's own works, as different as their positions are.

Both Arendt's and Sartre's empirical accounts of the actors' mental world and social psychology are without evidentiary foundation, indeed overwhelmingly falsified by the evidence. Contra Arendt, Eichmann, not to mention the many tens of thousands of other perpetrators—of whom Arendt did no general or systematic study—was a passionate antisemite, having gleefully boasted toward the end of the war to his deputy that "I [shall] laugh when I jump into the grave, because of the feeling that I have killed five million Jews. That gives me a lot of satisfaction and pleasure."[25] Sartre's claim that antisemitism is bad faith, meaning that antisemites somehow choose, despite knowledge of the falseness of such beliefs, to remain antisemites—in other words, they choose to deceive themselves—is, aside from its almost silly implausibility, belied by an enormous amount of evidence for Christians through the ages who believed that Jews were Christ-killers, minions of the devil, and so on, and for Hitler as well as for ordinary Germans during the Nazi period and before, who believed that Jews were pernicious people who had inflicted great harm on Germany.

The moral edifices that Arendt and Sartre construct, however interesting each construction may be, depend upon historical fictions. Thirty years after writing *Anti-Semite and Jew*, Sartre himself admitted the almost purely imaginary nature of the book. In a famous interview with Benny Lévy, he confessed that "the reality of the Jew is lacking in the book" and that he was not interested in that reality or in Jewish history because he believed at the time that there was no such thing. Incredulous at Sartre's admission of his ignorance, Lévy objected, "But when you wrote *Anti-Semite and Jew*, you surely had collected some documentation?" Sartre replied with one word: "No." Lévy queried, "What do you mean, no?" Sartre could not have made his meaning clearer. He explained: "None. I wrote without any documentation, without reading one book about Jews." Sartre's ignorance about antisemites was so great that he put forward the absurdity that "we find scarcely any anti-Semitism among workers."[26] Arendt at least knew something about Eichmann, having attended his trial, but much of what she wrote about him are her inventions and have been copiously and incontestably exposed as falsehoods.[27] How could anyone seriously maintain that Arendt or Sartre's views, however morally appealing, shed light on the correctness of any explanation of the perpetrators' actions?

The second flaw in this line of criticism is that it assumes, without justification, that a given explanation for why actors hold the views that they do, or choose to act as they do, admits only one moral conclusion about them. This is another odd, untenable position that is not adopted about other events or actors. A variety of moral, theological, or legal perspectives can be applied to the same explanation of an actor's deeds. The judgments of German courts are again pertinent, which held that the killers were moved to commit their crimes against Jews by their racist antisemitism *and* that (contrary to the claims of such critics) they were criminally culpable precisely for that reason. Depending on the deed, different moral perspectives may produce similar or different, even opposing, moral judgments. Here we see

Melding Nazi and Christian antisemitism in The Poisonous Mushroom: *The advertisement reads, "Julius Streicher speaks in the people's hall about 'The Jews Are Our Misfortune,'" the classic Nazi antisemitic phrase. The text below reads, "He who fights against the Jews, wrestles with the devil."*

that, like so many other basic procedures and conclusions of the social sciences and of philosophy that are often curiously ignored in discussions about the Holocaust, this incontestable fact—a fact that is at the foundation of the field of moral philosophy—is denied when assessing the German perpetrators.

In addition to these remarks on agency and moral evaluation (I take them up more systematically later), a few preliminary words of clarification are necessary regarding the terms "antisemitism," "eliminationist," "the Catholic Church," and the moral imperative "must."

The term "antisemitism" describes instances of persons thinking ill of, having animosity for, feeling enmity toward, or hating Jews simply because they are Jews or because those persons falsely attribute noxious qualities to their Jewishness and therefore to Jews in general. The classical example of such antisemitism is the libel that Jews are "Christ-killers." This charge has its origins in the false claim of the Christian Bible (the term used here for the "New Testament"), indeed its fantastical narrative, that "the whole [Jewish] people" was responsible for killing Jesus and that the Jews then alive, numbering a few million and scattered throughout the Mediterranean region, voluntarily, in unison, declared themselves guilty of this and also similarly declared their descendants, all Jews for all time, also guilty.[28] Another biblically based antisemitic charge, equally ludicrous, is that Jews are children of the devil; the belief that Jews are Satan's children or minions became extremely widespread in medieval Europe and, along with the Christ-killers accusation, formed the basis for many further accusations and injurious actions against Jews.[29] The Christian biblical charge identifying Jews with the devil remained a common theme through the Nazi period and was readily adopted by the Nazis, such as in the Nazis' illustrated educational book containing the hate-filled poem "The Father of the Jews Is the Devil,"[30] and in another famous Nazi children's book, *The Poisonous Mushroom,* which merged Christian and Nazi antisemitism, as one of its illustrations depicts.

These charges, which are, on the face of it, fantastical, originate in the Gospels. These texts were written many decades after Jesus' death by people who had no firsthand knowledge of the events of his life but who were embroiled in the nascent Christian community's intensive rivalry with Judaism and whose enmity for Jews was manifest and clearly stated. The Gospels' authors intended to deprecate Jews and Judaism in their efforts to persuade their contemporaries that Jews had forfeited the path to God, thereby consolidating their own Christian claim, repeated frequently in the Gospels, that the followers of Jesus had replaced Jews as the people of God. Any author who proclaims that Jews are a "brood of vipers" or children of the devil, or that all the Jews voluntarily cursed themselves and their descendants, or any of the other numerous antisemitic libels contained in the Gospels and other books of the Christian Bible (see part three for an in-depth discussion of this antisemitism) cannot be deemed a believable historical guide to what Jews did or what they thought about Jesus or anything else. He cannot be deemed a reliable historical source on the topic of Jews' relationship to Jesus because of his demonstrated hostility toward Jews and bias against them. This applies, of course, to the role of Jews in the critical events of Jesus' life, including the events surrounding his crucifixion by the

Romans. It is a truism about prejudice that a person's prejudices teach us not about the people whom he purports to describe but only about the prejudiced person himself and those who share in his prejudices. This applies also to the authors of the Christian Bible.

It is critical to keep in mind that just because these falsehoods, and the hatred and enmity that they have produced toward Jews, have their origins in a revered religious text, the Christian Bible, does not make them or the antisemitic portions of this Bible any less prejudiced, any less antisemitic. It is a widespread convention to deny that a member of the Church was antisemitic even when he believed, and may also have spread, the anti-Jewish libels of the Christian Bible or of the biblically based Catholic doctrine. This practice is most acutely evident in discussions of the Church and its clergy in the years immediately before, during, and after the Nazi period. If a member of the Church, whether he was a Pope or a rural parish priest, believed that the Jews of his time were guilty for killing Jesus, if he believed that Jews of his time were accursed for this alleged act, or if he believed any of the numerous other antisemitic charges current within the Church (such as that contact with Jews should be avoided or that the Jews were working to destroy the Catholic Church), then he was an antisemite. It is simply descriptively misleading to deny that people were antisemites who held or spread prejudice and hostility toward Jews and who caused unjust injury to them.

More, this convention—of absolving the Church and clergy of antisemitism if their antisemitism was "only" of the sort that was deeply embedded in Christianity itself—is morally unfathomable. The necessity of overturning this convention becomes immediately and ever more undeniably evident if the following maxim is observed. Every time you read in this book a statement about Jews coming from the Church, its clergy, or its sacred texts, that is characterized as antisemitic, consider what you would say if that same statement was made not about Jews, but about any other ethnic or religious group (that blacks, Mexicans, Turks, Italians, or Baptists, Lutherans, Muslims are a "brood of vipers" or children of their "father the devil"),[31] and that such statements were being put forward not by the Church, its clergy, or its sacred texts but by some other political organization or people or text. If you conclude that these statements, if said about non-Jews, are prejudiced or racist, then you must recognize that the actual Christian biblical statements about Jews, as well as the Catholic doctrinal, theological, and instructional positions about Jews that historically were derived from them are also prejudiced or racist against Jews—in other words, antisemitic.

A second manifestation of antisemitism is a person explaining a Jew's stances or deeds by reflexively and groundlessly attributing them to his identity as a Jew. A mark of a prejudiced person is to declare another person's identity as a member of a disliked, hated, dehumanized, or feared group as the explanation for that person's conduct, when that aspect of his identity obviously has no causal relationship to his actions, or before considering (and reasonably ruling out) other explanations for his conduct.

Antisemitism is also present when a person focuses on Jews or their conduct disproportionately (unless there is some fair and justifiable reason—such as dispassionate scholarly inquiry—for doing so). Fixating on Jews when non-Jews are doing similar things; disproportionately leveling criticism at Jews, their institutions, or Israel, while willfully ignoring non-Jewish people, institutions, or countries that deserve the same criticism, is another classic mark of an antisemite.

We see then that there are different ways that a person can be antisemitic. He can falsely accuse Jews of noxious qualities or malfeasance. He can essentialize Jews, which means that he reduces the complexity of a person to what is imputed to be his Jewish essence and proceeds as if a person's Jewishness determines his individual nature on a wide range of qualities, including his conduct, that have no necessary relationship to his identity as a Jew. And he can focus criticism disproportionately or exclusively on Jews, ignoring others who are similarly doing whatever it is he dislikes. An antisemite will often do all of these, even if they are, in principle, distinct from one another.

Just as there are several ways in which a person can be, or can express, his antisemitism, antisemitism exists in many varieties. Different antisemitisms contain different images of Jews, charges against them, degrees of intensity, and implied or proposed solutions to the so-called "Jewish Problem." When a person is described as an antisemite, or a statement as antisemitic, it does not necessarily mean that either *the way in which he or the statement is antisemitic* or *the quality of the antisemitism* is the same as the manner or quality of the antisemitism of other people or statements.[32] This should be particularly kept in mind as the analysis here unfolds.

Antisemitic beliefs and attitudes, like other prejudices, can lead an antisemite to want to act prejudicially or even in extremely harmful ways toward Jews. If the appropriate circumstances come about, he then can carry out his desires. Such discriminatory and injurious actions range from hurtful and damaging talk, to avoidance, to discrimination, to physical attacks, to elimination, to extermination.[33] It is often overlooked that spreading further prejudice against Jews, as well as willfully employing or

A nonlethal eliminationist epilogue to the murder of 2,900 Jews in Frankfurt: Copperplate engraving depicting the expulsion of the Jews of Frankfurt on August 23, 1614, by Georg Keller, published in Johann Ludwig Gottfried, Historische Chroniken, *Frankfurt, 1633.*

alluding to antisemitic images and tropes as a strategy to delegitimize Jews, especially in public life, constitutes antisemitic action.[34]

    Antisemitism has often resulted historically in the desire to eliminate Jews and their influence from society. When I refer to eliminationist antisemitism or, especially during the Nazi period, to an eliminationist persecution, program, or onslaught, *it does not necessarily mean killing*, because killing is but one of many eliminationist means. Eliminationist measures vary in their character and severity, from restricting Jews' economic, social, cultural, and political activities, to ghettoization, to forced conversion, to expulsion, to mass annihilation. In the 1930s, for example, the Germans' eliminationist program, already fully under way, consisted not of large-scale killing but of legal policies and social practices that removed Jews from professional and social contact with Germans, and that turned them into a hounded, immiserated, socially leprous community, with the intention of driving them from Germany. As I made clear throughout *Hitler's Willing Executioners,* the general term "eliminationist," therefore, *should not be understood to mean killing* but to mean instead the desire or endeavor to rid a locale of Jews and their real or imagined influence by one means or another—with the understanding that after mid-1941, the Germans' principal antisemitic eliminationist measure in Europe was mass killing.

The antisemitism that the Church had spread implied or even openly asserted that Jews had to be eliminated from Christian society, such as by forced conversion or expulsion, even though the Church and its bishops did not call for their mass murder, and even though they often made a point of enjoining their faithful against committing violence. So when I refer to the Church's "eliminationist antisemitism," unless specifically stated otherwise, it should be understood as an assertion either that the Church was calling for the nonlethal elimination of Jews or that its demonology of Jews was, however unintended, compatible with or implied eliminationist solutions, including perhaps extermination—even though the Catholic Church *was doctrinally opposed to, and itself did not advocate, killing Jews.*

The "Catholic Church" is a unified, centralized institution, with a hierarchical structure. At its apex is the Pope, seated with his clerical administration in the Church's capital, the Vatican. He governs and speaks for the Church authoritatively. Below him are national churches with their bishops and priests. When I refer to the Catholic Church or the Church, I mean either the Pope, the Vatican, and official Church policy, or the agglomeration of the national churches and their clergy in general. In using the monistic term "the Catholic Church" in this manner, for what is really often a diverse collection of national churches and their many members, I am following Catholics' own usage, while remaining cognizant that there were also often many exceptions or dissenters within the Church to what the Church as a whole or its members in general were thinking or doing. I often make note of such exceptions, but still, it should be clear that in discussing given issues I focus much more on the majority, which is often the overwhelming majority, of clergy than on the exceptions. Still, *unless I specifically state that there were no exceptions within the Church to a particular state of mind or practice, it should be assumed that I am implying that exceptions existed.* Lest there be a misunderstanding, everyone should note the following: During the Nazi period there were Catholics, clergy and lay, who were not antisemites or whose antisemitism was mild. There were Catholics, clergy and lay, who opposed the eliminationist persecution of the Jews, especially the use of physical violence, and most especially the mass murder. There were Catholics, clergy and lay, who aided Jews and who saved Jews from death.

The analysis and judgments here are about the Catholic Church and its clergy, not specifically about lay Catholics. When I speak here of the Catholic Church, without explicitly mentioning lay Catholics, it should be understood to mean the Church and its clergy but not lay Catholics, much less Christians more generally. The analysis and judgments here do, in principle, apply similarly to lay Catholics but only to those lay Catholics who were motivated by Catholic beliefs to harm or to approve of harm to Jews (the issue is not a person's identity as a Catholic but his beliefs derived from the Church's bible and its teachings). But I do not dwell on lay Catholics, and focus instead on the clergy for several reasons. Unlike lay Catholics, the clergy's overriding moral allegiance was to the Church, and the clergy, by their offices, spoke for the Church. It is also easier to identify the clergy's acts and their failures because they were public people, acting in an official capacity. And the burden upon these public shepherds of souls to act well was that much greater. None of this, however, means that lay Catholics or other people are immune from the fair application of our judgment.

To be sure, much of what I say here and the principles put forward could be applied to various Protestant churches, their clergy, and their lay members across Europe, just as they could be applied to lay Catholics and nonreligious actors during the Nazi period or to people involved in other historical or contemporary events. That I have not focused on Protestant churches does not imply that many of them and their clergy are not also fit subjects for an analogous moral reckoning. Some countries' Protestant churches and their clergy, such as Denmark's and Norway's, conducted themselves decidedly better than the Catholic Church.[35] The Protestant leadership in Germany, with the partial exception of the small Confessing Church, did not, having acted still less well than did the leadership of the Catholic Church. Because this moral reckoning is meant to be exemplary, not comprehensive, for the set of events under discussion, restricting its focus, and restricting it to the Catholic Church, is likely to etch the issues more clearly than would a broader study, even just of Christian churches.

Finally, in discussing this investigation's conclusions about the Catholic Church's appropriate course of future action, I often use the word "must." This is not meant to be preachy. It simply accords with moral philosophical writing and rectitude that when a conclusion inevitably follows from a premise or set of premises, it has the force of unavoidable obligation. It is a duty. It "must" be done. So the word "must"—as in "The Church must undertake . . ."—signifies my view that this is a moral necessity, impartially and appropriately derived from well-considered moral investigation (which I endeavor to lay out for the reader). Despite the temptation to eschew conventional moral philosophical linguistic usage on this point—because of the acute sensitivity of this book's topic and in order to avoid the charge of preachiness—I have chosen to adhere to the convention. It is my view that a major problem besetting discussion and understanding of the Holocaust is many academics' repeated violation of the canons of well-established standards of linguistic usage, methodology, and logic, so I would be particularly remiss if I chose consciously to contribute to this. Using the moral imperative, moreover, is in keeping with the Catholic Church's own view of these matters. The Church declares that "every offense committed against justice and truth entails the *duty of reparation.* . . . This reparation, moral and sometimes material, must be evaluated in terms of the extent of the damage inflicted." Reparation is a "duty," an unavoidable obligation, and the manner for evaluating it prescribed by the Church is a "must."[36]

This book is a moral reckoning. The reader should not be misled about its moral conclusions. When the logic of moral inquiry does produce an imperative, such as the Church's agreed "duty of repair," the best way to do that is with the verb that signifies it: "must."

THE BODY OF THE BOOK is divided into three parts, each building on the previous one. They roughly correspond to the three necessary components of a moral reckoning worthy of its name: moral investigation, moral judgment, and moral repair. Moral investigation is carried out in part one and part two, moral judgment in part two, and moral repair is explored in part three.

Part one recasts our understanding of how to think about the Pope's and the Church's actions during the Nazi period. Defenders as well as many critics of Pius XII make a variety of assumptions and mistakes that confuse the issues. They tend to focus overwhelmingly on the Pope as if the Pope were the Church. Yet Pius XII is but a small, if important, part of the story, and dwelling on him diverts attention from the actions of the rest of the Church (including his predecessor, Pope Pius XI, the national Catholic churches, bishops, priests, and others). When the Church's defenders do discuss parts of the Church other than the Pope, they pick those parts that display the Church in the most favorable light rather than analyzing systematically all parts of the Church, including those that acted badly. They also erect an artificial *cordon sanitaire* around the Church's antisemitism that dissociates it from that of the Nazis, creating the fiction that the two had nothing to do with each other. With such sleight of hand, the Church's defenders can at once extol the Church in the terms of a moral institution, and defend it in the terms of a political institution, without ever acknowledging that they are shifting the terms by which they are rendering their judgments. Such changing of evaluative criteria allows the Church to be presented and legitimized by one favorable standard that would normally bring with it an exacting set of expectations for its conduct, but then judged according to a different, far more lenient and expedient standard.

Each of these strategies distorts or obscures the historical and moral record. This part of the book, while analyzing these strategies, presents the relevant facts and a variety of perspectives that facilitate judging them, which become the basis for explaining the Pope's and the Church's actions causally and evaluating them morally. In sum, it recasts how we should think about the Church itself as an institution and about its and its clergy's actions during this period, and then evaluates what the Church and its clergy did do, could have done, and ought to have done.

Part two uses the conclusions from part one as the basis for taking up the broader questions of moral culpability generally, and specifically in the case of the Catholic Church. Much of the confusion surrounding the subject of moral culpability can be dispelled by clarifying the different kinds of moral culpability, and that moral culpability is not an existential state of a person or a collectivity but is always attached to a person's or an institution's bearing toward a specific stance or act, and then a series of stances or acts. Applying these notions to the inventory of stances and acts of the Church, of its many parts, and of its clergy is intended to produce a measured and nuanced account of the character and extent of their culpability for various aspects of the Holocaust. The judgments about the Church's conduct, moreover, are essentially the same whether we derive them from the Church's own moral precepts or those of a nonreligious-based moral universalism.[37]

The investigation should be seen as especially legitimate, including in the eyes of the Catholic Church, because it is predicated on today's Church's own clear and unequivocal position that it was the Church's and its clergy's moral duty to prevent Jews from being slaughtered. If the Church today were to maintain that it had no such moral duty, then our investigation would have to be altered somewhat to examine the meaning and consequences of such a position. But this is decidedly not the Church's moral position. This means that if someone were to say, "It is only normal that the Church would not care, so we are making a mountain out of a molehill," he would be wrong, because as the ensuing discussion makes clear, the Church's moral stance is that it had to care and its empirical claim is that it did care. The Church insists on both, repeatedly, unequivocally, and fervently. Whatever else we do here, we are being faithful to the Church by taking it at its word on this critical issue.

During the course of this moral reckoning, I often present the Church's own stated doctrinally based moral positions, in order to show their compatibility with my analysis. This compatibility should render my conclusions still that much more binding in the eyes of Catholics. With the exception of an occasional authoritative pronouncement from one of the Popes, I have used, as the source for Catholic doctrine and morality, the *Catechism of the Catholic Church*, the Catholic Church's lengthy (more than eight hundred pages) official instructional manual for all Catholics, children and adults, which has been commissioned, approved, and introduced by Pope John Paul II, who writes: "The *Catechism of the Catholic Church* . . . is a statement of the Church's faith and of catholic doctrine, attested to or illumined by Sacred Scripture, the Apostolic Tradition, and the Church's Magisterium. I declare it to be a sure norm for teaching the faith . . . a sure and authentic text for teaching catholic doctrine."[38] It should be clear from the outset that even though our analysis and conclusions are compatible with Catholic principles, however fortunate or significant that congruence may be, it is ultimately not important, indeed is irrelevant, for establishing our conclusions' value because, as part two makes clear, they rest on general moral categories that have full force independent of the Church's principles or authority.

Part three builds upon part one and part two to ask what the Church must do to make amends for its failures regarding the Jews, and to right itself. It considers the Church's postwar actions along these lines and finds that though the Church has taken many positive steps, its measures remain partial and glaringly insufficient according to our standards and according to those established by the Church's doctrine and principles. It argues, more generally, that the focus of the last few years on monetary restitution (important as it is) has obscured the critical need for a complementary moral restitution. For its moral failures, the Church should make moral amends. These would include, among other things, telling the truth, and reforming those of its doctrines and practices that helped to produce these failures.

MORAL INQUIRY BEYOND THE CATHOLIC CHURCH

The Church, though the specific subject of this inquiry, is incidental to the more general and most fundamental project of this book. Aside from the particular facts about the Catholic Church's and its clergy's conduct regarding the Germans' and their helpers' eliminationist persecution of the Jews, which is the principal subject of part one, the kinds of questions asked here, the framework of analysis used, and the kinds of conclusions drawn about culpability and restitution in part two and part three could be applied, in principle, to any other offenses, past or present, perpetrated by any institutions or people against any other people. The sort of investigation conducted here, in principle, could and should therefore be undertaken for all other institutions and people relevant to the eliminationist persecution of the Jews. It should be done about institutions and people regarding their stances and actions regarding the Germans' persecution of other groups during the Nazi period. It should be done about the perpetrators and bystanders of other mass murders, such as the Serbs' eliminationist assaults against Bosnian Muslims, Kosovars, and others in the former Yugoslavia. It should be done for institutions and people regarding any horrific system, event, or act, past or present, including the enslavement, segregation, and other forms of subjugation of African-Americans by the United States and its white citizens and, in particular, by southern states and their white citizens.

This book, therefore, in addition to being a moral investigation specifically of the Catholic Church, is a general investigation of how to conduct a moral reckoning. It offers a paradigm and set of procedures for conducting other ones as necessary. The general arguments and the mode of thinking presented here might be seen as relevant to ongoing and future discussions about responsibility and restitution—regarding the Holocaust (e.g., Swiss banks, slave labor) and regarding horrors unrelated to the Holocaust (e.g., South African apartheid, restitution to African-Americans for slavery).

The justifications for moral reckonings are plentiful and familiar, so I mention several additional ones here without elaborate explanation. Individuals should be held publicly accountable for their public actions. Institutions, including states, should be held accountable for their actions. The more we discuss our morality or moralities, in general and in particular applications, the more likely we are to become better-informed moral agents, with a greater potential to act well and to influence others to do the same. The more likely, then, it is for virtue to become a more integral part of our public life, including politics, where it is lacking and needed. If moral reckoning becomes routine, it may also serve as something of a deterrent to potential transgressors, because most people do not relish being the blameworthy subject of public moral reckonings, let alone being sanctioned in accord with the conclusions that such reckonings produce. So moral reckonings might succeed in deterring people from acting badly. Not only society but victims and perpetrators benefit from moral reckonings. Victims want justice, and justice in the broadest sense of the term includes telling the truth about transgressive deeds, naming their perpetrators, and judging the culpability. Ultimately, it is good for the perpetrators not to be allowed to let their deeds go quietly into the night, because forcing them to confront their own offenses increases the likelihood that they will honestly face them, repent, and reform themselves.

For conducting an exemplary moral reckoning, in general and specifically with regard to an institution's and its officials' actions toward eliminationist persecution of the Jews during the 1930s and 1940s, the Catholic Church seems to me a good choice, arguably even the best. I came to choose the Church and also the topic initially, however, not for this reason, but because it chose me.

Two years ago Martin Peretz, editor-in-chief of the *New Republic*, asked me to write a review of some books that were appearing on Pius XII and the Holocaust. I was in the midst of writing a book on genocide in the twentieth century, to which I am now returning, and wanted to keep interruptions to a minimum. I explained this, adding that I would do the review only if he really wanted me to. He told me that he did, adding that he was hoping for a major piece, not the usual book review.[39] Eventually about a dozen books collected for the review, and as I read them, I began to see that the subject matter was taking me in a totally unexpected direction, one that demanded not just a long article but also a book-length investigation and essay to answer our question: What must a religion of love and goodness do to confront its history of hatred and harm, and to perform restitution?

PART ONE

CLARIFYING
the Conduct

Since it violates the virtue of truthfulness, a lie does real violence to another. It affects his ability to know, which is a condition of every judgment and decision.
Catechism of the Catholic Church, parag. 2486

Feigned ignorance and hardness of heart do not diminish, but rather increase, the voluntary character of a sin.
Catechism of the Catholic Church, parag. 1859

IN THE LONG and sorry history of hatred that has shamed and demeaned the peoples of the Western world during the last two thousand years, more people have been deeply prejudiced against the Jews than against any other group. Antisemitism, the most hardy and poisonous of weeds, has flourished in all environments, outliving historical eras, transcending national boundaries, political systems, and modes of production, sinking its roots and undermining moral and social ecologies where there have been Jews and where there have been no Jews, where Jews have been wealthy and where they have been poor, where they have been socially and outwardly distinct from the Gentile population and where they have been socially assimilated and visibly indistinguishable.

Antisemitism's extreme durability is matched by its intensity and power. It has been, arguably, the European prejudice with the most fearsome content. Europeans in the Middle Ages commonly believed that Jews were servants of the devil (Antichrists) and in the modern period that they were immensely powerful, genetically programmed subhumans bent upon destroying humanity (antihumans). For centuries, most cataclysmically in the twentieth century, antisemitism was a binding force, Europe's common hatred that even adversary peoples and groups shared.

Antisemitism has also outdone all other European prejudices in engendering eliminationist violence, in the form of forced segregation, expulsions, and mass murders. All over Europe, Gentiles have expelled Jews, sometimes for hundreds of years: Crimea in 1016, Paris in 1182, England in 1290, France in 1306, Switzerland in 1348, Hungary in 1349, Provence in 1394, Austria in 1422, Lithuania in 1495, Portugal in 1497, and from most of the region that eventually became Germany during the course of the fourteenth through the sixteenth centuries. Most infamously, Spain expelled its Jews in 1492.

When these and other regions of Europe permitted Jews within their confines, they often, under the authority of papal bulls, sequestered them in ghettos, in order to restrict their movements, their activities, and their intercourse with Gentiles. Breslau established a ghetto in 1266. During the next six hundred years ghettos were erected in cities, among other places, in today's Austria, the Czech Republic, France, Germany, Greece, Italy, Poland, Portugal, and Spain, including in such major centers and capitals as Frankfurt (1460), Kraków (1494), Madrid (1480), Prague (1473), Rome (1555), Venice (1516), and Vienna (1570). From 1835 until the Bolshevik Revolution, Russia confined Jews to its western portion, known as the Pale of Settlement.

Christians' mass murdering of Jews began in 414, when the people of newly Christianized Roman Alexandria annihilated the city's Jewish community. During the First Crusade of 1096 the slaughter of Jews reached an especial frenzy. The Crusaders killed Jews of one community after another in northern France and Germany, with ten thousand victims. Such killings resumed in subsequent crusades and periodically around Europe during the next centuries. The larger instances can seem like precursors of the Holocaust: From 1348 to 1350, during the black plague, Germans slaughtered the Jews of roughly 350 communities, virtually every city and town, rendering Germany almost *judenrein*, "Jew-free." In 1391 Spaniards slew Jews all over Spain, and during the last phases of the Spanish Inquisition, many Jews were killed, often burned at the stake. The Chmielnicki massacres of 1648–1656 saw Ukrainians (then often called Cossacks) slaughter more than 100,000 Jews in cities and towns across Poland. The Russian pogroms from 1871 to 1906, though claiming a fraction of the victims of these earlier mass murders, shocked the Western world.[1]

Viewed historically, then, the Holocaust, perpetrated by antisemitic Germans who were aided by antisemitic Lithuanians, Ukrainians, Poles, French, and others, should be regarded as but the largest and most comprehensive in a long history of annihilative onslaughts. But it was not the final one. Immediately after the Holocaust, Jewish survivors were often greeted with hostility by their neighbors in Catholic Eastern Europe, who sometimes massacred them. The best-known such pogrom took place in Kielce, where in July 1946 rampaging Poles slaughtered forty Jews and injured others. The catalyst for this coda to the Holocaust? The medieval Christian ritual murder charge against the Jews. It is estimated that in the two years after the war ended, Poles killed fifteen hundred Jews.[2]

For considerably more than a millennium, antisemitism was an animating force in the social, political, and cultural lives of Western peoples, in whose mental and emotional maps of the world Jews had a prominent, malevolent place. The politics, economic development, and social and cultural histories of Europe cannot be understood without according antisemitism, its causes and consequences, a prominent place. Why, then, is antisemitism often accorded but a marginal place in Western history? When subjects to which it is centrally relevant are under discussion, it can be treated obliquely, minimized, or cordoned off—in the twentieth century, for example, as the property principally of some pathological small sect called Nazis.[3] Antisemitism's marginalized place in the canonical accounts of Western history may exist because the main responsibility for producing this all-time leading Western hatred lies with Christianity. More specifically, with the Catholic Church.

THE CATHOLIC CHURCH, ANTISEMITISM, AND THE HOLOCAUST

For centuries the Catholic Church, this pan-European institution of world-hegemonic aspirations, the central spiritual, moral, and instructional institution of European civilization, harbored antisemitism at its core, as an integral part of its doctrine, its theology, and its liturgy. It did so with the divine justification of the Christian Bible that Jews were Christ-killers, minions of the devil.

The Church spread antisemitism where its priests preached, ensuring that it would not be an ephemeral, territorially limited, and marginal hatred but would become within Christendom a powerful and enduring religious imperative. In medieval Europe, antisemitism was near universal.[4]

After the Reformation in the sixteenth century, antisemitism continued in roughly parallel forms in the Catholic and Protestant churches. It was something that even these bitter foes could share. Martin Luther propounded that the Jews "are for us a heavy burden, the calamity of our being; they are a pest in the midst of our lands." This was but one small part of his "homiletic massacre" of 1543, "On the Jews and Their Lies," a violently

A medieval version of the ritual murder of a Christian boy by Jews.

antisemitic treatise that, echoing the Catholic Church's eliminationist campaign against the Jews of Spain just fifty years earlier, called for the utter degradation and suppression, even elimination, of the Jews, including the destruction of their books and the burning of their homes and synagogues, so that "we may be free of this insufferable devilish burden—the Jews."[5] Luther's vicious antisemitism notwithstanding, it is not surprising that the Catholic Church denounced him and his followers as heretics and Jews, and that Catholics came to see Jews as instigators of the Reformation, which broke the Church's near European-wide monopoly on Christianity.[6] The Catholic demonology about the Jews made it second nature for many Catholics, at all levels of society, to blame the Jews for any natural or human calamity. King Philip II of Spain, the driving force behind the Spanish Inquisition and close ally of the papacy, declared in 1556 that "all the heresies which have occurred in Germany and France have been sown by descendants of Jews, as we have seen and still see daily in Spain."[7]

Antisemitism led to the Holocaust.[8] Antisemitism has been integral to the Catholic Church. The question of what the relationship is between the Church's antisemitism and the Holocaust should be at the center of any general treatment of either one. James Carroll, near the beginning of *Constantine's Sword*, his extraordinary investigation of this relationship, observes that "an inquiry into the origins of the Holocaust in the tortured past of Western civilization is necessarily an inquiry into the history of Catholicism."[9] However necessary, such an inquiry is for many people threatening and unwanted. As a result, there is a widespread and longstanding practice of deflecting attention from the central issues.

This practice of evasion and denial began as early as 1939 when Pope Pius XII suppressed *Humani Generis Unitas*, the not-yet-promulgated antiracism encyclical of his recently deceased predecessor, Pope Pius XI.

Pius XII had been born in 1876 in Rome as Eugenio Pacelli. He studied philosophy and then was ordained in 1899. He soon began his career as a Church politician by entering the Vatican's Secretariat of State in 1901. Obviously suited to his chosen path within the Church, Pacelli earned several promotions before he was made an archbishop in May 1917 and appointed the Nuncio in Bavaria. From 1920 to 1930 Pacelli served as the Papal Nuncio, the Vatican's emissary, to Germany. Having been named a cardinal in 1929, he rose in February 1930 to the Church's second-most-powerful position of Vatican Secretary of State, with the responsibilities of representing the Pope in supervising the Church bureaucracy and of conducting diplomatic relations with other states. In the beginning of March 1939, Pacelli completed his ascent, assuming the papacy and adopting the name Pius XII. (I refer to him as Pacelli for the years before he became Pope and as Pius XII for the years of his papacy.)

Upon taking this highest office, Pius XII had to make a momentous decision about what to do with Pius XI's draft encyclical. The decision was momentous because *Humani Generis Unitas* would finally, and publicly, have the Church defend the hounded Jews, by explicitly condemning the Nazis' antisemitism and calling for the cessation of the Germans' persecution of Jews: "It becomes clear that the struggle of racial purity ends by being uniquely the struggle against the Jews. Save for its systematic cruelty, this struggle is no different in true motives and methods from persecutions everywhere carried out against the Jews since antiquity."[10] That a Pope drew this direct connection, in motive and in method, between past persecutions—and by strong implication, the Church's persecutions—of the Jews and the Germans' contemporary assault on the Jews should give pause to anyone who wishes to dissociate the Church from any responsibility for the persecution and slaughter of the 1930s and 1940s. That a second Pope began his papacy by burying this remarkable document in defense of the Jews, now known as the Hidden Encyclical, in the "silence of the archives,"[11] and that the Vatican for half a century tried to hide Pius XII's act of suppression and the encyclical itself, tells us a great deal about Pius XII, and about the dissimulations that have surrounded that Pope's and the Church's relationship to the Holocaust.[12]

WAS PIUS XII REMISS?

Condemnatory and laudatory cases have been made about Pius XII. The basic issues seem straightforward. What did the Pope know of the Germans' ongoing slaughter of the Jews? What could he have done about it? What did he do, and what did he not do, and why? How honest has the Church been about all of this?

The critics have made the case that Pius XII was Hitler's Pope, that he let the Germans deport the Jews to Auschwitz from under his very windows, and that the postwar whitewashing of his papal sin is nothing less than a structure of deceit.[13] Various explanations are offered for his motives: his own antisemitism, his pursuit of papal power, the need to preserve the Church in threatening times, a personal timidity, a de facto alliance with Nazism against modernity, a strong preference for Nazism over communism, a fear of alienating German Catholics.[14] Pius XII's defenders portray him as an enemy of Hitler and a friend of the Jews, who worked to save as many people as possible. In their view, his failures, whatever they were, were those of a pious man who, with human shortcomings, had to act in tragic circumstances. They see the contemporary Church's reckoning with the Pope's and its own history as being, however imperfect, relatively forthright.

These contradictory portraits emerge because authors bring different values, perspectives, and agendas to their investigations, and also because some of the evidence can be read in multiple ways. Susan Zuccotti, for example, has recently exposed a central exculpating myth—in her view consciously fabricated or encouraged by the Pope and others, and sustained by Jews who themselves were misled or wanted to placate the powerful Church—that the Pope gave orders for Italian Church officials to hide Jews in churches and monasteries. The priests and others who took initiatives to save the lives of many Jews were certainly heroic, but there is no evidence of the Pope's guiding hand. Based on extensive, painstaking research into one locale after another, she methodically debunks claims that Pius XII was active on behalf of the Jews. These findings have devastated Pius XII's reputation.

In contrast, other authors give great weight to the Pope's representatives' quiet interventions on behalf of some Jews, even when the lucky Jews were not Jews at all but really Catholics who had converted from Judaism, or when the interventions were tepid and came only after the Germans and their local helpers had been killing Jews of a given country for months or years.[15] The Pope's defenders accept the assertions of Jews and Catholics that he was behind rescue efforts in Italy; however, this is hearsay, without foundation, and is contradicted by credible evidence.[16] The Pope's defenders also eagerly interpret public statements by Pius XII that were critical of violence or racism in general—no matter how glancing, weak, or tardy—as powerful and unequivocal defenses of the Jews, even though any mention of Jews is conspicuously absent.

Pius XII's Christmas message of 1942 is, for them, Exhibit A. At the end of a forty-five-minute speech dealing with other themes, the pontiff called for a just society: "We owe it to the innumerable dead . . . to the suffering groups of mothers, widows, and orphans . . . to the innumerable exiles . . . to the hundreds of thousands who, without personal guilt, are doomed to death or to a progressive deterioration of their condition, sometimes for no other reason than their nationality or descent . . . to the many thousands of noncombatants whom the air war has [harmed]."[17] Laudable as this statement might seem, its platitudinous vagueness is striking.

By Christmas 1942, the Germans and their helpers had been slaughtering millions of Jews across Europe for almost a year and a half. They were well on their way to annihilating the three million Jews of Catholic Poland. The *Einsatzgruppen*, the German army and other German units, and the Germans' local auxiliaries had machine-gunned and gassed a good portion of the million Jews in the Soviet Union whom they would ultimately kill. With the aid of locals, they had also killed most of the Jews of Catholic Lithuania, and of Latvia and Estonia, and had begun destroying the Jews of Romania. The German army had slaughtered most of the Jews of Serbia. Catholic Slovakia and Catholic Croatia had for months been "solving" their "Jewish Problem," the Slovaks by deporting the Jews to their deaths and the Croats by killing them themselves. The Germans had begun to annihilate the Jews of greater Germany itself, including prewar Austria, and the annexed territory that today is the Czech Republic. With their local helpers, they were annihilating the Jews of western Europe, of Belgium, France, Luxembourg, and the Netherlands. The death factories, with their gas chambers and crematoria, had long been consuming their victims day after day. For all this time that the Germans and their helpers were killing all these Jewish men, women, and children across the continent, Pius XII publicly said nothing. He uttered no protest even though he knew the broad contours of the destruction, having received a stream of detailed reports

Cardinal Secretary of State Eugenio Pacelli signs the Concordat between Nazi Germany and the Vatican at a formal ceremony in Rome. Vice-Chancellor Franz von Papen sits at the left and the German chargé d'affaires at the Vatican, Rudolf Buttmann, sits at the right.

about the ongoing mass murder. He watched in detached silence. Now, when he finally said something, he made no mention of Jews as victims, or Germans or Nazis as perpetrators, and no condemnation of racism or antisemitism. Pius XII made no attempt to provide usable information to the European peoples about the extent of the mass murder, and made no call to them to resist further slaughters.

Why, after such a long and lethal period of purposeful silence, did Pius XII say something, even something as inadequate as he did? He spoke out only after he had been strongly pressured by the Americans and the British to explicitly condemn the mass murder of the Jews, which he nevertheless steadfastly refused to do. Two weeks before his Christmas message, the British minister to the Vatican, Francis d'Arcy Osborne, was completely exasperated by the Pope's silence. On December 14 he even took the extraordinary diplomatic step of censuring Pius XII bluntly while speaking to the Vatican Secretary of State. Osborne recorded that he virtually commanded that the Vatican "should consider their duties in respect to the unprecedented crime against humanity of Hitler's campaign of extermination of the Jews."[18] But during the years when the Germans were mass-murdering the Jews, Pius XII chose again and again not to mention the Jews publicly. Nevertheless, his defenders insist that, his purposeful omissions notwithstanding, he was speaking about them all along; they ignore that until his vague Christmas utterance well over a year after the Germans had initiated that mass murder, Pius XII had been absolutely silent.[19]

The essential facts of the Pope's conduct are clear, even if what we make of some of them may be open to disagreement. As the Vatican's Secretary of State, Pacelli hastened to negotiate for the Church a treaty of cooperation, the Concordat, with Hitler's Germany.

Completed, signed, and publicized to the world in July 1933 and formally ratified that September, the Concordat was Nazi Germany's first great diplomatic triumph. It included the Church's liquidation of the democratic Catholic Center Party (the forerunner of postwar Germany's governing Christian Democratic Party), effectively legitimating Hitler's seizure of power and his destruction of democracy, which Pacelli and Pius XI welcomed. Cardinal Michael Faulhaber of Germany reported on Pius XI's support for Hitler's measures in a report to the Bavarian bishops. Cardinal Faulhaber had been in Rome, where he observed on March 13 "the Holy Father [saying], with special emphasis: 'Until recently the voice of the Roman Pope remained the only one to point out the serious danger threatening Christian culture which has been introduced into almost all nations.' Thus, public praise for Hitler." In March Pacelli conveyed to Hitler, in the words of Germany's envoy to the Holy See, the Vatican's "indirect acknowledgment of the action of the Reich Chancellor and the government against Communism."[20] The Concordat helped to legitimate the Nazi regime in the eyes of the world and consolidate its power at home.

Neither as Secretary of State nor later as Pope did Pacelli instruct Church officials to stop preaching the Church's antisemitism, which they continued to spread in their sermons and in the Church's own newspapers and other publications, many of which he could have easily influenced because they were under his supervision or ultimate control. This made him responsible for them.

Pacelli was no admirer of Hitler; in 1940, as Pope Pius XII, he conspired with some German generals and the British in a plot to overthrow Hitler that went nowhere. Yet he distinguished throughout between Hitler the man and Germany the country. To Germany he remained devoted. He wanted it to maintain its power. He identified with it during its war of extermination against the Soviet Union, because he considered Bolshevism to be the Church's mortal enemy. He wished for a German victory against the Soviets, even though they were then allied with Great Britain and the United

States in the fight to destroy Nazism. That this also meant that the Germans would virtually annihilate European Jewry, at the very least, did not seem to dampen Pius XII's ardor for German conquest in the East.[21] As late as 1941, he confessed a "special love" for Germans and regularly held audiences with German soldiers,[22] which he knew would be interpreted as an act of solidarity with them. In 1944, tired of hearing about the Jews, he got angry at the Polish ambassador for raising the subject. The ambassador, like other Allied diplomats, kept returning to the subject because the Pope refused to speak out publicly against the mass murder or discuss it with the German ambassador to the Vatican, Ernst von Weizsäcker, even though Pius XII met with Weizsäcker regularly.[23] From Pius XII's postwar stances, moreover, it is evident that this love of Germany held fast and even deepened, the crimes of many Germans notwithstanding.[24]

As to the Holocaust itself, Pius XII was briefed regularly about the details of the unfolding mass annihilation of the Jews, which he knew about almost from its start. During the war he never made a public statement condemning the Germans' persecution and extermination of the Jews. He never even informed the European peoples that the mass murder was taking place, which would have given every person the knowledge with which to make a choice. (When people made inquiries about the fate of the Jews, the Vatican, by withholding the facts, led them to believe things were less dire than they were.) Pius XII never privately instructed all European cardinals, bishops, priests, nuns, and lay Catholics to do whatever they could to save Jews. He did not protest or instruct others to hide the Jews when the Germans deported them from Italy or any other country, including from his own city, Rome.

Pius XII's diplomatic corps did sometimes intervene behind the scenes to help Jews of different countries. But these efforts came mainly late in the course of the mass murder, and without persistence or great vigor. (An exception was the timely and forceful intervention of his representative in Romania, Archbishop Andrea Cassulo.) Pius XII himself once protested to Miklós Horthy, the dictator of Hungary, about the deportation of Hungarian Jews in 1944. But he did this only after the Germans and their Hungarian helpers had already deported most of the more than 430,000 Jews they would deport (whom the Germans mainly gassed at Auschwitz), only after the Germans had clearly lost the war, and only after the Allied countries put him under great pressure to intervene. Occasionally, he also privately expressed sympathy for the victimized Jews, at least for the ears of the Allies' diplomats.[25] Since the war, he and other Church officials have asserted that he did things to help Jews that he did not do.

It cannot be reasonably maintained that Pius XII did everything he could to help the Jews. Yet many cling to this fiction, and continue to spread it. It needs to be dispelled step by step.

THE STRATEGIES OF EXCULPATION

The Pope's defenders engage in a series of exculpatory strategies that divert attention from a considered view of the more significant issues. Not surprisingly, these strategies are the stock-in-trade of those who try to exculpate ordinary Germans from their responsibility for, and participation in, the Holocaust.

The first strategy is direct exculpation. The Pope's defenders deny, delay in time, or underplay his knowledge of the ongoing extermination and its various features. The Church's cardinals, bishops, parish priests, and parishioners formed the most extensive information network in Europe. The Allies and Jewish organizations regularly passed on their often considerable knowledge about the unfolding mass murders to Pius XII. Yet his defenders fail to convey all of this. If they would acknowledge that the Pope had access to timely, sometimes immediate, and reliable information, often from multiple sources, about the killings, the camps, the intended fate of the deportees, then the question of why he did not act more quickly, forcefully, and consistently on the Jews' behalf becomes more pressing.[26]

The second strategy of Pius XII's defenders is to omit, casuistically conceal, or flatly deny that he was an antisemite and, by extension, that this animus influenced his reactions to the various phases (deprivation of rights, segregation, expulsion, ghettoization, and mass murder) of the Germans' eliminationist onslaught against the Jews. Such dissimulations and denials are exceedingly odd, because the evidence of Pius XII's antisemitism comes from an unimpeachable source: Pius XII. A letter that he wrote describing a scene of "absolute hell" from the Communist insurrection in Munich of April 1919, in the royal palace, is explicit:

> . . . in the midst of all this, a gang of young women, of dubious appearance, Jews like all the rest of them, hanging around in all the offices with lecherous demeanor and suggestive smiles. The boss of this female rabble was Levien's mistress, a young Russian woman, a Jew and a divorcée, who was in charge. And it was to her that the nunciature was obliged to pay homage in order to proceed.
>
> This Levien is a young man, of about thirty or thirty-five, also Russian and a Jew. Pale, dirty, with drugged eyes, hoarse voice, vulgar, repulsive, with a face that is both intelligent and sly.[27]

This passage is Pius XII's only relatively extensive utterance about Jews, not destined for publication, that has come to light. Recorded in a confidential letter about a scene that Pacelli had not even witnessed, it bears the stamp of authenticity, an expression of the then-future Pope's views of Jews. That his statement is not just an offhand remark but a concentrated barrage of antisemitic stereotypes and charges, which also echo the demonological views of Jews then current in Germany, around Europe, and in the Catholic Church itself, makes it that much more reasonable to believe that Pacelli's was not a fleeting opinion, a whimsical lapse into rank antisemitism, but an abiding sentiment that may be reflected in other similar statements, oral or written, the evidence of which would have expired with his interlocutors or would be safely secured in the locked archives of the Vatican.

The elements of Pacelli's antisemitic collage were of the kind that Julius Streicher would soon offer the German public in every issue of his notorious Nazi newspaper, *Der Stürmer*. Implicit in Pacelli's letter is the notion of Judeo-Bolshevism, the virtually axiomatic conviction among Nazis, modern antisemites in general, and within the Church itself that Jews were the principal bearers and even the authors of Bolshevism. The Communist revolutionaries, Pacelli averred in this letter, are "all" Jews. During the Weimar and Nazi period, anti-Communist diatribes and caricatures conflated Jews and Bolsheviks, pictorially depicting Communists with distorted Jewish visages as repulsive, licentious, and blood-lusting. Pacelli's description of the Bavarian Communist insurrectionists reads like a verbal rendition of one of the innumerable Nazi cartoons printed in Germany during Hitler's crusade against Bolshevism.

There was nothing that Pius XII dreaded more than Bolshevism. For him, it was the Antichrist, the ultimate evil that threatened the existence of the Church. Would it be unreasonable to believe that his stance toward the Germans' persecution of the Jews was colored in some measure by his apparent identification of communism with Jews?

Two decades after penning his antisemitic letter, Pacelli, then Vatican Secretary of State, either wrote or supervised the writing of a papal encyclical, *Mit brennender Sorge*, "With Burning Concern." It is often presented erroneously as evidence of the Church's, Pacelli's, or Pius XI's antipathy to Nazism, or as a sweeping condemnation of Nazism. The encyclical did object in clear and ringing language to violations of the Concordat, particularly the treatment of religion in Germany. In six sentences of its forty-three paragraphs it refers to race. It never mentions Jews. Its objection to the doctrine of race is not that it is false or inherently pernicious, but only that some would have race take precedence over the teachings of Christianity.

Race, no different from "time, space, [and] country," is too restrictive a basis for morality, which only God's universally valid commandments can supply.

The encyclical was not a general condemnation of Nazism itself. It never once mentioned Nazism by name. It pointedly made clear that its objection revolved around the narrow though important "systematic antagonism raised between national education and religious duty." But it also urged the young in Germany, in the canonical idiom of the Nazi regime itself, to embrace the new Germany: "No one would think of preventing the youth of Germany from establishing a true ethnic community (*Volksgemeinschaft*) in a noble love of freedom and unshakable fidelity to the Fatherland." Pacelli knew that, to German ears, the *Volksgemeinschaft* would by definition exclude Jews, because according to common belief and usage among Germans, and according to the well-known Nazi Party Program issued in 1920, "No Jew may be a member of the *Volk*."[28]

The encyclical did seek to educate the German people about Nazism's religious transgressions and about its raising of race above the universal commands of religion. In such an encyclical a friend of the Jews, or at least a non-antisemite, would have condemned Germany's intensive persecution of its Jews. Pacelli did not. He defended the Old Testament against the Nazis' charge that it was a Jewish book, but he couched the encyclical's explanation in explicitly antisemitic terms, presenting it as an anti-Jewish book that reveals "the story of the chosen people, bearers of the Revelation and the Promise, repeatedly straying from God and turning to the world."[29] Its value lies in "the luminous splendor of the divine light revealing the saving plan which finally triumphs over every fault and sin."

Pacelli's gratuitous affirmation of the sinfulness of the "straying from God" Jews could only strengthen the prevailing antisemitism among the many Germans who held that Jews should in some way be eliminated at least from German society. As if to drive home his point at a moment when Germans were subjecting Jews to a fierce persecution, he reminded Germans of "a people that was to crucify" Jesus, referring to the Jews corporately, as a people, as Jesus' "torturer." To ensure the maximum exposure and effect of this encyclical on religious practice (which also shows how little afraid Pacelli was of criticizing the regime's practices publicly), it was read from every German pulpit on Palm Sunday 1937.[30]

These expressions of Pius XII's obvious antisemitic sentiments combined with his oversight and repeated approval during the Nazi period of the publication of vicious antisemitic polemics in the Jesuit journal *Civiltà cattolica* (see pp. 82–85), and his failure during the time of maximum danger for the Jews to countermand the deep-rooted antisemitism of the Church leave no doubt that he was an antisemite. Why should this be astonishing? He had been brought up and lived his entire adult life in this profoundly antisemitic establishment of the Church, an institutional culture centrally animated by the belief, based in its holy Scripture, that Jews were Christ-killers and also by the notion that Jews were responsible for many of the perceived evils of modernity. It would have been noteworthy had he managed to remain free of anti-Jewish prejudice.

Do Pius XII's remarks mean that the character of his antisemitism was the same as Hitler's? Of course not. There are many kinds of antisemitism, and they vary enormously in their foundations, the nature of their charges, and their intensities.[31] Does Pius XII's antisemitism mean that he necessarily approved of every aspect of the Germans' persecution of the Jews? Of course not. But does it mean that his prejudices against Jews must be investigated in depth, and that their influence on his actions must be central to any evaluation of his conduct regarding the eliminationist persecution of the Jews? Of course it does. This would include not just why he chose to act or remain inactive with each new German initiative against the Jews but also why, in light of the obviously injurious, even murderous, consequences of antisemitism, he did not decree an end to antisemitic expression and practice from the Church or among Catholics (particularly among German Catholics, whose antisemitism in its demonology was often scarcely different from the Nazis'), and prevent its further dissemination by Church officials.

The nature of the relationship between antisemitic belief and anti-Jewish action is complex. Its explanation is open to disagreement. But two other things are beyond disagreement: that those who sidestep this central issue are de facto engaging in an exculpatory enterprise; and that, until the Vatican opens all its archives to all researchers—which it steadfastly refuses to do, attacking those who wish to learn the truth—much that might shed further light on the character of Pius XII's antisemitism and on how it affected his actions (and, more broadly, on the Church and its clergy) will remain hidden.

Pius XII's defenders attempt to exonerate him of antisemitism and to represent him as a friend of the endangered Jews who did everything that he believed possible to help them. Yet this depiction of him is riddled with weaknesses. Why, as a moral or practical matter, did Pius XII intervene in Germany on behalf of Catholics who had converted from Judaism but not on behalf of Jews? His defenders have no good answer. Why, as a moral or practical matter, did he cause *Mit brennender Sorge,* the fiery encyclical protesting the treatment of religion in Germany, to be read from pulpits across the country, but not similarly denounce the persecution of the Jews, either then or when the mass murder began? Again, there is no good answer.

Why, as a moral or practical matter, did he protest the Germans' invasion of Belgium, the Netherlands, and Luxembourg, with separate telegrams to the sovereigns of each (and printed in large type on the front page of the Vatican's official daily newspaper, *L'Osservatore Romano*)[32] but not the Germans' slaughter of the Jews? No good answer. Why, as a moral and practical matter, did he speak out publicly on behalf of the suffering Poles but not of the Jews? (On the instructions of Pius XII, Vatican Radio broadcast this in January 1940: "Conditions of religious, political, and economic life have thrown the Polish people, especially in those areas occupied by Germany, into a state of terror, of degradation, and, we dare say, of barbarism. . . . The Germans employ the same methods, perhaps even worse, as those used by the Soviets.")[33] Why, as a moral or practical matter, did Pius XII not direct all ecclesiastic personnel to defend and to help save Jews? Why, as a moral or practical matter, did he not lift a finger to forfend the deportation of the Jews of Rome or of other regions in Italy by denouncing this publicly and by instructing his priests and nuns to give the hunted Jewish men, women, and children sanctuary? Why, as a moral or practical matter, did Pius XII excommunicate all Communists in the world in 1949, including millions who never shed blood, but not excommunicate a single German or non-German who served Hitler—or even the Catholic-born Hitler himself—as the millionfold willing executioners of the Jewish people? To all of these questions there is no good answer.

To the extent that any of these questions are addressed (generally, they are ignored), the answers proffered by Pius XII's defenders form a third strategy to complement the first two of directly exculpating him and denying his antisemitism: inventing constraints. They claim without convincing evidence that he chose not to do more on behalf of Jews because he had to maintain the Vatican's neutrality, so as not to endanger the Church. Yet his demonstratively public condemnation of the Germans' invasion of Belgium, Luxembourg, and the Netherlands, and other acts, reveals this to be false. (I return to this claim below.) They also assert, perversely, that had Pius XII made concerted efforts to save Jews—as the critics maintain that he should have done—then he would have ended up only hastening more Jewish deaths. In 1963, no less a personage than the close wartime confidant of Pius XII, Cardinal Giovanni Battista Montini, shortly before his election as Pope Paul VI, made this argument: "An attitude of protest and condemnation [of the persecutions of the Jews] . . . would have been not only futile but harmful." But the cardinal's claim was not an argument at all. It was an imperious assertion, dismissing the need for further inquiry: "that is," the future Pope declared, "the long and the short of the matter."[34]

The contention that Pius XII would only have harmed Jews by trying to help them is patent nonsense. There is not a single instance where the intervention of Christian churches led to the deaths of more Jews. And there are many well-known instances where interventions on behalf of Jews saved many lives.

The best that the Pope's defenders can do is point to the Netherlands, where the Dutch Catholic Church's protest of the deportation of the Jews in July 1942 led the Germans to deport Catholics who had converted from Judaism. But this example is misleading in several ways.

The Germans' murder of these people is relevant to a discussion of the Church's solicitude for Catholics, which no one doubts or fails to applaud, but it is disingenuous to present this as an instance of the Church, attempting to help Jews, leading the Germans to kill Jews they would not have killed otherwise. Even if the Germans considered these victims to be Jews, in the eyes of the Church and the victims themselves, they were Catholics; they had renounced Judaism, been baptized, and declared themselves to be Catholics—believers in the divinity of Jesus and subordinate to the authority of his Catholic Church. Moreover, the Church quickly learned that these Catholics were doomed, destined to be murdered regardless of its protest. Soon after deporting these Catholics, the Germans deported the Dutch Protestants who had converted from Judaism, even though the Protestant churches had not publicly protested the deportation of the Jews.[35]

The contemporaneous French bishops' public protest of the deportation of Jews from France undermines any argument that the Church could have genuinely believed that silence in this context was golden. The French bishops' protests did not lead to more Jews dying or suffering. This was clear at the time. On the contrary, their protests spurred Catholics, clergy and lay, to save Jews.

The Pope's defenders typically fail to discuss the famous and most relevant case for assessing the efficacy of acting on behalf of Jews: that of Denmark. Leni Yahil writes:

> The struggle of the [Danish Lutheran State] Church against nazism in general and anti-Semitism in particular is a chapter in itself. We have already seen how the priests organized themselves within the underground movement even before the crisis broke out. But they did not hesitate throughout the entire occupation to express their views publicly and from the pulpit. Kaj Munk said in one of his sermons that in the event of the Germans trying to behave towards the Danish Jews as they had behaved toward the Norwegian Jews (who had been persecuted and deported), the Christian citizens of Denmark would publicly declare that the Nazis had thereby canceled all rights and turned the social order into chaos.

Many of the priests also found a way to express their views in articles published in newspapers or in the ecclesiastical press. In one such article pastor Johannes Nordentoft called for an active struggle against anti-Semitism. He wrote that to stand aside was the same as participating in anti-Semitic activities.[36]

The Danish Lutheran State Church, in the person of Bishop Hans Fuglsang-Damgaard of Copenhagen, supported by all its bishops, also sent a letter of protest to the German authorities before the deportations began, which their pastors read from every pulpit in Denmark on October 3, 1943, thereby helping to mobilize national sentiment and to move ordinary Danes to act on the Jews' behalf, secreting them away and ferrying them to safety in neutral Sweden:

> Whenever persecutions are undertaken for racial or religious reasons against the Jews, it is the duty of the Christian Church to raise a protest against it for the following reasons:
>
> . . . Because the persecution of the Jews is irreconcilable with the humanitarian concept of love of neighbors which follows from the message which the Church of Jesus Christ is commissioned to proclaim. With Christ there is no respect of persons, and he has taught us that every man is precious in the eyes of God. . . .
>
> . . . race and religion can never be in themselves a reason for depriving a man of his rights, freedom, or property. . . . We shall therefore struggle to ensure the continued guarantee to our Jewish brothers and sisters [of] the same freedom which we ourselves treasure more than life.
>
> . . . We are obliged by our conscience to maintain the law and to protest against any violation of human rights. Therefore we desire to declare unambiguously our allegiance to the word, *we must obey God rather than man.*[37]

What did the Germans do to the Danish Lutheran Church with all of its activities in defense of the Jews, including its ringing call for a national "struggle" against the Germans on behalf of the Jews? Nothing. What did Danes suffer for their collective thwarting of the Germans' exterminationist onslaught? Nothing. Did Pius XII know of the Danish church's protest? Of course he did. It happened two weeks before the Germans began deporting the Jews of Rome, and months before the Germans' deported Jews from other parts of Italy, such as Trieste (December 7, 1943, to February 24, 1945), and from other parts of Europe, including Hungary (starting in May 1944).

Here was a model of successful action against the annihilation of the Jews that Pius XII chose to reject. Here is a model of successful action that Pius XII's defenders choose not to mention—all the more striking in light of the fact that 100 percent of the more than 7,000 rescued Jews of Denmark survived the war. This cannot be said of the 1,900 Jews whom the Germans deported from Rome to Auschwitz in October 1943 and in the ensuing months. If the Catholics in Italy who did take the initiative to help Jews, sometimes to the Vatican's displeasure, had instead followed the Pope's lead and done nothing, then the Germans would have killed thousands more.

From the point of view of assessing the Pope, the fate of the close to five hundred Danish Jews whom the Germans did manage to deport is also important. In part because the Danish officials passionately demonstrated their concern for their country's Jews, the Germans sent them not to Auschwitz but to Theresienstadt, where the Germans permitted Danish officials and Red Cross officials to visit them and to monitor their well-being. Ninety percent of Denmark's deported Jews survived the war. The Pope and his representatives, however, made no genuine effort to look after the Jews deported from Rome or from other parts of Italy and other countries. The most they did was to make occasional, perfunctory inquiries.[38]

The fact is that in those dark years there were still other Christian church leaders besides the Danes, including the French Catholic bishops, the Orthodox Bulgarian Synod of bishops, and the Greek Orthodox archbishop of Athens, who publicly denounced the Germans' eliminationist onslaught against the Jews. There is every reason to believe that these ecclesiastical protests helped to save Jews' lives, and no reason to believe that they caused more Jews' deaths. All the Jews living within the borders of prewar Bulgaria, for example, numbering fifty thousand, survived the war.[39] These protests all occurred before the Germans began the deportation of Italy's Jews.

The Norwegian Protestant churches, upon the impending deportation of the Jews of Norway, also protested pointedly in a letter to Vidkun Quisling, the nation's collaborating leader. The letter was read from the pulpit twice in late 1942 all over Norway, and ministers led their congregations in saying prayers for the Jews. The letter was also published as the New Year's message for 1943, and broadcast to Norway and Sweden:

For ninety-one years Jews have had a legal right to reside and to earn a livelihood in our country. Now they are being deprived of their property without warning. . . . Jews have not been charged with transgression of the country's laws much less convicted of such transgressions by judicial procedure. Nevertheless, they are being punished as severely as the worst criminals are punished. They are being punished because of their racial background, wholly and solely because they are Jews. . . . According to God's Word, all people have, in the first instance, the same human worth and thereby the same human rights. Our state authorities are by law obliged to respect this basic view.

After speaking forthrightly in a manner that belies the Pope's defenders' claim that he never could or should have spoken out, the Norwegian bishops resumed: "To remain silent about this legalized injustice against the Jews would render ourselves co-guilty in this injustice." With the leadership provided by the Norwegian Protestant church leaders, Norwegians managed to help over 50 percent of the country's Jews escape to safety in Sweden. How did the Catholic Church of Norway contribute to the rescue? It did not, pointedly deciding not to participate in the protest. Its concern was restricted to five Christian families that had converts from Judaism.[40]

The Germans took no retribution on the Norwegian, French, Bulgarian, or Greek churches for championing the Jews, just as they had refrained from acting against the Danes. They took no retribution on Bishop Antonio Santin of Trieste, who during a mass in early November 1943, with Germans and Italian Fascists present, denounced in the name of Jesus the roundup of the Jews as violations of "charity, goodness, and humanity," and urged that within his diocese "every hand offer help" to them. The Germans did nothing to him, to his parishioners, to Jews married to Catholics, or to Catholics who had converted from Judaism. Having suffered no punishment for his actions, Bishop Santin wrote a letter imploring the Pope to help the Jews—"I humbly beg Your Holiness to intervene with the German ambassador to the Holy See in favor of these unhappy people." Two weeks later he traveled to the Vatican to make the same plea—all in vain.

That the Pope would bring danger upon himself and the Church for speaking out was then, and is now, a convenient fiction.[41] Moreover, the Pope himself proved definitively that such considerations played no role whatsoever in his decisions to remain publicly silent while the Germans murdered Jews. After the Allies liberated Rome on June 4, 1944, the Germans were in the process of gradually deporting the Jews of Trieste, which they still occupied. The Pope and the Vatican were completely safe. More than half a year had passed since Bishop Santin's appeal. Yet Pius XII still did absolutely nothing to help Trieste's Jews. Fifteen of the twenty-two trains that brought almost twelve hundred Jews mostly to Auschwitz departed Trieste when the Pope was safely under Allied protection.[42]

Quietly, behind the scenes, Pius XII personally could have also done many things to try to help the Jews, particularly of Italy, with no risk to himself or the Church. He chose not to.[43]

The notion that had the Pope spoken out and tried to mobilize Catholics, ecclesiastic and lay, and non-Catholics to resist the Germans' slaughters, then more Jews would have died is about as bizarre and nonsensical an argument as I have read by anyone writing about the Holocaust, except of course the fulminations of Holocaust deniers and their fellow travelers who blame the Jews for their own destruction or, now, for speaking the truth about the Holocaust after the fact.[44] No one has ever demonstrated—or even plausibly argued—that papal silence and the Church's inaction saved Jews anywhere. No one has ever demonstrated or even plausibly argued that there was a good reason at the time for the Pope to believe that abandoning the Jews to their German-ordained death sentence was the way to save them.

The hollowness of the excuses presented in defense of Pius XII and other Church leaders has been in a few strokes pithily conveyed by Settimio Sorani, who, as director of the Jewish refugee assistance agency Delasem in Rome, did save Jews. After the war, he wrote:

> Regarding the subject of the work of the Vatican, it must be specified precisely that much more was requested by many, and also much more was hoped for by the Jews: a more decisive attitude, more constructive, because if a certain number of human lives were saved, other results could have been achieved if the Church had acted differently from the beginning of the racial campaign in Germany, in Italy, and in the occupied countries, with an open condemnation of racism and the persecutions. In principle, no danger threatened the Pontifical state, and the Vatican was aware of the creation of the camps and of their real destructive purpose. Yet, in the Church, even in Italy, paintings were still shown that portrayed "ritual homicide." [Christian anti-semitic demonology held for centuries that Jews murdered Christians so they could use their blood in their rituals.][45]

Sorani knows what was really going on in the Vatican and, in an understated manner, concludes here with a hint at the real and obvious reason behind the Church's stance and conduct regarding Jews.

Let us step back for a moment from Pius XII and the stubbornly unflattering historical facts about him. Since when do we insist that religious men should not speak moral truths? That being silent in the face of mass murder is the right way to help the victims? That mobilizing people of conscience to resist radical evil would have the opposite effect of abetting that evil? I know of no other genocide where onlookers who genuinely opposed the mass murder adduced such arguments. Would the Pope's defenders have been happier had the world been silent and done even less than it did while the Hutu were slaughtering Tutsi in Rwanda, and while the Serbs slaughtered

Croats, Bosnian Muslims, or Kosovars?[46] It is curious that Pius XII—the man who had more moral authority in the 1940s than anyone else in Europe, who had the greatest capacity to get ordinary people to recognize their moral duty to resist the mass murdering, who more than any person could have spurred an enormous number of people across Europe either to stop aiding the mass murder or to resist it—only this man is deemed to have been wise to keep quiet. If the Danish church and ordinary Danes had emulated the Pope, then all the Jews of Denmark whom they saved would have ended up like the deported Jews of Rome whom the Pope abandoned: dead.

Imagine that Pius XII had instructed every bishop and priest across Europe, including in Germany, to declare in 1941 that the Jews are innocent human beings deserving, by divine right, every protection that their countrymen enjoyed, and that antisemitism is wrong, and that killing Jews is an unsurpassable transgression and mortal sin, and that any Catholic contributing to their mass murder would be excommunicated and would surely have to answer for his deeds in the next world. Imagine that Pius XII had broadcast the same declaration over Vatican Radio and the BBC throughout Europe, and that all Church publications around Europe had printed it on their front pages. Imagine that Pius XII and all European clergy, including German clergy, had then decreed it a moral duty for all Europeans to resist this evil. Does anyone really believe that many more Jews would not have been saved?

How many Catholics, Germans and non-Germans alike, working in the institutions of killing, how many Catholics around Europe who were helping the killers by identifying Jews, would have been given pause? How many more people, in addition to the Church with its vast human network and resources, would have been moved to help the hunted and forsaken Jews? Many people, antisemites included, needed desperately to be roused from their moral stupor to recognize the mass slaughter as evil. What almost all people needed additionally, and what the Danes received, was leadership. Pius XII and his clergy could have provided both.[47] Never mind the projections of how many people Pius XII would have saved; there is a good chance that the German government would not have tried to implement, or been able to implement, its murderous intentions in any manner resembling the way that it did. Was it not, plain and simple, the moral and spiritual duty of a Pope to declare that it is every person's responsibility to resist the this-worldly Satan and those who served him?

These various strategies to conceal Pius XII's culpability circumscribe the Pope's agency by feigning for him a lack of knowledge, a lack of animus toward Jesus, and the existence of debilitating practical constraints. Whatever isolated instances of aid to Jews that Pius XII's defenders point to

Pope Pius XII leading a service at the Vatican.

(which are often much less than what they seem), they ignore or deny the potential efficacy of all the other measures that were available to him to help Jews—measures that he repeatedly and consciously chose not to take.

Pius XII's defenders misrepresent him in another way. They heroize him as an actor by magnifying the significance of praiseworthy deeds by him, even inventing such deeds. The Church's own uncritical and false lionization of him is one such example. In "We Remember: A Reflection on the Shoah," issued in March 1998, the Church's generally welcomed official statement about its historical part in the Holocaust, the sum total of its discussion of Pius XII is to present him as an anti-antisemite and to laud him for what he allegedly "did personally or through his representatives to save hundreds of thousands of Jewish lives." According to the Pope's defenders, we are to believe that although Pius XII could not do much, he, being not an antisemite but a good friend of the Jews, did as much as it was possible for him to do. They maintain this even though Pius XII, at the height of the Germans' slaughter of European Jewry and shortly before the Germans began to deport Italian Jews, felt the need to declare to all Catholics, in graphic, gruesome terms, the falseness of Judaism and to express his antisemitism publicly. He did so by discussing the moment of the Jews' alleged deicide. In his *Mystici Corporis Christi,* the encyclical of June

1943, he declared: "But on the gibbet of his death Jesus made void the Law with its decrees, [and] fastened the handwriting of the Old Testament to the Cross, establishing the New Testament in His blood. . . . On the Cross then the Old Law died, soon to be buried and to be a *bearer of death*" (my emphasis).[48] What exactly Pius XII meant with his ominous pronouncement that the "Old Law"—which was often used and understood as a stand-in for the Jews—was to be a bearer of death is unclear. But to make such a false and inflammatory antisemitic charge when the Jews were being slaughtered in Christian and Catholic Europe tells us a great deal about the convictions and moral values of its author.

WHY SHOULD WE CARE so much whether Pius XII was a righteous man or a blameworthy man? After all, he was just a man, just one man, and as Garry Wills reminds us,

> Catholics have fallen out of the healthy old habit of reminding each other how sinful Popes can be. Painters of Last Judgments . . . used to include a figure wearing the papal crown in the fires of hell, presenting the Pope as a terminal sinner damned forever. This was not only a topos (commonplace), but a preacher's topos—a lesson of faith, not an attack on it. Authoritative as a Pope may be by his office, he is not impeccable as a man—he can sin, as can all humans.[49]

However important it is to expose the moral untenability of Pius XII's conduct and the hollowness of his defenders' arguments, it is still more important to recognize that Pius XII remains a sideshow, a diversionary topic, by which "the broader question of a massive Catholic failure is deflected."[50] The sound and fury engulfing this one man signifies more by what it omits and conceals about the Church than by what it reveals about him. What about the views and conduct of many thousands of clergy and their many-millionfold flock?

Pius XII was not the Catholic Church. The Church was an enormously powerful transnational institution, with a long, relevant history; a political culture; national churches with their cardinals, bishops, priests, and nuns; and its scores of millions of individual adherents, informed in their actions by their faith. Compared with all of this, one Pope must be but a small, if critical, part of any historical or moral reckoning.

The fixation on Pius XII is common among those who would figuratively or literally sanctify him, though it is also characteristic of some of his detractors. Given the charges against him, it is understandable that his defenders focus on him. Nevertheless, they proceed in the narrowest of terms, as if by refuting the accusations that the Pope was an antisemite, that he helped the Nazis, or that he stood with a hardened heart watching as the Germans slaughtered Jews, they would vindicate not only his conduct but also the conduct of the Catholic Church and of other Catholics qua Catholics.

To frame the issue as whether or not Pius XII spoke out or acted forcefully enough to save the Jews is to obscure broader themes that are, in many ways, more important. Even if the conclusions that people draw about Pius XII are not the ones that his champions wish, as long as the light shines principally on him, the Church's defenders have won a strategic victory in whitewashing the Church's past. Symptomatic of this strategy was the Church's restrictive mandate to the International Catholic-Jewish Historical Commission, which it formed in 1999 and which, owing to the Church's intransigence, is now defunct. The Church narrowly confined the commission's investigation to include only the highly restricted material that the Vatican itself had published on its own diplomatic activity and confined the time frame to only the war years. The Church thereby excluded its nondiplomatic activities and the conduct of its national churches from the investigation and prevented the commission from examining its actions during the first six years of the Germans' persecution of the Jews.

In order to forestall a systematic investigation of the Catholic Church's contribution to the German-led persecution and extermination of the Jews, the Church's defenders engage in many sleights of hand. Here I focus on only three major stratagems. The defenders shift their gaze from one part of the Church to another, depending on what is propitious for their arguments (that is, when not confining themselves to discussing only the Pope). They erect a *cordon sanitaire* around the antisemitism that moved the Germans to persecute and kill Jews, arguing that it had nothing to do with the Church's own deprecating and hate-filled views of Jews, which they consistently deny or underplay. And when it suits their exculpatory purposes, they shift from analyzing the Church as a moral institution to discussing it as a political institution.[51]

INVESTIGATE THE ENTIRE CHURCH

Like photographing a disfigured face only from its one good angle, shifting focus from some members or parts of the Church to other ones, as the issues change, systematically shows the Church off at its best and conceals its uglier aspects. When the Pope or a Church official did something laudable or at least defensible, such as intervening on behalf of Catholics who had converted from Judaism (which is typically falsely presented as an intervention on behalf of Jews), it is discussed and accorded great significance. When the Pope failed to do something he obviously should have done, such as intervening for or speaking out publicly on behalf of Jews, it is ignored and attention is diverted to, say, the French bishops who did protest, as if they spoke for and represented the entire Catholic Church (when the Pope and his representatives clearly failed to support these protests).[52] Italian clergy who helped Jews are praised rightly for their actions, but the utter failure of the German clergy's far more pressing need and greater duty to extend verbal and physical aid to Jews is passed over. The silence of other national churches' bishops, such as in Belgium, is ignored.[53]

Such bias in choosing which topics to discuss is guaranteed not to yield a faithful historical portrait of the Church's role, or its many components' roles, in these persecutions and mass murders. It is a prettifying procedure. This problem is exacerbated greatly by the convention—followed even by critics who bend over backward perhaps for fear of being falsely charged with being anti-Catholic (or anti-German or anti-Polish)—of presenting vivid anecdotes of righteous Catholics (or Germans or Poles) that offset summary statements of the Church's (or Germans' or Poles') enormously more widespread failures. This practice misleads readers with concrete stories and memorable images of the relatively rare instances of resistance while keeping abstract or vague the far more common cases of Catholics' (or Germans' or Poles') abandonment of Jews or of their complicity in the mass murder.[54]

Any serious investigation of the role of the Catholic Church during the Holocaust would have to assess systematically not just the Pope, not just the Vatican, but every national church. While across Europe there were a few diocesan efforts to help Jews, such as in Berlin and Italy, and there were individual clergy who helped Jews, such as Father Marie Benoît, in Marseilles, who shepherded hundreds of Jews to safety often in Switzerland or Spain, even a cursory inventory yields a depressing picture.[55]

The German Catholic Church, without hesitation, abandoned the Jews to their countrymen's ever-intensifying eliminationist persecution. Genealogical records, essential for determining who was a Jew according to Germany's new race laws, so that the regime would know whom to persecute and eventually to kill, were stored in churches. Catholic (and Protestant) bishops and priests in all corners of Germany had the needed genealogical investigations done, without protest and apparently without hesitation. It seems never to have occurred to them that they ought not generally help implement the race laws and the regime's identification of people whom, according to racist criteria, it would persecute as Jews. The voluntary and willful nature of the German Catholic Church's cooperation here is made that much more obvious by its reaction to government requests to use Church records to investigate Catholics who had converted from Judaism and people in mixed marriages. This the Church refused, denying the regime access to its records, while citing "pastoral secrecy."

In the eyes of Catholic clergy, helping their government in the persecution of the Jews, however, was an act of patriotism that promoted the welfare of Germans. In the authoritative *Klerusblatt*, the official organ of the Bavarian priests' association (Bavaria being the center of German Catholicism), a priest told its readers, already in 1934, that just as the Church had "always" aided the German people, it would also help with "pleasure" in the task of providing documentary Aryan proof to non-Jews in accordance with the wish of the Führer.[56] In January 1936 the *Klerusblatt* gave its stamp of approval to the recently passed Nuremberg Laws, seeing the race laws as measures designed to "preserve and refresh the German blood" as well as to "eliminate the Jews as bearers of civic and political rights."[57] How can any honest treatment of the Catholic Church during this period not put this racist-genealogical collaboration in the center of the discussion? Why, moreover, did Pius XII, as Vatican Secretary of State or as Pope, not prevent the German Catholic clergy's willful collaboration with this explicitly racist, eliminationist persecution? The Pope's defenders have no answer. They do not even mention the collaboration itself, the extent of which is vast.[58]

The German bishops consciously chose not to protest their government's extermination of the Jews of Germany and Europe. They also never protested publicly (or even privately to their government's leaders) against any other major aspect of their country's eliminationist persecution of the Jews, even as the horrors unfolded before their eyes. (Some had private misgivings, and one in particular, Bishop Konrad von Preysing, passionately but futilely urged both Pius XII and his German colleagues to try to save Jews.) This is in stark contrast to several German bishops' attacks on the German state's so-called Euthanasia program, which killed the putatively mentally and physically infirm. In a sermon in August 1941, German Bishop Clement August von Galen publicly condemned *this* program of mass murder: "If they start out by killing the insane, it can well be extended to the old, the infirm, sick, seriously crippled soldiers. What do you do to a machine which no longer runs, to an old horse which is incurably lame, a cow which does not give milk? They now want to treat humans the same way."[59] Bishop Galen did not mince his words. He explicitly called it "murder." Why did the German bishops and the Vatican, silent about the Germans' systematic mass murdering of the Jews, which had already begun, rally behind Bishop Galen when he spoke for the mentally ill and others who were not Jews? Earlier, in the second half of 1940, Cardinal Faulhaber protested to the Minister of Justice, and Cardinal Adolf Bertram protested to the head of the Reich Chancellery, against the so-called Euthanasia program, with Cardinal Faulhaber declaring: "I have deemed it my duty of conscience to speak out in this ethico-legal, nonpolitical question, for as a Catholic bishop I may not remain silent when the preservation of the moral foundations of all public order is at stake."[60] For Bishop Galen, were the Jews not "humans"? For Cardinal Faulhaber, was the mass murder of the Jews not an assault on "the moral foundations of all public order"? Why did the bishops not believe that protesting on behalf of the mentally ill and other victims of this program of mass murder would only hasten their deaths, as the Pope and the bishops are now alleged to have believed would have happened to Jews if they had defended them? Why did the German bishops' unqualified "duty of conscience to speak out" against mass murder not apply when the victims were Jews?

What did the Nazi leadership do to Bishop Galen, this man who had essentially denounced them as murderers? Nothing. The power of the Church was so great, as the Church itself knew, and the regime was so fearful of the Catholic Church's hold over Germans that it did not dare to move against Bishop Galen. Joseph Goebbels, Germany's Mephistophelean propaganda minister, acutely attuned to public opinion, explained, in the words of his interlocutor, that "the population of Münster could be regarded as lost during the war, if anything were done against the bishop, and in that fear one safely could include the whole of [the state] of Westphalia."[61] Hitler agreed with Goebbels.[62] Because of Church opposition and widespread public discontent the so-called Euthanasia program was soon formally halted, certainly saving some lives, even if the regime resumed killing mentally ill people secretly mainly in the now expanding camp system outside of Germany.

The German Catholic Church protested publicly many other regime policies, including governmental tolerance of dueling and cremation (but not the crematoria of Auschwitz, about which they knew).[63] The German Church protested against two attempts by the government to remove crucifixes from the schools of Bavaria, first in 1936 and then from April to September 1941, at the same time that the government began the systematic mass murdering of Jews. To safeguard the crucifixes, the Church helped to produce sustained, regional antigovernment public protests by ordinary Germans. What did the German government do to the Church, its bishops and priests? Virtually nothing. What happened to the policies? The government allowed the schools to display the crucifixes.[64] The German Church survived these and its many other conflicts with the German government essentially unscathed, which is the best indication that it would have survived, as the Catholic Church as a whole would have, had it defended the Jews. But the German bishops made no such protest. One priest, Provost Bernhard Lichtenberg of Berlin, said a daily prayer for the Jews. It took the regime years, until October 1941, to arrest him. He died two years later on his way to Dachau.[65] Father Lichtenberg and a few other lonely priests implicitly condemned the silent German Catholic leadership, who, like the Pope, abandoned him to his fate. The German bishops and priests were determinedly not the Jews' keepers—but then, unlike in Denmark, they by and large did not even see the Jews as "brothers and sisters."

What about the hundreds of German priests serving the German army and occupation forces in eastern Europe, who were in the thick of killing operations, holding services for and hearing the confessions of the killers? Did they see Jews as innocent and the mass slaughtering of Jews as wrong? Did the priests tell the many Catholics among the hundreds of thousands of Germans participating in the mass annihilation that they were sinning? The evidence strongly suggests that they did not. If they had viewed the killing of the Jews as a crime and a sin, then we would in all likelihood know about such a view and of their initiatives among the perpetrators, because it has been the practice of the Church to put forward any evidence that would cast a favorable light upon itself. The testimony that does exist is not heartening. Of an estimated one thousand Catholic and Protestant clergy serving as military chaplains, fewer than ten cases (most are Catholic priests) have come to light—some of which are dubious—where it can be said that the chaplains conveyed disapproval of or urged resistance to the mass murder. And some chaplains have recounted their clerical colleagues' approval of their countrymen's mass murdering.[66] One priest tells of the enthusiasm for the slaughter of the Jews that existed in the German occupying forces in the Soviet Union. "Among the Germans," he recalls, "one often heard the view: The Jews are parasites. They have exploited the *Volk*. So they should not wonder that we are now taking revenge on them" by exterminating them. He quotes another priest expressing approval of the mass murder, in scriptural terms, saying, "There is a curse on this people ever since the crucifixion of Jesus when they cried: 'Let his blood be on our heads and on the heads of our children.' " The priest who reported this explains that the second priest's approval of the mass murder was not shared by "most of the other" clergy, which means that a minority of the clergy did also support the mass annihilation of the Jews.[67]

That Catholic priests in the thick of the mass murder greeted the annihilation of the Jews with silence or worse should come as no surprise, since the Catholic military bishop, Franz Justus Rarkowski, the spiritual leader of the priests assigned to the Wehrmacht, was deeply Nazified. In his Christmas message of 1940, which all Catholic soldiers received, Bishop Rarkowski used well-known antisemitic tropes to vilify the putative progenitors of the war and explain Germany's suffering:

> The German people . . . has a good conscience and knows which people it is that before God and history bears the responsibility for this presently raging, gigantic struggle. The German people knows who lightheartedly unleashed the dogs of war. . . . Our opponents . . . believed in the power of their money bags and the repressive force of that shameful and un-Christian Treaty of Versailles.[68]

Doris Bergen has concluded that the great majority of German military chaplains, Catholics and Protestants, "weighed in on the side of the perpetrators, condoning and blessing their crimes through words, actions, and silence. One of the most obvious manifestations of this function was the provision of group absolution for soldiers."[69]

How could we not maintain that the German priests who gave succor to the genocidal executioners were at least collaborators with the Nazi regime, if not partners in this mass-murdering onslaught? (Why did the Pope not instruct them to counsel all Catholics among the executioners that they must stop murdering Jews?) This virtually unknown and unmentioned chapter of the Catholic Church and its clergy's role in the Holocaust has barely been investigated.

In Slovakia the Catholic Church was not just extremely influential, its priests were political founders and leaders of the newly independent state. The antisemitic Father Andre Hlinka established the Slovak People's Party in 1905. After his death in 1938 Monsignor Josef Tiso became his successor, and then in 1939 the first President of the German satellite state of Slovakia and the avowedly devout Catholic Vojtech Tuka became Prime Minister. Their government instituted comprehensive antisemitic laws modeled on Germany's and instigated the deportation of the country's Jews, by requesting at the beginning of 1942 that the Germans deport twenty thou-

Andre Hlinka (center) and Josef Tiso (left) receiving a delegation of American Slovaks.

sand Jews as a way for Slovakia to speciously fulfill its labor quota. Adolf Eichmann later commented that "Slovakian officials offered their Jews to us like someone throwing away sour beer."[70]

In August 1942, during the first phase of the deportation of the country's Jews to their deaths, the President-priest Tiso preached in a holiday mass, using Nazi antisemitic idioms and arguments, that expelling the Jews was a Christian act because Slovakia had to free itself of "its pests." He invoked the authority of his priestly predecessor, Father Hlinka, who, sharing the views of many Catholics of the time, had proclaimed—in violation of official Church policy—the racist doctrine: "A Jew remains a Jew even if he is baptized by a hundred Bishops."[71]

Although individual Slovak bishops decried these policies, the majority of the Church leadership supported its country's eliminationist program.

They themselves said as much. During the height of the deportations, in April 1942, the Slovak bishops collectively issued a pastoral letter that essentially justified the deportation of the Jews as Christ-killers: "The greatest tragedy of the Jewish nation lies in the fact of not having recognized the Redeemer and of having prepared a terrible and ignominious death for Him on the cross." They complemented this with modern antisemitic charges: "The influence of the Jews [has] been pernicious. In a short time they have taken control of almost all the economic and financial life of the country to the detriment of our people. Not only economically, but also in the cultural and moral spheres, they have harmed our people. The Church cannot be opposed, therefore, if the state with legal regulations hinders the dangerous influence of the Jews." Earlier the Slovak bishops had protested to their government, effectively, on behalf of Christians who had converted from Judaism but not on behalf of the Jews. These Christians were subsequently not deported.[72]

It should therefore come as no surprise how one priest in Slovakia counseled a critical perpetrator about the deportation of the Jews. Vojtech Tuka, Slovakia's mass-murdering Catholic Prime Minister, conveyed to a German diplomat that he had once told his father confessor that his conscience was clear about his deportation of Slovakia's Jews. As long as his deeds were, in Tuka's words, done "for the good of his people," the priest was "not opposed to his actions."[73]

The bishops waited until March 1943—almost one year after deportations, with all their visible brutalities, had begun and when three quarters of Slovakian Jewry had already been transported to their deaths—to issue a pastoral letter against the deportation. But they were clearly going on the record only because the war was going badly for the Germans, and even still, many bishops opposed the letter. The Slovakian bishops chose to have the letter read in Latin, which few Slovaks understood, so the letter would be guaranteed not to rally many people to sympathize with or aid the Jews. The letter was so opposed by the clergy that many priests refused to read it, or altered its content so that it no longer condemned the anti-Jewish onslaught.[74]

The Vatican did privately protest, in vain, several times to the Slovak government, though mainly on behalf of Catholics who had converted from Judaism and those in mixed marriages.[75] It was acutely worried that this avowedly Catholic regime would implicate the Church and the Pope in mass murder because in Slovakia the Church's fingerprints were undeniably on the trigger. The German government had earlier commented with "undisguised gratification" that the Slovaks' antisemitic laws "had been enacted in a state headed by a member of the Catholic clergy."[76] Pius XII's representative warned President Tiso in October 1944, when the Germans' defeat was around the corner, of the injury that further deportations would do to the Church: "The injustice wrought by his government is harmful to the prestige of his country and enemies will exploit it to discredit clergy and the Church the world over." This intervention, as the Church itself made clear, had much to do with the Church's selfish political interests and little to do with compassion for the soon-to-be slaughtered Jews.[77] As with the Pope's late appeal to Horthy in Hungary, the Church was donning a fig leaf of quarter-hearted intervention to cover up its indefensible stances for an expected postwar world under Allied domination.[78]

What did the Catholic Church do to President Tiso, the priest who, explicitly invoking the Church's authority as justification, contributed to the mass murder of Jews? What did it do to the Catholic clergy in the Slovak Parliament, not one of whom voted against the legislation legitimizing the deportation of the Jews to their deaths? No public condemnation. No excommunication. Nothing.[79] By allowing Father Tiso and the other priests to remain Catholics—not merely lay Catholics but priests who administered the sacraments—and by refusing to publicly and emphatically dissociate itself from him and the other priests who contributed to and gave their blessings to deportations and mass murder, and by refusing to excommunicate this man and the others acting publicly in the name of the Church, Pius XII and his bishops showed that they believed that people complicit in the mass murder of Jews were worthy of representing this Catholic Church in its most sacred duties.

This incredible state of affairs was even more starkly etched in Croatia, where many priests themselves committed mass murder, including as commanders of approximately half of the twenty death camps set up by the Nazi-like Ustasha regime: "Dozens, perhaps even hundreds of priests and monks shed their priestly apparel and donned Ustasha uniforms, in order to share in the 'sacred work' of murder, rape and robbery."[80]

The most notorious camp was Jasenovac, where the Croats killed 200,000 Jews, Serbs, and Gypsies. Forty thousand of them perished under the unusually cruel reign of "Brother Satan," the Franciscan friar Miroslav Filipovic-Majstorovic.[81] Pius XII neither reproached nor punished him or the other Croatian priest-executioners during or after the war. Instead, Pius XII supported their country's mass-murdering regime.[82]

The leaders of the various national Catholic churches (this is also true of Protestant churches) were deeply influenced in their views of Jews by the culture and politics of their own societies. This meant that the Catholic Church's overarching cultural and doctrinal patrimony of antisemitism was

At the celebration during the opening of the Ustasha headquarters in Zagreb, Rev. Stipe Vucetic and his assistant greeting the Ustasha dignitaries with a fascist salute.

refracted through each national political culture. In less antisemitic countries, such as Denmark, France, and Italy, the churches were, to varying degrees, also less antisemitic. This was also particularly true of the American Catholic Church, which was within the Catholic world notoriously independent, pluralistic, and tolerant, so much so that already in the late 1890s Pope Leo XII dubbed the tolerant ways of much of the American Catholic Church a heresy called "Americanism." The clergy in these countries more frequently reacted with genuine horror to the Germans' antisemitic onslaught and extended more aid to the Jews. In the most deeply antisemitic societies, such as Germany, Lithuania, Poland, Slovakia, and Ukraine, churchmen tended to reflect the intensity and the particular character of their local antisemitism.[83] In Lithuania in August 1941, when the Germans' and Lithuanians' slaughter of the country's Jews was in full swing, the leaders of the Lithuanian Catholic Church, in the words of a contemporaneous German report, "forbade the priests to help Jews in any way whatsoever"; and they issued this prohibition after representatives of the Jewish community had approached the Church leadership begging for help. Although some individual priests helped Jews, the Lithuanian Church as a whole collaborated with the Germans until the war turned against Germany (when a greater number began to help Jews, especially Jewish children), with some priests taking part in, and lending their authority to, the German and Lithuanian killing institutions.[84]

To understand its various and many roles during the Holocaust, then, the Catholic Church needs to be examined as an agglomeration of related, though distinct, this-worldly social and political institutions, at least as much as a unified institution, seated in the Vatican, whose character derives from the interpretation of religious doctrines or from its self-conceived political needs. A major research project into the political, social, and cultural histories of each national Catholic church's attitudes and actions toward the Jews—before and during the Nazi period—therefore is one essential prerequisite for fully evaluating the Catholic Church, and for the Church fully evaluating itself, during the Holocaust. It would have to produce for each country a series of in-depth, uncompromising volumes that would include, of course, an account of the small minority of individual bishops and priests across Europe who objected in principle to the persecution of Jews and sought to aid them, and of how their clerical brethren and parishioners reacted to their stances. Such an obviously needed investigative tack—which would necessitate full access to all Vatican, national, and local church archives, and which has not been pursued—would be a salutary departure from the current fixation on the person of the Pope and from the apologetic practice of superficially surveying the far-flung Church landscape with exculpatory bias.

The defenders of the Church complement their tactic of shifting focus to whatever parts or members of the Church show the Church in a favorable light on a given issue with another concealment tactic of asking certain questions to the exclusion of other ones. The most flagrant example is using Pius XII as a lightning rod that deflects attention from the rest of the Church. Equally misleading is the oft-discussed question of why the Church did not do more to help the hunted Jews. Although this question, like inquiries into the Pope's conduct, is important, it typically conceals the critically important, unexamined, and underlying question: What did the Church—its national churches, bishops, priests, nuns, and laity—think about Jews and about the eliminationist persecution of them in all of its facets, and not only in its most extreme manifestation of mass annihilation?

The Catholic Church and its national churches and clergy greeted many aspects of the Germans' pan-European eliminationist assault on the Jews, and of the national assaults in individual countries, with tacit or explicit approval, sometimes even with open enthusiasm, and rarely with principled disapproval. The Germans' antisemitism and eliminationist impulses were understood, found to be valid, and supported, exceptions notwithstanding, by the German (and Austrian), Croatian, Lithuanian, Polish, Slovak, and other parts of the Catholic Church. Differences over the means of implementing these goals (whether genocide was an acceptable and just response to the putative Jewish threat in which they commonly believed) is what separated portions of the Church from the many Germans and others who morally or physically supported mass murder.

LIFTING THE CHURCH'S IRON CURTAIN

Suppressing this question of the Catholic Church's and its clergy's view of Jews and of their persecution is one component of the second sleight of hand employed to falsely exonerate the Church: erecting an iron curtain between the Church's own virulent antisemitism and the virulent antisemitism that led the Germans and those who helped them persecute and then slaughter Jews. In one of the most glaring public historical falsehoods of recent times, the Holy See's Commission for Religious Relations with Jews declared in "We Remember: A Reflection on the Shoah" that the Nazis' "antisemitism had its roots outside of Christianity."[85]

The Catholic Church and today's Pope, who commissioned and wrote a letter of endorsement upon its publication, would have us believe that had the Church and its officials, high and low, never propagated the antisemitism that "We Remember" exculpatingly calls "anti-Judaism," and never imbued so many of its followers with this "anti-Judaism," then three things would still have happened: (1) the Nazis and other racist antisemites still would have invented exactly their murderous brand of antisemitism out of thin air; (2) all those people in Europe who were not "neo-pagan" antisemites (as the Church calls modern German antisemitism) but who were still supportive of the Germans' eliminationist persecution of the Jews—precisely because of their religious antisemitism (this is true, for example, of many complicit Croats, Lithuanians, Poles, Slovaks, and others)—still would have lent the same moral and physical support to the Germans' assault that they did; and (3) the Germans still would have met so little clerical and popular resistance and therefore they still would have been able to inflict as much suffering on Jews, including killing six million of them.

If people choose not to suspend their disbelief when beholding such improbable notions, then the Church's iron curtain separating its and the Germans' antisemitisms must be lifted. This inevitably leads to a consideration of the Church's culpability not just for its and its members' reactions to the eliminationist onslaught but also for the Holocaust itself. Several topics would have to be investigated, always keeping in mind that, according to a survey conducted in 1939, 95 percent of Germans still belonged to a Christian church and were hardly (as the Catholic Church would have us believe) "neo-pagans." Or is it the Church's position that the 43 percent of Germans who were Catholics were really neo-pagans? As Carroll observes: "The German people, whatever else they did, maintained their ostensible Christian identity—which is why the question about, at the very least, acquiescence in genocidal crimes is a question about the content of that identity."[86]

How did the Church perceive, characterize, and treat Jews over the centuries? How did the Church's antisemitic precept and practice contribute to the modern eliminationist antisemitism that animated the Nazis, the vast majority of the German people, and, by and large, the willing executioners? How did the Church's antisemitism prepare the social soil for Nazism, eventually tilled by others, to flourish and for the Nazis' eliminationist assault (both in its early and lethal stages) to find broad sympathy and many helpers in Germany and throughout Europe? (The same questions should be posed about the Protestant churches, particularly the German ones, bearers of the antisemitic legacy of Luther.)

Before investigating the complex of issues relevant to the Church's antisemitism and the Holocaust, it might be asked, Why is such an investigation lacking in most treatments of the Holocaust, not to mention in treatments of the Church during the Holocaust? How can it be that this overwhelming record of antisemitic enmity and hatred and its obvious, integral relationship to the genesis of the Holocaust be denied?

Defenders and even many critics of Pius XII fail to discuss the Church's antisemitism except in the most glancing, cursory, and often exculpating of ways.[87] It may seem extraordinary that people could write books about Pius XII, the Church, and the Holocaust without an in-depth exploration of the Church's long history of deeply rooted antisemitism and persecution of the Jews, or of the extent and the character of antisemitism within the Church during the Nazi era. Given that this unapologetically ahistorical approach to the study of the Holocaust has been a common, though not universal, practice among academic historians who have focused on the mass murder itself, this particular neglect becomes just another unremarkable part of a general neglect.[88]

Those who speak obvious and plain truths about the antisemitism of the European past, including of Catholic officials, often meet ferocious opposition. Given that roughly two billion people in the world today, including most Americans and Europeans, are Christians (with more than one billion Catholics among them), and that the most visible, respected, and powerful religious leader in the world is the leader of the Catholic Church, speaking the truth about Christianity and antisemitism, and especially about Christianity and the Holocaust, is too rare. Those who are deeply invested in defending the indefensible—whether they be Germans, Christians, or academics—can become enraged when someone exposes the falsehoods of their claims. Their accusations that such people are anti-German or anti-Catholic are no less surreal than if those who stated the obvious truths that widespread racism undergirded American slavery and Jim Crow, and that the enslaving or segregating whites thought blacks to be inferior or dangerous, were branded anti-white.

To dig into the historical development and nature of the Church's antisemitism is to excavate the ideational seedbed from which the ideas grew that animated the perpetrators of the Holocaust. Such an account can be structured around four main themes.[89]

First, the supersessionist creed of Christianity, often called its "replacement theology," held that once Jesus fulfilled the messianic prophecy of Judaism, a new Christian era had begun that replaced the now anachronistic Judaic one. Just as Judaism had become Christianity, Jews were to become Christians. Since the refusal of the Jews to accept the Christian demands that they renounce their Judaism implicitly posed a fundamental challenge to the Christian claims, and since that challenge came from the once acknowledged people of God, the disparagement of the Jews became central to Christianity. If the Jews, the people of God, rejected the divinity of Jesus and his Church, then either Jesus was not divine and the Church was wrong, or that people had strayed from God's path. So the Gospel According to John has Jesus saying to the Jews, "Whoever belongs to God hears the words of God; for this reason you do not listen, because you do not belong to God."[90] If not to God, then to whom? According to John, Jesus recognizes the true identity and nature of the Jews, saying, "You belong to your father the devil and you willingly carry out your father's desires. He was a murderer from the beginning and does not stand in truth, because there is no truth in him."[91]

That the Jews were capable of any evil—including serving the devil—became the pan-European view in the Middle Ages. This alleged alliance with the devil was made plausible and fueled by the foundational libel that Jews had killed Jesus, and that all Jews, dubbed "Christ-killers," are forever responsible for the crime. Carroll writes that while Christianity, historically, has needed living Jews to be a negative Other, against which the true

Christian claims could be pressed, "replacement implied the elimination of the replaced. This strain would lead to conversionism and expulsions, and ultimately it would be reduced to its perverted essence by the attempted genocide."[92]

Second, Christian antisemitism has been divorced from the nature of actual Jews. "The age-old 'Jewish Problem' . . . is, was and remains a Christian problem, spawned by an ignorant Christian imagination."[93] The claim that prejudices—against Jews, blacks, gays, women, and so on—are provoked by those who are hated or deemed odious, in this case the Jews, is transparently false. (Such an assertion is itself typically an expression of the prejudice that it purports to explain.) The responsibility for antisemitism and other prejudices lies with the people who are prejudiced, and with their societies and cultures, which teach them their prejudices. Even though most antisemites throughout history have not known actual Jews (just think of all those parts of Europe that expelled Jews sometimes for hundreds of years and continued throughout that time to be thoroughly antisemitic), they were nonetheless animated by the vivid, often demonic images of Jews of their cultures' and religions' imagination. Real, living Jews had nothing to do with generating the antisemites' prejudices.

Third, antisemitism has been characterized by a direct yet complex relationship of beliefs to actions. The basic supersessionist tenet of Christianity, given an inexhaustible supply of emotional fuel by the foundational charge of Christ-killing, was elaborated through the centuries in a variety of ways, producing a series of evolving and related antisemitisms that were often distinct in their precise demonology, which then frequently inspired Christians to adopt eliminationist strategies and undertake assaults that assumed a wide variety of forms depending on doctrine and social and political circumstances. The Christian supersessionist creed was multipotential in action, meaning that depending on the circumstances in which it was acted upon, it produced different anti-Jewish eliminationist programs, because there were a variety of logical eliminationist solutions to the Christian "Jewish Problem": expulsions, pogroms, forced conversions, ghettoization, and sustained murderous assaults. Although there can be no doubt that antisemitic belief and antisemitic action do not correspond in a one-to-one relationship—because other social, cultural, and especially political factors shape the relationship—there can also be no doubt that, when activated and channeled by political leaders, beliefs about Jews suggest certain courses of action to their bearers. In the case of antisemitism, it has often been sufficient to motivate leaders and ordinary people alike to seek to eliminate Jews from their midst, at times with deadly violence.

It should also be clear that antisemitism itself does not generate a program of systematic mass murder. Those who want to deny that the Church's antisemitism or the antisemitism of ordinary Germans had a significant role, or any causal role at all, in producing the Holocaust claim that if either kind of antisemitism was critical to producing the Holocaust, then the Holocaust, or something like it, would have happened long before it did or have happened in other antisemitic countries. This line of argumentation is transparently false. It neglects the well-established fact that for a large program of mass murder to occur, two factors are necessary but neither one alone is sufficient: a political leadership that initiates and organizes the mass murder, and people willing to implement its policies. Either one (a deeply antisemitic populace) without the other (a political leadership that, for whatever reason, refuses to engage in a politics of systematic extermination) does not lead to large-scale mass murder.[94] Only in Germany under the Nazis, and then among some of their satellites, did the two come together in modern times.

The fourth central feature of antisemitism, then, is the tendency among antisemites toward violence, even mass murder, against Jews. The Church adopted a catastrophic posture, physically and socially for the Jews, and doctrinally and morally for itself. It counseled that the Jews were not to be attacked because of the Augustinian-derived notion, codified first during the reign of Pope Gregory I in various proclamations, including in 598 in *Sicut Judaeis* that the Jews should not be destroyed and should be granted legal protection. The Jews were, however, to live with substantial restrictions and disabilities as befitting those who reject the Church.[95] Yet the same Church repeatedly found it hard to prevent the flood of rage against the Jews that it engendered among its followers from bursting the weak dams of its formal injunctions against violence. "For a thousand years," Carroll writes, "the compulsively repeated pattern of that ambivalence would show in bishops and Popes protecting Jews—but from expressly Christian mobs that wanted to kill Jews because of what bishops and Popes had taught about Jews." The bishops' and Popes' weak restraining impulses were "bound to fail" whenever "Jews presumed, whether economically or culturally or both, to even think of thriving,"[96] or for that matter when, for any reason whatsoever, Christians projected responsibility for natural or social maladies upon the demonized Jews. One such instance, mentioned earlier, occurred during the black plague of the mid–fourteenth century, when Christians, mainly in Germanic lands, annihilated the Jews of roughly 350 communities, including such major centers as Mainz, Trier, and Cologne. This murderous logic, of Popes' and bishops' needing to restrain Catholics from acting on what Popes and bishops had inculcated into them, was also operative in the 1930s and 1940s. The Pope and most bishops watched the Germans and their local helpers—many of whom had imbibed Church-inspired antisemitism—deport and slaughter the Jews of one Catholic country after the next, and also of non-Catholic Christian countries. This time they did not even try to protect them.

As Carroll argues, all of this comes together in the most central and sacred symbol of Christianity: the cross. Christianity developed from a religion that initially celebrated Jesus' life to a religion fixated on his death with all its consequences (a contingent turn that the Catholic Church and other Christian churches could reverse). The most catastrophic consequence was a Christian fixation on the people who allegedly caused the crucifixion, which led to the rise of the cross as a concomitant weapon against the "Christ-killers." Carroll observes that the cause of this age-old "Jewish problem," born of Christian ignorance, "is so plain we can hardly see it as such, and it has been there all along. A miscarried cult of the cross is ubiquitous in this story, from the Milvian Bridge [where the night before a victorious battle for his Roman Empire in 312, Constantine saw a cross in the sky, which led him and his empire to become Christian] to Auschwitz."[97] The Crusades were wars of the cross, intended to free Jerusalem from Muslim control, yet in 1096 the First Crusade's first victims were—perfectly logically—Jews, the Jews of Mainz. A Jewish chronicler captures the annihilatory logic of the antisemitism:

> [The Crusaders] said to one another: "Behold we travel to a distant land to do battle with the kings of that land. 'We take our souls in our hands' in order to kill and subjugate all those kingdoms that do not believe in the Crucified. How much more so [should we kill and subjugate] the Jews, who killed and crucified him." They taunted us from every direction. They took counsel, ordering that either we turn to their abominable faith or they would destroy us "from infant to suckling." They—both princes and common folk—placed an evil sign upon their garments, a cross.[98]

The cross's development as an antisemitic symbol and weapon can be traced from Constantine's Christianized Roman Empire to the medieval Crusades to modern times, culminating in some Catholics' recent attempts to dejudaize Auschwitz by colonizing it with a convent and a huge cross. For the better part of two millennia, since the time of Constantine's adoption of Christianity for the Roman Empire in the fourth century, the cross has stood for the murder of Jesus, implicitly invoking the Jews as his putative

A house marked by a cross to the left of the door in the last days of June 1941, indicating that no Jews lived there. Non-Jewish families reportedly marked their homes and businesses with crosses three days before the roundup and slaughter of thousands of Jews in Iaşi, Romania.

murderers. "In a dozen ways," Carroll writes, "the cross itself had been conscripted into this campaign . . . and now every cross in Western Christendom would become an infallible promulgation of the same doctrine."[99]

Given the many historical fabrications and libels about Jews contained in the Christian Bible (discussed here extensively in part three), including the explicit, false, and immoral blaming of *all* the Jews of Jesus' time *and their descendants* for his death, it is all too likely that many Christians will continue to blame Jews for Jesus' death. The Gospel According to Matthew fabricates the whole Jewish people demanding Jesus' crucifixion, shouting, "Let him be crucified!," willingly accepting their guilt, and willingly pronouncing a curse of that guilt upon their own descendants: "And the whole people said in reply [to Pilate's declaration of his own innocence], 'His blood be upon us and upon our children.' "[100]

Here is the paradigmatic accusation of collective guilt, imputed as an indelible stamp on all Jews forever even though the Jewish people did not kill Jesus and were not, in any sense, responsible for his death. It was the Romans who decided to kill him, and who executed him in their trademark Roman manner of crucifixion. In light of these indisputable facts, why, it has been asked, have the Catholic Church and other Christian churches, if they need to cast a collective villain in the drama of Jesus' death, not focused on the Romans and their descendants, who would be today's Italians, for the role? But then while Rome was the Western world's superpower during the time of the Gospels' composition, and Italy supplies the ground for, and most of the people who have populated the highest echelons of, the Catholic Church, the Jews were the weak and vulnerable people, and remained the weak and vulnerable people, whom Christians and the Church were trying to delegitimize, and whose tradition they were trying to appropriate as their own, and whose God they were saying was now theirs and only theirs. Even though the Catholic Church finally declared in 1965 that it is false to blame Jews today for the death of Jesus, and has since removed much of the explicit antisemitism from its doctrine, theology, and liturgy, the cross, Catholicism's central and most evocative symbol, bound up in the biblically derived antisemitic libel of "Christ-killers" is, as Carroll argues, all too likely to provoke further antipathy toward Jews.

This analysis of Catholicism's antisemitism does not substitute for the long story itself, which has been told many times.[101] I will not retell it here, as much as it bears retelling in Christian cultures. Suffice it to say that the once pan-European antisemitism, which one scholar describes as "a hatred so vast and abysmal, so intense, that it leaves one gasping for comprehension"[102] and which frequently led to eliminationist onslaughts including proto-genocidal violence, did not generally dissipate with the Enlightenment and modernity, though it did gradually decline in some countries and among certain groups. Instead, it continued to be spread systematically by the Church at the same time that a new, derivative form of antisemitism, racist in character, began to flourish by its side.

This occurred most centrally, though not only, in Germany in the nineteenth century, where Christianity's litany of anti-Jewish charges and the emotional force that came with them was reinforced with a new pseudoscientific foundation of race and augmented with a new set of accusations appropriate to the age—accusations that were taken up by Christian antisemites and racist antisemites alike. Christian antisemitism had always adapted itself to the idiom and social conditions of the day, with new antisemitic charges cropping up in response to political, economic, social, and cultural developments. The modern world was the age of nations, so Jews were said to undermine the national corpus. It was the age of industrializing capitalism, so Jews were said to pull its levers, to prey on entire economies. It was the age of secularization, so the Jews were said to be assaulting Christianity and morality in general. It was the age of growing demands for political and economic inclusion and justice, including Marxist demands, so the Jews were said to be the instigators of destabilizing politics and revolution.

The Christian age-old view of the Jews as authors of so much evil was naturally adopted by racist antisemites, most noticeably in Germany. Germanness was fused with Christianity, rendering Jewishness the nefarious Other, not just for Christendom but also for Germania. Christianity bequeathed to modern racist antisemites a powerful demonology, a fierce emotional antipathy toward Jews and an image of the Jew as the sinister Other perpetually seeking to destroy goodness root and branch, in the case of Germany the root being the German *Volk*.

It is not surprising, therefore, that the Catholic Church, whose publications and preachers continued to pour forth antisemitic canards and hatred throughout the nineteenth century and into the twentieth, including the 1930s and 1940s, could find common cause with most of what racist antisemites were saying and urging, even if they did not usually share the racists' belief that the source of the Jews' putative perniciousness was biological, which meant that Jews could not be redeemed by conversion to Christianity and the act of baptism. To the ear of the common folk, not focused on every tonal variation of the antisemitic battle cry, the fearsome charges and hatred of one kind of antisemite (the religious, such as the Catholic Church) echoed and reinforced the fearsome charges and hatred of another kind of antisemite (the racist, such as the Nazis). That the antisemites' respective accusations that demonized Jews were not 100 percent congruent but only a figurative 90 percent made little difference to their antisemitic followers.

It was in the 1930s, when Hitler was weak and the Church was indisputably in no danger, that Pacelli, then Vatican Secretary of State, engineered Catholicism's legitimation of Nazi dictatorship with a deal, the aforementioned Concordat, pledging the German Church's loyalty to Germany's Nazi leadership (Catholic bishops, at the behest of Pius XI and Pacelli's Church, swore an oath of allegiance to the Nazi state) and forbidding the Church from participating in politics. The Concordat effectively conceded to the regime the right to pursue, without Church criticism or opposition, its political goals, which included its openly militarist, imperialist, and racist program.[103] Pacelli even agreed to a subsequent "secret annex" to the Concordat that effectively gave the Church's approval to German rearmament, still forbidden by the Versailles Treaty.[104] Hitler's existentially central, loudly trumpeted, though still vague in detail, eliminationist enterprise against the Jews was well known to the Catholic Church. Before signing the Concordat, Hitler even boasted to two German Church leaders of his affinity with the Church in his hostility to the Jews, explicitly telling them that he would "drive the Jews out more and more."[105]

The Catholic Church gained with the Concordat a recognized sphere of religious and cultural immunity for itself in Germany, where its newspapers and organizations were under pressure from the regime. Pacelli's political bargain with Hitler might have appeared less reprehensible had the Church made it with a heavy heart weighed down by utter repulsion toward the eliminationist antisemitism that reigned in Germany, and with firm resolve to fight it, however possible. But this was not the case. In a note that he submitted to the German government at the time of the Concordat's ratification, which reflected the views of the German Catholic Church leaders, Pacelli conveyed the Church's intention to let the Germans have a free hand with the Jews, except Catholics who had been born Jews, by stating, "The Holy See has no intention of interfering in Germany's internal political affairs," which had been the sentence dictated to Pacelli by Eugen Klee, the German government's representative, to mean that the Church would not interfere with the Germans' policies on Jews.[106]

Both in the Vatican and in Germany itself the Catholic Church continued to spread antisemitism and, certain exceptions notwithstanding, to be greatly sympathetic to the Germans' eliminationist impulses—even if some clergy had private misgivings about the violence, such as *Kristallnacht*, the protogenocidal nationwide assault on the Jewish community and its property on November 9–10, 1938. This is evident by the failure of the Catholic Church, its Popes Pius XI and Pius XII, and its national bishops to oppose the dehumanizing, inherently eliminationist antisemitic legislation that Germany, Italy, and many other countries issued in the 1930s and 1940s. There is no evidence that clerical expressions of approval, or clerical silence, regarding these policies concealed an inward opposition to them born of the belief that the Jews were innocent. If the Church archives contained evidence of such opposition, especially on the part of the Popes, how likely is it that the Church, desperate to clear Pius XII and itself, would insist on keeping such evidence hidden from the public?

ASIDE FROM THE INDISPUTABLE FACT that the Church's antisemitism was the trunk that never ceased bringing nourishment to the modern European antisemitism that had branched off from it, just a cursory glance at what the Church was preaching about Jews from the second half of the nineteenth century through the Nazi years renders untenable the claim of an unbridgeable difference between the Church's "anti-Judaism" and its offshoot European "antisemitism." Those asserting such a difference as fact do not do the minimum necessary to show it, such as seriously discussing the nature of antisemitism and its varieties, and compare the two kinds of antisemitism in depth according to clear evaluative criteria, in order to ascertain what their relationship is. They do not discuss the actual historical relationship of the Church's antisemitism and modern European anti-semitism. Surely that relationship is not nonexistent, as Pope John Paul II and other apologists would have us believe.[107]

Even if they did adequately compare the different antisemitisms as they choose to portray them, it would not suffice because this distinction between anti-Judaism and antisemitism is itself founded on a fiction, a sanitized account of the Church's so-called anti-Judaism. The antisemitism of the Church, certainly since the last part of the nineteenth century and throughout the Nazi period, was far more "modern" and far closer, in precept and practice, to the Nazis' antisemitism than has been acknowledged. David Kertzer even ascribes responsibility for engendering the modern antisemitism that came to predominate in Germany and elsewhere to the Catholic Church, which he calls "one of its important architects."[108]

Kertzer has refocused attention away from the difference between the formal religious foundation of the Church's antisemitism and the racist foundation of modern European antisemitism toward the great similarities in content and demonology of these kindred ideologies of prejudice. There was even a new tendency among Catholic writers to define Jews as a race. In 1880 the Jesuit fortnightly *Civiltà cattolica*, which was the official, authoritative, and critically important Vatican publication, explained: "Oh how wrong and deluded are those who think that Judaism is just a religion, like Catholicism, Paganism, Protestantism, and not in fact a race, a people, a nation!"[109] In 1897 *Civiltà cattolica* was still more emphatic: "The Jew remains always in every place immutably a Jew. His nationality is not in the soil where he is born, nor in the language that he speaks, but in his seed." Regardless of whether given churchmen were formally sticking to the religious explanation for the alleged evil of the Jews or propagating the new racist explanation, the content of the Church's antisemitic demonology was modern. "As modern anti-Semitic movements took shape at the end of the nineteenth century," Kertzer observes, "the Church was a major player in them, constantly warning people of the rising 'Jewish peril.' "[110] A typical and classical statement of this kind was to be found in an article in *Civiltà cattolica* from 1893, called "Jewish Morality":

[The Jewish nation] does not work, but traffics in the property and the work of others; it does not produce, but lives and grows fat with the products of the arts and industry of the nations that give it refuge. It is the giant octopus that

The cover of an issue of the radical antisemitic Deutschvölkische Monatshefte *from 1921, recalling* Civiltà cattolica, *depicts an octopus, caricatured as a Jew, wrapping its tentacles around a blond woman representing the Germanic world. On the ground next to the woman lie her Valkyrie helmet and broken shield and sword. The caption reads: "The master of the world!"*

with its oversized tentacles envelops everything. It has its stomach in the banks . . . and its suction cups everywhere: in contracts and monopolies, . . . in postal services and telegraph companies, in shipping and in the railroads, in the town treasuries and in state finance. It represents the kingdom of capital . . . the aristocracy of gold. . . . It reigns unopposed.[111]

The Church's accusations against Jews were often virtually indistinguishable from those of the racist antisemites.[112] Even Pius XI's suppressed antiracism encyclical is animated by modern antisemitic charges that might be termed soft Nazism.

This should come as no surprise because Pius XI had long been a committed antisemite. In 1918, immediately after the end of World War I and less than four years before Achille Ratti was to be elevated to the papacy as Pope Pius XI, Pope Benedict XV sent him to Poland as his representative with the assignment of working to improve the lot of the Jews, whom Catholic Poles were intensely persecuting, even with some pogroms. Kertzer concludes: "Ratti did nothing of the sort. . . . On the contrary, he did everything he could to impede any Vatican action on behalf of the Jews and prevent any Vatican intervention that would discourage the violence. . . . [His] reports to the Vatican on the situation of the Jews in Poland . . . rather than warning about the Jews' persecutors, were aimed at alerting the Vatican to the dangers posed by the Jews themselves."

Why did he disobey his Pope's order? Because of his antisemitism. Not only, according to Ratti, do the Jews in Polish cities "only subsist through small commerce involving contraband, fraud, and usury," but, he also declared in his report, "one of the most evil and strongest influences that is felt here, perhaps the strongest and most evil, is that of the Jews."[113] Like his successor, Pius XII, he subscribed to the modern antisemitic demonology that identified Bolshevism with Jews, maintaining in his report to the Vatican that "the Jews form the principal force [of Bolshevism] in Poland."[114] In 1932 he even confided his profound animosity toward Jews, which stayed with him at least through most of his papacy, to Mussolini. The persecution of the Church around the world, Pius XI volunteered, was partly a result of "Judaism's antipathy for Christianity," and with the exception of Italian Jews, the Jews of Europe, especially of central and eastern Europe, were a threat to Christian society. As his own experience in Warsaw had supposedly taught him, "I saw that the [Bolshevik] Commissioners . . . were all Jews."[115] With views such as those of Pius XI and Pius XII—especially their false common identification of Jews with communism and of Communist leaders all being Jews—leading the Church, it is no wonder that Mussolini and Hitler believed that the Church would not be an impediment to them regarding the Jews. (But it is a wonder that the Church's self-exculpatory "We Remember" presents Pius XI, like Pius XII, only as an anti-antisemite.)

How far gone this modern antisemitic Church was by the 1930s is suggested by Pius XI's attempt, late in his life, to atone for his and the Church's transgressions (including the antisemitism of his and Pacelli's encyclical *Mit brennender Sorge,* and his suppression of a Catholic organization that sought to put an end to the deicide charge),[116] and for his silence in the face of the Germans' racist antisemitic assault upon the Jews. Shortly before he was to die, he decided to commission a new encyclical, the so-called Hidden Encyclical, that explicitly condemned the Germans' assault. Because he so distrusted the antisemitic Vatican establishment, presumably including Pacelli himself, from whom he concealed his initiative, he went to an outsider, an American Jesuit named John LaFarge, who was the editor of the Jesuit journal *America* and had written an antiracism book that attacked segregation in the American South. Father LaFarge informed the superior general of the Society of Jesus, Father Wladimir Ledóchowski, who had collaborated closely with the Pope on earlier encyclicals but whose views about the Jews led the Pope to want to keep this new initiative a secret from him. When Father LaFarge eventually turned his draft over to him, Father Ledóchowski strategically gave it for evaluation to another priest, Enrico Rosa, the former longtime editor and notorious antisemitic polemicist of the Vatican's authoritative *Civiltà cattolica*.[117]

In *Civiltà cattolica*, "the boundary seems very fluid" between the Church's "anti-Judaism" and the "average" antisemitism of the period.[118] Even a sampling of the hate-filled charges against the Jews that *Civiltà cattolica* was printing in the 1920s and 1930s shows them to be Nazi-like. In 1922 it declared that "the world is sick. . . . Everywhere peoples are in the grip of inexplicable convulsions." Who is responsible? "The Synagogue." "Jewish intruders" control the principal threat to world order, Russia and the Communist International. In 1936, after the Nuremberg Laws had been published and the Jews had been under sustained assault in Germany for some years, it echoed standard Nazi antisemitic rhetoric in accusing the Jews of being "uniquely endowed with the qualities of parasites and destroyers," as pulling the levers of both capitalism and communism, in a pincer assault to control the entire world. In 1938 it warned of "the Jews' continual persecution of Christians, particularly the Catholic Church, and their alliance with Freemasons, socialists, and other anti-Christian groups."

A year earlier this authoritative Vatican journal disseminated as "an obvious fact that the Jews are a disruptive element because of their dominating spirit and their revolutionary tendency. Judaism is . . . a foreign body that irritates and provokes the reactions of the organism it has contaminated." It went on to discuss solutions to the "Jewish Problem" ambivalently and explicitly considered various forms of "elimination" as functional equivalents. It thereby indicated that the different solutions were, in principle, compatible with its assessment of the evil of the Jews and of the danger that they posed to Christian society. In addition to the solution of "segregation" (which it did not categorize as "elimination"), *Civiltà cattolica* discussed undertaking the "expulsion" of the Jews. It also proposed a still more extreme way of solving the putative problem of the Jews, which it called the "clearly hostile manner" of "destruction." So in 1937—after the Nuremberg Laws, when the Germans' destructive vise was tightening on the Jews of Germany—this authoritative Vatican journal made it unequivocal that its own antisemitism (though it rejected the term) was eliminationist, and then discussed the annihilation of the Jews as an actual thinkable option.

This authoritative journal of the Vatican tells us how fearsome the Church's demonology about the Jews was, so fearsome that this organ of the Church acknowledged the logic of adopting eliminationist solutions, so fearsome that it presented expulsion and mass annihilation as self-evidently flowing from its conception of the Jews. It assumed that its readers—clergy, editors of Catholic newspapers and journals around the world—required no elaborate explanation in order to understand why the Jews' destruction would be considered necessary and could be considered an appropriate solution, and also why the Vatican's journal, whose views had to be in harmony with those of the Pope and Secretary of State, would be presenting it as such. In the end, the journal rejected such solutions as un-Christian and urged its readers to show Christian charity toward the Jews in the hope that the Jews would reform themselves. But since *Civiltà cattolica*—and the Church—had for decades insistently described the Jews as an incorrigible threat to the well-being of the world, why should a Catholic who believed that the Jews were so dangerous have taken these words of Christian charity to be an effective prescription for a cure? Why should such a person have chosen anything but one of the eliminationist solutions?

The proximity between the Catholic Church's antisemitism and modern antisemitism, even Nazi antisemitism, did not go unrecognized by the most vicious antisemites. The Nazi newspaper *Der Stürmer* and the Italian Fascist newspaper *Il Regime fascista* applauded *Civiltà cattolica* as an antisemitic model. *Il Regime fascista* opined in 1938 that all countries, including Italy and Germany, "still have much to learn from the Fathers of the Society of Jesus."

The significance and importance of this kind of antisemitism appearing in *Civiltà cattolica*'s was immense. *Civiltà cattolica* was known throughout the Church and beyond to express the views of the Holy See, having been founded by Pius IX in 1850 and run by a collective of Jesuits under a director appointed by the Pope, and for the purpose of representing the Pope's views. Its influence among clergy and ultimately lay Catholics was therefore bound to be great. The journal's unusual authoritativeness derived from its close supervision by the Vatican Secretary of State, who was Pacelli during the 1930s, and by the Pope, who during the Nazi period was Pius XI and then Pacelli, now Pius XII. Prior to publication the Secretary of State and often the Pope himself formally reviewed each issue of *Civiltà cattolica* to ensure that its contents properly represented the Church's teachings and the Pope's views and interests. Therefore, *Civiltà cattolica*'s damaging and incendiary antisemitism, only a sampling of which is presented here, was published under the approving eye of Pacelli himself. He must have deemed such antisemitic accusations and incitements to accurately represent the views of the Church and believed their publication to further the interests of the Church. If he had not, then they would not have been published. Would a man of God who did not share such antisemitism, such deprecating and injurious views of others, repeatedly approve of their publication in one of the chief organs of his religion?[119]

Against what other group did prominent Catholic clergy, in an authoritative Vatican-approved publication no less, even consider, if only to reject, mass annihilation as a possibility? The Church had many real enemies, including secularizers, rival Christian movements that disparaged and hated Catholicism, Nazism, and, of course, communism. But its authoritative voices did not consider exterminating these enemies en masse. How great must the antisemitism of the Church have been, how demonic a phantasmagoric image of Jews must it have had that a prominent member of the Church would explicitly discuss such an idea, already in 1937, and that the most influential Vatican journal would choose to print it and be permitted by Pacelli to do so? The Church's images of Jews made Jews worse than the worst criminals. Given the Church's official endorsement of the death penalty, did not the logic of its enmity toward Jews, of the great crimes of which it deemed Jews guilty, suggest that the death penalty was an appropriate punishment? *Civiltà cattolica* admitted as much. That would make the pursuit of such a lethal policy not murder but a just execution—even if the Church's position, that the Jews should be allowed to live but subjected to severe restrictions and disabilities as a warning to others who would reject Jesus, formally inhibited the Church from propounding or accepting this logic as a guide to action.

Father Rosa himself, just as he was receiving the draft encyclical, was publishing his own article on what to do with the Jews. This occurred two weeks after Italy's first antisemitic decree in September 1938, expelling foreign Jews. In the article he endorsed a series of articles that *Civiltà cattolica* had published in 1890, in which the Jewish exceptions to the Jewish norm are defended: "Not all Jews are thieves, agitators, deceivers, usurers, freemasons, crooks and corruptors of morals. Everywhere, there is a certain number of them who are not accomplices in the evil actions of the others."

(Even Hitler believed that there had been one good Jew. He had been an antisemite and committed suicide.)[120] According to Father Rosa, experience showed that the polemicist in 1890 was correct when he wrote that granting the Jews civil equality "has had the effect of bringing Judaism and freemasonry together in persecuting the Catholic Church and elevating the Jewish race over Christians, as much in hidden power as in manifest opulence." Father Rosa's views were all but official Church pronouncements, and known throughout the Catholic world to be such, as his obituary in the Jesuit journal testified: "It is no exaggeration to say that Father Enrico Rosa remained for thirty years at the head of Italian Catholic journalism as interpreter and intrepid champion of the directives of the Holy See."[121]

Even the antiracism encyclical, this defense of the Jews which Pius XII quashed, calls for an understanding of the "authentic basis for the social separation of the Jews from the rest of humanity," namely, religion, which becomes an occasion for the author's advancement of vicious antisemitic notions. The encyclical conjures up the image of Christ-killers, "the Jewish people [who] put to death their Savior and King," the resulting "Divine malediction, doom[ing them]", as it were, to perpetually wander over the face of the earth," and "the wrath of God, because it [the Jewish people] has rejected the Gospel." It warns of "the spiritual dangers to which contact with Jews can expose souls," and, in the contemporary antisemitic idiom, that Jews "promote revolutionary movements that aim to destroy society and to obliterate from the minds of men the knowledge, reverence, and love of God."[122]

This was what Jews could hope for from their "friends" within the Church: a condemnation of violence and racist persecution in one breath, undermined in the next by the expression of the then still seemingly irrepressible age-old desire of Church leaders to make it clear that the Jews were indeed a great evil, which, de facto, lent support to the ideational grounding of the eliminationist assault on the Jews.

National churches (Polish, Slovakian, French, and others) were no better, and some were worse, with Catholic publications around Europe—especially in Germany before and during the Nazi period, including while Germans were slaughtering Jews—disseminating antisemitic vitriol that was often indistinguishable from the Nazis' fare. In Germany they justified the elimination of the Jewish "alien bodies" from the country, often in racist terms. Antisemitic policies, according to the German Catholic publications, were "justifiable self-defense to prevent the harmful characteristics and influences of the Jewish race."[123] Archbishop Conrad Gröber published an antisemitic pastoral letter in March 1941, blaming the Jews for the death of

A sign warning: "Jews in the Blossersberg community are not welcome! To know the Jew is to know the devil!"

Jesus and, quoting the Gospel According to Matthew, implying that the Germans' current eliminationist policies were justified: "The self-imposed curse of the Jews, 'His blood be on our heads and on our children's,' has come true terribly until the present time, until today."[124] Why was this German bishop not censured by the other German bishops? Why was he not censured by Pius XII? If we consider all that the antisemitic Pius XII permitted *Civiltà cattolica* to publish and that he himself felt the need, during the height of the mass murder, to conjure up the deicide charge and impugn the "Old Law" as "a bearer of death" in his June 1943 encyclical, *Mystici Corporis Christi,* perhaps it becomes clearer.

We might think about the effect of the Church's antisemitic doctrines upon the willingness of ordinary Germans, Poles, and others to support the violent elimination of Jews. Take a person who believed in the demonology that the Jews are Christ-killers, minions of the devil, that they threaten the German, Lithuanian, or Slovak people, that they are responsible for Bolshevism, that they cause economic crises, like the worldwide depression of the 1930s, that they corrode morals, and so on, and ask, What would such an individual do when political leaders said that we must eliminate these evil people who cause you, your family, and your countrymen so much suffering? Would he resist an initiative to get rid of the people about whom he believed such things, merely because he might believe that the source of their great evil is their religion (something that the Church decidedly did not emphasize during these years), particularly when he knew that wholesale conversion was not even a remote possibility? Or would he recognize that while the Church may have helped, along with others, to alert him to the extreme threat of the diabolical Jews, it is the government, not the Church, that fashions and implements practical solutions to political problems, which across Europe is what the grave "Jewish Problem" was widely understood, ultimately, to be?

The striking inability of Church writers to propose a workable noneliminationist political solution to the putative world historical problem of the Jews, which they asserted repeatedly to be so severe, helps explain why their acolytes and even the clergy themselves—the German Catholic Church choosing to collaborate actively with the government to enforce the eliminationist race laws, and Slovakian clergy and Croatian clergy lending a hand to mass murder—were so susceptible to the Germans' practical, sometimes even "final" eliminationist initiatives.

MORAL OR POLITICAL INSTITUTION?

In the discussion of the role of the Catholic Church in the destruction of European Jewry, a third diversionary strategy is often encountered: oscillating between presenting the Church as a moral institution and presenting it as a political institution without acknowledging its political essence or taking note of the shifting ground. The Church is legitimized as a moral institution, and its failings are defended by appealing to the constraints, real or invented, that it faced as a political institution.

Moral institutions, even when they take part in the material world, must be centrally concerned with the moral content of people's lives and guided in their actions by defensible moral principles. Political institutions, whatever moral notions should or do animate their members, are concerned with public power—acquiring, using, and sustaining it. If the Church is to be defended as a moral institution, then one set of criteria should be employed. If it is to be defended as a political institution, then different criteria would be used.

Political institutions do make moral claims, even when they are manifestly disingenuous: to care for and protect their people, to enhance their welfare, perhaps even to bring about their salvation. These typically are particular, self-interested, nonuniversal claims. For the Catholic Church to have a special status as a universal moral institution, which is its explicit claim for itself—after all, "catholic" means universal—it must really predominately tend the souls and moral lives, and be concerned for the welfare, of all human beings.[125]

The Church's moral status stands on its claim to be the earthly representative or embodiment of Jesus, at once the Son of God and God, and on its faithfulness to his teachings.[126] Its mission is to bring people to salvation through him, and to get them to live according to his moral instruction. If we take the Church's self-presentation seriously and assess it as a moral, not a political, institution, and its leaders as moral, not political, actors, then we must address a series of troubling issues.

What was wrong with this moral institution and its moral leaders that it did not recognize that Nazism was an unsurpassed evil? Already in 1933 Hitler presented, as a blueprint for world transformation, a racist, lethal view of humanity that was anathema to Jesus' ministry. Hitler preached passionate hatred of Jews and called explicitly for their elimination in 1920, practically from the beginning of his political career. Even then he made it clear that his preferred form of elimination was extermination. "We are animated," he declared, "with an inexorable resolve to seize the Evil [the Jews] by the roots and to exterminate it root and branch. To attain our aim we should stop at nothing even if we must join forces with the devil."[127] He glorified war. He urged foreign conquest. By 1939, not to mention 1941, Hitler was undeniably practicing what he had proudly and insistently preached. Catholics should know as well as anyone that one does not make pacts with the devil, in this case the world's closest human approximation of him. But that is precisely what the Church did with its Concordat, which, the Germans' gargantuan mass murdering notwithstanding, the Church, Pius XII, and the German national church "honored" through the war.

Why did this moral institution and its moral leaders not direct even an iota of the ire against Hitler and the Nazis that it hurled at the innocent and harmless Jews during these years? Why did this moral institution and its moral leaders speak relatively temperately about Nazism, its mass murdering notwithstanding, yet assault the Soviet Union with the most vitriolic imprecations? Compared with the Church's kid-glove criticism of Nazism itself (as opposed to its ringing condemnation of some religious practices in Germany) in *Mit brennender Sorge,* the encyclical of 1937, Pius XI's contemporaneous anticommunist encyclical, *Divini Redemptoris,* is a thundering, thorough condemnation: Communism destroys Christianity and Christians "with a hatred and a savage barbarity one would not have believed possible in our age." It is a "satanic scourge," a "false messianic idea," and "the fatal plague, which insinuates itself into the very marrow of human society only to bring about its ruin." It produces "violent hate and destruction" and deems that all those who "resist such systematic violence, must be annihilated as hostile to the human race."[128] Turning to Pius XII himself, why in the 1930s, as Vatican Secretary of State, did he work hard to soften those statements critical of Nazism or Germany that did emanate from Church officials?[129]

What principles governed when this moral institution compromised morality for expediency, namely, its own power? During the 1930s, for example, the Nazis conducted their intensive, violent, eliminationist assault upon the Jews, created concentration camps (to which they initially consigned the regime's and the Church's common Communist and socialist enemies), and institutionalized torture as a regime practice. Although the existence of the Church was not then in any conceivable sense imperiled, the Church kept silent and in some of these areas even lent tacit or active support to the murderous regime.

Also lost in the discussion of the Church's eschewal of its moral duty toward the victims is its duty to, yes, the perpetrators. After all, it is not bodies but souls that are the Church's self-appointed, primary responsibility. So why did it fail utterly to tend the souls of the mass murderers and of the other persecutors of Jews? Why did it not warn them, educate them, make clear to them that the mortal sins they were committing would endanger their souls?[130] During these years this moral institution thought nothing of warning its flock against all manner of lesser danger and lesser sin, including the putative threat to Christian souls of fantasized Jewish infiltration. Why did this moral institution not raise a voice, let alone trumpet with all its power, the danger of damnation into which the willing executioners plunged themselves, so that some of them might not transgress or, if they already had, might work to redeem themselves first by refusing to kill (which the Nazi regime allowed them to do) and then by aiding the Jews however they could? Why did this moral institution not forcefully preach to Catholics: Do not hate Jews. Do not persecute them. Do not commit mass murder. Resist murderers with all your might.

Any evaluation of the Catholic Church as a moral institution must centrally take into account that in effect the Church was serving—because not to choose is to choose—the closest human analogue to the Antichrist, Hitler, and that it tacitly and sometimes materially aided in mass murder. There were righteous individuals within the Church. There were bishops, priests, nuns, and laity who spoke out and helped to hide Jews. They are honored by Yad Vashem, the Israeli memorial to the Holocaust, as "Righteous among the Nations." Many of them (even when they were also anti-semites) were moved by their religious beliefs, such as some members of Zegota, the largely Catholic Polish organization, to save Jews. But they acted on their own, in sharp contrast to official Church policy.

It is hard to defend the Church of this era as a moral institution, at least with regard to Nazism and the Holocaust. Not surprisingly, its defenders hardly try. Instead, they take refuge in defending the Church as a political institution. They say that it had diplomatic considerations; that it had to remain neutral in the war or it would be endangered; that it believed it had to support the fight against communism.[131] How, then, does the Church look if we evaluate it using the standard appropriate to its true political nature?

The reality is that, almost since its inception, the Church has been a political institution, vying for this-worldly power at least as much as it tended to otherworldly affairs. In the nineteenth century the Church made a fatal political turn when it rejected liberalism, democracy, and capitalism, when it rejected modernity itself. This the Church itself declared in one of the most important encyclicals in its history, Pope Pius IX's *Quanta Cura* in 1864. It explicitly rejected as an "error" the notion that "the Roman Pontiff can, and ought to, reconcile himself, and come to terms with progress, liberalism, and modern civilization."[132]

It was natural for the Church, a reflex, to use antisemitism to fight modernity. It identified the Jews as responsible for modernity, blaming them for the hated political, social, economic, and cultural changes that threatened it and its hold over its people. In the words of the encyclical, "It is from them [a conspiracy of secret sects] that the *synagogue of Satan*, which gathers its troops against the Church of Christ, takes its strength." This encyclical, according to Kertzer, "would shape Catholic attitudes for decades to come," particularly its invocation of the "synagogue of Satan"— the name given in the Christian Bible to the Jews' place of worship—as the font of the modern evil.[133]

Appealing to all people beholden to embattled institutions, practices, and traditions, the Church sought to mobilize the vast reservoir of European antisemitism in its political battle against modernity. So it attacked Jews relentlessly. The political tactic, which was also true to the churchmen's genuine belief, was clear. If modernity could be identified with the Jews, then half the battle against it was won. The Church was availing itself of a common, time-honored trans-European political strategy, born of belief and expediency, of attacking institutions by identifying them with Jews. This, of course, was most successful in Germany, where racist antisemites were turning the Jews into the central symbol of everything that they deemed to be awry with Germany and with modernity. (The Church's role—antisemitism and the Holocaust aside—in producing the antimodern, antidemocratic cultural and political climate that contributed to the rise of Nazism, fascism, and other antidemocratic, antimodern institutions in the twentieth-century is underappreciated and also something that a full assessment of the Church must address squarely.)

The defenders of the Church argue that with the outbreak of World War II it felt beleaguered on all sides, afraid for its existence. Even someone who is hardly a defender of the Church can write somewhat sympathetically in this vein:

> Never had the term "Fortress Church" seemed more apt. Under these circumstances, many Vatican officials became more suspicious, timid, and inflexible than ever. Their activities became equally narrow and defensive, directed exclusively toward their own constituency. There was little room for concern about the poverty, oppression, or violations of the human rights of non-Catholics, who were, by definition, enemies of the Church.[134]

Perhaps the Church should have been more outward-looking and active, its defenders say, but its reaction is both understandable and in the end justifiable, given the real danger that it faced from Nazism, which they are right to say was profoundly anti-Christian, even if the Nazis concealed their hostility well enough so that most Germans, even ecclesiastical Germans, did not understand this. If the German Catholic bishops and the Pope had believed that they were in mortal danger from Nazism, then would they have been wishing for Germany to defeat the Soviet Union, thereby strengthening Nazism immeasurably and consolidating its control over Europe? How fearful of Nazism could the Church's leadership truly have been?[135]

We are asked to show understanding for this embattled political institution, which had an independent sovereign state, Vatican City, with an absolute ruler, the Pope, and diplomatic relations with other states. But why should the Church's situation vis-à-vis the Germans be judged so different from that of all the other countries and peoples, and why should the difficult circumstances that everyone in Europe was facing (in many places far more direly than the Church) so readily excuse or extenuate only this political institution and its political leaders' pattern of action and inaction?

Many people around Europe came to terms politically and ideologically with the Germans, abetting them in at least some of their important political goals, even as they claimed that they did so in order to safeguard their people and some semblance of independence for their country. Such people—Quisling in Norway, Marshal Pétain and Pierre Laval in Vichy—are often called collaborators, and their regimes collaborationist.[136] Using this frame of evaluation, one might conclude that Pius XII, too, must be classified as a Nazi collaborator, even if one does not share the overly harshly drawn portrait of him as "Hitler's Pope."

Analytical rigor and moral honesty demand that this comparison be considered. That the words "collaborator" and "collaborationist" are not frequently uttered in connection with Pius XII and the Catholic Church (or its national churches, bishops, and so on) is a symptom of the failure of writers and commentators in our Christian societies to speak plainly about this most prominent Christian leader and institution. This failure is even more glaring in light of certain facts about France, the country that gave us the concept of "collaborator": the declaration in November 1941 by Monsignor Beaussart, the representative of Paris's Cardinal Emmanuel Suhard, who was the Church's Assembly of Cardinals and Archbishops' liaison with the Germans, that "collaboration is the only reasonable course for France and for the Church";[137] Charles de Gaulle's wish, after the war, to have at least twenty-seven bishops removed for collaborating with Vichy;[138] the French legal codification of the crime of collaboration, the principles of which would certainly apply to the Catholic Church and many of its clergy within and outside of France.

After all, the Catholic Church was the first international political institution to sign and announce a major agreement with Hitler, and it did so in order to sustain its worldly power. Presenting itself as a moral institution, it conferred de facto moral legitimacy upon his regime. It aided in the Germans' persecution of their country's Jews by willingly supplying its genealogical records. It joined the regime in denouncing the Jews and then stood by, all but mute, as the Germans and their helpers committed genocide. It allowed its German clergy to give succor to the soldiers of his apocalyptic, mass-murdering war. In Slovakia prominent clergy were genocidal allies of the Germans. In Croatia a significant number of clergy committed mass murder themselves. As Vichy was putatively safeguarding France, the Church was safeguarding its material and spiritual domain, namely, itself. Each betrayed an enormous number of people—in exchange for these, in the modern currency of power, few pieces of gold. Whatever answers may be given, the questions must be asked. With regard to the Jews, was the Catholic Church more like Vichy France or like Denmark? Was Pius XII more like Pétain or Laval or more like the Protestant Bishop Fuglsang-Damgaard of Copenhagen and King Christian X of Denmark?

Any evaluation of the Church as a political institution, the terms in which it is defended, must begin with the facts that while many of the world's political institutions were, with all their power, resisting the Hitlerian scourge, including by fighting an apocalyptic war for the future of civilization, the Church cut a self-interested, Nazi-legitimizing deal, sparing itself inconvenience and conserving its own power; the Church was obviously content enough to watch more or less passively as the Germans conquered Europe, made war against the hated Soviet Union, and pitilessly exterminated the Jews.

A principal difficulty with moral evaluation is the array of available evaluative frameworks and therefore the need to state clearly and then justify the one chosen. This is rarely done by academics writing about the Holocaust, let alone defenders of the Church, though they readily render convenient judgments. Comparison, for example, can be used as an analytic framework and also to suggest a framework of moral evaluation. Even though comparison is often used, the examples chosen are seldom justified. Defenders of Pius XII, for example, make much of the alleged effects of the Dutch Catholic Church's protests in making the Pope reluctant to help Jews, while being silent about the effective protests of other national churches; they fail to compare the Church to Denmark on the one hand, or to Vichy or Quisling's Norway on the other.

What moral standard should be used? The defenders fail to state the clear moral principles that the Pope and the Church should have been employing in deciding whether to help the Jews or the moral standard that we should adopt to evaluate their actions. Presumably, Pius XII and his Church subscribed to the Catholic principle that murder is a sin and to the doctrine derived from the Fifth Commandment to resist murder. Since no one could honestly maintain that the Church did everything it could, or even made a substantial good-faith effort, to resist the murder of the Jews, its defenders must articulate the criteria by which the Church might rightly have violated this principle in the case of the Jews. A conjecture, not a fact, that to resist the mass murder—even to do something as little as expressing public disapproval of it—would cripple its power? A conjecture, not a fact, that German Catholics, because they were so antisemitic, would, in a conflict between the Church and Nazism, choose Nazism over Catholicism? If the Church's defenders think that mere conjectures of these kinds provide a sufficient standard to justify the abandonment of millions of people to their deaths, then they ought to say so openly. They should further state what the acceptable moral calculus would be: how many Jews' lives would it be right for the Church to have sacrificed for its desire to preserve how much of its power (the danger to which was hypothetical) or to keep how many of its German Catholics from leaving the fold (that they would do so, again, was only hypothetical)? How high would the Church's defenders go? Would they say that the Church rightly would stand by quietly for the mass murder of eight million, ten million, fifteen million, for the mass murder of the entire Jewish people? Until a defender of the Pope's and the Church's conduct during the Holocaust answers such questions, he has not made a good-faith attempt to address the real issues.

Even if the Church's defenders were willing to sketch such a calculus, this would still not settle the matter. To put forward their position that the Church's inaction was not owing to the identity of the victims, in other words not owing to the Church leaders' views about Jews, and that the

Church was right to act so prudently, as it did, the defenders would have to be able also to argue the following: that had the Nazis set out to exterminate systematically eleven million Catholics in Germany or Italy, or for that matter eleven million Protestants in Germany (the number of Jews whom the Nazis slated for extermination at the Wannsee Conference) only and precisely because the victims were Catholic or Christian, and had the Germans been carrying out the mass annihilation over the course of almost four years, until six million Christian martyrs had perished, that the Church would have employed the same moral calculus and done as little to help these victims as it did to help the Jews; that Pius XII would have never spoken out explicitly in public against the mass murder; that the bishops of, say, the German Catholic Church would have remained silent; and that the Pope and the Church would have continued to legitimize the regime and aid it in the myriad ways that it did, including by "honoring" its Concordat.

The Church's and the Pope's defenders, I suppose, would not be willing to argue this. After all, what Catholic (or non-Catholic) could believe, or find it anything but utterly delegitimizing of the Catholic Church, that the Church and the Pope would, under his very window, without protest, and with differing degrees of aid by some national Catholic churches, watch six million or eleven million Catholics or Protestants be annihilated only because of their faith? If the Church's defenders would refuse to make such a claim, then they are, de facto, conceding more generally that the Church was not using defensible moral principles in its response to the Holocaust, and, effectively, that antisemitism prejudicially influenced its response. Why should it be any less delegitimating of the Church when the actual victims of its wrongful actions and inactions were Jews?

Imagine something else: that the powerless Jews were really as powerful as the Nazis' and the Church's respective fantastical demonologies held them to be, and that Jews, not German Catholics and Protestants, were engaged in slaughtering six million of an intended eleven million Catholics or Protestants. Would the Catholic Church have been silent and have been content to do as little to help the victims as it did during the Holocaust? Would anyone argue in this scenario that prudence dictated that the Pope should remain silent as Jews were slaughtering Catholics because his protest would lead only to more dead Catholics?

IF IT IS FAIR to judge any individual or institution by the highest moral standard, surely that individual is the Pope and that institution is the Catholic Church. Moreover, the obligation of the Pope, the Church, and the national churches—specifically, the German bishops and priests whose country initiated, organized, and was the driving force behind the annihilation—to protect Jews might reasonably be deemed greater than that of other individuals and other institutions, because the Church and the national churches were so extensively culpable for spreading the beliefs that led many Germans, Poles, French, and others to support an eliminationist assault upon the Jews. But leaving behind the powerful arguments for the Church and its leaders' higher responsibility to save Jews, they can be judged according to a variety of familiar, widely held moral perspectives. And leaving principle aside for a moment, on a practical level the Church and its leadership can be compared with the Danes. The Danes vigorously and loudly defended the Jews among them, insisting to their German occupiers that the Jews of Denmark not be discriminated against, that they not suffer indignities, that they be allowed to work and socialize with all other Danes, that they be allowed to worship undisturbed in their synagogues. The Germans accepted this. And when, only after years of occupation, the Germans moved to deport the Danish Jews to their deaths, the Danes with the encouragement of the Danish Lutheran State Church saved virtually all of them, ferrying them to safety in Sweden. Here was a practical model of action. Therefore, to expect the Pope, the Church, and the national Catholic churches to have made a substantial effort to save Jews is actually not to expect more of them than of the others who did so, it is only to refuse to tolerate the disingenuous excuses for why they as individuals and as institutions did so much less good and so much more harm than others did.

So what moral standard should be used? The Church's own doctrines, which include Christianity's universalism? A Kantian universalism? A liberal utilitarianism? The application of any or all of these standards produces nothing other than condemnation of the Pope's and the Church's silences and relative inaction. The issue is also clear if we employ the Church's own doctrine, derived from the Fifth Commandment: "The moral law prohibits exposing someone to mortal danger without grave reasons, as well as refusing assistance to a person in danger."[139] What may be the most famous parable of the Christian Bible, that of the Good Samaritan—which proclaims the alleged superiority of Christian morality over Jewish morality—makes vivid this Christian duty to help those in dire need.[140] Perhaps the Church's status as a political institution, whose first priority is the maintenance and furtherance of its power, could be invoked in its defense? But this position would immediately delegitimize the Church as a moral institution and edge it toward a confession of collaborationism. Although each one of these (or other) conventional evaluative standards could be plausibly adopted, the Pope's defenders employ none of them (or in the case of the political justification, at least not openly), because each one would lead to the condemnation of the Church.

In effect, the Church's defenders try to justify the Church's failure with the aforementioned hybrid of the selective, bizarre moral consequentialism of a political institution covered by the distracting gloss of presenting the Church as if it had been a moral institution. The defenders present uncertain, hypothetical consequences as having been near certainties or facts. They then use these "facts" as justification for the Church's not having undertaken indisputably right and necessary moral action. The Church, its intentions pure, runs its defenders' argumentation, could not have done more to help Jews (therefore abdicating its moral responsibility) because it had to safeguard its own allegedly threatened survival (the tenuous consequentialist hypothesis), and it realized in its solicitude for Jews (the Church's false claim of a governing morality) that not to help them was the only way to help them (a bizarre, still more tenuous consequentialism).

It is hard to imagine Catholics justifying moral consequentialism of this sort openly according to theological or moral principles, particularly because the Church and its doctrine explicitly reject such precept and practice: "One may not do evil so that good may result from it."[141] Such moral consequentialism is employed by the Church and its defenders when discussing the Holocaust as long as it can be smuggled in and slipped past the many people who are predisposed to accepting the moral legitimacy and the goodwill of the Church. But to state it openly? And the moral consequentialism is so manifestly hypocritical because no one can believe that the Church would have applied it consistently to an explicit mass-extermination program directed at Catholics for being Catholic.

In truth, the Catholic Church was acting not as a moral institution but as a political one. We should recognize this. We should accept its consequences. One such consequence is that the notion that we cannot criticize Catholic doctrine and actions is nonsense. Like other political institutions, the Church is fit to be criticized by outsiders. The Church has a state, vast material holdings, formal diplomacy; it makes treaties of cooperation and has more than one billion adherents. Its doctrine, like the ideology of a state, is political, and it has consequences for people who are not Catholic. Historically, the Church has been animated by an analogue of aggressive nationalism, preaching exclusivity, a conquering imperialism of the soul, and disdain and hatred of others, particularly Jews. Other institutions, including states, that share any number of these characteristics are rightly subjected to calls for change by nonmembers. Why should the Catholic Church be granted immunity? Everything the Church does that has political consequences or implications for non-Catholics should be subjected by outsiders and Catholics alike to critical, which means fair, scrutiny and evaluation and, when necessary, to calls for change.

THE STRATEGIES of diversion—direct exculpation of Pius XII, tactical shifts to favorable subjects, the dance around antisemitism, and concealing that the Church was really a political institution and therefore should be evaluated as one—are bankrupt. As Garry Wills writes about another aspect of these issues, "A man condemns himself in his own eyes if he tries to claim that he agrees with [them]."[142] Little remains that can exonerate the Church, Pius XII, and many bishops and priests for their many undeniably harmful actions and inactions and ultimately for their weighty moral culpability in the Germans' and their helpers' slaughter of the Jews.

WHAT WOULD JESUS HAVE DONE?

When all the argumentation for and against the conduct of Pius XII and the Catholic Church before and during the Holocaust has been made, when all the discussion of particular deeds, circumstances, and motives is cleared away, everything comes down to two unavoidable questions. The first: Would Jesus, a man who spoke truth to power, have said that his Church should have shouted protest, have spoken moral truth to evil, instead of being virtually silent, as the Jews were being hounded, tortured, and exterminated? Would Jesus himself, in the face of such evil, have publicly condemned the evildoers?

There are three possible responses. To say no, with all the moral and doctrinal devastation that this implies for Christianity. To say nothing, to avoid answering this morally unavoidable question, which would concede that for a defender of Pius XII or of the Church and its clergy this plainest and most pertinent question has no morally palatable answer. Or to say that Jesus would have told his Church that it must not be a silent witness, complicit in the evil of the slaughtering of his people or, for that matter, of any people, that Jesus himself, this forthright man of goodness, would, of course, have publicly, repeatedly decried the evil in explicit, unambiguous, powerful, and ringing language. By admitting this, a person would necessarily concede that Pope Pius XII, the Catholic Church, and its silent clergy sinned against God, betrayed their faith, their flock, and the Jews, and that they bear a weighty moral responsibility in the death of the Jews.

No matter what a person's response to the question of what Jesus would have done, each answer leads to the second unavoidable question: What should be the future of this Church that has not fully faced its antisemitic history, that still has antisemitic elements embedded in its foundational texts, doctrine, and theology, and that still leads its followers to believe that Judaism has been superseded and that Jews are excluded from salvation?

PART TWO

JUDGING
the Culpability

It is therefore an error to judge the morality of human acts by considering only the intention that inspires them or the circumstances (environment, social pressure, duress or emergency, etc.) which supply their context. There are acts which, in and of themselves, independently of circumstances and intentions, are always gravely illicit by reason of their object; such as ... murder ... One may not do evil so that good may result from it.

Catechism of the Catholic Church, parag. 1756

THE CATHOLIC CHURCH and many of its national churches, Pope Pius XI and Pope Pius XII, and many bishops and priests acted badly in the decades before or during the Holocaust. Establishing this is not the end of an investigation but the foundation for beginning a sustained inquiry into the causes and character of the Church's and its clergy's culpability, which we take up here in part two, and then into the Church's duty to redress these wrongs, which we explore in part three.

THE MATRIX OF THE CHURCH'S FAILURES

The patterns of the Catholic Church's actions need to be mapped and explained. This means expanding the view beyond Pius XII to the various national churches and their clergy, and also beyond what a certain person or group of people did or did not do only with respect to the killing itself. The scope of the investigation should include the full range of the Church's and its clergy's actions toward Jews—the good, the bad, and the nonexistent. It also means eschewing the endless anecdotal ad hoc explaining that passes for genuine explanation, such as claiming, typically without evidence, that for this bad act someone was afraid of the Germans and for that bad act someone else did not quite understand what he was doing, explanations that, as we saw in part one, are confounded once they are applied more broadly even to the most obvious relevant facts, such as to other actions by the same person or to other actors facing the same situation. Instead, since people's choices and actions fall into general patterns that have recognizable contours, we must find a general explanation for these patterns, acknowledging that there are always idiosyncratic aspects and therefore exceptions to the rule.

During the Nazi period much of people's stances and actions—including those of ordinary Germans—regarding the Germans' eliminationist persecution of the Jews can be captured by distinguishing and then systematically investigating two dimensions of their beliefs, which until now have been consistently and confusingly lumped together: (1) a person's beliefs about Jews' innocence or guilt, and (2) his beliefs about the rightness of a given punishment. Keeping this distinction in mind can also help us understand the conduct of the Catholic Church, its national churches, and its clergy during these years. And it can help us do so comparatively in two senses, compared with the Church's own stances regarding other criminal actions of the Germans, and compared with how other actors, such as the Danish Lutheran State Church and its clergy, responded to the eliminationist persecution of the Jews. Just a preliminary word on the first issue. Even though, during the Nazi period, the Catholic Church failed to act well regarding other peoples and in many other ways, against no group other than the Jews did the Church itself willfully, actively, and consistently do harm and promote suffering, let alone harm and suffering on such a vast scale. This central fact must be kept in focus and is itself in need of explanation.

There is no doubt that the Germans—originators, engineers, and principal though not sole implementers of the Europe-wide eliminationist onslaught against the Jews—were, with exceptions, animated by an image of the Jews that, whatever its manifold features, essentially held them to be guilty of the greatest crimes and most damaging offenses against Germans and humanity, and an ongoing threat to Germany's well-being and existence.[1] The question to be posed about each member of every country's clergy, from the lowest parish priest to the Pope, is one that is almost always ignored by those writing about these issues: Did these men believe that the Jews were innocent or guilty of the charges? In other words, did they deem the extrajudicial, de facto criminal conviction of the Jews by the Germans, the Slovaks, the Croats, and others to be just or unjust? If they did think the Jews guilty of inflicting great harm on non-Jews, to be justly seen as responsible for great evil, then a second question must be asked: Did Catholic clergy believe that the punishment that the Germans and their helpers were meting out to Jews, which changed with time, fit the crime? Did the clergy hold the various punishments to be just or unjust?

Let us look first at the preexterminationist phase of the Germans' persecution of the Jews, which included all those policies dehumanizing them and seeking to eliminate them and their influence from country after country. Virtually all Catholic clergy and a large percentage of their parishioners held the Jews to be guilty of grave crimes and offenses. This conclusion seems incontestable. The guilt of the Jews, of *all* Jews—a collective and intergenerational guilt—is a Christian biblical pronouncement ("And the whole [Jewish] people said in reply, 'His [Jesus'] blood be upon us and upon our children' ").[2] This collective guilt imputed to the Jewish people, as a people, was a core doctrine of the Catholic Church, which the Church had spread assiduously for centuries. Furthermore, the Church and much of its clergy and laity, particularly in central and eastern Europe, held, as a form of common sense derived mainly from their religion, that Jews had a singular propensity for evildoing, were the authors of enormous social and political harm against their host countries, and were the creators or managers of the communist ogre.

Catholic bishops and priests around Europe wanted Catholics to know that they did not consider the Jews innocent, so they and their publications were passionately vocal about the Jews' guilt. Listen to their leaders. During the height of the mass murder Adolf Bertram, perhaps the leading cardinal of the German Church, wrote to Nazi officials "the harmful Jewish influences upon German culture and national interests." A leading Austrian bishop, Johannes Maria Gföllner of Linz, issued a pastoral letter shortly before Hitler took power blaming the Jews for international capitalism, socialism, and communism, the principal threats to the well-being of humanity. He declared, "It is beyond any doubt that many Jews, unrelated to any religious concern, exercise an extremely pernicious influence in almost all sectors of modern civilization. The economy and business . . . law and medicine, society and politics are all being infiltrated and polluted by materialistic and liberal principles that derive primarily from Judaism." What should the response be? "Not only is it legitimate to combat and to end Judaism's pernicious influence," according to the bishop, "it is indeed the strict duty of conscience of every informed Christian. One can only hope that Aryans and Christians will increasingly come to recognize the dangers and troubles created by the Jewish spirit and to fight them more tenaciously."[3] Not just Austrians but Catholics in other countries learned of Bishop Gföllner's views, as his letter was reprinted in the Catholic press across Europe.

Cardinal August Hlond, the head of the Polish Catholic Church, in February 1936 issued a pastoral letter "On the Principles of Catholic Morality":

> So long as Jews remain Jews, a Jewish problem exists and will continue to exist. . . .
>
> It is a fact that Jews are waging war against the Catholic Church and that they are steeped in free-thinking, and constitute the vanguard of atheism, the Bolshevik movement, and revolutionary activity. It is a fact that Jews have a corruptive influence on morals and that their publishing houses are spreading pornography. It is true that Jews are perpetrating fraud, practicing usury, and dealing in prostitution. It is true that, from a religious and ethical point of view, Jewish youth are having a negative influence on the Catholic youth in our schools.

Cardinal Hlond's pithy enumeration of the "facts," which led him to call for Poles to "stay away from the harmful moral influence of Jews," which could easily be understood to mean from Jews themselves, and to boycott Jewish stores and newspapers, was a good summary of the prevalent views among the European Church leadership. But Cardinal Hlond tempered his verbal assault and call to anti-Jewish action by differentiating himself from racist antisemites and by urging Poles to adopt a Christian attitude toward the Jews. One should not hate them but "honor and love Jews as human beings and neighbors, even though we do not honor the indescribable tragedy of that nation" for having rejected Jesus. Unlike the racists, Cardinal Hlond also acknowledged and emphatically declared that there are many exceptions to the rule, "honest, just, kind, and philanthropic" Jews. He emphatically opposed violence against Jews. Cardinal Hlond tempered his dominant message about the enormous evil that Jews were doing and always would do to Poles and his call to anti-Jewish action by invoking Christian principles of love and ultimately a degree of tolerance, which in the Polish context meant that he did not call for their elimination from Poland. For this he was considered too moderate by most of the Polish Church, whose other leaders and publications routinely called for the elimination of Jews from Poland, often urging their expulsion. As a Polish Jesuit brochure summarized: "Jews should be expelled from Christian societies." Jews must leave "so that the Polish nation could live and develop normally."[4]

Archbishop Aloys Stepinac of Zagreb, head of the Croatian Catholic Church and certainly one of the least extreme Croatian Church leaders, held that the Jews, together with the Serbs, should be removed from Croatia's social and economic life, that Jews were pornographers, and that their doctors were the primary perpetrators of the "evil" of abortion.[5] His colleague Bishop Ivan Saric of Sarajevo was less "moderate." In May 1941 his diocesan newspaper published an article entitled "Why Are the Jews Persecuted?" It explained:

> The descendants of those who hated Jesus, persecuted him to death, crucified him and persecuted his disciples, are guilty of greater sins than their forebears. Jewish greed increases. The Jews have led Europe and the world towards disaster—moral and economic disaster. Their appetite grows till only domination of the whole world will satisfy it . . . Satan aided them in the invention of Socialism and Communism. There is a limit to love. The movement of liberation of the world from the Jews is a movement for the renewal of human dignity. Omniscient and omnipotent God stands behind this movement.[6]

As here, the Christ-killing biblically based antisemitism often melded seamlessly with the shared Church and secular modern antisemitic idiom of the Jews' alleged social and political despoliation. Much of the bishop's fulminations could have appeared in a publication of that "movement of liberation of the world from the Jews," to which he gave God's endorsement: Nazism.

In Slovakia the Catholic bishops issued a pastoral letter to the entire nation justifying the deportation of the Jews to their deaths. The bishops declared that "the influence of the Jews [has] been pernicious. In a short time they have taken control of almost all the economic and financial life of the country to the detriment of our people. Not only economically, but also in the cultural and moral spheres, they have harmed our people. The Church cannot be opposed, therefore, if the state with legal regulations hinders the dangerous influence of the Jews." In France Bishop Delay of Marseilles, one of the bishops best disposed toward the Jews, was nevertheless an antisemite: "We do not ignore the fact that the Jewish question poses difficult national and international problems. We are well aware that our country has the right to take all appropriate steps to defend itself against those who, especially in recent years, have done her so much harm and to punish those who abuse the hospitality that has so liberally been extended to them."[7]

In Hungary, when discussing whether the Church should protest the deportation of the Jews (to their deaths in Auschwitz), the country's second-ranking churchman, Archbishop Gyula Czapik, reflecting the views of the Hungarian Church leaders, counseled the head of their Church, Cardinal Justinian Serédi, to remain silent because many Jews "sinned against

Hungarian Christianity while none of their community ever reprimanded them for this." Cardinal Serédi nevertheless decided that the Church must go on record as opposed to the mass murder, but did so in a manner that could only further inflame the already intense antisemitism in Hungary:

> We do not deny that a number of Jews exercised a wicked, destructive influence upon Hungarian economic, social, and moral life. It is also a fact that the others did nothing to protest against their coreligionists in this matter. We do not doubt that the Jewish question must be solved in a legal and just manner. And so, we do not voice any opposition to the steps which have been taken against them until now in the economic field in the interests of the state. Similarly, we lodge no protest against the eradication of their undesirable influence. On the contrary, we would like to see it disappear.

With this "Shepherds' Epistle," which was to be read before every congregation, the Hungarian Synod of Bishops as a group justified the notions that the Jews are all guilty, guilty of inflicting great injury to non-Jewish Hungarians or of allowing other Jews to do so, that all the Hungarian government's criminal anti-Jewish measures (expulsion from homes, jobs, et cetera) leading to the deportation are to be endorsed, and that the Jews' influence (effectively the Jews themselves) should be eliminated from Hungarian society.[8] The Catholic bishops issued this epistle at the end of June 1944, during the height of the deportation of Hungarian Jews to their deaths.

In Slovenia, Bishop Gregory Rožman of Llubljana, the capital, was a powerful ally of the Germans. He organized Catholic armed forces to fight alongside the Germans and the Italians, with priests serving in important roles. After Italy's surrender in September 1943, Bishop Rožman helped the Germans assume control of Slovenia for themselves. He also initiated the creation of a Slovenian Homeguard under German control, which took part in many crimes, including mass murder. One existing photo shows the bishop on the dais with the local SS commander and the Fascist president of Slovenia reviewing the troops.

Bishop Rožman frequently urged Slovenes to support the Germans, doing so in a pastoral letter in November 1943 when the Germans were consolidating their rule in Slovenia. Why should Slovenes tie their fate to the Germans? The bishop explained that only "by this courageous fighting and industrious work for God, for the people and Fatherland will we, under the leadership of Germany, assure our existence and better future, in the fight against [the] Jewish conspiracy."[9]

In Italy, where two Popes identified Bolshevism with Jews, the Vatican endorsed and itself disseminated the country's Nazi-like antisemitic laws when the Fascist government issued them in 1938. This public approval was echoed by Italy's bishops.[10] The archbishop of Florence, one of the leading Italian cardinals, conveyed to his priests and parishioners in early 1939 in the archdiocesan bulletin that the Italian racial laws do not conflict with divine law: "As for the Jews, no one can forget the ruinous work that they have often undertaken not only against the spirit of the Church, but also to the detriment of civil coexistence." So, according to the archbishop, the Church, above all, "has in every epoch judged living together with the Jews to be dangerous to the Faith and to the tranquility of Christian people. Hence the laws promulgated by the Church for centuries aimed at isolating the Jews"[11]—laws that, in many respects, the Italian Fascist laws were emulating.

The Catholic Church, its national churches, and its clergy proclaimed, in official declarations and letters, in newspapers and other publications, and in sermons their belief in the Jews' guilt, guilt of such alleged deeds as having killed the Son of God, being the progenitors of Bolshevism, harming grievously the nations among whom they lived, and producing financial privation the world over. There is, moreover, every reason to believe that the antisemitism of the leading bishops and lower clergy around Europe, and their openly stated belief that the Jews were guilty of the gravest crimes, was indicative of the character of many of their parishioners' views of Jews—even if there were exceptions, in some countries, such as Italy, many exceptions among clerical and lay Catholics. Guenter Lewy, historian of the German Catholic Church during the Nazi period, sees German Catholics to have been so antisemitic, so poisoned in their view of Jews by their own Church, that had the Catholic bishops taken the implausible step of declaring the Jews innocent, he believes that "their own followers would probably have failed to understand and approve such sympathy for the Jews."[12]

The common beliefs of ecclesiastical and lay Catholics in the guilt of the Jews, not to mention the often common eliminationist character of those beliefs, was perhaps nowhere better illustrated than in the Hungarian town of Veszprem, where after the deportation of its Jews, a flier, issued by the local fascist party, the Arrow Cross, announced a thanksgiving prayer service:

> With the help of Divine Providence our ancient city and province have been liberated from that Judaism which sullied our nation. In our thousand-year national history, this is not the first time we have been freed from some

scourge which had befallen us. However, no previous event can compare in its importance with this event, for no previous foe threatening us, whether by force or by a political takeover, had ever succeeded in overcoming us to the extent that the Jews had succeeded, with the aid of their poisoned roots which penetrated our national body and took hold of it. We are following in the foot-steps of our fathers in coming to express our thanks to our God who saves us whenever we are in distress. Come and gather for the thanksgiving service which will take place on June 25 at 11:30 A.M. at the Franciscan Church.

The local priest agreed to hold the service in his church, which overflowed with Hungarian Catholics joyous because their Jewish neighbors had been deported. The local bishop did not forbid the service but chose not to attend it not because he dissented from the celebratory sentiments but because some Christians who had converted from Judaism were among the deported.[13]

Had the Catholic Church, its national churches, and its clergy believed that the Jews were innocent, were not offenders against Christianity, society, and goodness, then we would certainly know it. They would have proclaimed it, publicly, all over Europe, in country after country. Instead there was a powerful and continual ecclesiastical chorus condemning Jews and sometimes celebrating their elimination. Among churchmen the few audible exceptions to this condemnatory chorus were lonely voices. Not even Father Lichtenberg of Berlin was one, his devoted opposition to his countrymen's violent persecution of the Jews notwithstanding. Before he was shocked by *Kristallnacht* to stand up for the Jews, Father Lichtenberg, just like other German bishops and priests, vocalized antisemitism against Otto von Corvin, the Protestant author of an anticlerical book, whom the Catholic establishment was alleging to be half Jewish. In a 1935 letter he claimed that Corvin "according to the latest research, was not of Aryan descent."[14] Father Lichtenberg appears to have believed that just being a Jew, or even a half-Jew by "race," was sufficient to render someone suspect, unwholesome, indeed, prima facie guilty of some substantial transgression. It was to Hitler that Father Lichtenberg addressed this antisemitic appeal.

Individuals aside, to find Christian churches that corporately found the Jews innocent of the grave crimes and other transgressions of which antisemites around Europe were accusing them, we would have to look to non-Catholic churches, like the Protestant churches of Denmark and Norway.

Again, it is worth pausing to reflect on the content of the leading Catholic bishops' antisemitic invective and accusations. Imagine if today people would assert such things about blacks (or any other group, such as Italians or Lutherans)—that they "exercise a wicked, destructive influence" upon "economic, social and moral life," that they seek to dominate "the whole world," that "Satan aided them" in their machinations, and that the appropriate response was to eliminate their influence, to liberate the world, which would be "a movement for the renewal of human dignity." Would we say that those propagating such vicious nonsense about blacks were deeply prejudiced and filled with hatred? Of course. Would we say that they thought blacks guilty of inflicting great harm upon nonblacks? Of course. Would we pretend that such people were not leading racists, and that their profound racist views were irrelevant to understanding whatever harmful stances or actions they adopted towards blacks? Of course not. Why, then, do so many people adopt obviously nonsensical positions, ones that are exactly the opposite of these, when discussing the Catholic clergy who held such views about Jews and who acted or remained inactive in ways that harmed them?

Precisely because the Church and its leaders deemed the Jews guilty and an ongoing danger, they fought their emancipation all over Europe throughout the nineteenth century, and after the Church's defeat in this battle against the Jews, it never stopped lamenting its loss. So it is no surprise that in the 1930s, when the Germans promised and began to implement the rescission of that emancipation, few Church officials found this punishment fundamentally unjust. Some objected to particular features, such as the pitiless brutality of the actual eliminationist program and, to be sure, of its ancillary harmful consequences for Catholics who had converted from Judaism or Catholics married to Jews. But in no way is this the same as believing that the punishment *in its essence* did not fit the "crime," or that the Jews were guiltless. Of course, there were exceptions. Those few in Germany who, like the Danish and Norwegian churches, saw the Jews as innocent naturally saw the eliminationist onslaught against the Jews, in its early and in its later phases, to be unjust, indeed criminal.

The first phase of eliminationist policies can be mapped by two dimensions of people's beliefs about Jews: (1) a person's beliefs about the Jews' guilt or innocence of committing grievous crimes or other serious offenses or of being a threat, and (2) his beliefs about the justness of the preexterminationist punishment. For churchmen, the results are striking.[15]

People who understood that the Jews were innocent, naturally, did not behold the eliminationist onslaught as just, so cell 4 in the table (see next page) is empty. Cell 2, believing the Jews were guilty but that the punishment was unjust, was also virtually empty. Almost all Catholic clergy fell into the two other cells. The evidence suggests that virtually the entire clergy of the Catholic Church believed the Jews were guilty and the nonlethal eliminationist punishments just (cell 1). The clergy were vocal on both points. Cell 3, for people holding the Jews to be innocent and the pun-

BELIEFS ABOUT JEWS' GUILT AND THE JUSTICE
OF NON-EXTERMINATIONIST PUNISHMENT

		Punishment	
		Just	Unjust
		1	**2**
Crime	Guilty	most clergy	very few clergy
		4	**3**
	Innocent	no clergy	few clergy

ishment unjust, is occupied by a small number of Catholic clergy, though when looking to Scandinavia we see that this cell would be well populated by Protestant clergy.

Notable is Pope Pius XI. He seems to have had a change of heart late in life, shocked by the horror of the protogenocidal assault known as *Kristallnacht* coming on the heels of Italy promulgating its own antisemitic laws. A committed self-professed antisemite, he did not believe the Jews to be innocent or, initially, object to anti-Jewish laws—he had earlier volunteered his principled approval of such laws to Mussolini. Yet Pius XI eventually found the inner resources to reconsider the justice of these measures. As late as September 1938 he affirmed that he retained his antisemitic view of Jews by stating that Christians had the right to defend themselves against Jews, but this time he indicated that limits existed to what could be done. He rejected the Germans' and their imitators' brand of violent eliminationist antisemitism as "a hateful movement" and declared that "spiritually, we are all Semites." How heartfelt this was is unclear, since he said this over Belgian Catholic Radio, personally requested that it be printed in *La libre belgique*, but never had it printed in Italy—as if he had said it mainly for foreign consumption.[16] Still, Pius XI's Hidden Encyclical made clear that he partly moved himself from cell 1 to cell 2, retaining his belief in the Jews' guilt but now decrying at least the Germans' particular brand of inhumane treatment of them.

For the second phase of the Germans' assault on the Jews—the exterminationist phase—the cells of the matrix look much the same but with the migration of some unknown but probably significant part of the Catholic Church's clergy from cell 1 to cell 2. Nothing happened to change the clergy's beliefs about the innocence or guilt of the Jews—which, being based on the evaluation of the Jews' nature, aspirations, and actions, remained the same no matter what punishment was proposed. Churchmen who believed the punishment of the preexterminationist phase was unjust naturally also believed that annihilating the Jews was unjust. With the annihilation, however, some clergy who beheld the Jews as guilty and a perpetual danger, and who themselves could affirm the fundamental justness of the eliminationist enterprise believed that mass annihilation was too extreme an eliminationist punishment. Bishop Delay, who spoke of the need to defend France and "punish" the Jews who had done "much harm," still maintained that "the rights of the state have limits" and protested the deportations of Jews that might "send them possibly to their deaths."[17] Bishop Gföllner of Austria, Cardinal Hlond of Poland, and Archbishop Stepinac of Croatia also opposed exterminationist violence. Cardinal Hlond had already told Poles, in his pastoral letter of 1936, "I warn against that moral stance, imported from abroad, that is basically and ruthlessly anti-Jewish. . . . One is forbidden to assault, beat up, maim, or slander Jews."[18] In May 1942 Archbishop Stepinac denounced the mass murder in a sermon to thousands: "All races and nations were created in the image of God . . . therefore the Church criticized in the past and does so in the present all deeds of injustice or violence, perpetrated in the name of class, race or nationality. It is forbidden to exterminate Gypsies and Jews because they are said to belong to an inferior race."[19]

Why did they and some others draw the line at mass murder? It is possible that they did not think that the crimes they ascribed to Jews in principle warranted such an extreme penalty. But this may not have been the reason, given that they did believe that the Jews' putative crimes were heinous in the extreme. It seems at least as likely that they believed that, even if as a matter of degree the "punishment fits the crime," it was nonetheless immoral to carry it out. They may have been moved by the Church's tradition that the Jews, their putative crimes notwithstanding, must be kept alive or by some objection to the death penalty. Or given that the antisemitism of many of them was not racist but religious in foundation, they still held to the principle that Jews could be redeemed through conversion, and to the possibility that at least some of them could be converted. The racist antisemitism of the Nazis and of most Germans meant that the Jews were incorrigible, their putative propensity to do evil genetic, and the great danger they allegedly posed to others, therefore, to persist as long as Jews exist.

That is why so many Germans willingly lent themselves to or supported the mass murder, as the only "Final Solution" to the so-called Jewish Problem, and why the historically unprecedented measure of seeking out and destroying the Jews not just in their own country but the world over made sense to them. The religion-based antisemitism of the Church meant, formally, that Jews could change. And indeed, the Church's own experience with converts from Judaism taught it that some Jews did become Christians. It is true that the Church's demonology about Jews in the twentieth century had taken on a cast and content that were similar to the demonology propounded by racist antisemites, with some leading churchmen adopting and propagating a racist conception of the Jews. Nevertheless, the possibility of redeeming the Jews, the very possibility that had informed the Church's degrading and injurious though not formally lethal eliminationist policy toward Jews for centuries, probably led many clergy during the Nazi period to conclude that killing Jews was neither necessary nor right. In the end, many clergy might have finally said *no* to the final stage of the methodically escalating eliminationist persecution of the Jews when that stage became mass murder for no reason more complicated than, when they confronted the prospect of human beings slaughtering so many children and the parents of so many children, they balked.

What remains indeterminate—given the absence of detailed investigations about national Catholic churches and their clergy (the need for which we saw in part one)—is the percentage of the clergy of each national church and then of the Catholic Church as a whole that approved of the killing, and the percentage that saw the mass annihilation as traversing a moral boundary that it was impermissible to cross, even for punishing the great criminals that they, exceptions notwithstanding, generally believed the Jews to be.

Once we separate the two dimensions of beliefs about the eliminationist onslaught—the Jews' innocence or guilt and the justness of their punishment—the patterns of the Church's actions and inactions, the good, the bad, and the nonexistent, become more comprehensible. In the case of the Church, the relationship of antisemitic belief to anti-Jewish action, the cause and effect, are easily discernible.

The Church's and its clergy's belief in the Jews' guilt makes it, in a sense, obvious and unremarkable that, during the 1930s and even afterward, they would continue to teach Catholics, even urge them, to be antisemites, and generally approve of the Germans' and their helpers' nonlethal eliminationist policies. It is equally unremarkable, given this belief, that they would in various ways aid—including in Germany by providing the genealogies and sometimes vocally applauding the policies—in these avowed eliminationist measures. It follows that they would not themselves defend, or urge

Catholics to defend, the Jews from the antisemitic verbal onslaught or from the legal and physical assault. It is also no wonder that the Catholic Church, two Popes, and national churches never declared the Jews innocent. Why would they have? They did not believe it.

The Germans then moved from the nonlethal eliminationist policies—which, if more violent and brutal, essentially accorded with the Church's desire for the rescission of the emancipation of the Jews—to mass murder. Some heretofore supportive clergy could no longer go along with the Jews' persecutors because they did not think that the new punishment was just. But since the clergy still believed the Jews to be guilty and a danger, they must have felt enormous ambivalence about how they should act. They could not bring themselves to declare what, from a non-antisemite's perspective, needed to be told to everyone, namely, that the Jews were innocent. They could not in their hearts blame those people who genuinely believed, as the churchmen themselves did, in the Jews' extreme guilt but who, acting on their shared beliefs, went too far in meting out punishment. Hence, the Church's failure to excommunicate, condemn, or seek the punishment of the perpetrators of the Holocaust, even though it excommunicated in one fell swoop all Communists around the world, irrespective of whether they had committed any crimes.

WHEN THE CLERGY confronted the unjust punishment, they found it difficult to act. Much of the Church, including the German Church, was deeply implicated *morally,* or more, in the mass murder, not to mention in the earlier aspects of the criminal eliminationist onslaught. (I elaborate on this shortly.) For the churches to condemn the mass murder was all but to condemn themselves because it was one logical, though not the only logical or an inevitable, policy extension of the antisemitism they had propagated and the earlier eliminationist policies they had supported. Even if the churchmen disapproved of this most extreme eliminationist punishment, their antisemitism was such that it was hard to rouse themselves in sympathy for the Jews. The weight and recent history of the Church was against acting on behalf of Jews. Suddenly and without delay, bishops and priests had to find a way to turn themselves around on behalf of a people for whom they felt great enmity, whom they believed to be responsible for killing Jesus and posing, with their putative Bolshevism, a dire threat to the very existence of the Church and human flourishing.

This was not easy. Those clergy who managed to do it often acted with ambivalence and insufficient energy. Some roused themselves to act well: Dutch bishops, French bishops, a sizable number of clergy in Italy, and

even the Vatican's own representative in Italy, Monsignor Francesco Bor-
gongini Duca, who vigorously urged the Italian government not to allow the
Jews of Italian-occupied southern France to be deported.[20] But even many
of these clergy waited until the last moment, when the anticipated deportations were imminent, and did not act insistently, with passion and determination. Others acted after the last moment, when the perpetrators had
already helped kill enormous numbers of Jews. Pius XII intervened late in
Hungary with his telegram to Horthy, only after the soon-to-be-victorious
Allies had intensively pressured him. Similarly, the Vatican intervened late
in Slovakia, motivated, according to the admission of its own representative, by its concern for the Church's standing in the postwar world.

Given the clergy's ambivalence, it is not surprising that such interventions lacked the timeliness and fervor that the Church lent to its protests
against things it really cared about, like the well-being of Catholics who had
converted from Judaism or the sacrament of marriage, how religion was
being taught in Germany, or, in Germany, the so-called Euthanasia program, whose principal victims were Christians.

Let us not make the mistake of believing, as it appears the Church and its
defenders would like, that speaking out once against one aspect of the Germans' eliminationist program, and then never again, or doing nothing more
than critically alluding to the mass murder, was a sufficient protest in the
face of such gargantuan evil unfolding over a long time. Let us not make the
mistake of believing that saying something not until long after the killing
began, when millions had already perished, retroactively covers the earlier
period of total silence. But a single, late statement is typically what the
churchmen who did criticize the exterminationist measures, like almost all
the French bishops, tended to do. People, especially political and religious
leaders, who condemn deeds that they believe are great crimes, especially
when done in their name, are typically not content with a single late, brief
expression of their dissent. They tend to protest immediately, vigorously,
again and again. But not here.

And certainly not Pius XII, with little more to show than his two brief
and late public references to people dying because of their nationality or
descent and his very late appeal to Horthy. Pius XII was absolutely silent for
well over a year while the Germans and their helpers killed millions. He
spoke out only after a German victory was no longer likely and when he was
under intense pressure from the Allies. He kept his message vague, and in
his Christmas 1942 message he buried it at the end of a long speech as part
of a list of other items. He did not even mention the perpetrators (Germans)
or victims (Jews) by name, or the animating idea of the mass slaughter (antisemitism). He did not convey extensive, sufficient knowledge of the mass

murder and offer moral guidance to Catholics and non-Catholics regarding the necessity of acting on behalf of the Jews.[21] The notions that these wan, elliptical, evasive statements constituted a stirring and impassioned defense of the Jews, a people then on its way to total extinction within Europe, and that such statements are the proof that shows that Pius XII was a committed defender of the Jews, are not even superficially credible.

Think of the crippling emotional and practical predicament in which the Pope, bishops, and priests found themselves. They had felt great animosity and enmity toward the Jews, who, among their many other supposed historical and contemporary transgressions, were allegedly guilty for killing Jesus. They believed that they and their beloved Church had suffered and continued to suffer great injuries at the hands of the Jews, whom they deemed responsible for the grave Bolshevik threat. They had called for the Jews to be curtailed; many even called for severe punishment. They had participated in the Jews' disenfranchisement. They had looked with approval on the Jews' exclusion from civic and social life. Then suddenly, perhaps because they still conceived of the killing of the Jews as murder rather than a just death sentence or perhaps because of a Church policy that the Jews should be kept alive in misery (but that did not adequately address the grave problem of what to do with them), the churchmen had to defend the Jews— all because other people had gone too far in the common battle against the Jews. Some clergy managed to rouse themselves to take up the challenge. But they were a small minority.

How difficult and unlikely would such a switch-over be, psychologically, particularly when the Church itself was so deeply implicated in the harmful policies that culminated in this most extreme one? Defending the Jews also meant that the Pope and the bishops would have to acknowledge, at least implicitly, that what they had been teaching their parishioners about Jews was pernicious. This would put their religious credibility and authority at risk. And they had so much work to undo. Lewy contends that the antisemitic German populace would have probably been deaf to a protest by their bishops on behalf of the Jews—the very people "whom the Church, after all, had herself long been branding as a harmful factor in German life. Consequently, at the very moment when the bishops might perhaps have wanted to protest the inhuman treatment of the Jews, they found themselves the prisoners of their own antisemitic teachings."[22]

The Catholic Church and its clergy were like many people who oppose the death penalty as a matter of principle or because of practical problems with applying it fairly, yet who nonetheless feel little sympathy for murderers who are put to death. The moral and psychological gravity of the crime, the palpable heinousness of the flesh-and-blood criminal, tend to outweigh the principle that leads people to disapprove of the punishment. Hence, the reticence to protest, much less to protest vigorously. After all, protesting means that a person inevitably comes to champion and identify with, and, perhaps more important psychologically, often be identified by others with, the person whom he considers a villainous criminal. It is hardly surprising that even when Church leaders condemned the deportations or killings of Jews, they almost always restricted their condemnations to these specific punishments, or made sure to make clear that they believed that the Jews were pernicious and harmful to the well-being of non-Jews, which only served to weaken the churchmen's admonitions against violence. It is also not surprising that Church leaders did not tell their countrymen that the Jews were completely innocent, let alone emphatically stand up for the notion, did not call the Jews brothers and sisters, did not insistently counsel that Catholics and others must treat the Jews with love, compassion, and solicitude.

How hard it must have been psychologically for the Church and its clergy, after all these years of warning their followers of the great dangers posed by the Jews, suddenly to have to start publicly defending these very people.[23] That is why, for example, so many Slovakian priests refused to read even a late protest from their own bishops against the deportation of the Jews, and even though the bishops had made the protest pro forma anyway by composing it in Latin. It may be why, when the French bishops instructed priests to read to their parishioners their protest against the deportation of Jews to their deaths, more than half of the priests in Vichy refused.[24] And it is probably why, even though the French bishops, as a collective, issued this protest, only six of them would, as individuals, protest the deportations. How complex is the moral psychology of defending those whom a person feels enmity toward, or feels threatened by, or hates. The internal resistance is difficult to overcome. The Norwegian and Danish Protestant churches, precisely because they understood that the Jews were unambiguously innocent, could defend them without difficulty and with passion, not just as objects of unjust punishment but as people. In Scandinavia the Jews, like "all people," have "the same human worth and thereby the same human rights."[25]

The paradoxical consequences of the Church's stance toward the Jews should not go unnoticed. The Church, more than probably any other major non-Nazi institution in Europe, taught people a hate-filled, dehumanizing, and eliminationist view of Jews—that they were a guilt-laden and pernicious people—a view that led many of its adherents to support and often willingly to participate in the Jews' persecution. Some clergy even contributed to the Jews' annihilation. Nevertheless, the Church's formal position condemning physical violence mobilized some clergy, their anti-semitism notwithstanding, to aid Jews. These bishops and priests took seriously the Church's long-standing and oft stated position that the Jews should live in a reduced state, which means that they should *live*, and the Christian moral injunction against murder. Or maybe these professional shepherds of human beings saved Jews for no doctrinal reason at all, but simply because they could not bear seeing so many people slaughtered. Although the clergy who helped Jews were a small minority of the Church (we need more research into them as well) and a noticeably small part of the German Catholic Church, they still were a substantial number of people commanding considerable resources, including hiding places in churches, monasteries, and educational institutions that they used to save Jews. Even when employing but a small percentage of their tens of thousands of churches and religious institutions across Europe, Catholic clergy and nuns acting on their own, without support from the Vatican or national church leaderships, easily hid tens of thousands of Jews, mainly Jewish children, whom they often baptized as Christians.[26] But in only two places did the institutional Church undertake rescue efforts at the diocesan level: Berlin, under Bishop Konrad Preysing's leadership, and Italy, where many bishops

A priest in Dembniki, Poland, poses with a group of altar boys on the steps of the church; two of them are hidden Jewish children.

and priests organized networks to save Jews. In Italy and elsewhere, priests and lay Catholics acted heroically. Churchmen even hid some Jews within the Vatican itself, the evidence suggesting that the Pope tolerated this at least for a while, though he did not initiate or encourage it. The Pope's role in the infamous order of early 1944 expelling all "nonclerics" from the Vatican properties, which did lead to Jews being expelled but which was not strictly enforced, is murky, but at the very least it is hard to believe that had the Pope been a genuine friend of the Jews, the order, issued by his direct subordinates, would have ever been given in the first place. In the rest of Catholic Europe, the bishops were generally unwilling to help the Jews. Michael Phayer concludes that "in every European country except Poland, the church's diocesan structure was in place, but it was not infused with the spirit and vigor found in Italy and Berlin."[27]

The contrast between the general failure of the Catholic Church and, for that matter, of most ordinary Germans, whether Catholics or Protestants, to act well regarding Jews, and the exemplary conduct of the Danish church and the Danish people toward the Jews could not be starker. The cause of these differences is equally clear. The Danish Lutheran State Church and the Danish people understood that the Jews were innocent. So they defended them as people, not merely as the despised objects of overly harsh and morally impermissible punishment. They defended them not only at the last moment—immediately before the Germans were about to deport and kill them, or well after the Germans and their helpers had already killed millions across Europe—but at the first moment, when the Germans occupied Denmark. The Danes neither aided nor supported the initial eliminationist measures; they did not stand by or remain silent, and they did not allow the Germans to implement such measures.[28]

All this they did because the Jews were innocent. And when the moment of peril came, Danes easily, immediately rose to the Jews' defense and aided them with determination, insistence, and fervor. And, as we know, they succeeded in their rescue operations.

To make sense out of the various and sometimes inconsistent actions and inaction on the part of Catholic churchmen, one must understand the complex constellation of their beliefs in the innocence or guilt of the Jews and in the justice of the evolving punishment policies. That is not to say that other factors, such as the political calculations of this political Church, did not provide some of the detailed contouring to the pattern's overall shape. But these other factors, including the Pope's anti-Bolshevism, his alleged fear for the safety of the Church, his putative personal timidity, are either confounded by the evidence or cannot begin to explain the general pattern of the Church's conduct, including the Pope's own and the actions of the national churches and their clergy, who, it can be assumed, did not all share the Pope's imputed personality trait. None of these can explain one of the most basic and central facts of this period of maximum danger for Jews: that the Pope, the Church, and the national churches and their clergy continued to spread antisemitism. Indeed, when we behold the conduct of the Danish Lutheran Church and its clergy, all of these proposed explanations of the Catholic Church's and its clergy's manifold failures in the face of the eliminationist assault on the Jews look silly. Only the Catholic Church's and its clergy's view of the Jews' guilt and the justness of the given punishments can explain the general pattern of their actions. At the root of these views was the Church's and its clergy's profound antisemitism.

THE OBLIGATION TO JUDGE

Now that we have described, analyzed, and explained the central aspects of the Church's actions during the Nazi period, the analytically distinct task of a methodical moral reckoning can begin.

A moral reckoning is predicated upon four notions: (1) that human beings are responsible for their actions; (2) that it is right for us to judge other people's actions; (3) that to do so, we must have fair and clear criteria; and (4) that our judgments must be transparent in their reasoning to conclusions.

The Church and its members, from the Pope down to parish priests and their parishioners, like other human beings, were agents. Agency is a person's capacity to understand, to judge whether something is right according to his moral notions, and to act. It is the capacity to say no. The Catholic Church agrees that human beings are moral agents. Its fundamental doctrine of "freedom" or "free will"—"the power, rooted in reason and will, to act or not to act, to do this or that, and so to perform deliberate actions on one's own responsibility"—is another word for agency. In principle, philosophically and theologically, the agency of the Church and its members cannot be denied. In a practical sense, the opportunities for the Church and its clergy to act without suffering greatly, were generally expansive. With regard to many of their actions, such as whether they would continue to impart antisemitism to Catholics, they were completely unfettered. The discussion in part one leaves no doubt about this. As agents, as moral actors, the Church and its clergy were morally responsible for their stances and actions, and are worthy of praise or blame accordingly. The Catholic

Church agrees that when someone is a voluntary agent, "freedom makes man *responsible* for his acts."[29]

Second, it is our right and obligation, as people who were not actors of the time or "in their shoes," to adjudicate such praise or blame. That anyone would assert otherwise is odd. We judge people all the time in our daily lives: the man who fired someone, perhaps unjustly; the woman who extends or fails to extend aid to a friend or relative in need; the man who spreads vicious rumors about another; the woman who harms someone with a lie so that she can advance her fortunes.[30] We regularly judge people for their extraordinary deeds: Hitler, Saddam Hussein, the perpetrators of the Holocaust, the Serbs who tortured and killed Muslims in Bosnia or Kosovo, the perpetrators of the September 11, 2001, World Trade Center bombing and mass murder, people who commit or conspire to commit other crimes in the past and today. We judge people who, in every imaginable way, act badly or fail to act well. We also dole out praise to all manner of actors during all periods, including the Nazi years. We honor the people who saved Jews, anointed at Yad Vashem "Righteous among the Nations." Father Peter Gumpel, the all but official Church spokesman regarding Pius XII, not only praises him but also judges him saintly. And when Father Gumpel and others attack Pius XII's critics as malevolent (Father Gumpel invents a "Jewish faction" that has something "against Catholics"), they are judging others.[31] If praising is morally permissible and obligatory, then so is its counterpart, blaming.

Why should people be excused from all responsibility just because the Nazis were brutal? They deserve such immunity only if three things had been true: (1) that they wanted to act well, (2) that they themselves were clearly subjected to that brutality, and (3) that this is the reason they did not act on their good convictions. In this case that would mean that churchmen thought the Jews were innocent, or, if they did not, then they still felt great compassion for the Jews and wanted to aid them, but were prevented from doing so because and only because of the alleged terror. The Church cannot show these conditions to be true (moreover, it was the Church's own desire and choice to preach the most damning antisemitic charges about Jews). If there were records of internal discussions in the Vatican, or among national church leaders, about the innocence of the Jews and the great injustice of *all* the eliminationist measures, including those of the Germans in the 1930s— and surely there would have been such discussions, had the churchmen believed such things—then it cannot be doubted that the Church would have long ago made them public. Even the sanitized selection of materials in the Church's official publication of wartime diplomatic material, contrary to the Church's claims about it, does not help the Church's case. In addition to all of the self-indicting correspondence and reports in the eleven volumes, the repeated absence in them of a recognition on the part of Vatican officials that the Jews were wholly innocent, and of a display of general concern for the general well-being of Jews, is striking.[32] The Church and its defenders, when trying to exonerate the Church, do not even attempt to show that the three conditions obtained that are necessary for the Church to be absolved of responsibility for its failures. The extensive evidence from this period incontrovertibly confounds such a notion. The best that the Church and its defenders can do is say, mantralike, the equivalent of "The Nazis were brutal."

Why should only the Church, Pius XI and Pius XII, bishops, and priests be immune from our moral judgment, and be immune specifically for their conduct with respect to one of the greatest crimes in human history? Because they claim to be servants of God, and therefore devoted to living moral lives? That would, if anything, make them subject to a *more* exacting application of our moral judgment. The Church itself doctrinally supports judging others and itself. For example, it judges people who do not accept its authority to be unworthy of entering heaven ("outside the Church there is no salvation") with the strong doctrinal implication, notwithstanding some official claims to the contrary, that they will tend to end up in hell.[33] And it judges itself to be innocence incarnate ("the Church . . . is held, as a matter of faith, to be unfailingly holy").[34] Regarding the Holocaust, the Church is not bashful to judge itself and its leading members loudly and insistently. Its judgment, the self-critical French bishops' statement from 1997 notwithstanding (see part three), is a finding, by and large, of innocence. Since when are those who may be culpable, or their representatives, allowed to dictate the terms of judgment? Since when are they allowed to be their own sole and definitive judges, attacking and denigrating as prejudiced those who do not share their allegiances, identities, or institutional affiliations, who would dare to critically investigate and judge them?

To assert that we may not judge the Pope and other Catholics acting as Catholics during the Holocaust is to maintain that we may not judge people in circumstances we have not faced. Virtually no one accepts or, whatever he might say, practices such a precept. This would mean that there is no morality, because morality consists of rules of good conduct that apply, and that we may apply, to people regardless of whether we have found ourselves exactly in their situation. Not to judge is to deny that people can do good, can do praiseworthy things. No one, least of all the Church, trumpeting its belief in its own infallible praiseworthiness, denies this. Not to judge is to deny the existence of morality. It is therefore to deny our human agency, which is to deny our humanity, philosophically, theologically, and just plain and simply. Judging the Pope, bishops, and others is not a transgressive act, but the fulfillment of our moral duties to one another as people.

Third, in judging, we must establish a set of clear and fair general evaluative criteria, which we then apply dispassionately to the particular events of the Holocaust. Just as the criteria apply to people in other times and places, they would, in principle, apply to all individuals during the Nazi period— Catholics, Germans, French, Poles, Jews. In this case, they would apply also to the Church as an institution and, particularly, to Church leaders, its bishops and priests.

Leaders, political and religious, have a greater responsibility to act morally, for example, to defend those who need defending. They accept this responsibility when they enter important positions in public life. They say to others, I am worthy of being a leader of your spiritual or political community because I am a person who can be relied upon to do what is in your best interests and what is right. Their vocation is to act well. So it is entirely appropriate to expect more of the Church leadership than of ordinary Catholics, and to condemn them more stringently for their bad actions. When they fail, they fail twice: in the duty that all people share to act well, and in the additional vocational obligation to act well, which they have freely chosen and declared themselves worthy to bear.

We should, of course, be careful to understand all of their circumstances, including any difficult ones they might have faced. A critical part of their "circumstances," which is typically elided or obscured by those who claim to want to understand what it was like to be in the shoes of perpetrators or bystanders during the Nazi period, are the people's views, values, and beliefs about Jews and about the different components of the eliminationist onslaught against them. Ignoring such views, values, and beliefs effectively removes perhaps the most critical (and often damning) factor from all consideration. This is why it is particularly important to investigate systematically and in depth what churchmen across Europe thought of Jews and their persecutors' various punishments of them. Did they think the Jews innocent or guilty? Did they think the punishments just or unjust?

Finally, a moral reckoning requires that we judge openly, explicitly, and in a sustained manner. Let us be honest. People judge the Catholic Church, Popes, Germans, Poles, French, and others for their conduct during this period all the time. So do academic historians who deny or try to conceal that they do. When people judge, they do so fleetingly and, if they are critical, often seemingly fearfully. They typically use unarticulated criteria that are inconsistent, confused, and not backed by principles, in other words, criteria that are indefensible. The realm of actions to be judged is confined to the most egregious offenses, often only the mass murder itself. If Pius XII, for example, can be cleared of charges of complicity in the genocide, then he is deemed innocent of all wrongdoing. Many other censorious deeds of the period—whether committed by Pius XII, other churchmen, or nonchurchmen—are tacitly ignored, as if they did not occur or are unworthy of moral scrutiny. The antisemitism of Pius XII and others is often not addressed directly and in depth, or gingerly skirted over as some relatively inconsequential vestige of the Church's so-called anti-Judaism. The criteria of judgment are often set up to be exculpatory, as is the limited range of actions chosen for consideration. This multifaceted narrowing of the moral field is intellectually dishonest, no less so than are the people who, in proposing explanations of the actions of the perpetrators of the Holocaust, confine themselves to addressing only the deeds functionally related to the act of killing itself, pretending that the perpetrators did not do things that flatly falsify their explanations—even though it is common knowledge that the perpetrators routinely did these things, such as willingly torturing, beating, degrading, and taunting their victims.[35]

Moral blinders are used for Pius XII and the Catholic Church as much as they have been used for the perpetrators of the Holocaust and ordinary Germans. The judging that goes on all the time, which is narrow, incidental, casual, confusing, and attenuated, and which follows no clear and defensible principles, is a far cry from the genuine moral reckoning that a moral institution, such as the one the Catholic Church presents itself to be, deserves. It is a far cry from the genuine moral reckoning that a crime such as the Holocaust deserves. Because we cannot but judge, we might as well not be timid or furtive about doing it. Because judgments are rendered in any case, we ought to judge well. We ought to raise the task of judging to a central and valued practice, and carry it out regularly, in a sustained and concerted way.[36]

The empirical and analytical foundation for judging the Church now exists. The Church, the Pope, the national churches, bishops, and priests generally failed during the Holocaust. They failed because they believed the Jews to be evil and harmful, and because they did not object in principle to punishing Jews substantially and therefore at least to many of the eliminationist measures taken by the Germans and their helpers. Thus, in a general sense, the Church and so many of its clergy committed an offense. Eliminationist antisemitism—the desire, by some means (which is not necessarily lethal) to rid society of Jews and of their real and putative influence, the central motive for the Holocaust—had been spread by the Church and its clergy throughout Germany and Catholic Europe. Many clergy, in their capacities as clergy, acted badly in other ways. Many others failed to act well. They evinced a breathtaking lack of empathy for the victims. Some national churches made some effort to defend Jews from the worst of the overwhelming assault. Within these churches and even within the national churches that did not defend the Jews, there were individual bishops and priests who disapproved of the killing and tried to help the victims. Part of any judgment is to praise those clergy in a manner commensurate with their good acts, which is a much more straightforward undertaking and has already been done frequently.

The general failure, the general offense, of the Church and its clergy needs to be evaluated more precisely. This proceeds in several stages. As a practical matter, it would facilitate the analysis to separate, and take up sequentially, two issues: (1) what the Church and its clergy did to harm Jews; and (2) what they did not do to help Jews. Existing evaluations of the Church, both the defenses and the critiques, generally struggle over the second one, asking principally whether the Pope (or occasionally the Church in general) helped the Jews and why he and the Church did not help them more.[37] In other words, was there a failure to lend necessary aid, to act well? In part one we focused extensively on these issues. But these themes compose only a figurative half of the story. The other half—indeed, the still more problematic half—has been, owing to the strategies discussed in part one, mainly excised from our view and our analyses: The Church and its members themselves did many blameworthy things.

The Church's and its clergy's blameworthy acts need to be brought into focus, and evaluated, as we have seen, according to fair and clear criteria and in an open and transparent manner. To do so requires that we establish a set of general categories that distinguish two sets of things: the different kinds of offenses and the different kinds of culpability attached to each type of offense. Then we need to place the Church's and its clergy's specific actions and stances in these general categories, in order to assess their culpability for what they did. After this is done, we can take up the second theme, of the Church's and its clergy's widespread failure to help Jews, and assess it more carefully. From this fine-grained evaluation, we can construct a more accurate portrait of the Church's and its clergy's deeds, offenses, and culpability.

VARIETIES OF CULPABILITY

A person has committed an offense in a general sense if (1) a second person has been unjustly harmed, and (2) the first person approves of that harm.[38]

There are two basic kinds of unjust harm: criminal and noncriminal. The criminal violates criminal law, whether domestic or international. Murder is a criminal harm. The noncriminal violates clear moral norms but not criminal law.[39] Teaching bigotry is a noncriminal harm.

There are also two kinds of approval: action and belief. A person can

TYPE OF OFFENSE

	Type of Approval	
	Action	Belief
Criminal	1 crime (e.g., murder)	3 supporting crime (e.g., murder)
Noncriminal	2 noncriminal transgression (e.g., teaching bigotry)	4 supporting noncriminal transgression (e.g., teaching bigotry)

Type of Harm

approve of an unjust harm by willfully contributing to it, becoming a perpetrator. He can, for example, choose to murder someone. He can urge people to be bigots, namely teach bigotry. A person can also believe the unjust harm to be right or praiseworthy but not contribute to it, be a bystander, because he is not needed, lacks the opportunity, or has some disqualifying incapacity. The word "support" is used here throughout to mean such a belief without its holder acting upon this belief. He can support the murderer's killing of his victim. He can support the bigotry.

It needs to be emphasized that communication—speaking and writing—is action. Spreading libels about another person, for example, is an act, one that can cause great harm. It alters the world unjustly by encouraging people to believe ill of someone who does not deserve it; it may even lead them to inflict further harm upon him. In the law, injurious speech is recognized as an act. When it meets certain legal standards, it is the tort of libel.

These two dimensions, unjust harm and approval, generate four distinct kinds of offenses:

1. Committing a criminal transgression or crime, such as murder
2. Committing a noncriminal transgression, such as teaching bigotry
3. Supporting a criminal transgression or crime, such as murder
4. Supporting a noncriminal transgression, such as teaching bigotry

Just as these four transgressions differ in their nature, so too does the nature of a person's culpability for each one.

Focusing on the dimension of unjust harm, just as the nature of the act varies, so does the degree of culpability. A person who is culpable for a crime, following conventional legal usage, is guilty. A person who is culpable for a noncriminal transgression, following conventional nonlegal usage, bears blame.[40]

Focusing on the dimension of approval, harming a targeted group of people is by definition political, so the type of culpability for contributing to such an assault is also political. Murdering someone, for example, as part of a political program of mass murder, or teaching bigotry are each political. Supporting such political action is inherently part of the realm of morality, so the type of culpability for such support is moral.

Therefore, the dimensions of unjust harm and approval specify, in addition to the four distinct kinds of offense, four parallel kinds of culpability:

1. A person committing a crime, such as murder, bears political guilt, which in accordance with conventional legal usage can be called legal guilt.
2. A person committing a noncriminal transgression, such as teaching bigotry, bears political blame.
3. A person supporting a crime, such as murder, bears moral guilt.
4. A person supporting a noncriminal transgression, such as teaching bigotry, bears moral blame.

These categories of offense and the attendant categories of culpability are relatively straightforward. They are general categories that are applicable to any persons and any deeds during any time. Their derivation, from the two dimensions of offense—unjust harm and approval—and the intellectual justification for them are independent of any consideration of the Catholic Church itself. Just as they could be used for ordinary Germans during the Nazi period or American southerners during the eras of slavery or Jim Crow, they can be and are used for the Catholic Church and its members, in order to sharpen our focus and to judge them. Before doing so, it is worth noting that the Church's own doctrines and maxims, which can be found in its official, authoritative instructional text, the *Catechism of the Catholic Church*, closely mirror our analysis, albeit in the Church's theological terms.

The Catholic Church's basic moral framework, its grounding in a divinity aside, is compatible with, indeed is very close to, our own. Our insistence on individual agency and responsibility, and on deeming that an individual commits an offense when he unjustly injures others and is therefore blameworthy both when he participates in the offense and when he, without par-

TYPE OF CULPABILITY

Type of Approval

	Action	Belief
Criminal	1 offense: crime culpability: legal guilt	3 offense: supporting crime culpability: moral guilt
Noncriminal	2 offense: noncriminal transgression culpability: political blame	4 offense: supporting noncriminal transgression culpability: moral blame

Type of Harm labels the left side (Criminal / Noncriminal).

ticipating, approves of it, is the same or directly analogous to the Church's own moral principles.

Just as we hold that individual agency is real and the source of a person's offenses and moral responsibility, the Church understands that "free will" is "the root of sin."[41] Just as we see unjust harm against another to be a blameworthy offense, the Church holds sin to be an "offense" and act of "evil" "against God" and also against "reason, truth, and right conscience," which "wounds the nature of man and injures human solidarity." For the Church, sin is "an utterance, a deed, or a desire contrary to the eternal law." Just as we hold guilt or blame to be individual, never collective, the Church maintains that "sin is a personal act."[42] Just as we hold that someone is not relieved of responsibility for his actions just because he acted in concert with, or under the authority of, others, the Church maintains, "we have a responsibility for the sins committed by others when *we cooperate in them*." Just as we maintain that committing unjust harm against others brings guilt or blame, the Church maintains that "participating directly and voluntarily" in sins incurs "responsibility for the sins." Just as we hold that support for the unjust harm perpetrated by someone else brings guilt or blame, the Church maintains that "approving" sins of others incurs "responsibility for the sins." The Church is adamant that "every attitude and word likely to cause [persons] unjust injury" incurs "guilt."[43]

The Church does not follow as closely our distinction between criminal and noncriminal acts, instead grading the types of transgressive acts and therefore degree of sin according to its own notions of mortal and venial sin. A mortal sin, by gravely violating God's law, destroys what a venial sin only wounds: "charity in the heart of man," charity being the "theological virtue by which we love God above all things for its own sake, and our neighbor as ourselves for the love of God." The Church explains: "For a *sin* to be *mortal*, three conditions must together be met: 'Mortal sin is a sin whose object is grave matter and which is also committed with full knowledge and deliberate consent.' " Grave matter, according to the Church, is "specified by the Ten Commandments" and includes "Do not kill," "Do not steal," and "Do not bear false witness."[44] Our distinction between committing a crime, for which a person incurs criminal guilt, and supporting a crime, for which a person incurs moral guilt, is not followed in the Church's moral system. It holds that if the violation is grave, both the perpetrator and his supporter commit the same kind of transgression: a mortal sin.[45] In the Church's terms, the spreading of prejudice and hatred, in this case antisemitism, is a sin. Although the Church's *Catechism* does not address this directly, John Paul II and many Church publications have repeatedly confirmed this conclusion. It is a sin because it is bearing false witness, which is "misrepresenting the truth in our relations with others." For the Church the sin of spreading antisemitism would not fall into the lesser, venial category of offense, as it does in ours of blame (instead of guilt). It follows from the Church's doctrinal principles that spreading prejudice or hatred, including antisemitism, is a mortal sin because "bearing false witness" is a mortal sin.[46]

The Catholic Church's moral principles, though closely mapping our own, are at least as censorious of the offenses under consideration here as ours are. Indeed, in the eyes of the Church, the offender who does not repent his mortal sin—such as the spreading of antisemitism—faces "the eternal death of hell."[47] This is important to keep in mind for the discussion of part three, where repentance is a central theme. There and elsewhere, we periodically return to the Church's own doctrines and teachings, in order to show the affinity of this investigation with its own precepts. The Church itself, if applying its own principles fairly to its own and its members' stances and actions toward Jews, would come to conclusions that closely mirror ours. But for now, let us return to our categories, keeping in mind that each of them has a moral component. A person who incurs legal guilt or political blame also incurs the moral culpability inherent to each one.

A person bears *legal guilt* if he commits a crime according to domestic or international law. International law includes many provisions that bear on this discussion. The principles of international law include punishment for war crimes and crimes against humanity. Following the Charter of the Nuremberg Tribunal, war crimes include "violations of the laws or customs of war which include, but are not limited to, murder, ill-treatment or deportation to slave-labor or for any other purpose of civilian population of or in occupied territory." Crimes against humanity are "murder, extermination, enslavement, deportation, and other inhuman acts done against any civilian population, or persecutions on political, racial, or religious grounds, when such acts are done or such persecutions are carried on in execution of or in connection with any crime against peace or any war crime." The principles of international law also state that just because national law does not impose a penalty for a criminal act, this "does not relieve the person who committed the act from responsibility under international law."[48]

In the United Nations International Law Commission's "Draft Code of Offenses against the Peace and Security of Mankind" acts that are "offenses against the peace and security of mankind" include "Acts by authorities of a State or by private individuals committed with intent to destroy, in whole or in part, a national, ethnic, racial or religious group as such, including: (i) Killing members of the group; (ii) Causing serious bodily or mental harm to members of the group; (iii) Deliberately inflicting on the group conditions of life calculated to bring about its physical destruction in whole or in part." It also includes as offenses acts that are part of a "conspiracy to commit" any of these offenses, "direct incitement to commit" any of these offenses, "complicity in the commission" of any of these offenses, and "attempts to commit" any of these offenses.[49] The statutes of the United Nations' International Tribunals for Yugoslavia and Rwanda include as punishable offenses an even longer list of acts, including "murder," "extermination," "deportation," "persecutions on political, racial and religious grounds," and "other inhumane acts." The statute states specifically that "a person who planned, instigated, ordered, committed or otherwise aided and abetted in the planning, preparation or execution" of such crimes "shall be individually responsible for the crime."[50]

Since this is not a legal proceeding but a moral reckoning, we should not be restricted here to the letter of a country's law of the time, particularly since those laws were promulgated by unlawful and immoral governments that were responsible for great crimes themselves. As these and other international statutes make clear, it is by now a well-established principle in international law that domestic laws that violate international laws and norms of human rights are invalid and do not protect people who commit crimes under their unlawful auspices.[51] Also, since this is an exercise in moral judgment and moral repair—not in legal judgment and legal punishment—we do the actors no injustice or disservice by using the broadly accepted legal categories of the time and of today. Therefore, when appropriate, we should apply such standards.

Regarding the Jews, legal guilt would apply to anyone who killed Jews or contributed to their deaths.[52] It would apply to anyone who persecuted or contributed to their persecution in other ways, such as enforcing racial laws, which were a clear violation of the Jews' human rights and therefore criminal. A person who chose to be a member of a criminal organization, such as the SS (certainly after 1933), is also criminally liable, and therefore, in our terms, legally guilty. This principle, that voluntary membership in a criminal organization is itself a crime, was established at the Nuremberg trials.[53] The reasoning is simple. If a person chooses to become a member or to maintain membership in an organization that is known to be criminal in its essence, or has as a principal activity its members' criminal conduct, he, as an individual, by dint of his membership choice, adopts for himself the burden of that criminality. In essence, he is part of a conspiracy to commit crimes. It follows that a person willfully aiding such a criminal organization is legally guilty. Legal guilt would also apply to a superior, such as the Pope or a bishop who failed to try to prevent a subordinate from committing a crime that he knew the subordinate was intending to commit.

A person bears *moral guilt* if he, without committing a crime, supports a criminal act. The notion of moral guilt is straightforward. A person has morally thrown in his lot with the criminal. By his support he holds that the criminal has acted justly and that, in principle, he would do the same if called upon or if presented with the opportunity. A person who supports a criminal act is not, however, legally guilty because we do not convict people of crimes, we do not say that they bear legal guilt, for their thoughts and attitudes. But we can render moral judgment upon them. By supporting the crime, by being in moral solidarity with the criminal, a person becomes morally implicated in the crime. Just as he lends his moral support to the crime, we must extend our moral condemnation to him. If the actor is a criminal, then his supporter is a moral offender. The actor is criminally or legally guilty. His supporter is morally guilty. Regarding the Jews, anyone who supported the mass murder or other criminal acts against them bears moral guilt.

A person bears *political blame* if he commits a political act that is not criminal, but that nevertheless unjustly harms others. A person spreading false accusations about others unjustly harms them and, therefore, bears political blame. The same is true for a person teaching others to hate or feel enmity toward innocent people. Prejudice, the hatred and enmity it produces, is by definition a form of unjust discrimination. Propagating and disseminating antisemitism is a political transgression and incurs political blame. The Church similarly maintains that "every attitude and word likely to cause" a person "unjust injury" violates the "*respect for the reputation* of persons." This includes "calumny," which is therefore "forbidden" and brings with it "guilt."[54] A second type of political transgression for which a person bears political blame is lending general aid to a person or government engaged in crime, without specifically aiding the crime itself; here the unjust act does not rise to the level of criminality, because it does not violate a law. Telling people, for example, to serve and sustain a political regime that is systematically perpetrating crime or that is in its essence criminal incurs political blame.

A person bears *moral blame* if he, without committing a political transgression, himself supports one. The relationship of moral blame to political blame is the same as that of moral guilt to legal guilt. A person inwardly giving his blessing to a political transgression—the spreading of prejudice or lending aid to a criminal regime—bears moral blame.

It should be clear that any analysis of culpability that grapples with complex, multifaceted stances and actions is difficult. Inevitably some acts shade from one category to another and are hard to place definitively, or would require far too lengthy a discussion for all their nuances to be presented here. Many actors, such as Pius XII, also bear several different kinds of culpability for their related, if different acts, which are also sometimes difficult to distinguish clearly from one another. All the difficulties notwithstanding, the categorization here helps to disentangle and clarify a variety of transgressions and types of culpability, and thereby facilitates us rendering well-grounded moral judgments and then undertaking the process of moral repair.

THE CHURCH'S AFFIRMATIVE OFFENSES

This is not meant to be an exhaustive inventory and assessment of the Catholic Church's offenses. As discussed in part one, until many detailed studies of each national church's conduct during this period are available, we are not in a position to evaluate the Church and its officials comprehensively. Even if we know *for sure* of many offenses committed by the Church and its clergy, we do not know the full extent of the wrongdoing of various national churches, or even of the two Popes and the Vatican, or how many of its bishops and priests took part in any of a range of blameworthy deeds. Here I provide a preliminary inventory of the kinds of offenses committed by the Church and its clergy, some assessments of their typicality, and some examples and explanation.

In many ways, Catholic bishops and priests across Europe supported political transgressions. Many supported the destruction of democracy and the establishment of persecutionist dictatorships, which they continued to support as they watched the persecution. In country after country there is every reason to believe that the desire for democracy's destruction and support for tyranny was not confined to a scattered few clergy. The Church's pervasive hostility to modernity, particularly to modernity's political and cultural democratic creed and institutions, and its belief that Bolshevism must be fought ruthlessly all but guaranteed that in Germany, Italy, and elsewhere the Nazis, Fascists, and rightist tyrannies would be greeted by churchmen with relief if not acclaim. We do not know exactly how widespread such broad support was, but all those who did support these political transgressions are morally blameworthy. All those who actively sustained them bear political blame. Pius XII, first as Vatican Secretary of State and then as Pope, bears such moral blame and political blame. The German, Croatian, French, Italian, and Slovakian national churches were pleased with the replacement of democratic and constitutional systems by authoritarian regimes that would persecute their opponents.[55] The same censure applies to the German Catholic Church for its support of the imperialist war that Germany initiated. The German Church shared Germany's international ambitions, including the political transgression of aggressive war, defined at the Nuremberg trials as a crime (but which we will consider here to be a political offense). Two weeks after Germany set off World War II by attacking Poland, the German bishops issued a joint pastoral letter, which reflected their belief in the justness of this aggressive war, which was for the conquest of *Lebensraum:* "In this decisive hour we encourage and admonish our Catholic soldiers, in obedience to the Führer, to do their duty and to be ready to sacrifice their whole person. We appeal to the faithful to join in ardent prayers that God's providence may lead this war to blessed success and peace for the fatherland and people."[56]

The bishops' support for Germany's victory in its apocalyptic and annihilative war continued unabated, even though they knew that with every German advance and then with every day that Germany warded off defeat, their countrymen would slaughter more Jews, moving Hitler and those who shared his goal closer to achieving the total extermination of the Jewish people. Gordon Zahn explains "that the German Catholic who looked to his religious superiors for spiritual guidance and direction regarding service in Hitler's wars received virtually the same answers he would have received from the Nazi ruler himself."

So Cardinal Faulhaber declared in October 1943 that "nobody in his heart can possibly wish an unsuccessful outcome of the war. Every reasonable person knows that in such a case the State and the Church, and organized society altogether, would be overturned by the Russian chaos." In January 1945 the German Archbishop Lorenz Jäger urged Catholics to continue to contribute to Germany's war against democracy and communism, or as he put it, "liberalism and individualism on one side, collectivism on the other"—both of which the Catholic Church and the German Catholic Church tended to blame on the Jews. (The archbishop appeared to be suggesting even in 1945 that Nazism was preferable to democracy.) Bishop Galen confessed at Easter in his first public statement after the Allied occupation of Germany had begun that his heart had bled at "the sight of the passing troops of our enemy." In one respect it is understandable that a person would be saddened by the sight of his country being occupied, but this was the "enemy" that right-thinking Germans rightly saw as the liberators of Germany from Nazism. And Bishop Galen decidedly did not say that his heart had bled for the slaughtered Jews.

Lewy concludes that with the exception of Bishop Preysing, "all German bishops until the very last days of the conflict called on the faithful to do their patriotic duty. This position, we may assume, represented sincerely felt loyalty to their country. The fact that Germany was ruled by the Nazis, who harassed and persecuted the Church and were guilty of untold other crimes, made no difference."[57] He might have added that it made no difference either because the bishops subscribed to the imperialist and apocalyptic ambitions of the Nazis or because their countrymen's crimes, including the mass annihilation of the Jews, did not seem to them to be transgressions of sufficient magnitude to warrant withdrawing their aid and support from the very war that made the crimes possible and from the regime that was perpetrating them. For the German bishops, in deciding which was more important to them—the victory of a regime that in the eyes of the rest of the world was utterly criminal, or putting an end to the mass murder of the Jews—everything indicates that the decision was easy to make.

For their aid and support of such general political transgressions as the overthrow of democratic institutions and the rule of law and their replacement by authoritarian regimes, churchmen in Germany, Italy, and elsewhere incurred political blame and moral blame.

Regarding Jews in particular, the Church's and its clergy's antisemitism incurred the different kinds of moral culpability that are attached to each of a range of offenses. Antisemitism was the Church's, its national churches', and their clergy's central, most multifaceted, and pervasive offense, so the theme of antisemitism will recur repeatedly in this moral accounting. What are antisemitism's offending features?

Supporting Political Transgressions, Incurring Moral Blame

Antisemitism, and this is true of other kinds of prejudice, is baseless antipathy or animus, which in itself constitutes unjust discrimination. In the Church's terms, it is a violation of the Eighth Commandment, "You shall not bear false witness against your neighbor," which, according to Church doctrine, mandates that "*respect for the reputation* of persons forbids every attitude and word likely to cause them unjust injury." When Jews live in a profoundly antisemitic culture, they live in a culture of hostility, a culture that not only inevitably leads to further unjust discriminatory acts but is itself, by definition, harmfully discriminatory. It is discriminatory and injurious because a Jew, a Jewish child, is disliked, thought ill of, hated, before the antisemites know anything else about her as an individual, and for alleged attributes that are not, and will never be, hers. The antisemites think ill of her only because of her identity as a Jew. Feeling antipathy or animus toward a person for such a reason is to perpetrate an injustice, which is to inflict harm. The Catholic Church agrees. It maintains that he who commits "calumny . . . by remarks contrary to the truth, harms the reputation of others and gives occasion for false judgments concerning them." "Calumny," it continues, "destroy[s] the *reputation and honor of one's neighbor*. Honor is the social witness given to human dignity, and everyone enjoys a natural right to the honor of his name and reputation and to respect. Thus . . . calumny offend[s] against the virtues of justice and charity."[58]

Antisemitism, a culture of hatred, denies individuals virtually all opportunity to define themselves for other people. It imposes on Jews an overriding identity and an explanation, sometimes unwanted and almost always wrong: "He is a Jew, therefore he is bad or does bad things." Or "He is like that because he is a Jew, and he did that noxious thing because he is a Jew"— even when neither the quality nor the act is related to his identity as a Jew. Antisemites dislike Jews and are likely to act harmfully toward them (1) for false reasons and (2) for an attribute of the victims—that they are identified as Jews—that is irrelevant to the disapproved act.

Antisemitism, a culture of hatred, coursed through the politics and societies of Europe during the 1930s and 1940s and through the corridors of the Church, from St. Peter's to the most humble parish chapel. It was an unremarkable feature of European Catholics' outlook, derived from the Christian Bible and from Church teachings. In many European countries it was well nigh impossible, especially for Catholic clergy, not to be exposed to antisemitism. The clergy knew that it was central to the political cultures of much of Europe, that it was being spread by politicians, secular and Church alike. All those who supported the offense of antisemitism, in this instance the offense being the political transgression of teaching and spreading it, bear moral blame for their approving stance. Given that antisemitism was the common sense of the institutional culture of the Catholic Church during this period—indeed it was at the time hard to be a Catholic priest and not to be antisemitic, since among the many other commonly held antisemitic charges, it was a central Catholic doctrine, based in Scripture, that contemporary Jews were guilty for the death of Jesus—it is safe to say that support for this offense and its attendant moral blame applies to the vast majority of clergy of these years, even if the character and intensity of their antisemitism varied widely.

Committing Political Transgressions, Incurring Political Blame

For many of the Catholic bishops and priests who supported tyranny and antisemitism, their moral blame is mirrored by political blame for their political activities on behalf of the cause of tyranny and for spreading antisemitism. No one bears a greater burden of this kind than the two Popes, Pius XI and Pius XII (as Vatican Secretary of State), in their welcoming of the Nazis to power, which ushered in the destruction of the democratic institutions that they generally despised. Their Concordat lent early political legitimacy to the Hitler-led Nazi regime.

This made them and the Church for which they spoke during the 1930s (until later disillusionment partly set in) an important political aid to the regime. In a 1937 sermon Cardinal Faulhaber boasted about how much the Church with its Concordat had buttressed Nazism:

> At a time when the heads of the major nations in the world faced the new Germany with cool reserve and considerable suspicion, the Catholic Church, the greatest moral power on earth, through the Concordat expressed its confidence in the new German government. This was a deed of immeasurable significance for the reputation of the new government abroad.[59]

German Catholics attend a thanksgiving service at the St. Hedwig Cathedral in Berlin on September 17, 1933, after the ratification of the Concordat.

The political blame incurred by the Popes is shared by the German Church's clergy, who, exceptions notwithstanding, helped to legitimize Nazism. This is generally true also for Catholicism's national churches in Italy, France, Slovakia, Austria, and Croatia for their support of their own countries' criminal regimes.

It would be hard to exaggerate the extent of the Church's political blame for the political transgression of teaching millions of people libelous notions about Jews and therefore to feel animus and enmity toward them. The Vatican, national churches across Europe—in Germany, Poland, France, Italy, and elsewhere—published in their newspapers and periodicals the most damaging antisemitic libels, including especially identifying

German Catholic clergy give the Nazi salute with government officials including Wilhelm Frick, Minister of the Interior and later governor of Bohemia and Moravia (second from right), and Joseph Goebbels, the Propaganda Minister (far right).

The Archbishop of Croatia, Aloys Stepinac (far right), at an official ceremony in 1941.

Nuns marching together with Ustasha legionnaires.

Jews with the Bolshevik threat. Ronald Modras, at the end of his study of the Polish Catholic Church and antisemitism, writes of the clergy's teaching of antisemitism and the character of their responsibility for the violence that they helped to produce:

> The Catholic clergy, as represented by the Catholic press and the pronouncements of bishops, were not innocent bystanders or passive observers in the wave of antisemitism that encompassed Poland in the later half of the 1930s. Along with the [enormously influential antisemitic political party, the] National Democrats, they were very much integral to it, as their liberal opponents testified and the sheer volume of the material I have surveyed here confirms. Even when nationalistic youth translated antisemitic attitudes into violence, one did not hear ringing denunciations from Catholic church leaders or the Catholic press. Instead of subjecting the violence to unambiguous criticism, church leaders rather gave explanations for antisemitism that ultimately served to justify it.[60]

Teaching Catholics that all Jews are guilty for crucifying Jesus, which was perhaps the most injurious antisemitic charge ever put forward, was official

Catholic Church policy. Antisemitic hatred and enmity was embedded in the doctrine, theology, and liturgy of the Catholic Church, doled out in larger and smaller doses to Catholics not just in Poland but also around Europe on a yearly, weekly, and daily basis, with the most fervent period of antisemitic agitation, of course, being Holy Week, the week leading up to Easter when the Church would focus its ire squarely on the liturgically dubbed "perfidious" Jews for their alleged killing of Jesus.[61]

The Nazis found the teachings of the Church to be such fertile soil that they naturally and routinely drew on Christian antisemitic motifs to facilitate, politically and culturally, the spreading and reinforcing of their own antisemitism. Julius Streicher in a 1936 Christmas address to two thousand children in Nuremberg effortlessly mobilized the Christian knowledge that the children already possessed: " 'Do you know who the Devil is?' he asked his breathlessly listening audience. 'The Jew, the Jew,' resounded from a thousand children's voices."[62]

This was but one drop in a continuous stream of catechistic lessons and exchanges between Nazi teachers and their already well-schooled German Catholic (and Protestant) pupils which included signs posted in German cities, at the entrances to towns, and in the countryside linking Jews to the Christian devil. Streicher a year earlier drew on one of the Nazis' favorite and frequently used Christian images, in declaring, "Only one people remained victorious in that dreadful war, a people whom Christ said that its father is the Devil." Streicher, like tens of millions in Germany and across Europe, knew his Christian Bible, here recalling the notorious accusation in the Gospel According to John that the Jews wanted to kill Jesus. John has Jesus saying, "You belong to your father the devil and you willingly carry out your father's desires. He was a murderer from the beginning and does not stand in truth, because there is no truth in him."[63] Identifying the Jews with the devil of the Christian imagination was one of the standard tropes of Streicher's newspaper, *Der Stürmer*. At its height *Der Stürmer* had a circulation of 500,000 and was read by many more because it was displayed throughout Germany in showcases at bus stops, busy pedestrian areas, factory canteens, and other places where people congregated. Streicher was among the most obsessed antisemites the Nazis had to offer. His flock in Nuremberg and his readership around Germany, thanks to Catholic and Protestant schooling, were in step with him on this and many other core antisemitic issues.

As we saw in part one, it is an absurdity to maintain that the Nazis would have invented their antisemitism out of thin air, or that their tens of millions of eager antisemitic followers would have thrown their lot in with the

Caricature of a Jew on the front page of Der Stürmer *in October 1937. The caption reads, "Mother Europe / If I had to leave even one of my children to this devil it would be my death."*

Eschenbach in central Franconia, July 1935. The sign declares: "The father of the Jews is the devil."

Nazis' dehumanizing and violent policies that followed on this wild, phantasmagoric prejudice, had the Catholic Church not already poisoned much of German and European culture with antisemitism. Cardinal Edward Cassidy, head of the Holy See's Commission for Religious Relations with the Jews, when addressing Jewish leaders in Washington in 1998, was not uninformed when he pointed a finger at the Catholic Church, declaring that "the ghetto, which came into being in 1555 with a papal bull, became in Nazi Germany the antechamber of the extermination."[64] It would also be absurd to think that the Church's sustained propagation of antisemitism during the Nazi period did not reinforce popular support around Europe for the eliminationist persecution of the Jews. Had the two Popes, the Church leaders and lower clergy used their pulpits and their enormous number of newspapers and diocesan publications with their huge, faithful readerships in Germany and around Europe to declare antisemitism a vicious delusion and to denounce the persecution of the Jews as a grievous crime and sin, then the political history of Europe would have been different, and the fate of the Jews much better.

But this did not happen. Pius XI and Pius XII were antisemites. They were prone, as they themselves gave evidence—Pius XI with his reports from Poland of 1918 and Pius XII with his report of 1919 on the Communist insurrection in Munich—to almost Nazi-like fantasies and libels about Jews. Their supervision, approval, and tolerance of *Civiltà cattolica* and other Church publications spreading the most incendiary kind of antisemitic libels and accusations continued steadily during the Nazi period. Catholic bishops and priests in Germany and across Europe were also antisemites. Even Pius XI's buried encyclical protesting the Germans' exceptionally brutal persecution of the Jews is a document filled with fearsome antisemitism. The two Popes, their bishops, and their priests had adopted as their own their antisemitic Church's image, animus, and idiom about Jews. When confronted by the prospect of doing something effective against the putative Jewish menace, they, with exceptions, did not say no to the deeds.

The likelihood that the popes and clergy alike would act prejudicially to the detriment of Jews was especially great because they, like the Nazi leadership and many Germans, (1) identified communism with Jews; (2) considered communism to be their greatest political enemy; and (3) saw the Germans' apocalyptic war against communism combined with an annihilative war against the Jews (even if a substantial number of clergy may have opposed the mass killing itself) as a fight against their common foe: Judeo-Bolshevism. This ominous identification of the Jews with Bolshevism was all but the official position of the most politically critical of the national Catholic churches, the one, with the possible exception of the Italian Church, closest to Pius XII's heart, the German Church.

The German Catholic clergy's beliefs about the nature of contemporary Jewry had much in common with those of the Nazis. The clergy viewed the Jews as a harmful and malevolent people, the source of many of the ills that had afflicted Germany before Hitler's accession to power. They believed that Jews authored or promoted the trends in the modern world that they held to be inimical to Catholicism, indeed to social and religious wholesomeness. They alleged that Jews spread moral libertinism, preached unbelief, mocked hallowed traditions, preyed on Christians economically, eroded national and communal solidarity, and fostered decadence, including modern art.

Of all the Jews' alleged evil activities, the most destructive was the putative preeminent role they played in the Bolshevik movement. The Jews were considered to be Bolshevism's hidden animating force, its invisible "wire pullers." The belief that the Jews were the inspirers and movers of Bolshevism was the most potent contemporary impetus for the Catholic clergy's hostility toward Jews and for their concomitant support of the Nazi measures against them, short of outright murder. They believed the Jews to be the driving spirit of the most dangerous political movement to confront the Catholic Church in its history. Bolshevism was conceived as a "satanic" force bent upon annihilating not only all of Christendom but European civilization itself. The German Catholic Church's authoritative *Handbook of Contemporary Religious Questions,* composed in 1937, defined Bolshevism as "an Asiatic state despotism." Who was behind it? "In point of fact," the German bishops declared in the handbook, which they published as a sure guide to enlighten "the ranks of the Church that are threatened by confusion," Bolshevism was "in the service of a group of terrorists led by Jews." The German Church described the encounter with Bolshevism in well nigh apocalyptic terms. The conflict with Bolshevism was a modern-day crusade. Allegedly led mainly by Jews, Bolshevism threatened all the nations of the world. A titanic struggle for the future of humankind was being waged. The handbook quotes approvingly Hitler's declaration that the encounter with Bolshevism was a struggle between European *Kultur* and Asian *Unkultur.* Surely the harshest measures were permissible against those who lead, promote, and sustain this satanic movement.

It would be difficult to find in the records of the German Catholic Church during the Nazi period, even in its known internal confidential discussions and communications, dissenting opinions from these dominant beliefs about the perniciousness and guilt of the Jews. There were voices in the Church questioning or opposing particular measures against the Jews; there were some who doubted the truth of this or that unwholesome trait or propensity attributed to the Jews. But seldom do we meet within the ranks of the clergy the recognition that the entire web of beliefs about the Jews was a tissue of pernicious delusions; seldom do we encounter an opinion akin to that of Sebastian Haffner, an uncompromising German opponent of the Nazis, who wrote in 1939 that the Nazis' assertions about the Jews are "such plain nonsense that one demeans oneself when one discusses them even if only to refute them."[65] What a sober, clear-sighted non-antisemitic German apprehended as a corpus of contemptible nonsense, Catholic clergy and theologians, erudite exponents of the Christian creed, held to be axiomatic truths.

Only in one major respect did the German Catholic Church's conception of the Jews differ from that of the Nazis, namely, in its view of the source of the Jewish proclivity to do evil. According to Nazi racial doctrine the evil of the Jews derived from their bodily constitution, from a biological drive, like that which impels predatory animals or microorganisms to prey and to destroy. The Jews were therefore unreformable. They had to be incarcerated in perpetuity or killed.

The theological doctrines of the Catholic Church would not formally allow it to subscribe to such a crude species of racism. It held to its ancient doctrine that the evil of the Jews had its roots in their putatively obsolete and pernicious religion, their willful rejection of Jesus. The Jews were therefore, at least in principle, redeemable. They could be reformed by conversion; the waters of baptism would cleanse them.

Although Nazi racism was incompatible with the Catholic creed, the German Church did not reject it completely, because its clergy, including its leading bishops, were not immune from the racist thinking prevalent in their society. Thus, in its official pronouncements, the German Church equivocated about racism, finding merit in some of its aspects, while rejecting other elements that clashed directly with the core of its own creed. The German bishops affirmed that the different races making up humanity were endowed with different qualities and attributes, but they implicitly rejected the Nazi doctrine that the races form a hierarchical order, those at the top being superior to those below them and those on the lowest rung being so primitive, so destitute of moral and intellectual worth, as to be deemed subhumans. The German Catholic Church held to Catholicism's fundamental tenet that in the eyes of God all races are equal and capable of salvation.

But the German bishops did not apply these notions to Jews because their beliefs about their tangible evil and perniciousness overrode these abstract considerations of the moral equality of all people. They did not reject the Nazi race laws, particularly the Nuremberg Laws. Instead, they affirmed them. The German bishops proclaimed that the preservation of racial distinctiveness was a good thing. "Every people," their authoritative handbook explains, "bears itself the responsibility for its successful existence, and the intake of entirely foreign blood will always represent a risk for a nationality that has proven its historical worth. Hence, no people may be denied the right to maintain undisturbed its previous racial stock and to employ safeguards for this purpose. The Christian religion demanded only that the methods employed should not violate the ethical precepts and natural justice." "The racial legislation of the day," the Nuremberg Laws, "make sense . . . if the native racial qualities and culture are to be fostered

During the war a sign at the entrance to a Dutch town declares "Jews not welcome."

and protected from degeneration (*Entartung*)." Here the German bishops adopted one of the key terms of the Nazi racist lexicon, "degenerate," used by the Nazis to denounce and defame that which they sought to undo or eradicate.

The German Church's corporate belief in the need to protect the Germans' "racial qualities," their "blood," from degeneration, the role of the Jews, and the threat of Bolshevism form an inextricably entangled ideological complex. The bishops warned: "No people can avoid this clash between its national tradition and Marxism, which is opposed to national ties and led mostly by Jewish agitators and revolutionaries." The bishops emphatically declared that "Christianity can only welcome a scientifically founded racial inquiry and racial fostering."[66]

What was true about the German Catholic Church was also true, to a greater or lesser degree, of other national Catholic churches, especially with regard to warning their peoples of the alleged, dire Jewish-Bolshevik danger. The Catholic clergy, in teaching, in exhorting ordinary Germans, French, Poles, and others to be wary of the alleged Jewish peril and thereby breeding enmity toward Jews, were also teaching them to discriminate against them: not to trust Jews, not to mix with Jews freely or intimately, and to keep them at bay as much as possible. Shunning people, discriminating against people in private relations, is not a crime, but it certainly is a harmful act. When done systematically, as it was in Germany and elsewhere, it is political in nature, because it has harmful social and political consequences. For this, all those bishops and priests who spread, preached, or taught antisemitism are also politically blameworthy, thus inherently morally blameworthy as well.

Others would judge the Church still more harshly. Today's Germany, and several other countries, have criminal laws against hate speech. In Germany a person commits the crime of *Volksverhetzung* if he "incites to hatred against parts of the population or instigates violence or arbitrary measures against them or . . . attacks the human dignity of others by insulting, maliciously disparaging or slandering parts of the population." Today's Germany would judge the Catholic Church's vilifications, slanders, and condemnations of the Jews in which members of the hierarchy freely indulged before and during the Nazi period, if made today, as criminal. The German justice system would have to bring criminal charges for *Volksverhetzung* against a bishop or priest who spread such antisemitism today.[67]

Supporting Crime, Incurring Moral Guilt

The moral guilt that accrues to people for supporting crime was extremely widespread within the Church although it varied substantially depending on the given crime. The Church as a whole and bishops and priests across Europe supported the anti-Jewish laws passed in Germany and then in similar form in Italy, Vichy, Slovakia, Croatia, and other countries. How could they not, when the laws merely codified what many organs of the Church had themselves been urging, and of which the Church officially approved? These laws, containing scores of provisions that gravely violated the Jews' human rights, were clearly criminal. The understanding and support for such laws was especially substantial in the German Catholic Church, where the belief in the Jews' putative criminal nature and the alleged great danger they posed was strong.

To be more specific, the Germans (and their helpers abroad) subjected Jews to a range of criminal policies. Before the war these anti-Jewish policies included legal and administrative measures that forbade Jews from holding government jobs, especially in the civil service, and from practicing their professions and participating in the economy; that isolated Jews from non-Jews by excluding them from using public facilities, including schools and swimming pools; that turned them into political and social pariahs by stripping them of their citizenship and prohibiting them from marrying or having sexual relations with non-Jews; that drove them to emigrate; and that subjected them to violence including physical assault, incarceration in concentration camps, burning of their synagogues and communal buildings, and episodic murder.

During the war the Germans augmented these policies with a set of new ones: forced deportation, ghettoization, murder through starvation, debilitation, and disease (even prior to the formal program of total annihilation), a greatly expanded and ever more brutal camp system, enslavement, and systematic, comprehensive mass murder. All of these policies furthered the Germans' two central objectives: producing the "social death" of Jews (turning them into violently dominated, natally alienated, and generally dishonored beings, against whom one might do anything) and eliminating the Jews and their "influence" wherever Germany ruled, eventually with the essentially open policy of extermination.[68]

These policies were at the heartless core of Germany's politics during the 1930s and 1940s. Knowledge of them, indeed contact with them, was all but unavoidable. The German bishops and priests knew them all well (as did the Vatican and clergy across Europe). How did they view them? There is no evidence that even a significant minority of them viewed the two central German anti-Jewish policy objectives of these years with disapproval. These interrelated criminal aims—making the Jews socially dead and eliminating their influence and contact with Germans—were based on an image of Jewish infiltration and danger that accorded with what the Church had been preaching all along. Individual churchmen sometimes disapproved of individual aspects of this eliminationist assault. Some looked upon the violence with distaste and some with disapproval and horror, but we have little evidence even of this or that the disapproval was a heartfelt, deep strain within the German Catholic Church. In fact, the evidence of the German Church's acceptance and approval of Germany's criminal eliminationist program, short of the murderous violence, is overwhelming. The compatibility of the Nazi regime's and the German Catholic Church's aspirations in this matter is striking. Even after *Kristallnacht,* the German Catholic Church, its bishops and priests, were silent.

These obvious conclusions about the failure of the German Catholic Church are not only mine. In 1979 even the German Catholic Church itself in a declaration from the Secretariat of its National Bishops' Conference conceded the facts:

All the more difficult is it to understand today that neither to the boycott of Jewish stores on April 1, 1933, nor to the promulgation of the Nuremberg

A Catholic shrine and an antisemitic sign watch together over a town in Franconia in 1935. The sign declares: "Jews are not welcome here."

Laws in September 1935 nor to the excesses that occurred in the course of the so-called Kristallnacht on 9/10 November 1938 did a sufficiently clear and immediate reaction on the part of the Church occur.[69]

Only mass murder may have failed to find overwhelming understanding within the German Church hierarchy. Yet the evidence of widespread principled, unequivocal moral condemnation among the German clergy even of their countrymen's slaughter of the Jews is also not substantial. And the priestly servicing of the German occupation and mass-murdering forces in eastern Europe might suggest that German clergy approved of the annihilation of the Jews in greater numbers than anyone has dared to say. If indeed it is true in this matter, as it is with antisemitism in general, that the Catholic clergy of a nation greatly reflect the character of the prejudices of the society that nurtures them and in which they live, then why should we be surprised if many German clergy did share the belief widespread in German society that the total and final elimination of the Jews, already socially dead, by physical slaughter, was necessary and just?

Many other national Catholic churches, including the Croatian, French, and Slovakian, appear to have supported the Germans' and their national helpers' local eliminationist onslaughts. Prior to the policies of deportation and slaughter, the national Catholic churches around Europe did not protest or demonstrate that their leadership opposed the eliminationist persecution of the Jews. In many countries even deportation, the violent uprooting and expulsion of Jews from their homes and their countries, was not widely condemned morally by the national churches, although for some clergy, particularly in the Netherlands, France, and Italy, the deportations and the mass murder went too far.

There was a symbiosis between the Nazis' antisemitism and the Church's conception and teachings about Jews. The significant differences between the racial foundation of the first and the religious foundation of the second notwithstanding, they shared a common foundational feature that marked them as being of the most dangerous kind of antisemitisms, distinguishing them from all lesser varieties of this prejudice. Unlike most forms of anti-semitism, and most forms of prejudice, each conceived of Jews in terms of the fundamental moral order of the world. In this view, Jews are more than grave transgressors of moral norms. They are beings whose very existence constitutes a violation of the moral fabric of society. For the Nazis the Jews were genetically evil, an inveterate and powerful force for harm. For the Church they were the ontological enemies of God, inflicting great injuries on his earthly flock. Antisemitisms of this ilk are more tenacious than other kinds of antisemitism, arouse more passion, usually provoke and support a wider variety of more serious and inflammatory charges against the Jews, and inhere within them a greater potential for violent and deadly anti-Jewish action.[70]

The Nazis and the Church could therefore conclude in common that the Jews were so threatening that the danger they putatively posed could not be neutralized so long as they mixed freely among the nations. In light of this, the silence of national church after national church, of bishops and priests in country after country, as they watched, sometimes with mixed emotions, others implementing eliminationist anti-Jewish policies becomes more understandable. As I have already discussed, the absence of protest on the part of an institution and people who are all but professional critics, com-mentators on the immorality of policies, deeds, and ideas that they oppose confirms this obvious conclusion. Furthermore, the testimony of the lead-ing churchmen themselves makes it clear that the Church was in sync with the intellectual and nonlethal programmatic core of the Germans' elimina-tionist enterprise.

At least twice Pius XII and the Vatican were offered the opportunity to speak freely, without any risk whatsoever, for the emendation of anti-Jewish laws. In August 1941 the Vichy government asked the Vatican for its opinion on its anti-Jewish laws. Vichy's ambassador to the Vatican, Léon Bérard, reported on the Church's reply, affirming, "I have never been told anything which—from the standpoint of the Holy See—implied criticism and disapproval of the legislative and administrative acts in question." For the church, Bérard explained, "It would be unreasonable, in a Christian state, to permit them [Jews] to exercise the functions of government and thus to submit the Catholics to their authority. Consequently it is legitimate to bar them from public functions." Except for protecting the sacrament of marriage for Catholics (with Jewish spouses) and the reflexive refrain that Vichy should show "justice and charity" when implementing its measures, "as I was told by an authorized spokesman at the Vatican: we shall not in the least be reprimanded for this statute on the Jews."

Shortly thereafter Vichy issued a press release in which it legitimized its anti-Jewish measures by invoking the Catholic Church's blessing: "From information obtained at the most authorized sources it results that nothing in the legislation designed to protect France from the Jewish influence is opposed to the doctrine of the Church."[71] The Catholic Church—not the Pope, not the Vatican—did not contest the essential truth of this statement and thereby allowed its public voice to be a weighty voice in support of Vichy's criminal anti-Jewish measures; this was also, by implication, an endorsement of Germany's similar measures. The Vichy ambassador had received his go-ahead from the highest officials of the Vatican Secretariat of State, one of whom was Monsignor Giovanni Battista Montini, who would eventually become Pope Paul VI.

Even more telling is the episode from August 1943 when, after the fall of Mussolini, Italy's new anti-Fascist government of Marshal Pietro Badoglio was in power and was expected to rescind the worst laws of Fascism. Pius XII's representative, Father Pietro Tacchi Venturi, met with the new Minister of the Interior and asked only for the abrogation of two provisions of the anti-Jewish laws that harmed Catholics who had converted from Judaism and for an exemption from them of Jews who had been in the process of converting to Catholicism when the laws were instituted. A delegation of Italian Jews had begged Father Tacchi Venturi to request the abolition of the oppressive and degrading laws of the defunct Fascist regime and to support, as he reported, "the complete return to the legislation that had been introduced by the liberal regimes and which had remained in effect until November 1938."

Father Tacchi Venturi did no such thing, even though the newly created Allied military government in liberated Sicily had already abrogated all Italy's antisemitic legislation in that part of Italy. After the meeting, Father

Tacchi Venturi reported to Cardinal Luigi Maglione, the Vatican Secretary of State, that he had implemented his assignment, which must have been an expression of Pius XII's own wishes. Father Tacchi Venturi wrote, "I took care not to call for the total abrogation of a law [i.e. the race laws] which, according to the principles and the traditions of the Catholic Church, certainly has some clauses that should be abolished, but which clearly contains others that have merit and should be confirmed."[72] These Nazi-like laws were an extensive catalogue of human-rights violations. They revoked Jews' personal, economic, social, civil, and political rights in extreme ways: prohibiting them from marrying non-Jews; from owning property, including businesses, over a certain value; from working in the civil service, being in the army, or working as doctors, lawyers, agronomists, and in other professions; from employing non-Jews in their homes; from being visible in public by being listed in telephone directories or having death notices in newspapers; from contact with non-Jewish Italians on vacation.[73]

Whatever objections the Church might have had to this or that aspect of the anti-Jewish laws, its position was decidedly not that they were fundamentally wrong or evil and should be abolished. Instead, the Church held that, as a body, they should be "confirmed." And that is exactly what the Church did. After all, these laws were, according to the Church's highest authority, an expression of the Church's own self-declared antisemitic "principles."

What makes the Catholic Church's unabashed affirmation of these laws even more significant is that they—the Pope, the Vatican Secretary of State, Father Tacchi Venturi, indeed, well nigh the entire upper and probably lower Church hierarchy—knew that these anti-Jewish laws were a foundational element in the Germans' and their helpers' exterminationist onslaught. Here is irrefutable evidence that, on the moral faculties and consciences of Pius XII and of those around him, these criminal laws did not weigh heavily, and that they did not do so because the Pope and others did not view them as morally repugnant. Their decision to "confirm" the wisdom and desirability of these laws came in August 1943. They knew all about the mass murder of Jewish men, women, and children by the millions. They had received extensive reports about the slaughter, its extent, its pitilessness, and its gruesome details, and the Pope himself received regular updates about the unfolding mass murder, often from British and American diplomats, who beseeched him to intervene. The Church leadership knew about the gas chambers.

How do we know that they knew and believed all this? From many sources, including the Vatican itself. On May 5, 1943, just three months before the Pope's emissary Father Tacchi Venturi confirmed the desirability of Italy's Nazi-like anti-Jewish laws, an official of the Vatican Secretariat of State summarized the Church's extensive knowledge about the genocide in Poland:

> In Poland, there were, before the war, about 4,500,000 Jews; it is calculated now that there remain (including all those who came there from other countries occupied by the Germans) only 100,000.
>
> In Warsaw a ghetto containing about 650,000 was created: now there are only 20–25,000 Jews there.
>
> Naturally many Jews have gotten away; but there is no doubt that the majority has been killed. After months and months of transport of thousands and thousands of people, they have made nothing more known of themselves: something that can only be explained by their deaths. . . .
>
> Special death camps at Lublin (Treblinka) and near Brest Litovsk. It is said that several hundred at a time are jammed into large rooms, where they die by gassing.[74]

The knowledge that the Germans and their helpers were slaughtering Jews by the millions—making it easily foreseeable that they would also want to murder the Jews of Italy—did not deter the Pope and his Church from conveying their approval of Italy's criminal anti-Jewish laws. For Pius XII and his Church, expressing their own antisemitism and conveying their solidarity with many of the murderers' nonlethal policies was closer to their hearts than was speaking for the lives of the victims.

Committing Crimes, Incurring Guilt

As part of the Germans' and their helpers' eliminationist persecution of the Jews, some substantial number of Catholic Church officials, high and low, themselves committed a range of crimes. They played a part in the crimes of the preexterminationist phase. They contributed to and in some cases engineered aspects of the mass murder itself. More pervasively, for many Germans, Croats, Lithuanians, and others who slaughtered Jews, and the many more who aided in their slaughter, Catholic clergy, even if not by design, supplied the rationale for them to act as they did.

In communicating their lack of dissent from—in other words, their support for—Vichy's and Italy's criminal antisemitic laws, the Pope and those around him were not only morally guilty of approving of criminal deeds, but they also committed a criminal act. This is true regardless of whether they conceived of it this way; they made it easier for, even gave encouragement to, those who were or would be committing crimes; they directly facilitated the crime of the anti-Jewish laws.

Again, the Church's criminality in this regard should come as no surprise. Prior to their proclamation in Italy, the Church, in its authoritative organs, had made its favorable disposition toward anti-Jewish laws clear.[75] The ones eventually promulgated clearly were some approximate expression of what the Church had urged. Representative of the Church's position was an article written in June 1938 in the Vatican's newspaper, L'Osservatore Romano. Commenting on the Germans' and Austrians' assault on Austria's Jews after Germany had annexed Austria in March, the article decried the general violence in a backhanded way, by affirming a laundry list of standard, vicious antisemitic charges as true but insufficient as a basis for "the unjust and violent hunting down of everyone together, guilty and innocent." (Who and how many the innocent were, it does not say, though the clear sense was that they were the few. And, of course, it did not expand upon the notion of innocence or plead with passion for those whom it considered innocent.)[76] It continued: "Nor in this brutal process, without legal status, can we recognize an equable and lasting solution to the formidable Jewish problem."[77] Looking at Germany, where the already draconian, criminal anti-Jewish laws were squeezing the life out of Jews and their communities, the antisemitic Church urged the criminal promulgation of severe laws to solve "the formidable Jewish problem." If the Church was not also explicitly giving its blessings to the imminent Italian anti-Jewish legislation, it could have come as no surprise to the politically savvy Church that such statements would be taken as an indication of its approval.

And when, on October 7, Mussolini presented his "Declaration on Race," the model for the comprehensive anti-Jewish laws that he promulgated November 17 (containing the core of the antisemitic measures discussed above), it was greeted with approval by the Church both through diplomatic channels (Mussolini's ambassador to the Vatican reported that the Vatican "point[ed] out some good aspects of the deliberations") and in L'Osservatore Romano, which printed the declaration in full. The Catholic Church wanted its endorsement of the antisemitic laws known to everyone—indeed, its only criticism, as was the Church's habit, was over the Church's control of the sacrament of marriage.[78]

Essentially, the Church, for decades including during the 1930s, even in 1938, had been loudly calling for the rescission of the despised Jews' emancipation, their legal and civil emergence during the nineteenth century from the Church-constructed ghetto. As has often been pointed out, many of the Germans' eliminationist policies, forcing Jews into ghettos, expelling them from entire regions, prohibiting them from taking part in all kinds of economic and professional activities, forbidding them from holding public office, reimposed measures first instituted by the Catholic Church. Less well known is that the Church still enforced many of these measures in its own lands, including in Rome, in the nineteenth century. According to David Kertzer, "Church ideology held that any contact with Jews was polluting to the larger society, that Jews were perpetual foreigners, a perennial threat to Christians."[79] As Bishop Alois Hudal, the head of the German Church in Rome and close friend of Pius XII, lamented in 1937, when giving his approval to the Nuremberg race laws, "The walls of the Ghetto had been torn down in the nineteenth century by the liberal state first and not by the Church."[80]

In January 1939, after Mussolini's promulgation of Italy's race laws, *L'Osservatore Romano* published a long homily from "a lower-level prelate indicat[ing] that many Vatican officials, if not the pope himself, approved of [it]."[81] Of what were they approving? The fulfillment by Mussolini (and Hitler) of the Church's desired rollback of the emancipation of the Jews. The prelater, a bishop, declared:

> The Church has always regarded living side by side with Jews, as long as they remain Jews, as dangerous to the faith and tranquility of Christian people. It is for this reason that you find an old and long tradition of ecclesiastical legislation and discipline, intended to brake and limit the action and influence of the Jews in the midst of Christians, and the contact of Christians with them, isolating the Jews and not allowing them the exercise of those offices and professions in which they could dominate or influence the spirit, the education, the customs of Christians.

The Vatican's newspaper explained that the bishop had discussed "the horrendous deicide, the odious Jewish persecution of the Messiah, his apostles and disciples, and the nascent Church."[82] The bishop and the Church believed that contemporary Jews bore the alleged guilt of their forebears—that Jews were collectively and intergenerationally guilty—and that the Jews were pernicious evildoers whose influence in Christian society needed to be eradicated. To those who would carry out this eliminationist aspiration, they granted legitimacy and gave their blessing.[83]

If the Church harbored the wish for the rescission of the Jews' emancipation, if not the ghetto's resurrection, Hitler, Mussolini, Pétain, and others fulfilled the wish. They turned the clock back with more hellish intent and effect than the Church had expected, but even then the Church, with minor criticisms, easily adjusted and continued to support much of the effort. Few in the Church appeared very upset.

The support that two Popes and the Vatican gave to criminal laws and persecutions against the Jews was mirrored wholly or to some substantial degree in national churches, including in Croatia, France, Poland, Slovakia, and, most critically, in Germany. Even before Bishop Hudal gave the laws his blessing, the *Klerusblatt,* the official organ of the Bavarian priests' association, declared in January 1936 the Nuremberg race laws to be essential for the well-being of the German people.[84] And the German Catholic Church, in the "race" entry in its authoritative 1937 *Handbook of Contemporary Religious Questions,* adopted for itself the foundational logic of the Nuremberg Laws, endorsing the rejection of "foreign blood," namely, Jewish blood, and affirming that "no people may be denied the right to maintain undisturbed their previous racial stock and to enact safeguards for this purpose."[85] In acknowledging the need for race purity, the German Church was publicly contravening a fundamental Catholic doctrine, essentially communicating to its faithful its endorsement, whatever the Church's qualifications, of the racism and antisemitism then pervasive in German society and central to Germany's politics.

That the Catholic Church, whether the German Catholic Church or the Vatican speaking for the Church as a whole, would endorse dehumanizing racist anti-Jewish laws, should come as no surprise to anyone familiar with the Church's own practices, its self-professed universalism notwithstanding. After all, the Germans, in passing the 1935 race laws that denied civic membership and privileges to Jews within Germany, were emulating not only the Church's long history of holding Jews corporately dangerous and therefore necessary to exclude in critical ways from full membership in society. They were also emulating the anti-Jewish racism that the most eminent and powerful order of the Catholic Church had been practicing for 342 years.

The Society of Jesus, known as the Jesuits, established racist membership criteria in 1593, with its so-called pure-blood decree, expelling all Jesuits who had Jewish ancestry, and forbidding admission to all Christians who were tainted by Jewish blood, no matter how small the quantity. Fifteen years later the Jesuits, according to the order's superior general, "moderate[d]" the racism. The moderation consisted of allowing Christians who could prove no Jewish ancestry for five generations to be admitted if they were of "honest family" or "honorable reputation."[86] This still meant that if a Christian who wanted to devote his life to serving Jesus had even one Jewish ancestor five generations in the past, of whose existence the devout great-great-great-grandchild did not even know, the Church considered the applicant too racially polluted to become a Jesuit. If among all his ancestors he had only one who was Jewish, who had lived, say, two hundred years earlier, the Church deemed the Jewishness of his blood sufficiently diluted that it was at least theoretically possible for him to gain an exemption from the prohibition, and to be admitted to the Jesuit order. In 1923 the Jesuits further "moderated" their racism by reducing the blood purity requirement to four generations.

The Nazis were well aware of the racism of the Jesuits. Deeply impressed by the Church's racist exclusion of Jewish blood from its highest order, Eugen Klee, Germany's representative at the Vatican who had helped negotiate the Concordat with Pacelli, expressed his admiration to Pacelli's Undersecretary of State, Bishop Giuseppe Pizzardo, in 1933, just a few days after Klee exchanged the Concordat's documents of ratification with Pacelli. Klee told Bishop Pizzardo, who was the head of the Vatican's Section for Extraordinary Ecclesiastical Affairs, that Germany needed to do for itself what the Church had long been doing. Klee reported to Berlin:

> I explained to undersecretary Pizzardo also orally that these laws of one of the most eminent orders of the Catholic Church, which had been upheld throughout centuries and which must have therefore well proven to be necessary, go still beyond the measures that were adopted in Germany. They therefore show clearly how justified the concerns of the German government are for the racial preservation of the German people.[87]

Klee gave no indication that Bishop Pizzardo had disagreed. The Germans' Nuremberg Laws were not passed until two years later. In forbidding Jews from being citizens, in defining who was considered a Jew, the Germans' race laws concerned themselves with the generation of a person's grandparents (and even people with some Jewish blood in that generation were not excluded). Thus the Jesuits' membership criteria remained "superior" to the Germans' Nuremberg Laws in the severity of their racism. So much for the spurious distinction in kind between the Church's so-called anti-Judaism and modern racist antisemitism.

The Germans' assault on the Jews of Germany and then of Europe evolved to take advantage of new opportunities as they developed, and therefore had different stages and many components. There were, however, the two constants of making the Jews socially dead and of preventing them, as thoroughly as possible, from having contact with and influence over non-Jews. The foundation for each of these policies was the race laws, initially passed in Nuremberg in 1935 and then emulated during the war in many European countries, including under the Pope's nose in Italy. The race laws defined the criteria used to classify people as Jews. Certifying that a given person of mixed religious background was "racially" a Jew was a sine qua non of the Germans' eliminationist assault upon them, and could be done only with the aid of genealogical records. As we have seen, Catholic bishops and priests across Germany supplied the genealogical records under their care, thereby making the general implementation of the race laws possible and also making it possible for their countrymen to identify Jews, to turn them into the socially dead, and to eliminate them from German society. All bishops and priests who did this bear legal guilt for the myriad grave violations of human rights that the regime was then committing against Jews.

The culpability of the German Catholic Church and its collaborating members is still greater. During the 1930s the German clergy could not know for sure that Hitler would, when the time was ripe, opt for the "final solution" that he had long wanted, the exterminationist variant of his proudly and insistently proclaimed eliminationist program.[88] But they knew that he was undertaking a violent eliminationist campaign, which already included physical assaults upon and the murder of Jews. This was broadcast to the entire world after the nationwide protogenocidal assault of November 1938, called *Kristallnacht*. Any clergyman could easily foresee that by furnishing the regime with the Church's genealogical records he would be helping the regime to identify people who might then be subjected to violence. Indeed, one prominent German Catholic in exile, Waldemar Gurian, denounced the Nuremberg Laws as immoral, telling his German Catholic colleagues that the legislation was "only a stage on the way toward the complete physical destruction of the Jews."[89] By implication, he was warning the German Catholic bishops and priests that they were potentially complicit in that destruction if they should facilitate the application of these immoral and criminal statutes. The legal principle that a person willingly involving himself in a crime is responsible for crimes that result from that initial criminal act applies here as well. By giving access to the genealogical records the German Catholic Church and its complicit bishops and priests bear legal guilt (not to mention moral guilt) for the murder of some substantial number of people. Pius XI and Pius XII, who was until 1939 the Vatican's Secretary of State, share in this legal guilt; they did not prevent German bishops and priests from aiding in these crimes.

Catholic clergy serving the mass-murdering security forces, including the German army in those areas and cases where it was involved in the annihilation, and those attached to the occupation forces in certain areas, especially in the Soviet Union and Poland, were serving in criminal organizations and therefore implicated in their criminal deeds. This was also true of Catholic clergy in Croatia, Slovakia, and elsewhere. Catholic clergy gave succor to mass murderers.

Indeed, the clergy's very presence among the killers was, in the eyes of the Church, predicated upon the view that Nazism was compatible with Catholic principles (even if Christianity was anathema to the leading Nazis). In 1934 this was stated openly by the prominent Catholic theologian Michael Schmaus, after the German bishops revoked their short-lived prohibition against Catholic membership in the Nazi Party.[90] The Church throughout this period did ban Catholics from joining Communist parties, precisely because it held Communism to be incompatible with Catholicism. But Nazism, its eliminationist antisemitism and volcanic murderousness notwithstanding, was another matter.

Many in the German Catholic Church, its dissatisfactions with the Nazis' treatment of religion aside, believed that important aspects of Nazism and its policies to be the fulfillment of Catholic principles. Some of the greatest Catholic theologians in Germany developed a powerful Nazified Catholic body of thought called *Reichstheologie.*[91] Karl Adam, perhaps the leading German Catholic theologian of his era, whose writings remained standard theological works for decades after the war, was spouting Nazi-like racist pronouncements already in 1933. Adam presented Hitler as the savior of the German people and the preservation of Germany's blood purity—"our unity of blood, our German self, the *Homo Germanus*"—as justified self-defense because all thinking and feeling had its basis in a people's blood. "The myth of the German," Adam wrote, "his culture and his history are decisively shaped by blood."[92] In this spirit, Adam deemed it necessary to cleanse Germany of the corrupting Jewish mentality, though he averred that the Christian conscience demands it be done with justice and love.[93] Such racism, which was by no means confined to Adam, was a direct violation of fundamental Catholic doctrine. Adam, Schmaus, and other well-known Catholic thinkers and leaders, by embracing Hitler and Nazism, served to legitimize the regime to Catholics.[94] Similarly, Catholic priests in the killing fields served to further legitimize the annihilation of the Jews to the executioners.

A priest lending his presence to the forces of a mass-murdering war, without objection, is a priest lending his approval. This is understood by believers and nonbelievers alike, and the clergy also know that their presence is interpreted in this way. The vocation of spiritual and moral guidance renders a present religious authority's silence into not tacit but active approval. But many German clergy were not silent about the unabashed exterminatory, criminal German war against Bolshevism. At Catholic services in the field, the prayers included "Let us all, under [Hitler's] leadership, see in the devotion to people and fatherland a holy task, so that through faith, obedience and fidelity we will obtain the eternal resting place in Your light and Your peace." This holy task that they all knew their country, with the aid of the German army, was undertaking included, of course, the total annihilation of the Jews of the Soviet Union.

The silence of German priests in the apocalyptic killing fields of the east—when they were not actively lending approval with their words—was reproduced by Catholic clergy across Europe. During the Nazi period the Church emanated a great deal of silence. Silence is a critical issue here. It has two aspects. Silence constitutes a decision not to act against something, an act of omission, which I take up shortly. It may also be an affirmative act indicating support for the uncommented-upon deed. In the face of great evil, silence from those who are publicly deemed morally responsible for speaking out can reasonably be construed as approval.

The Church, its national churches, individual bishops and priests were virtually professional critics of things they deemed to violate the moral law. After all, their vocational duty, in the words of Pius XII's inaugural encyclical of 1939, was "to testify to the truth with Apostolic Firmness."[95] Their self-understood calling, therefore, was to bring to the attention of their parishioners and of communal and political authorities matters that threatened the physical or moral well-being of their flock. The Church and its clergy habitually rendered judgment, criticism, condemnation of aspects of politics or society of which they disapproved. Even a cursory look at Popes' pronouncements, bishops' statements, and priests' sermons and at Church publications, its journals and newspapers, reveals a highly outspoken, interventionist institution and staff, both before and during World War II. Yet with regard to the brutal eliminationist persecution of the Jews, overwhelmingly there was silence. The Church, when it was not expressing its explicit approval of one or another aspect of the persecution, thundered silence.[96]

When silence is so widespread, when thousands of bishops and priests do not protest and leave no record of dissent over what was undoubtedly one of the most insistent and immediately present moral issues of the day, it is reasonable to conclude that they did not disapprove of the deeds in question.[97] Silence communicates an absence of disapproval. The Church must have known that the Germans and other European peoples, perpetrators and onlookers, would, or at the very least could, understand the Church's silence to mean a lack of disapproval, to mean approval. After all, Catholics know—and bishops and priests know that Catholics know—that it is the clergy's solemn religious duty to warn Catholics against committing sin. In a candid private moment after the Germans had already begun the systematic mass murdering of Jews, Pius XII told Cardinal Angelo Roncalli, later his successor as Pope John XXIII, in Cardinal Roncalli's words "of his generosity towards the Germans who visit him," and then asked "if his silence regarding Nazism is not judged badly."[98] Yet Pius XII and most of the Church willingly let the Germans and the European peoples and their leaders hear his silence and its implied approval.

In some instances Catholic clergy went still further in contributing to the annihilation of the Jews. Slovakia and Croatia are the most striking cases of Catholic bishops and priests directly lending a hand to mass murder. In light of the Vatican's own approval of anti-Jewish legislation, it becomes easier to understand why it did not object to the president-priest Tiso's preaching to the Slovak people that it was a Christian act to expel the Jews so that Slovakia could free itself of "its pests." After all, he was drawing on the "principles and the traditions of the Catholic Church," which the Pope's representative, Father Tacchi Venturi, would soon call upon as justification for Italy's own anti-Jewish laws.

The Pope and the Vatican watched its own bishops and priests participate in and vocally support the killing of Jews in Croatia and the deportation of Jews to their deaths from Slovakia. The Pope and the Vatican watched as these priestly mass murderers and justifiers of mass murder and its preparatory measures (e.g., antisemitic laws and deportations) invoked the Church's name and its principles to publicly legitimize their deeds. The Pope and the Vatican did not use every means at their disposal to prevent the crimes of their subordinates, of which they had foreknowledge. In fact, they did very little. Does this mean that the Pope and the responsible Vatican officials, that those who led and spoke authoritatively for the Catholic Church and who were the superiors of these criminals, are implicated directly in this aspect of the annihilation of the Jews? The United Nations International Law Commission's "Draft Code of Crimes Against the Peace and Security of Mankind, 1996" confirms standard intuitions that they would be. It states, "The fact that a crime against the peace and security of mankind was committed by a subordinate does not relieve his superiors of criminal responsibility, if they knew or had reason to know, in the circumstances at the time, that the subordinate was committing or was going to commit such a crime and if they did not take all necessary measures within their power to prevent or repress the crime."[99]

There is also evidence that suggests that the Pope and the responsible Vatican officials agreed with this, believing themselves implicated directly in these aspects of the mass murder carried out by their subordinates. Take Slovakia. It was a Catholic country, which by itself does not, according to our rejection of the practice of ascribing blame based on people's identities, make the Catholic Church responsible for the country's policies, even though in the eyes of the Church itself the country's Catholicism *was* relevant for assessing its own responsibility for those policies. A priest was the country's president. An avowedly Catholic party governed the country, seeking to mold it according to Catholic principles. Many priests served in the country's legislature, which voted, as did all its legislator priests, to deport the country's Jews to their deaths. The Slovakian clergy, like other clergy, were under the discipline of the Pope. He had absolute authority over them. He could have commanded them to desist from acting in ways that violated the Church's doctrine and practices. Yet he did not command them not to deport their country's Jews to their deaths.

Knowing this state of affairs, the authoritative Monsignor Domenico Tardini, one of two undersecretaries in the Vatican's Secretariat of State and the head of its Section for Extraordinary Ecclesiastical Affairs, warned in an internal Vatican memo of April 7, 1943, that if the Church did not do something to dissociate itself from the mass murder that had by then been going on for over a year, it might not be able to avoid being blamed for it. With the fingerprints of the president-priest Tiso clearly on the mass murder of Slovakia's Jews, Tardini acknowledged "the danger that the responsibility can be shifted [*sic*] to the Catholic Church itself." The Church's priest, the president of Slovakia, he was implicitly acknowledging, was a mass murderer. The Church, he was saying, could be held responsible. Monsignor Tardini did not deny the Church's "responsibility," which would reasonably be construed by others as its guilt, but only counseled that the Vatican act. He did say that it should protest out of a moral obligation to help the afflicted, though the memo is unclear as to whether he justified Church intervention because Jews are imperiled or because Christians who had converted from Judaism are. Either way, the central concern of this part of the memo was propaganda, specifically how to create an appearance of the Church aiding the Jews in order to prevent the Church from being blamed.

Knowing that the actions of its clergy in Slovakia, subject to the Pope's absolute authority, would likely be blamed on "the Catholic Church itself," having had this declared in an authoritative internal Church document, what did "the Catholic Church" do? On the day of the memo, the Vatican representative to Slovakia, Monsignor Giuseppe Burzio, was already acting to try to preclude the Church from being blamed for the deportations. Monsignor Burzio made a toothless protest to Prime Minister Tuka regarding further planned deportations. When Tuka rejected the Vatican's arguments, and repeatedly and forcefully asserted that the Slovaks had to deport the "Jewish plague," Monsignor Burzio politely objected, invoking Christian principles. But he did nothing more than gently try to persuade the mass murderer, and thereby do nothing more than put the Vatican's position on record, without any realistic hope that his arguments would convince a man already committed to the elimination of his country's Jews to suddenly see the criminality of his ways. At the end of the meeting, Monsignor Burzio came to the crucial point of Tardini's strategy of trying to dissociate the Church from the mass murder. He reported back to the Secretary of State that "I asked [Tuka] a final question: 'May I at least, this being the opinion, indeed the current conviction, communicate to the Holy See that the deportation of the Jews of Slovakia did not occur through the initiative of the Slovak government, but under external pressure?' "

Both the Vatican's representative, who had just listened to Tuka rant about "his mission" to "rid Slovakia of this plague, this band of malefactors and gangsters," and the Vatican knew fully well that what Monsignor Burzio was asking Tuka to agree to was a lie. Tuka said as much: "I assure you as a Christian that it is our will and our initiative." He added that "this, yes, is true, that I was offered the possibility of realizing my plan, and I certainly did not refuse it." Tuka then assured Monsignor Burzio that the people about whom the Vatican really cared, Christians who had converted from Judaism, would not be deported.[100]

The Pope and his representatives still did not publicly condemn the mass murder and call on Slovaks to resist it. They still did not privately or publicly prohibit its priests, including the country's president, from deporting the Jews. They still did not threaten the mass murderers with excommunication. They still did not even pressure them forcefully behind the scenes then or a few weeks later when the Slovak government formally informed the Vatican that it would press forward with its eliminationist measures. They did not take these steps even though Monsignor Tardini had acknowledged that "the Catholic Church itself" could be deemed guilty for the Slovaks' crimes against the Jews.[101]

The Concordat became the Church's own statement of its official complicity in many of the regime's crimes. Although when negotiating it Pacelli did not intend it as such, the Concordat became his, the Vatican's, and the

German Church's tacit compact with the German government's progressively increasing criminality, its antisemitic laws, its creation and steady expansion of the brutal concentration-camp system, and eventually its mass murdering. This is also true of the regime's other crimes within Germany, such as persecuting and incarcerating Communists, gays, and others.[102] In a moment of rare insight and honesty, the antisemitic Archbishop Gröber declared after the war that with the Concordat, the Church had deceived German Catholics and the rest of the world.[103]

Perhaps, most broadly, the Catholic Church was implicated in crime by providing the motive for many of the criminals. The evidence is overwhelming that, exceptions notwithstanding, the perpetrators of the Holocaust, the ordinary Germans and their helpers around Europe, willingly killed Jews because, moved by antisemitism, they believed that the Jews ought to die. To whatever extent this antisemitism of the perpetrators—high officials, those who rounded up Jews, those who guarded them in camps, those who shot them, those who manned the extermination facilities—had been directly or indirectly learned from Church sources, the Church in effect provided the motive for murder. This is so even if murder was not the Church's expressed intention or wish. More than a few of the perpetrators—Germans, Croats, French, Lithuanians, Poles, and others—derived their motivating antisemitism, wholly or in part, from what their trusted religious and moral shepherds had taught them.[104]

Throughout Europe, bishops and priests knew this. (After all, many clergy continued to spread antisemitism.) Yet they chose, day after day, neither to condemn nor to repudiate the antisemitic beliefs, the crimes and other offenses that followed on these beliefs, or the people who, inspired by the beliefs, committed those crimes and offenses.

Criminal Incitement?

As I discussed in part one, the kind of antisemitism that predominated in much of Europe, particularly central and eastern Europe, was the Church's. Unlike in predominantly racially antisemitic Germany itself, the hatred of the Jews in many countries derived to a large extent from the Church's teachings. Its image of the Jew as a socially corrosive evildoer was clearly motive enough for many Croats, French, Lithuanians, Poles, Slovaks, and others to help the Germans, even in the slaughter of Jews, once the Germans brought their eliminationist onslaught to those countries or created the conditions that made local ones possible.

If a person assiduously teaches another person to hate and feel enmity toward a third person, if the second person then acts upon what he has learned by deciding to kill the third person, and if the first person knows of the plan, understands his role in supplying the motive, in inciting him to kill, and nevertheless does not try to dissuade the person about to commit murder from acting, then the first person too has contributed intimately to the crime, and bears legal guilt for it. This principle was applied to the Holocaust at the Nuremberg trials in the case of Julius Streicher, the publisher of the viciously antisemitic popular newspaper *Der Stürmer*, which had, during the 1930s, expressed admiration for the antisemitism of the Church's official *Civiltà cattolica*. Indeed, at Nuremberg, the underlying legal principle for Streicher's conviction was incitement to murder and extermination.

Streicher asserted at Nuremberg that if he had to stand before the court to answer for his contribution to the mass murder of the Jews, then Luther—the father of the Lutheran antisemitic tradition, whose own antisemitism derived from the Catholic tradition and who four centuries after his death still inspired people, especially in Germany, to feel animus and enmity toward Jews, and to want to eliminate them—should be standing shoulder to shoulder with him. Leaving aside whether Streicher was correct about someone dead for four hundred years, Streicher, this man who knew Nazi antisemitism, its religious sources, and the affinities between the two, to which he would refer, and who understood the power of the religious-produced animus, was certainly correct that the religious authorities who spread the hatred were also culpable. The prosecutor spoke the undeniable truth about the catastrophic consequences of those who spread antisemitism. Streicher

made these things possible—made these crimes possible—which could never have happened had it not been for him and for those like him. He led the propaganda and the education of the German people in those ways. Without him the Kaltenbrunners, the Himmlers, the General Stroops would have had nobody to carry out their orders. And, as we have seen, he has concentrated upon the youth and the childhood of Germany. In its extent his crime is probably greater and more far-reaching than that of any of the other defendants. The misery that they caused finished with their incarceration. The effects of this man's crime, of the poison that he had injected into the minds of millions and millions of young boys and girls and young men and women lives on. He leaves behind him a legacy of almost a whole people poisoned with hate, sadism, and murder, and perverted by him.[105]

Illustration on the front page of Der Stürmer *from May 1936, depicting a group of Hitler Youth. The caption reads "We youth step happily forward facing the sun . . . With our faith we drive the devil from the land."*

The overstatement in the last sentence notwithstanding, if all of this applies to this one man for inculcating the poison of antisemitism into the minds of Germany's youth, then how does it not also apply to the enormously more influential antisemitic institution and teacher of children, the Catholic Church? The Church's antisemitism was in tone and color nothing like the licentious, lurid, and pornographic antisemitism of Streicher. But that is beside the point. Relevant is the Church's image of the Jew as a powerful evildoer and dangerous threat, and the effects of this image upon its faithful. The Church certainly "poisoned" the "minds" of many more millions of "young men and girls and young men and women" than did Streicher. If his deed was a "crime," then the "extent" of the Church's crime was far "more far-reaching" than Streicher's.

Streicher explicitly exhorted Germans to annihilate the Jews. The Church as an institution did not, even if individual churchmen around Europe themselves willingly contributed to the mass murder by telling their followers to support exterminatory measures or measures that they knew were integral to the destruction process. Still, it is worth asking whether the Church more broadly provided, however unwittingly, a rationale, indeed an incitement to kill. It kept silent as it knowingly watched the murderers make preparations and, over the course of years, in one part of Europe after another carry out their crime, a crime that for some of them had been at least partly inspired by the Church's teachings. Why should the Church, with its pan-European antisemitic incitement stretching across the generations, and its vast influence, be held any less responsible than one newspaper publisher who himself did not have any national policy role? For his antisemitic incitement, Streicher was convicted of crimes against humanity.[106]

Examples of the Church's incitement to radical anti-Jewish action are legion. On January 30, 1939, the same day that Hitler announced to the world that if a war came, he intended to annihilate the Jewish people, Archbishop Gröber, one of the most esteemed and influential Catholic leaders in Germany, libeled the Jews in a manner that might suggest to ordinary Germans that they ought to make good on Hitler's prophecy. After six years of the Germans' pitiless, violent persecution of the Jews, Archbishop Gröber did not urge the German people to sympathize with and to help the afflicted victims but, in a pastoral letter, told them that the Jews hated Jesus and so crucified him, and that their lethality endlessly continued to afflict the world: The Jews' "murderous hatred has continued in later centuries."[107] What might a Catholic German think necessary to preserve himself, his family, and his people, when reminded by his bishop of what he had already been taught for years, of the Jews' putative "murderous hatred" that threatens them all? If the Jews are ceaselessly at war with Germans, then perhaps Germans undertaking a war to eradicate the Jews would be necessary self-defense. Archbishop Gröber had his pastoral letter officially published less than two weeks after Hitler pronounced his prophecy. Anyone who believed, as virtually everyone did, that Hitler was intent on ridding Germany of Jews, including by using violence, could have likely and reasonably understood Archbishop Gröber to be supporting that intent.

The antisemitism that the Catholic Church had directly or indirectly taught throughout Europe was a powerful motivator for Catholics to perpetrate anti-Jewish action. If a person believes that Jews are minions of the devil, or Christ-killers, or Bolshevik revolutionaries determined to destroy religion and civilization, malevolent financiers causing global economic depression, or spiritual polluters and corroders of Christian values and goodness—all then part of the Catholic Church's standard antisemitic litany—then he will want someone to solve this, in the authoritative words of Father Rosa, "formidable Jewish Problem." If he is given the opportunity to help by taking radical action, including perhaps by destroying the people who would allegedly destroy him, it is obvious that many people will find, and did find, such beliefs to be adequate and necessary reasons to defend themselves.

Church Antisemitism, Church Culpability

For anyone who finds it hard to believe that Christian clergy, men of God, could tolerate, support, let alone advocate the mass slaughter of men, women, and children, just a brief glance at portions of the historical record would be sobering. The Crusades, the Inquisition, the contribution of priests to the Spaniards' annihilation of Native Americans in Latin America, the mass-murdering Croatian priests, president-priest Tiso's role in the slaughter of Slovakian Jews, and more recently, Hutu priests and nuns in Rwanda helping to slaughter Tutsi, show that many Catholic churchmen have been capable of sanctioning mass murder and of directly taking a hand in it. And many German Christian leaders during the Holocaust were no better. A large group of Protestant Church leaders, fully aware of their countrymen's mass extermination of the Jews, publicly went on record urging their government to prosecute its policies with zeal.

In December 1941, Protestant Evangelical Church leaders of seven regions of Germany collectively issued an official proclamation that declared the Jews incapable of being saved by baptism, owing to their racial constitution; to be responsible for the war; and to be "born enemies of the world and Germany." They therefore urged that the "severest measures against the Jews be adopted and that they be banished from German lands." Would not the superlative the "severest measures" encompass the death penalty? And with the context of the apocalyptic war with the Soviet Union and of the Germans' already ongoing extermination of Soviet Jewry, it could have meant only one thing. With these words, the Protestant Church leadership of a good part of Germany—collectively as a corporate group, and with the authority of their offices—on their own initiative implicitly endorsed the mass slaughter of Jews or at least knew that many would understand them to be endorsing the annihilation, which amounts to the same result.[108]

If Christian antisemitism could motivate Church leaders to support the slaughter of Jews, then it could, and did, certainly motivate many lay Christians across Europe to do the same. For all such people who participated in the murder of Jews, the Church bears, in addition to its grievous moral guilt, legal guilt. The Church's formal position against violence is all but irrelevant to this judgment, because during these years it did not teach the repudiation of anti-Jewish killing to its flock.

You place the straw around the houses of one town, teach the people of the next town to hate and fear the inhabitants of the first town. An incendiary comes along to give your followers a match. Your followers together with others light the flames that torch one building, then another, then another, systematically but slowly destroying them all. You save a few of the people, though only a few, from the buildings that the killers have not yet reached. You do not warn the other intended victims. You do not urge all those who work for you to save as many as they can. You do not tell all those who support the incendiary or even help him light his fires that they are committing crimes and sins and consigning themselves to hell. Indeed, all the while you continue to teach your followers to hate and fear the victims. After the flames die down and the incendiary is dead, you say that you never told him or your followers explicitly to kill and indeed had as little to do with him as possible. Your proof, you say, is that you and the incendiary never got along and that you even saved a few people along the way.

Would you believe that, under such a scenario, others would hold you innocent of all blame, all guilt, all culpability? Would you believe that you would not have to answer for your offenses? If you believe that you would have to, then you must also believe that the Catholic Church has much to answer for.

Let me be clear. I am not saying that the Pope and the clergy in general actively wanted the Jews to die. But aside from the small percentage of clergy who aided the Jews, we cannot be sure that the Catholic clergy in general opposed the mass annihilation. We cannot be sure that if they did, then they opposed it unequivocally and with all their hearts. We cannot be sure that they beheld the killing of the Jews, whom many of them deemed guilty of the gravest offenses, unambiguously as a crime and a sin. And we have such doubts because of the widespread antisemitism among them and because of the things that many of them did. We can be sure that a significant number of bishops and priests willingly contributed to the annihilation of the Jews. We can also be sure that the Pope's and the clergy's stunning lack of public sympathy for the Jews, their aid for critical acts of criminality, their support for so many more, and their extensive political blame and guilt definitively implicate the Catholic Church broadly and deeply in the crimes of the Germans, Croats, Lithuanians, Slovaks, and others against the Jews.

The Ambiguities of Church Interventions for Jews

The Catholic churchmen's multiple offenses and considerable culpability notwithstanding, we should bear in mind that the Church and its officials occasionally did try to help Jews, and some also did feel qualms or more over the eliminationist violence, especially the mass murder.

The Catholic Church, Pius XII, and the leadership of a few national churches made occasional attempts to help Jews. They were not particularly vigorous or sustained attempts, and they tended to come late in the war, after the Germans had already killed most of the Jews of a given country, and when the Allies were clearly going to win the war. When defending the Jews mattered a great deal, before the killing operations began or while they were just getting going, the Church watched silently. When it might have done the most good, namely, during the 1930s at the initial stages of the Germans' violent eliminationist persecution, when the Jews' persecutors passed dehumanizing race laws and robbed them of their livelihoods, professions, and homes, the Catholic Church, across Europe, was an antagonist of the Jews. And the most significant possible interventions—thunderous public condemnation by Pius XI or Pius XII, excommunication of all those persecuting Jews, an explicit call to all Europeans to help Jews—never came at all. This unwillingness to help Jews stands in the starkest contrast to the Church's regular interventions on behalf of Catholics who had converted from Judaism or of Jews covered by the sacrament of marriage to Catholics. For their welfare, the Church was genuinely concerned, and it intervened for them immediately, vigorously, and with evident passion. The Church's rare, weak, and late interventions on behalf of just some Jews have the unmistakable earmarks of halfhearted moves by people wanting to cover their backs for the coming postwar world.

It appears this way because, according to the Church's highest leaders, that is what it was. They said as much in their secret conversations as they were discussing and instituting their strategy of disinformation. This strategy consisted of taking measures, or pretending to take measures, that would convince the world that the Church was doing precisely what its leaders had not undertaken, and were still not undertaking: effective steps to save Jews from being harmed and killed.

As we have seen, a few explicit public condemnations of the mass murder of the Jews came from national Church leaders—although none from the Vatican or from Pius XII. Some churchmen also expressed private disapproval of certain elements of the eliminationist persecution, particularly the killing, and the sincere desire that the Church do more to help the Jews. Some were heartfelt, as when Germany's Bishop Preysing passionately urged his German colleagues and the Pope, utterly in vain, to speak out forcefully in defense of the Jews. Some were obviously hypocritical declarations, in private to foreign diplomats crafted for their consumption.[109]

Churchmen knew that many people, especially outside of continental Europe, especially in Britain and in the United States, if aware of the truth, would see the Church as blameworthy for its role in the Germans' eliminationist persecution of the Jews. The Church, to shore itself up politically, and under pressure from abroad, needed to transfigure its inaction into the appearance of dedicated action on behalf of the Jews. After all, once it appeared that the Germans would not be victorious, it became important for the Church to create a pseudorecord of concern for the Jews in order to protect itself from the critical scrutiny of the Allies. The Pope's perfunctory and deeply inadequate Christmas message of 1942, which fleetingly and wanly alluded to the killing—and which came after the Allies had pressured him intensively to condemn the mass murder but in which he chose not to mention Jews, Germans, or the mass murder explicitly—may have been the first initiative in a political campaign, emanating from the center of the Church, to create a foundation for what has since come to be called plausible deniability.

Less than four months later, on April 7, 1943, such a strategy was articulated, if not codified, in the internal Vatican memo, written by the authoritative Monsignor Tardini, that summarized the state of the Vatican's measures regarding Jews. As we just saw, he expressed the Church's fear that the president-priest Tiso's hands on the mass murder of Slovakia's Jews produced "the danger that the responsibility can be shifted [*sic*] to the Catholic Church itself." To safeguard the Church's political standing, he recommended that the Vatican protest to President Tiso, and that it do so for the explicit purpose of then leaking the warning to the world. Monsignor Tardini explained that "it would not be out of place to discreetly make known to the public this diplomatic note of the Holy See (the fact of its being sent, the content of the document rather then the text). This will make known to the world that the Holy See fulfills its duty of charity." Monsignor Tardini then put into writing a self-evidently shared antisemitic fantasy about Jewish power—self-evidently shared because he did not bother to explain what to a non-antisemite was a preposterous notion. He considered that the Jews who had no country, no army, no power, and were being only slaughtered would somehow be counted among the "victors," so he reflected on the significance of this for the Church's propaganda initiatives. Monsignor Tardini reminded his superiors that his proposal to issue a protest that could be leaked would not "attract the sympathy of the Jews in case they are among the victors (given the fact that the Jews—as much as can be foreseen—will never be too friendly to the Holy See and to the Catholic Church)." It appears that to Monsignor Tardini this imputed hostility was, at least in this respect, not to be lamented, since the Church's apparent (but empty) gesture of aid was being made to people allegedly hostile to it, which "will render more meritorious any charitable efforts" by the Church.[110]

The priority of creating the illusion of effective action over actually taking effective action was reaffirmed just three weeks later. Pius XII was formalizing his already long-decided rejection of Bishop Preysing's plea that he take real action against the mass murder. The Pope conveyed to Bishop Preysing that the bishop's wish that he issue a public condemnation of the annihilation of the Jews would go unheeded, simultaneously making clear that it was appearances that were paramount in his mind. The Pope counseled the German bishops that their earlier statement urging humane treatment of "other races" was already sufficient because it was enough to gain for them, after the war, "the respect of world opinion."[111] As far as the Pope was concerned, the German bishops had already done enough to satisfy their public-relations needs. That the German bishops' statement was so perfunctory, so meaninglessly vague, and therefore had done nothing to help Jews did not deter the Pope from counseling them as he did.

It was less than half a year later, in October, that Father Tacchi Venturi, under pressure from Jewish relatives, urged a symbolic and therefore sham inquiry into the fate of the Jews of Rome. Machiavelli-like, he explained its advisability to the Vatican's Secretary of State: "A step like this by the Holy See, even if it does not obtain the desired effect, will without doubt help increase the veneration and gratitude toward the August Person of the Holy Father."[112] The political cynicism of these high Church officials could hardly have been exceeded given that the Jews under discussion were the ones whom the Pope had knowingly abandoned to be murdered by allowing the Germans to deport them from his doorstep without a murmur.

Just two months later, in mid-December, even though the Pope had demonstrated repeatedly that he would not appeal for the lives of the Jews of Italy, the archbishop of Ferrara implored him to do precisely that. Internal correspondence of the Vatican Secretariat of State discusses proposed responses that were crafted precisely in order to give the false appearance that the Pope was trying to help the Jews while actually achieving virtually nothing. A memo that lays out such steps declares their wisdom: "If nothing else, it will always be possible to say that the Holy See has done everything possible to help these unhappy people."[113]

By mid-1944, the end of the war was approaching, Allied pressure on the Vatican was intensifying, and the need for the Church to position itself politically for a post–German-dominated Europe was growing. In June Pius XII sent his telegram to the Hungarian leader Horthy, thereby creating what would turn out to be the part of his fictive alibi that has been rhetorically the most useful—remarkably effective given that, before caving in to the Allies' pressure that he appeal to Horthy, Pius XII had watched in quiet detachment while the Hungarians and Germans had deported hundreds of thousands of Jews from Hungary for extermination.

A few months later, in October, the Vatican tried to do something about one of the greatest messes that the Church had created for itself, the one in Slovakia. The Pope and the Vatican had done next to nothing to stay the hand of the mass-murdering president-priest Tiso of Slovakia. The Vatican's desperation to position the Church politically for the imminent Allied victory by dissociating itself from its Slovakian clergy's deeds was by October undisguised, as it appealed precisely in such terms to Father Tiso. The problem for the Pope's emissary was that neither he, nor the Pope, nor the Vatican could hope that another toothless moral appeal would influence their own Father Tiso and Slovakia's many other politician-priests who had willingly handed over most of their country's Jews, like "sour beer," for slaughter. So the Pope's emissary appealed to President Tiso openly about the Church's cynical political considerations. He warned him that the mass annihilation "is harmful to the prestige of his country and enemies will exploit it to discredit clergy and the Church the world over."[114] The political strategy of disinformation, perhaps initiated by Pius XII himself in his Christmas address two years earlier, and then articulated a few months later in Monsignor Tardini's internal memo for the Vatican, had by then been implemented in a variety of ways. Now, in late 1944, the Vatican was using its strategy as a political argument to try to win over Father Tiso, so that the Church could better protect its political standing.

The Church's highest leaders, the Pope, the Vatican's Secretary of State, and other critical Vatican officials, pursued strategies that, sometimes by their own admission, were designed to convince people that the Church, and particularly Pius XII, had with all their hearts tried to protect the Jews, even though it was not true. Whether this pattern was part of a formal policy or merely a repeatedly employed technique of deception may become clear—as would other such buried instances—when the Church's locked-away documents are unlocked.

Whichever it was, as the Church's highest officials themselves repeatedly made clear, pseudoprotection for the Jews was good politics because it provided real protection for what the Church genuinely and passionately cared about: its reputation and political standing. Even if this illusionistic campaign of disguising offenses as virtues was certainly not the Church's worst transgression during this period, it was its most nakedly cynical. It also was the first and most critical component of the Church's and its apologists' bad-faith campaign of systematic disinformation that continues to this day.

Aside from the heroic efforts by individual or small groups of clergy and nuns to save Jews, typically undertaken without the Church leadership's initiative or aid, the Church and its leadership's more positive stances and actions regarding Jews were often far less praiseworthy than they at first appear.

THE CHURCH'S OFFENSES OF OMISSION

It might be that no historical event has provoked discussion of acts of omission as much as the Holocaust has. Whatever philosophical or legal arguments may undergird the notion that an offense of omission, namely, the failure to prevent unjust harm, is not blameworthy, these arguments do not seem forceful when the issue is mass murder. Not surprisingly, such arguments have not influenced actual discussions about culpability during the Holocaust, which have depended upon the virtually unquestioned assumption that acts of omission can be offenses. Few people are willing to assert that those who were able to thwart the mass murder of Jews were not bound by moral duty to do so. Or that the failure to try, especially if the risk incurred was low, is not blameworthy in the extreme. The Church itself concedes the principle that acts of omission are really offenses of omission, in its continual attempts to convince people that it really did do whatever it reasonably could have done to save Jews. The Church and its defenders make their false assertion that Pius XII was not silent, and they have made it so insistently, precisely because such silence is, in the Church's terms, a sin, and in ours, an offense. The Church explicitly declares that people incur "a responsibility for the sins committed by others" by "not hindering them when we have an obligation to do so."[115]

I will not go over in detail the arguments for why someone should be seen as morally, even legally, guilty for doing nothing to help to save human beings whom others are about to murder en masse. It seems self-evident, and the Catholic Church holds the same unambiguous position on this point. Still, it is worth saying a few clarifying words on the subject.

When a person fails to hinder something that he could prevent, he is really choosing to allow it to happen. As Bernard Williams writes, "Allowing is best understood as an action, and it is usually an intentional action; whether it is allowing someone to do something, or allowing things to take their course."[116] People ordinarily oppose and, when in their power, try to stop deeds that confront them that they consider unjust and of great harm, deeds that violate their deepest moral values. A person does not willingly allow another person to break into a neighbor's house or kill a neighbor's child. At the very least he warns his neighbor of the impending break-in or calls the police. If a person allows someone to commit an offense that he could try to stop but chooses not to, his willful inaction constitutes a willful act to support the deed, the act being his decision not to prevent it. This is especially the case when a person is part of what can be called the "system of prevention," people formally charged with preventing the harm in question, as the Catholic Church was—in its own eyes and those of its faithful— for grave moral matters. An act of omission, when a person knows of the harm being done, therefore constitutes a choice to let harm occur, and therefore approval of the harmful act. This makes the act of omission an offense. A failure of this kind to try to prevent harm constitutes approval of the harm no less than verbally sanctioning it does.[117]

A failure to try to prevent unjust harm can rise to the level of a criminal transgression. Often such an act of omission is a political transgression. If you have good reason to believe someone is about to be killed, not warning that person is, in many countries, a crime; in the Church's terms it is a sin. If so, then the churchmen from Pius XII on down who failed to warn the Jews of impending roundups, and deportations, of which they knew, and that the Germans intended to murder them—bear legal guilt. Not trying to prevent a crime that one could conceivably prevent is also in many countries a crime. It is probably the case, however, that there was enough risk involved in hiding Jews that the failure on the part of individual clergy to have done more to hide Jews should not prima facie be deemed a crime. So in principle each instance where churchmen could reasonably be thought to have been able to try to save Jews would have to be investigated in depth, in order to determine whether or not the inaction was a crime or the fear-inspired acquiescence of well-intentioned people.

Arguably the most effective thing that members of the Catholic Church could have done to help Jews, and certainly the easiest, was to talk. Just as teaching or urging people to be hostile and feel enmity toward others is a form of action (often, certainly in this case, leading to catastrophic consequences), the failure to say necessary things, in being a failure to act well, is to act badly.

For all the times and ways that Pope Pius XI and Pius XII, other Vatican officials, and clergy around Europe did not speak out against the eliminationist persecution of the Jews, both during the 1930s and in its exterminationist phase of the 1940s, they committed offenses. In the view of the contemporaneous Norwegian Protestant Churches, declared for all of Norway and the world to hear and certainly known to the upper echelons of the Catholic Church, silence rendered the silent (which would include the Catholic Church and its clergy) "co-guilty in this injustice."[118] The Catholic Church and its clergy's silence was understood to be approval, and in many cases it was. The Church and its clergy had a duty to dispel any false notions on this score. That they did not was a moral failing. Each individual's culpability varies with the specific offense. For some, moral guilt is incurred, for others moral blame.

That the Church failed to fight, obstruct, and speak out with all its considerable might against the evil emanating from Germany is certainly at least an act of political omission. Its duty to do so was greater than the ordinary duty people have to resist evil because of the Church's role as a moral

Priests giving the Hitler salute at a Catholic youth rally in the Berlin-Neukölln stadium in August 1933.

steward, and because centuries of its antisemitic teachings prepared the soil, then planted by others, from which *Kristallnacht,* Babi Yar, and Auschwitz emerged. How much greater was the Church's duty to have fought Hitler, given that he was, if not its child, then its bastard child, progeny that the Church wanted in part to disown? This too needs to be said: The Church had incurred, by its own actions, a still greater duty to help the Jews than to help other victims, precisely because its antisemitic and sometimes racist libels and hatred were the foundation for the unjust harm that so many Germans and others inflicted upon the Jews. Guenter Lewy observes that "from the time Hitler came to power all the German bishops began declaring their appreciation of the important natural values of race and racial purity." The consequence of this was that "when Hitler started to pursue the purity of the German blood in his own ruthless way, the overwhelming majority of the German Catholics . . . dutifully obeyed his orders and promptly forgot the warnings against using extreme and immoral means in the defense of one's race given out by the bishops."[119]

The Church's antisemitism itself was a necessary cause of the Holocaust. This does not mean that it was sufficient cause. It was not.[120] The Church itself would not have initiated and carried out a program for the annihilation of the Jews. It could not have done so. It did not do so. Among other reasons, its own doctrine prohibited such a course of action. That its antisemitism was nevertheless a necessary cause of this annihilative onslaught only increases the Church's political and moral blame for not trying to thwart or mitigate the Germans' and the others' mass murdering.

POSTWAR OFFENSES

The Catholic Church's offenses and culpability did not end with the war. After the war the Church could have spoken about the guilt of the perpetrators and called for justice. We might consider it to have been the Church's duty. After all, for generations it had publicly called for the punishment of the innocent Jews. So why did the Church not advocate the same for the Germans, Croats, Dutch, French, Italians, Poles, Slovaks, and others who were actually guilty of great crimes? Why did Pius XII not excommunicate a single German or non-German mass murderer of Jews? Instead of condemning the German criminals with even an iota of the ire that it and its clergy heaped upon the innocent Jews, the Church maintained its criminal solidarity with them. Even the Germans' defeat did not change this.

What the Vatican had not done to help the unjustly hunted Jews, it gladly did for Germans and others who murdered them. Highly placed members of the Church systematically aided the leading slayers of European Jewry in escaping justice by providing them with false documents and shepherding them to South America. The roster of Vatican transgressions includes seeking clemency for convicted war criminals; resisting the extradition of potential German war criminals; hiding fugitives on Vatican properties; and abetting the escape of mass murderers by appointing Nazi sympathizers inside the Church to critical positions.[121]

One of the ringleaders of this substantial criminal conspiracy was the friend and confidant of Pope Pius XII and of the later Pope Paul VI, the head of the German Church in Rome, and a known passionate supporter of Nazism, Bishop Hudal. Bishop Hudal himself has testified that "after 1945 all my charitable work was primarily devoted to the former members of National Socialism and Fascism, particularly to the so-called 'war criminals' . . . who were being persecuted" and whom he considered to be "frequently personally completely without guilt." He boasted that he "by means of false personal documents, rescued not a few of them so that they could flee their tormentors to happier lands."[122] Whom did this important Catholic bishop at the Vatican see as these so-called tormentors? The Allies' legal authorities. The men whom Bishop Hudal and many others at the heart of the Church believed to be more innocent than the Jews included some of the greatest criminals of all time: Adolf Eichmann, who coordinated the annihilation of millions of Jews; Franz Stangl, the commander successively of two extermination camps, Sobibór and Treblinka; Kurt Christmann, the commander of Sonderkommando 10a, which slaughtered Jews in the Soviet Union; Walter Rauff, in charge of developing the gas vans used in the mass murder of hundreds of thousands; Klaus Barbie, "the Butcher of Lyon"; Ante Pavelič, the head of the mass-murdering Croatian Ustasha regime; and most infamous of all, Auschwitz's Dr. Josef Mengele.[123] The efforts of Bishop Hudal and the other clergy were deeply appreciated. Eichmann, who landed safely in Argentina, decided to inscribe himself in his newly minted passport as a Catholic even though he was a Protestant. He explained: "I recall with deep gratitude the aid given to me by Catholic priests in my flight from Europe and decided to honor the Catholic faith by becoming an honorary member."[124]

The activities of Bishop Hudal and others were widely known around the Vatican. Pius XII certainly knew of at least some of Bishop Hudal's and other high Church officials' aid to the mass murderers, whom the bishop, clearly not alone, believed to be "completely innocent." One of the high Church officials actively involved in these activities, who gave extensive reports to Pius XII twice a day, was his right-hand man, Monsignor Montini, the future Pope Paul VI.[125] By allowing members of their church to help the mass murderers circumvent the Allied justice authorities, Monsignor Montini and Pius XII indicated their approval of such aid.

Helping criminals to escape justice is itself a criminal offense, for which those involved and those who approved of it bear guilt and blame. The Church again agrees with our assessment, declaring that if we "protect evil-doers," then "we have a responsibility for the sins committed by others."[126]

FORSAKING CATHOLICS' SOULS

The act that may be, in a certain sense, the Church's greatest offense has not been even mentioned: its failure to Catholics.

This moral reckoning with the Catholic Church is predicated upon the view that there is a universal duty not to commit unjust harm and, if possible within reasonable bounds, to prevent others from perpetrating such harm. The Church's obligation to heed this investigation's conclusions is doubly strong because the Church's own particular principles, its doctrine, unambiguously accept the rightness of these universal principles and their application to the eliminationist persecution of the Jews. But of course—and this is what the Church and its defenders today so desperately try to cover up—the Catholic Church of the 1930s and 1940s did not practice these principles; if anything something like their opposite. To a person of the time, say a Catholic or a Jew, who was not looking back on the events through the distorting lenses of the current fictionalized benevolent image of the Church, the notion that the Catholic Church would have vigorously and readily given substantial moral and material aid to Jews would have come as a great surprise. Jews did not expect the Church to tend to them and champion their safety, because the Church was unmistakably and vocally hostile to them. (Though in desperate moments Jews would appeal to individual churchmen, and a small percentage of clergy did respond with aid.)

But unlike Jews, Catholics did expect the Church to tend to their own moral and spiritual safety because that is the Church's highest duty and reason for being. The Church is the shepherd. Catholics are its flock. Yet Catholics received no such care from the Church but something like its opposite. In every act and nonact by which the Church failed Jews, it also failed Catholics.

The Church did not tell Catholics that with every antisemitic act of omission or of participation—most obviously by actively participating, in any way, in the mass annihilation of the Jews—they committed a crime against humanity and a sin against God. The Church thereby allowed Catholics to place their souls at risk for an eternity in hell. According to the Church, the failure to have warned Catholics is a sin because we incur the "responsibility for the sins committed by others" by "not disclosing them when we have an obligation to do so." With this offense (and this is, of course, also true of the failure to warn Jews), the Catholic Church, its national churches, two popes, its bishops and priests offended God and failed Catholics as badly as a religious leader can fail those who look to him for guidance.

The Church, Pius XII, and the clergy (some of this applies also to Pius XI) allowed Catholics to persecute and perpetrate unjust harm upon Jews for one of two reasons: because the churchmen did not conceive of the anti-Jewish onslaught, including the mass killing, as crimes; or because they thought the various components of the German-led violent eliminationist persecution were crimes and, with their silence, chose to allow (act of omission) Catholics to commit them (that is, when they were not also encouraging the criminal acts themselves). From the standpoint of Catholics, I am not sure which is worse: a Church and Church leaders morally bankrupt or even criminal because they were so besotted by doctrinal hatred and enmity that they gave their moral blessing to one of the

Cardinal Michael Faulhaber marches between rows of SA men at a Nazi rally in Munich.

greatest crimes in human history, or a Church and Church leaders morally bankrupt or even criminal because, for their own, perhaps political, reasons, they willfully ignored their duty to warn their members against committing deeds they knew to be criminal, and therefore willfully permitted millions of their members to imperil their souls.

It is likely that some combination of both existed, but I find it hard to believe that the overwhelming majority of the Church's European clergy thought that Catholics were committing grievous crimes and mortal sins (including in the nonlethal phases of the eliminationist onslaught) and allowed them to do so by saying nothing. The bishops and priests would have had to be adopting this difficult and inexplicable position day after day, for years on end. After all, the Church made clear, right up front, that its fiery encyclical *Mit brennender Sorge* was "prompted by the desire, as it behooves Us, to secure for Germany the freedom of the Church's beneficent mission and the salvation of the souls in her care . . ."[127] By implication, the silent churchmen did not judge "the salvation of the souls in her care" to be endangered by Catholics' participation in the eliminationist persecution of the Jews. Germany's Cardinal Faulhaber had declared it "a duty of conscience to speak out" against the so-called Euthanasia program, "for as a Catholic bishop I may not remain silent when the preservation of the moral foundations of all public order is at stake."[128] Yet he remained silent as Catholics persecuted and killed Jews, so he must have thought that in this case the "moral foundations" remained secure. Pius XII himself had proclaimed in his first encyclical that his greatest duty was "to testify to the truth with Apostolic Firmness."[129] Surely, if there was any truth to which he had to testify, then it was to the criminality and mortal sinfulness of the Germans' onslaught against European Jews, and the peril to which Catholics who contributed to it were subjecting their souls. The Church's willingness to allow Catholics and its clergy to persecute and even kill Jews appears, therefore, more likely to have resulted from the belief that the members of their flock were not endangering their souls—that such acts were not crimes, offenses, or sins.

Karl Barth, the great German protestant theologian, speaking for Christians in general, seems to concur that such a belief existed. In December 1938 shortly after *Kristallnacht,* the violent nationwide assault on the Jewish communities of Germany, Barth asked rhetorically, "How is it possible that our ears, the ears of Christians, do not ring in the presence of the . . . misery and malice" suffered by the Jews? Toward the end of the war, in July 1944, he answered his own question, "We do not like the Jews as a rule, it is therefore not easy for us to apply to them as well the general love for humankind." Barth however left the source of this antipathy unmentioned. After the war other members of his Confessing Church pointed to the source. Pastor Wolfgang Raupach-Rudnick, an expert on Christian-Jewish relations in the Protestant church, explains that they attributed this antipathy to their Christian beliefs, namely (according to a report about his lecture) the "double prejudice of Christianity—its own antisemitic history and its theological blindness, that the persecution of this people could have been willed by God." These beliefs were the common property even of this most liberal and anti-Nazi of German protestant churches, of other protestant churches, as well as of the Catholic Church. The French Catholic bishops confirmed this, though somewhat imprecisely, in their "Declaration of Repentance" of 1997. The Church's "centuries-old ideas and attitudes" towards Jews, antisemitism, had had, according to the Church's own bishops, a "soporific effect on the people's consciences, reducing their capacity to resist when the full violence of National Socialist antisemitism rose up." More accurately, the antisemitism that the Church taught its faithful led them to believe that the Jews were guilty, reduced their capacity to feel for the Jews, and gave them reason not to want to come to the Jews' defense.[130]

To recognize that the clergy failed the laity in this way is decidedly not to imply that ordinary Catholics were not also agents. They too were moral actors; in the Church's terms they had free will and therefore were also culpable for their offenses. As we have made clear, the analysis and judgments here apply similarly to ordinary Catholics who were motivated by Catholic beliefs to harm or to approve of harm to Jews—although they have not formally been the subjects of our investigation. And just because they too, as agents, were responsible for their actions does not mean that they were not also forsaken by their Church.

We see then that it is not just the Jewish victims and their families who should be calling for a moral reckoning with the Catholic Church. The call should be coming (and to a small degree is coming) also from Catholics. The Church betrayed its Catholic flock by the tens of millions. Although each one, victimized Jew and morally abandoned Catholic, has a special claim on witnessing such a reckoning, we need not be Jew or Catholic to have a legitimate stake in it. We need not be afflicted Jews or Catholics, or their actual or spiritual descendants. All people have the right, indeed the duty, to engage in moral judgment of significant public events, institutions, and actors. All people have the right and the duty to urge that the conclusions that correctly follow on that moral judgment be widely known and be acted upon. Although such a moral reckoning will serve everyone, no one has a more urgent need for it than the Catholic Church itself, which does not yet know how to call for what it must.

PART THREE

REPAIRING
the Harm

Many sins wrong our neighbor. One must do what is possible in order to repair the harm (e.g., return stolen goods, restore the reputation of someone slandered, pay compensation for injuries). Simple justice requires as much.

Catechism of the Catholic Church, parag. 1459

INSTITUTIONS and moral philosophies need to be grounded in principles that are defensible in their own terms. Even so, practically all foundational principles, including Catholic principles, can be challenged by good-faith champions of other principles. But because no court of judgment can, with authoritative finality, decree anyone's principles to be wrong, no higher authority exists than an individual's own thoughts and passions. This is why, self-interests and advantages aside, it is often difficult to get institutions or people to replace their own principles—no matter how wrong they seem to others—with different ones. Humility and self-doubt should also inform those who would convince or convert others. The severe limitations of the human mind and heart to make sense of the overwhelming quantity of data about this world, and the total absence of verifiable information about a possible afterlife, should render all of us that much more doubtful about the rightness of our ways. For all these reasons, we should do two things: err on the side of tolerance, and regularly test and reinvestigate the wisdom of our own first principles. The world in all its complexities and the hereafter in all its unknowability admit a plurality of plausibly good orientations toward this world.

When certain principles, views, or institutional practices produce outcomes that either contradict other foundational principles or that are undeniably catastrophic (in which case they usually contradict some important principle), it should lead a person of good faith to want to revisit, reconsider, and possibly recast or jettison altogether those principles, views, or practices. Thomas Hobbes, a system builder of the first rank, advised:

> By this it appears how necessary it is for any man that aspires to true knowledge to examine the definitions of former authors, and either to correct them where they are negligently set down or to make them himself. For the errors of definitions multiply themselves according as the reckoning proceeds, and lead men into absurdities which at last they see but cannot avoid without reckoning anew from the beginning, in which lies the foundation of their errors.[1]

Such was the situation, the need, of the Catholic Church to "reckon anew" in 1945.

The Church's views, and its principles, about Jews systematically led its followers to commit deeds that violated the most fundamental Church principles, sometimes including "You shall not kill."[2] The results were unquestionably catastrophic ones that no one of good faith would defend today. Although the Church has instituted some important changes, it has not gone far enough. In critical respects its situation remains unaltered to this day. A reconsideration of certain aspects of the Catholic Church is, therefore, still necessary. This reconsideration requires a rethinking of central features of the Church, from the definition of the kind of entity it is, to the sorts and character of investigations we do, to how we think about remedying its problems.

The Catholic Church should be acknowledged, generally and particularly in its relations with Jews, for what it always has been, including during the Nazi period, and still is today: a political institution. The Pope has been and remains a political leader. These truths are obvious to students of Church history, to political scientists, and to Jews. They were obvious to politicians who were Pius XII's contemporaries. The Church had for centuries been a temporal political ruler in Europe and maintained its rule over a significant portion of Italy until the second half of the nineteenth century. Even where it did not rule it had enormous political influence, shaping the politics of the continent for centuries. Much of the history of Europe, including during the modern period, has been informed by secular authorities' attempts to reduce the political reach and power of the Church. Although the Church has, for centuries, been fighting a losing battle to maintain or extend its political power (losses that, fantastically, it sometimes blamed on the politically all-but-powerless Jews), it has remained political at its core throughout the twentieth century and into the twenty-first. Ernst von Weizsäcker, the German ambassador to the Vatican starting in 1943, captured the dual, though decidedly political, nature of the Church, as encapsulated in the Pope, whom he knew well: "My general impression was that I met more a man of religious devotion than a politician—yet he is a politician to a high degree."[3]

Today many people in the West are not aware of the Catholic Church's political nature, a false view that the Church itself has fostered, particularly its character and conduct during the Nazi period, a view that seemingly is believed by many who write about its conduct during that time. But to the professional experts on politics, it is incontestable that the Catholic Church is a political institution and should be analyzed and treated as such.[4]

What kind of political institution is it? Its governing structure and culture is authoritarian. The Church and its internal critics agree on this point, their differences being that the critics decry the authoritarianism while the Church celebrates it. A dissident Catholic "shadow synod" convening in Rome in 2001 called for "the world's last absolute monarchy" to be replaced by "democracy."[5] The Church, by contrast, declares with pride that the Pope "by reason of his office as Vicar of Christ, and as pastor of the entire Church has full, supreme, and universal power over the whole Church, a power which he can always exercise unhindered."[6] By "virtue of his office" the Pope is proclaimed "infallible." The Church itself is also "infallible."[7]

The doctrine of infallibility means several things. When the Pope speaks authoritatively, God is said to be speaking through him. Within the Church there can be no efficacious discussion of the rightness of the words of a man possessing "supreme and universal power over the whole Church," no dissent, no review or recourse, no official tolerance of other ways, no revision of his positions. This is a doctrine, and I mean this now in a neutral way, of intolerance. If the truth conflicts with authoritative declarations of the Pope or calls into question the doctrine of infallibility or the Pope's supreme power, then the Church and its clergy have to maintain that truth is fiction and fiction is truth.

The authoritarian structure and culture of the Church, undergirded by the infallibility doctrine, is inherently dishonest. Time and again truth is "subordinated to ecclesiastical tactics,"[8] sacrificed to buttress papal authority. No person and no institution is infallible.[9] It is true that the Pope is deemed infallible only when speaking ex cathedra authoritatively on Church doctrine. But there is a strong tendency on the part of the Church to deny that Popes err, even on other matters, because admitting that a Pope is wrong would inevitably erode his aura of infallibility and therefore his authority. This penchant for denying Popes' past errors, falsehoods, and transgressions is particularly evident regarding Jews, since Popes' conduct toward Jews has been, if not explicitly grounded in Church scripture and doctrine, then derived from them. The admission of fundamental errors regarding Jews would therefore have profound, disequilibrating implications for the viability of the underlying religious doctrine of Church and papal infallibility.[10]

Doctrinally the Church maintains imperial aspirations to subject all of humanity to the Pope's unquestioned and untrammeled power—even if the Church is no longer militant or martial.[11] The Church continues to impart to its faithful notions that indicate that except for those who have not heard of Christianity non-Christians are excluded from heaven, which itself strongly implies and which will be understood by many to mean that they will go to hell. (Hell, whatever else it also is, and however it is variously understood by lay Catholics, is officially described as the "state of definitive self-exclusion from communion with God and the blessed" and its punishments as "eternal fire".) In its section on "hell" the *Catechism*, citing the Gospel According to Matthew, declares, "Jesus often speaks of 'Gehenna,' of 'the unquenchable fire' reserved for those who to the end of their lives *refuse to believe and be converted,* where both body and soul can be lost" [my emphasis].[12] What are Catholics supposed to think about the moral status of people whom they know will for all eternity be excluded from heaven—the only place one would want to be—and from salvation? Regarding Jews, the Catholic Church continues to contain, at its core, Scripture, doctrine, and theology that deprecate and disparage them and their religion. As long as such Scripture, doctrine, and theology exist, they will continue to produce suspicion, antipathy, and for some, hatred toward Jews. This is so whatever the well-meaning self-conceptions and conscious intent of Church leaders may be—and undoubtedly are. Whatever some Church leaders formally profess, the belief within the upper echelons of the Church (even if this is not true for many lay Catholics) is that Jews ought to become Christians. Jews qua Jews ought to disappear. How could it be otherwise for a Church that holds that the salvation of humanity depends upon the conversion of Jews to Christianity?[13]

Given what the Christian Bible and the Church's own teaching proclaim to Catholics in so many ways, every day, indeed what is at the heart of the Catholic Church's claim about itself—"Outside the Church there is no salvation" and "the Church still has the obligation and also the sacred right to evangelize all men"[14]—it is no surprise that the Church and its clergy as a whole do not embrace the notions that Jews ought to remain Jews and can find salvation as Jews. If the Church leaders did not believe that Jews needed to become Christians, then they would loudly declare the falseness of this doctrine and renounce the Church's position that the Catholic Church is universal and that all people ought to be subjected to its authority.

There are indications that elements within the Catholic Church are rethinking these matters. Certainly, there have long been important dissenting voices within the Church and local initiatives in the United States, Germany, and elsewhere that suggest more pluralistic and accommodating views. Perhaps with time these voices will grow more powerful and come to predominate within the Church, and will lead to revised Church doctrine and teaching on these matters. Whatever genuine pluralism and respect for non-Christians exist within sectors of the Church and among individual Catholics, whatever the substantial good work Catholics direct at non-Catholics, and whatever the frequent heartfelt community-level cooperation, especially in the United States, of Catholics and their churches with Jews and their religious and cultural institutions, the Catholic Church, in the end, still speaks determinatively on critical matters in the voice of the infallible Pope, still has its binding doctrine and an official policy, and still maintains an orthodoxy of belief and conduct on matters it deems essential, including its conception of Jews and of the Church's relationship to them and their religion.

Seen from the outside, and certainly from the vantage point of a political scientist, Catholic doctrine, theology, and liturgy looks, historically and even today, more like the ideology of an imperial power, sometimes an antagonistic power, than a mere set of beliefs about God. Knowing that such a body of ideas is harnessed to even a small state like the Vatican that is a powerful transnational institution, with a charismatic leader (which the Pope is by definition) and formal diplomatic relations with states around the world, it becomes ever more difficult to see the Church as not being in its essence political.

The Catholic Church, then, vies for the distinction of being the largest authoritarian political institution in the world, even if many critical factors make the Church ultimately a constrained and weak authoritarian institution. Aside from doctrine, two are worth mentioning here: the Church's expectations of obedience are confined mainly to the moral sphere, and then to areas where its religious doctrines intersect politics. The Church, though populous, is weak (its state is small, it has no army and no other means of physical coercion), and is politically incapable of enforcing its wishes on its members and those over whom it would like to gain suzerainty. These limiting features reduce the likelihood of physical danger resulting from the Church's doctrines, the parallel organizational structure that embodies them, and its practices. But this does not change the Church's authoritarian nature. It does not mean that the Church does not powerfully shape people's values and beliefs.

Recognizing the political and authoritarian nature of the Catholic Church allows us to reframe the evaluation of the Church and its leaders in the normal terms that we use for other political entities and actors. It removes the halo of immunity, which the Church so often enjoys, against full scrutiny and criticism, and against the unmasking use of direct language. If a Pope is not to be accorded the deference owed to the infallible voice of God on earth (or at least to somebody who many believe is that person), then the crippling moral and linguistic manacles come off, freeing us to discuss and evaluate Pius XII as we would any other political (and moral) leader.

It is precisely such a calm and open discussion of the Church's and its clergy's stances toward Jews, especially during the Nazi period, that the Church and its defenders cannot abide. Eugene Fisher, the associate director of the Secretariat for Ecumenical and Interreligious Affairs of the National Conference of Catholic Bishops and the American Church's point man on these issues, illustrated this recently. In May 2001 he reacted with indignation that anyone would dare speak the truth that Pope Pius XII had been absolutely silent in public about the mass murder of the Jews for well over a year after the Holocaust began and then, the Pope's allusions aside, never publicly protested against the extermination of the Jews. In *The New York Times* Fisher labeled people who would use the accurate phrase "the silence of the Pope," and thereby utter the truth that Fisher and the Church wish to bury, as engaging in "bigotry" and motivated by "anti-Catholicism."[15] This is just one example of the Church's and its defenders' attempts to intimidate people who would speak plain truths about the Church or its clergy. Such political attacks also simultaneously seek to prevent a sober scholarly appraisal of the Church's and its clergy's deeds and misdeeds by impugning the moral or psychological character of the unwanted messenger and thereby creating a discussion not about the real issue, the veracity of the message, but about a diversionary and fictive issue, the moral or mental fitness of its bearer.

Because the Catholic Church is a political institution, which still has substantial power, we may investigate its culture, ideology, and practices, just as we would those of any other state. This includes investigating the Church's doctrine, theology, and liturgy. We must do so in a hardheaded way, asking the same sorts of questions about its intolerant or harmful doctrines that we would ask about those of any other political institution. If we find that its ideology is hate-filled or noxious, or that its practices are unjust and harmful, then we would be remiss if we did not call for their cessation or revision—even if this means altering fundamental Catholic beliefs or practices (again this pertains to only those that are political). It is worth emphasizing that surveying those Catholic beliefs and practices that have implications or consequences for non-Catholics, especially when they are political, should be as much the province of non-Catholics as Catholics. And non-Catholics should not hesitate to call for remedies when remedies are needed, just as Catholics and non-Catholics alike would not hesitate to do so for other political institutions. Although William Donohue, president of the Catholic League for Religious and Civil Rights, reacts to the truth about the Catholic Church and the Holocaust with the accusation of anti-Catholic bigotry, when discussing another matter he has made clear that he shares principles of scrutiny that are similar to our own. Donohue says that "house rules," such as celibacy, should be left alone by non-Catholics, but since "the Catholic Church has a tremendous public effect on society," it can be examined and criticized as any other institution. "Non-Catholics," he declares, "have every right to speak out."[16]

It is therefore that much more wrong for the Church and its defenders to label someone anti-Catholic just because he criticizes the Church as an institution, or its doctrine, theology, liturgy, or practices. We do not call someone anti-American or anti-German just because he criticizes aspects of American or German politics, such as their respective laws on freedom of speech or taxes or even citizenship requirements, or because he condemns some aspect of the country's foreign policy or treatment of minorities. We do not call someone antisemitic just because he criticizes some aspect of Judaism, Jewish institutions, or Israel. We do not call someone prejudiced against any of these institutions, even if he subjects it to a thoroughgoing critique, when that critique is empirically, morally, and analytically well-grounded and fairly applied.

The tendency among some representatives and defenders of the Church to deem anti-Catholic anyone who explicitly criticizes or questions some aspect of the Church stems in part from the Church's self-definition as the embodiment of God on earth and therefore as infallible. The critic is deemed "anti-Catholic" merely because he is *against* the *Catholic* Church's own imperious claim that it and its core doctrine are not subject to criticism. Essentially, such defenders of the Church define "anti-Catholic" as any statement or person that takes issue with the Church's claim to its infallible monopoly on truth or its claim to an infallible incapacity to commit crimes or other offenses. Because the Church's defenders take their own definition of their Church as the sole legitimate basis on which statements about the Church may be evaluated, and because that definition is at odds with the basis used for evaluating the possible prejudicial nature of criticism of other political institutions or religions, the Church's defenders falsely brand otherwise ordinary and legitimate criticism, when it is directed at the Church as an institution, its clergy, or its doctrine, as being anti-Catholic prejudice or bigotry. Because such ordinary and legitimate criticism violates the Church's definition of what it *is,* the Church's defenders can raise the polemical stakes still higher by defaming the authors of such legitimate criticism as wanting to destroy the Church.

Leaving aside the Church's defenders' institutionally idiosyncratic penchant for attacking a person as an anti-Catholic bigot because he refuses to recognize their claim to the Church's monopoly on truth, the Catholic Church has not taken criticism from outsiders well. This is not surprising, because political institutions commonly react badly to criticism. However, the Church's sensitivity in this respect, unlike the sensitivity of many institutions, is particularly understandable because there has been much ill will and much genuine bigotry toward Catholics and their Church. So the obvious must be said. The principles that qualify a person or a statement as anti-semitic also qualify a person or a statement as anti-Catholic.

First, it is wrong to criticize the Catholic Church or its clerical or lay members untruthfully (keeping in mind that inevitably there are occasional innocent mistakes). Second, it is wrong to criticize Catholics based solely on their identity as Catholics or to say that their identity as Catholics caused them to believe or do certain blameworthy things. Such assertions are different from legitimate criticism, criticism of the Church for its doctrine and practices or criticism of Catholics based on the justifiable conclusion that they, as individuals, held certain beliefs and that those beliefs were derived from their religion or taught them by the Church or its clergy and led them to take blameworthy stances and actions. (The issue is not *Catholic identity* but *Catholics' beliefs and practices,* such as of those Catholics who have believed what the Church, for centuries, taught and what is stated clearly in the Christian Bible, namely that all Jews are guilty for Jesus' death.) Third, it is wrong to criticize the Church, its clergy, or its members exclusively or more harshly than other institutions or people that deserve similar criticism (unless specific, justifiable circumstances warranted a focus on the Church—such as scholarly inquiry—or the singular harshness). All of these wrong stances qualify as prejudice against Catholics, Catholicism, or the Catholic Church as an institution. Adopting them is anti-Catholic.[17]

Being anti-Catholic is self-evidently wrong. But—as has become recently increasingly clear, especially in the United States—it is also wrong and sometimes dangerous to give the Church and its leadership the free ride that they have so often received owing to faulty assumptions about their nature, to the Church's and its defenders' successful dissemination of disinformation about its past and its practices, or to fear of speaking the truth about such a powerful institution that can mobilize so many people and resources in its often aggressive defense, and which does not hesitate to fend off fair-minded critics and legitimate criticism by branding them falsely as anti-Catholic.

Many Catholics wish to reflect critically on their religion and on their Church. Many Catholics already dissent from a variety of Church doctrines, indicating that the contemporary Church's claim to a monopoly of thought and practice on critical matters is not accepted by a good portion of the Catholic faithful. These include personal and social matters, such as divorce, contraception, and abortion, the ordination of women, priestly celibacy, and homosexuality, and many other doctrinal and political matters, such as who may attain salvation and how the Church is governed. Of late in the United States, Catholics have grown vocal and insistent in their dissent and criticism, demanding that the Church finally listen and heed their concerns. Catholics, as we are witnessing now in the United States, also sometimes seek to change Catholic institutional structures, practices, or doctrines with which they disagree. Indeed, our criticism of the Church's, its clergy's, and lay Catholics' past moral choices and offenses, predicated upon their agency or, in the Church's terms, free will, necessarily implies, encourages, and takes heart in the Church's, its clergy's, and lay Catholics' capacities after the war and today to make good moral choices to refashion those aspects of their Church and their religion that require it.[18]

Good moral choices depend on a clear-eyed view of the moral field, which can be facilitated by stripping away our personal attachments. Imagine that we donned the Rawlsian veil of ignorance, which means that we must make our moral decisions and craft just institutions without knowing our own identities or the particular identities of any other people or institutions.[19] We would not know anything about the identity of the Catholic Church—Catholicism's status as one of the main religions of the world, its members' identities, et cetera. Imagine then that, without reference to our personal identities (which we do not know), we would have to judge this now-unnamed institution on the record that the Church has compiled toward the Jews, applying only fair principles of justice. What would we say? We would say that this institution has engaged in systematic deceit and intellectual fraud, spread vast hatred and enmity, and helped to produce colossal suffering and the deaths of millions of innocent people. Granted, the most infamous and destructive of the mass murders was initiated by others and without the explicit encouragement or blessing of the institution, some number of whose members, including its leading members, thought it to be a crime. Yet many of the institution's relevant national branches and individual officials did approve, encourage, abet, or participate in the mass murder or its preparatory measures, and the institution's leaders did not at the time or since then discipline or repudiate them.

If this institution were judged impartially on this record, then the calls for it to remove or reform all its wholesome aspects pertinent to this past would likely have become thunderous long ago. From the viewpoint of its victims—people who have just wanted to be left alone—this institution had for centuries been the doctrinal inspiration of hatred, suffering, violence, and occasional large-scale mass murder. Whatever good this institution had done for its members, would the continuing existence of its features that helped to produce such suffering ever be justified—if the institution had some name other than the Catholic Church, had nothing like its roughly one billion adherents, and was not the custodian of the most populous branch of the world's dominant religion, Christianity?[20]

Fortunately, the Catholic Church has, in the past several decades, changed a great deal for the better, and has the potential to redress what has been left untended. If that potential is to be realized, we need to ponder what this would entail: a clear-sighted view of the Church, its offenses, and those of its features that are pernicious; an understanding of its duty to redress its wrongs and deficiencies; and an investigation of what such redress might look like.

To do this, we should employ common and correct standards of evaluation. We should not make the mistake of suspending ordinary methods of analysis and principles of judgment.[21] We already employed these maxims in part two; just by doing something as simple and obviously necessary as this, we produced—following general, neutral evaluative principles—a portrait of, and a set of conclusions about, the Church and its clergy in the years immediately preceding, during, and after the Holocaust that are at odds with received ones, devastating to the Church's image and moral standing, and with far-reaching implications for today's Church that we need to explore.

This means that, for assessing the Church's and its clergy's actions during the Nazi period up to today, we must employ the conventional evaluative standards that we apply to other political (or social) institutions, politicians, or actors: looking at the Church's and churchmen's conduct in a variety of comparative perspectives, assessing explanations (and excuses) with skepticism and logical rigor, and using direct, nonobfuscating language. Antisemitism is antisemitism, libel is libel, and hatred is hatred, even when they come from the Church as holy biblical pronouncements or dressed up in hair-splitting doctrinal garb (as "anti-Judaism" rather than antisemitism). We should expect that, when the Church and its clergy have committed offenses, their deeds and they should be judged no more leniently than non-clerical offenders. We should expect that they should act to undo or rectify what they can. We should expose and reject the euphemisms, descriptive distortions, conceptual sleights of hand, narrative incompleteness, interpretive contortions, and moral excuse making that is so often evident in the writing about the Catholic Church and the Holocaust. When describing, analyzing, and judging the Church before, during, and after the Holocaust, we should call a spade a spade.

THE CHURCH'S FAILURES IN DEALING WITH THE PAST

In the introduction and part one we saw that in several critical ways the understanding and investigation of the Catholic Church need to be reframed. We need to have a dispassionate approach to it, asking the standard questions about both its internal workings and its external relations that we would ask about any political or social institution. We need to look beyond the Pope, who often serves as a lightning rod and alibi for others, to the Church as a whole and in its many parts. We need to recognize that antisemitism has been at the center of Church doctrine and theology and the Church's historical development more generally and that the Church has been fully a political institution whatever its attendant moral status. In part two we saw that the Church, parts of the Church, and individual clergy, from the Pope on down, committed a wide range of criminal and noncriminal transgressions and bear substantial culpability—criminal, political, and moral—for them. Building on the findings of the first two parts, we can explore their implications here, and draw conclusions about the kinds of tasks, including self-transformations, that the Church, the Pope, and its bishops and priests must undertake. The Church is morally bound to right the wrongs, and repair the harm, that it can.

We have shown that the Catholic Church and its clergy committed many substantial offenses, incurring a range and weight of guilt and blame grave enough to warrant a thorough reexamination of the institution. That the obvious facts and simple truths stated here will undoubtedly startle many people shows how effective the Church has been in its self-exculpating strategies, and how indulgent and uncritical many writers about the Holocaust and the Church have been toward it. The Church is a human institution within human societies, which means that, whatever its claimed relationship to God, on this earth it is still governed by the laws, and subject to the good moral principles, of those societies. Therefore, in each society in which the Church and its clergy committed offenses, people should ask: Which of their offenses are subject to legal, political, and social punishment, and what should such punishment be? The Catholic Church itself also had the duty, after the war, to confront its transgressions. What did the Church do to address its offenses? Was that sufficient? If not, what must it now do?

We can begin to answer these questions by considering basic legal and political facts. Clergy who committed crimes, no different from nonclergy who committed crimes, ought to have been prosecuted. The priestly cloth ought not bring legal or social immunity and does not, at least when clergy commit other kinds of crimes and offenses. If today a priest commits murder or some other crime, he is prosecuted. All those who directly participated in the deportations and mass murder of Jews ought to have been held criminally liable. Determining exactly which activities properly rise to the level of criminal involvement would require a discussion of complex legal issues, which vary from country to country.

Legal considerations of this kind, though worth stating, are somewhat beside the point. Prosecuting people for crimes is often, certainly in the case of the Holocaust and other mass murders, a political decision. No country after World War II put on trial all the people, or even any but a small percentage of its people, who committed crimes against Jews or other victim groups during the Nazi period. In many countries there were simply too many criminals, and no political will or popular support, to put thousands, tens of thousands, or, in the most obvious case of Germany, even hundreds of thousands on trial. It was quite the opposite.[22] So as a matter of politics and public policy, few churchmen were sufficiently high-profile criminals— the president-priest Tiso's conviction and execution in Czechoslovakia in April 1947 being an exception—to have fallen within the range of the small prosecutorial net that was used in Germany and elsewhere.[23] And of course the passage of time renders trials moot for the twenty-first century.

Aside from legal prosecutions, the peoples of the different countries could censure the Church and call for nonlegal investigations of the Church's and churchmen's full range of offenses. They could pressure the national churches and the Vatican to come clean about what their institutions and members did during the Nazi period, and to adopt remedies and other measures deemed necessary in light of the Church's offenses. This would include, of course, making it known to everyone that the Church and many clergy did commit the offenses. At the very least, appropriately severe moral censure could be directed at the Church and the relevant clergy for their transgressions.

Virtually none of this has occurred, for many reasons. For the peoples of European countries to seek an investigation of, and to censure, Christian churches, including the Catholic Church, their own national churches and clergy, they would have had to countenance the widespread condemnation of aspects of their own religious tradition, its institutions and leaders. They would have also implicated many of their countrymen. And they would have had to do this all because the Jews—still hated in many of these societies for years after the war—had in large numbers perished. Until recently, none of this has been even remotely possible.[24]

Although socially and politically in country after country there was all but a total failure after the war to address the Church's offenses, it is not too late to call for such investigations and to direct appropriate moral censure at the Church and its national churches both for what they did during the Nazi period (and before) and also for their failures after the war to undertake a genuine moral reckoning with their offenses. Several German companies and institutions have in the last several years initiated such investigations of their companies' misdeeds during the Nazi period. Similar investigations have been initiated by institutions in other countries. In March 2002 the commission of independent historians set up by the Swiss government, and given full access to the necessary archives and records, issued an eleven-thousand-plus-page report that documents the many failures and offenses against Jews by Switzerland, Swiss companies, and individual Swiss during the war, and that explodes the myth that the Swiss committed these offenses because they were coerced by the Germans.[25] This twenty-six volume report is a far cry from the Church's meager "We Remember," only a few pages long and often self-exculpatory in its reflections. Among other things, this book is a call for an investigation, a set of investigations, of the Church no less thorough than that issued by the commission on Switzerland. We must examine the actions and inactions not narrowly of Pius XII, but of the Catholic Church and its clergy throughout Europe, country by country, region by region, locale by locale.

Turning to the Church's own duty after the war to address its and its clergy's offenses, we can say that in the broadest sense, the Church needed to do three things: (1) address its specific offenses, in order to see who was culpable for which of them and to bring the offenders to justice (whether within legal systems or socially and institutionally); (2) make amends with the victims as best as the Church could; and more generally (3) investigate within the Church itself the sources of its offenses and then countermand them. These three tasks, though logically distinct, intersect; making appropriate amends with the victims, for example, also requires that the Church change those elements within it that led it and its clergy to perpetrate the unjust harm in the first place.

In each of these three tasks the Church has generally failed. There is little indication that it has undertaken a genuine confrontation with the range of its specific offenses. It has not even honestly addressed its past antisemitism. A break with such antisemitism, as Garry Wills observes,

> is not easily accomplished, not for any institution, and least of all for an institution that claims never to have been wrong, never to have persecuted, never to have inflicted injustice. Given so much to hide, the impulse to keep on hiding becomes imperative, automatic, almost inevitable. The structures of deceit are ever less escapable. . . . It is thought, no doubt, that to let the truth slip through . . . would embarrass the Church. But to keep on evading the truth is a worse embarrassment, and a crime—an insult to those who have been wronged, and whose wrong will not be recognized.[26]

We should not be satisfied with vague, uplifting words that get in the way of a full and honest confrontation with the Church's wrongdoings, and the wrongdoings of two Popes and many bishops and priests, which would necessarily result in an extensive and explicit truthful discussion about this past.

As has been said about Germany so often that it has become a cliché, the Catholic Church has a "past that will not fade away."[27] The Church's way of dealing with its dishonorable past has been, essentially, to blind itself to the truth or to try to cover it up. (I refer here to Popes, the Vatican, and many national churches, though in some countries, such as France, bishops and others eventually acknowledged some essential truths about the Church's past, and individual churchmen in many countries have also been more forthright.) The Church denies or fails to address fully the antisemitism that was central to its precept and practice for centuries. It denies that its antisemitism led to the suffering of tens of millions of people over two millennia, including many violent assaults, expulsions, murders, and other crimes. It denies its central contribution to modern antisemitism and therefore Nazi antisemitism. It denies that its antisemitism influenced Church officials and laity to have insufficient sympathy for, and to be inadequately vigorous in aiding, the hounded and imperiled Jews. It denies that many of its officials and laity, influenced by the Church's antisemitism, actively aided the Germans' eliminationist assault upon the Jews. All one has to do is read "We Remember" or the Church's "Memory and Reconciliation: The Church and the Faults of the Past" from 2000 to see how much the Church denies and how little it acknowledges and seemingly takes to heart.[28]

Some national churches have at least partly confronted the past, yet the evidence suggests that even the best of these attempts remains vague and superficial, failing to focus on each of the kinds of transgressions that we discussed in part two and on those people who were culpable for them.[29] Indeed, the Church's principal bearing toward its offenses has been to cover up, dissimulate, make excuses, and divert attention. That the Church could seriously be considering declaring Pius XII a saint shows how far it is from a genuine confrontation with and understanding of its offenses, which include his.

The spate of recent books dwelling on the misconduct of Pius XII during the Holocaust has put the Church under pressure, as it wishes formally to begin the process that would typically lead to his canonization. That it would declare this man with his record a saint should not surprise anyone who knows that, in 2000, Pope John Paul II beatified Pius IX, the nineteenth-century father of modern Church antisemitism who declared in 1871 that by rejecting Christianity, Jews had become "dogs" and that "we have today in Rome unfortunately too many of these dogs, and we hear them barking in all the streets, and going around molesting people everywhere." Pius IX's antisemitism was not confined to his vivid invective. He was also a passionate persecutor of Jews and infamously refused to return the Jewish child Edgardo Mortara, abducted from his parents by one of the Church's inquisitors.[30]

Trying to quell the criticism about Pius XII, the Vatican announced in October 1999 its creation of a commission of three Catholic and three Jewish historians to investigate the Pope's conduct during the Holocaust. The commission's initial task was to review the Church's own published wartime diplomatic documents, ask questions, and produce a report.

In October 2000 the commission issued "The Vatican and the Holocaust: A Preliminary Report." Its members requested a broad range of materials necessary for them to complete their work, which indicated how much the Church was keeping buried and suggested, with their forty-seven questions, how damaging that unseen material might be. When after ten months of inaction it became clear to the commission that the Vatican had no intention of providing the materials, the commission suspended its work. The Vatican responded by accusing the Jewish members of the commission of conducting a "defamatory campaign" against the Church. (The Vatican did this even though the commission in its report bent over backward to be inoffensive, nonjudgmental, and understanding.[31]) The commission's Catholic members did not contest their Jewish colleagues' disclosure that they had always expected that the Church would give them access to the documents necessary for their work. Yet the Vatican did not attack the non-Jews. If, as the Church maintained, the Jews were lying, then so were the Catholics. Why, then, attack only the Jews, and why use the classical antisemitic trope that Jews are conducting a "campaign" against the Church?

That the Church was not going to allow the commission to undertake a serious probe of Pius XII might have been obvious from the beginning, because the priest whom the Vatican designated to be its representative to the commission, and the author of the Church's official public attack on the Jewish historians, the Jesuit Father Gumpel, is the Church's official handler of, and main public advocate for furthering, Pius XII's candidacy for canonization. Against all the evidence, Father Gumpel maintains that Pius XII was saintly regarding the Jews, "laboring ceaselessly" for them. Speaking in this regard, officially for the Church, he brands Jews who criticize Pius XII as responsible for "calumnious attacks against this great and saintly man" and even as "massive accomplices in the destruction of the Catholic Church," just as "Jews were the managers of Communism" (a Nazi-like charge), which "persecuted the Catholic Church."[32] As if such antisemitic slurs were not enough, Father Gumpel made a special point of stirring up antisemitism by emphatically declaring on *CBS News* to millions of people: "Let us be frank and open about this. . . . It is a fact that the Jews have killed Christ. This is an undeniable historical fact."[33]

John Paul II has not censured Father Gumpel. Father Gumpel has, however, been denounced by Gerhard Bodendorfer, the chief of the coordinating body for Christian-Jewish dialogue in Austria, as a man "hawking" such "old, obviously undistilled prejudices," such as "conspiracy theories about world Judaism" that "come out of the lowest drawer of antisemitism."[34] Yet Father Gumpel maintains a place of great honor and responsibility in the Church, which gave him the platform to defame Jews who merely seek the records they need for the work that the Church set them to do.

What is the Church hiding? Why does it forbid researchers from using its archives? If Pius XII were as blameless, heroic, and "saintly" as the Church maintains, then why does it not produce the evidence that would show this? Perhaps because the sequestered material does not support the Church's claims about Pius XII. As we have noted, even the sanitized selection of materials that the Church has published in its collection of wartime diplomatic material is powerfully indicting of him (no matter that the Church and its defenders continue to insist, Orwellian-like, the opposite). Why should Catholics, Jews, or anyone else continue to indulge the Church's obstinacy in not owning up to its past, as if it were an irresponsible child, rather than an almost two-millennia-old institution that teaches its members individual responsibility before God and humanity, and the necessity of doing penance before humanity as well as God?

How can this Church, with its history, continue to spread and teach demeaning notions about Jews and their religion, specifically, that Jews refuse to accept the truth that they can plainly see, that their religion has been superseded by Christianity?[35] The recently published new *Catechism of the Catholic Church*—for all of its improvements and its noticeable attempts to be as inoffensive toward and respectful of Jews as is possible within the limits of unbending doctrine—remains a supersessionist and deeply flawed document. Echoing the Christian Bible, it asserts among other things that the Jews bear a terrible burden because they willfully insist on being an obstacle to the well-being of the rest of humanity, preventing the arrival of the Messiah and human salvation because of their "unbelief" in Jesus.[36] Half a century after the Holocaust, the Catholic Church still promulgates a doctrine that explicitly holds the Jews, in their desire to remain Jews, to be the greatest obstacle to the well-being of Christians. The Central Committee of German Catholics, to its credit, has explicitly criticized the *Catechism* for this, for its replacement theology, its partly supersessionist presentation of the relationship of the Christian Bible to the Jewish Bible, and for its failure to address "the church's anti-Judaism . . . at all," which the German Catholics concede "is hard to understand today."[37]

In 1994, at the time of the publication of the new *Catechism*, John Paul II further confirmed this supersessionism in his book *Crossing the Threshold of Hope:* "The time when the people of the Old Covenant will be able to see themselves as part of the New is, naturally, a question to be left to the Holy Spirit."[38] When will the misguided Jews "be able" to see that they must accept the divinity of Jesus? Even the terminology that the Church uses to describe the Bibles, as "Old" and "New" Testaments, has a supersessionist dimension, particularly in light of the Church's centuries of teaching the "Old" Testament as a flawed and partly superseded book that pointed the way toward the new, better dispensation of the "New" Testament, and that heralded the coming of Jesus. Although there is disagreement among Catholic clergy and theologians on the relationship of the two Bibles, and some of them explicitly reject this supersessionist reading of that relationship, this is how the Catholic Church still doctrinally presents the relationship in its *Catechism*. The *Catechism* declares that "the economy of the Old Testament was deliberately so oriented that it should prepare for and declare in prophecy the coming of Christ, redeemer of all men." While the Church denies that the "New" Testament has rendered its predecessor "void" and affirms that "the books of the Old Testament" are "indispensable" and are "divinely inspired," it is adamant that "they contain matters imperfect and provisional," which are then replaced by the perfection of the "New" Testament.[39]

The Church has not done well in its first task of dealing with its offenses. It has barely investigated who was culpable for them. It has not brought them to justice. On the second task of making amends with the victims, it has offered vague words of regret and sometimes apology for only a small portion of the offenses that it, its national churches, and its Popes, bishops, and priests committed. Never has the Church issued the necessary explicit acknowledgment of the broad range of its members' transgressions. Why has there been no genuine mea culpa from the Church? After all, Catholics are supposed to do penance, which in addition to confessing one's sins to a priest includes the admission "of faults to one's brethren."[40] Even the welcomed words of apology, when coming from the Vatican in particular, have been simultaneously undermined by the obfuscation and the self-exculpatory excuse making of the kind found in "We Remember."

Why have the Church and its defenders fabricated the idea that Pius XII engineered behind the scenes an extensive Church rescue effort of Jews? Why, in August 1946, did Pius XII utter the falsehood that "in the past we condemned repeatedly the persecutions that a fanatical anti-Semitism unleashed against the Hebrew people"?[41] Even in this historical fabrication the Pope could bring himself to speak only in the most perfunctory and oblique manner about the Holocaust. Why did Pius XII's Church after the war give refuge, protection, and aid to the mass murderers of Jews, helping them to evade justice, instead of helping those who sought to punish them? Why in the first days of May 1945 did Germany's Cardinal Bertram, upon learning of Hitler's death, order that in all the churches of his archdiocese a special requiem, namely, "a solemn requiem mass be held in commemoration of the Führer," so that his Catholic flock could pray to the Almighty, in accord with the requiem's liturgy, that the Almighty's son, Hitler, be admitted to paradise? Why would one of Germany's leading cardinals pay homage to this executioner of the Jewish people with a solemn requiem mass, which the Church allows to be celebrated only for a believing member of

Cardinal Adolf Bertram (middle) during his seventy-fifth birthday celebration, at which he received a letter of congratulations from Hitler.

the Church (which Hitler was not) when the Church deems it to be in its public interest?[42] With this revealing deed, Cardinal Bertram symbolically closed the Catholic Church's role in the Nazi period while inaugurating the coming era of the Church's moral evasion over its past.

The current Pope, John Paul II, and many national churches, their bishops and priests, have taken some evident, often heartfelt measures to acknowledge officially the horrors of the past and to make amends with Jews. These too are welcomed, although they were tardy in their arrival, more than half a century after the end of the Holocaust. And what they contain does not come close to meeting the Church's needs in these respects, the nature of which is elaborated below.

On the third task, eradicating the sources of the offenses, the Church's forward steps have been slow in coming, though eventually they have been substantial.

If the Church and Pius XII, as their defenders insist, had really not been antisemitic and had really tried to do everything they could to help Jews, then why, after the defeat of Germany, did they choose to devote energy to helping the mass murderers escape justice and choose not to do some simple things to help the victimized Jews?

Pius XII lived for thirteen years after the war, but he did not publicly condemn the extermination of the Jews explicitly. Nor did he repudiate the Church's antisemitism. He refused again and again to make public statements condemning antisemitism, even though he was repeatedly beseeched by some Church leaders, foreign diplomats, and Jewish leaders to do so,[43] and even though other Christian churches were doing so. In 1948 the World Council of Churches Assembly declared at its inaugural meeting: "We call upon all the churches we represent to denounce anti-Semitism, no matter what its origin, as absolutely irreconcilable with the profession and practice of the Christian faith. Anti-Semitism is a sin against God and man."[44] Why did the many Protestant churches that were there denounce antisemitism, "no matter what its origin," as a sin in 1948 but Pius XII could not? The World Council of Churches also asked German Protestant churches for a statement of guilt. Pius XII would not do the same for the German Catholic Church. Instead, he went in the opposite direction. He pretended that German Catholics had been a model, and to persuade others, he pronounced the blatant lie that they had "wholeheartedly" opposed Nazism.[45]

Why, when a putative threat to the Catholic Church's existence could no longer be invoked, did this Pope, supposedly a friend of the Jews, not speak critically and forcefully about the crime of the Holocaust and the evil of antisemitism? Did he not think that all the Catholics who aided in the slaughter, that all the Germans and Austrians who passionately supported Hitler, the eliminationist assault on the Jews, and even the extermination itself, all the Catholics in Europe who were antisemites, did he not think that they might benefit from moral and practical instruction on the evils of their antisemitic beliefs and actions? Did he not think that Catholics coming of age after the war in continuing antisemitic environments across Europe (and beyond) should be warned about the evils of Jew-hatred? Pius XII's postwar failure to work to remove the stain of antisemitism from the hearts of Catholics aside, did he not simply want to express his condemnation of, and publicly reflect upon, this unsurpassed evil of his age and of his papacy?

Instead of doing this, Pius XII's Church continued to preach its age-old antisemitism in its doctrine, theology, and liturgy. Pius XII also sought to stop others in the Church from fighting antisemitism, such as Gertrud Luckner. Luckner, a member of the Catholic charity organization Caritas, tried during the Nazi period to create a Catholic network to rescue Jews. Even though she had difficulty rousing others to participate, she did manage to save some Jews, and for her lonely efforts the regime arrested her and sent her to the Ravensbrück concentration camp in 1943. After the war she became the leader of a small, avowedly philosemitic German Catholic group that was the only Catholic group in Germany seeking to reconcile Christians and Jews. Luckner "innocently sought the pope's support for her work." How did Pius XII greet the request of this courageous woman who had given so much to help Jews, trying only to do what the Pope and his apologists have claimed he too wanted to do? He refused to lend her aid, Luckner "discovered instead that the Holy See intended to investigate her. In June of 1948 the Holy Office issued a *monitum* (warning) to the German church charging that efforts of religious groups to attack antisemitism were encouraging religious indifferentism (the belief that one religion is as good as the next)."[46] (After two years, she was cleared of the charge.) Also in light of all these actions of Pius XII after the war, and all his failures to act, how can we take seriously the whitewashing notion that the Pope was moved during the war principally by a beneficent concern for the general welfare of Jews?

What was wrong with this Church that, after an antisemitic catastrophe of the Holocaust's magnitude, it did not immediately renounce the antisemitism that had been at its core? What was wrong with this Church that it continued to spread antisemitism throughout the Catholic world, including the Christ-killing blood libel that all Jews are responsible for Jesus' death and many other calumnies?[47] The Catholic Church taught such hate-filled and enmity-inspiring notions explicitly and purposely, as it had for centuries, in its instruction to the young. Examples abound from the postwar period. An Italian Catholic textbook declared about Jews: "This people will be torn from their land . . . scattered through the world . . . under the burden of a divine curse which will accompany them through the course of their history." A French Catholic textbook: "The Jews remain those who reject Christ, and the people whose ancestors solemnly asked that his blood fall upon them." A Spanish Catholic textbook: "The wretched Jews could not imagine the accumulation of calamities that would befall them and their descendants for having taken upon themselves the responsibility for the blood of the Just One, the Son of God." Given these teachings, read by the children of Catholic Europe during the postwar period, how could the Holocaust *not* be in some senses understood as just punishment?[48]

It took the Church twenty years after the Holocaust before it produced the reforms of the Second Vatican Council. Twenty more years of explicitly teaching the most damaging antisemitism to hundreds of millions of people. What could be more egregious? What could be more shocking from the perspective of reforming the Church? Why did this supposedly non-antisemitic Church continue to cling, as it did, to its hate-filled views of Jews before promulgating some necessary though still insufficient reforms announced in October 1965 in *Nostra Aetate*, "In Our Time," the Second Vatican Council's "Declaration on the Relation of the Church to Non-Christian Religions"? And even then, there was so much resistance within the Church even to its halting, forward steps. Why has the Church, even when it moves forward, been so timid in fighting antisemitism?[49]

Vatican II was convened by Pope John XXIII, a progressive and humble man who wanted to drag the Church politically and, in the eyes of many, theologically into the modern world. He was a genuine friend of the Jews, having himself, as papal legate in Turkey during the war, tried his best to help Jews and managed to save many Jews' lives by providing them with immigration certificates. But within the Church the resistance to an official renunciation of even aspects of the Church's antisemitism was great. Certain cardinals made several attempts to sabotage the reforms, which only the Pope's intervention forfended. Although John XXIII's sudden death meant that Vatican II would go only a small way toward acknowledging and redressing the problems with its doctrine, theology, and practices toward Jews, the momentum that he established was too great for Vatican II to be completely short-circuited.

The bishops' maneuverings during the Council and the various drafts of the Council's statement on the Jews show how resistant the assembled bishops were to rectifying the Church's antisemitic injustices, including its historical fabrications. They rejected a draft proposal that explicitly and unequivocally declared that "the Chosen people cannot without injustice be termed a deicidal race." Wills comments that "the same Council fathers who did not want a reference to deicide also sought to exclude any mention of past persecutions by the church, or of Christian guilt for them. They won [against the liberal bishops] on all three issues." The deeply flawed and tepid statement on the Jews that the Council did promulgate contained the historically misleading assertion that the "authorities of the Jews and those who followed their lead pressed for the death of Christ." This is not surprising since Pope Paul VI—the former confidant and whitewasher of Pius XII and contributor to the program that aided the German mass murderers to flee abroad and escape justice after the war—at a crucial time during the deliberation, Passion Sunday 1965, gave a sermon that explicitly accused the Jews of deicide, saying that the Jewish people, when Jesus came to them as the Messiah, "derided, scorned, and ridiculed him, and finally killed him." It is therefore also not surprising that the Council's statement also fails to mention a most basic fact that would go a long way to demythologizing Jesus' death and correcting the record for all misled Catholics, namely, that it was the Roman authorities alone who passed the death sentence on, and then crucified, Jesus. The Council's statement did lift "blame" from "the Jews of today" and from Jews alive then, though not from all of them. But the explicit clearing of the Jews of "deicide" is gone. Wills writes:

> In an item-by-item vote of the whole Council, the vote against the sentence that opposed blaming Jews for the death of Christ was 188, and that against opposition to calling the Jews cursed was 245. Admittedly, this is a small minority—the votes for the statements were 1,875 and 1,821 respectively. But it is astounding that even the weakened form of the statement, unaccompanied by any recognition of past persecution or any expression of sorrow and repentance, could still be rejected by hundreds of Catholic bishops.[50]

The tardiness and obstructionism of the reforms notwithstanding, the Church produced significant, necessary changes in its stance toward Jews at Vatican II, and since then.

Nostra Aetate did formally lift the blood libel of Christ-killers from the heads of all Jews not alive during the time of Jesus. For all *Nostra Aetate*'s substantial failings, because the Church's depiction of Jews for the previous two millennia had been so injurious and hate-inducing, the Vatican II statement was an enormous step forward, and this is how it is, almost without criticism, portrayed. It initiated an era of greater Church tolerance toward Jews and of the Church working to put an end to aspects of its and many of its members' antisemitism. Building on Vatican II, the Church has progressively altered Catholic doctrine, liturgy, and teachings (including textbooks) about Jews in a manner that, although far from perfect, has been substantial and has, with the stubborn exception of the Christian Bible itself, put a halt to most of the contempt and enmity for Jews that the Church used to explicitly teach Catholics. Along with excising many of its own antisemitic features, the Church has begun to teach a degree of tolerance and acceptance of Jews (and peoples of other faiths) that was previously all but unimaginable in the Catholic world. John Paul II, who has done much to foster these initiatives, can today speak of Jews in glowing terms, declaring, "This extraordinary people continues to bear signs of its divine election."[51]

Still, the substantive progress of Vatican II, when it finally came, was itself a figurative half measure at best. The forward steps toward internal reform, welcomed and beneficial though they may be, have been halting, selective, often superficial, and deeply inadequate. Among many other examples of antisemitic passages being taught by the Church to the Catholic faithful, the citation of the Jews as killers of Jesus remains in the Good Friday liturgy to this day.[52] The official prayer book of the American Catholic Church still includes the "reproaches," which are antisemitic chants blaming the Jews for the death of Jesus. They are not taken from the Christian Bible but are traditional works that incite antipathies, or worse, toward Jews, some of which date from the ninth century. The reproaches take the form of Jesus reminding the Jewish people of his beneficence to the Jews in events recounted in the Jewish Bible, which Jesus then contrasts with the Jews' imputed cruelty to him. "My people," asks Jesus, "what have I done to you? How have I offended you? Answer me! I led you out of Egypt, from slavery to freedom, but you led your Savior to the cross." The Good Friday reproaches repeatedly adopt the form of the Jews inverting goodness by repaying Jesus' good acts with their own allegedly wicked analogues. Jesus reproaches the Jews with "for your sake I scourged your captors and their first-born sons, but you brought your scourges down on me." He reproaches them with "I led you on your way in a pillar of cloud, but you led me to Pilate's court." He reproaches them with "for you I struck down the kings of Canaan, but you struck my head with a reed." He reproaches them with "I raised you to the height of majesty, but you raised me high on a cross." The American Catholic Church, in choosing to begin the third millennium by portraying the Jews as the dark side of these Manichean oppositions, reminiscent in this sense of the devil himself, continues the Church's centuries-long antisemitic traditions. Because the reproaches are not sacred Scripture, there is no religious argument for continuing to spread their libelous message among the more than sixty million American Catholics on one of the most important occasions in the Christian year and a peak time for Church attendance. The reproaches are a discretionary, willful addition by the American Catholic Church to the Good Friday liturgy. Though they are not obligatory for the service itself, indeed the American Catholic Church designates them as optional, an official in the United States bishops' liturgy secretariat estimates that 40 percent of the country's parishes chant them.[53]

More significantly, the Church's lectionaries for mass, despite several revisions since the war, have for decades included significant antisemitism, or as Norman Beck, who has studied them, calls the passages, "defamatory anti-Jewish polemic." The Church's anti-Jewish supersessionist creed lives well within the Church in many other ways: in its doctrine that the Christian Bible, which it calls the "New Testament," partly supersedes the

Jewish Bible, to which it gives the appellation of the "Old Testament"; in statements in the Christian Bible itself to this effect; in the Church's inter- pretation and presentation of the Jewish Bible as a flawed book that points the way to the true revelation of the Christian Bible; and many Christian biblical passages and in its doctrine that continues to make it at least unlikely that Jews can enter heaven, and, whatever some Church teachings and the- ologians may otherwise say or imply, which will reasonably be understood to mean that Jews will go to hell. In its Bible the Catholic Church continues to impart to all Catholics that Jews are the children of hell's master.[54]

These are instances of what euphemistically might be called the Catholic Church's Bible problem: Its foundational text is the source of, and conse- crating authority for, the most damaging antisemitism.[55]

Take, as one of many examples, the unambiguous language of the Chris- tian Bible in the Gospel According to Matthew regarding Jesus' death: "And the whole [Jewish] people said in reply, 'His blood be upon us and upon our children.' " To an ordinary reader, this would suggest exactly what it sug- gests: that the whole Jewish people and all their children, including Jews today, bear the guilt for Jesus' death. Even though Vatican II lifted the charge of guilt from the Jewish people as a whole and the Catholic Church's commentary in its own official Bible says as much, that same official com- mentary nevertheless first confirms that the obvious meaning of this text is its actual meaning. Regarding the phrase "the whole people," the Catholic Church's commentary confirms that "Matthew sees in those who speak these words *the* entire *people* (Greek *laos*) of Israel." Regarding what the Christian Bible has the entire Jewish people declaring with alacrity, "His blood be upon us and upon our children," the Church's commentary states that "the responsibility for Jesus' death is accepted by the nation that was God's special possession . . . his own *people* . . . and they thereby lose that high privilege."[56]

Or take Paul's First Letter to the Thessalonians, where he tells them of "the Jews, who killed both the Lord Jesus and the prophets and persecuted us." Paul then adopts a typological and apocalyptic mode of discussing Jews, telling the Thessalonians that the Jews have not changed because "they do not please God, and are opposed to everyone, trying to prevent us from speaking to the Gentiles that they may be saved, thus constantly filling up the measure of their sins." For their sins, the Jews are to be punished. According to Paul, "the wrath of God has finally begun to come upon them."[57]

The Church certainly urges Catholics to accept the Christian Bible as God's word, believe its lessons, and learn to live their lives according to its content. The Church certainly hopes that they will and certainly believes that its efforts in this regard are not in vain, that many Catholics are indeed learning the Christian Bible's content and using it as a guide to their outlooks on the world and their conduct. The Church is certainly not entirely wrong. So why would we, why would the Catholic Church believe that many Catholics do not also believe and use as a guide to this world the Christian Bible's enormously damaging statements about Jews? Why would we and the Catholic Church not believe that many devout Catholic readers wonder, who are these Jews today, the spiritual descendants of that people who rejected Jesus and who the Christian Bible says bear the guilt of his blood, and whom it repeatedly deprecates as an inherently sinister force? Is it not reasonable to suppose that of the hundreds of millions of people who read the Christian Bible as a divine text, a large number of them come away thinking ill of contemporary Jews? How could we, how could the Church, come to any other conclusion?

More than twenty years after Vatican II, almost 25 percent of Germans could not disagree with the statement that "one sometimes hears that the Jews have so many problems because God is punishing them for crucifying Jesus Christ." Given that only 35 percent of Germans categorized themselves as "religious, devout people," the 25 percent who do not deny the link between the Jews being Christ-killers and their persecution takes on much greater weight as a percentage of those who are devout. Catholics endorsed the Christ-killer libel twice as frequently as Protestants. The good news in Germany is that younger people, including those who are religious, reject this canard much more than do older people.[58] Still, one researcher who, around the same time, plumbed the nature of antisemitism deeper than the superficial survey data ever do concluded that 80 percent of the antisemites in Germany still grounded their antisemitism in Christian antisemitic characterizations of Jews.[59]

In Austria, a Catholic country, where the education about the Nazi period has been much less extensive than in Germany, one third of the people would not say in 1991 that it is wrong to maintain that "Jews are still responsible for the death of Jesus Christ."[60] The Italian people are almost famously less than devout in their Catholicism, and compared with other European peoples during the twentieth century, they have been relatively less antisemitic and their antisemitism has been milder in quality. Yet today 43 percent of Italians still consider Jews to be guilty for the crucifixion of Jesus, and 23 percent of them are "sure of the existence of dangerous and powerful Jewish lobbies."[61]

Just from these data about Germany, a country of then roughly sixty million people, Austria with a population of about eight million, and Italy with a population of more than fifty-five million people, we see that many tens of millions of Christians, and Catholics in particular, subscribe to the central biblical blood libel about Jews. Surely, still many more, who reject the notion that the Jews today are guilty for Jesus' death (though they may still believe the falsehood that the Jews of Jesus' time are guilty for his death) still harbor other Christian and Catholic antisemitic notions, whether these notions come directly from the Christian Bible or from the teachings of the churches that have become embedded in the culture of antisemitism in Europe and around the world.[62] The significance and damaging nature of the belief that Jews are Christ-killers or are responsible for the death of Jesus is even greater. It has been firmly established that this belief predisposes people to believing other, even secular antisemitic accusations about Jews, to have hostile feelings toward Jews, and to countenance discriminatory conduct toward them.[63]

Notwithstanding this continuing troubling state of the views of Jews held by Christians and specifically by Catholics, everyone should recognize that there has been considerable goodwill toward Jews on the part of many people in the Church. John XXIII was, and John Paul II continues to be, distraught over the Holocaust. Each has seen it as the Church's obligation to repair relations with Jews, and within the Church they are not alone. In national churches around Europe, the United States, and elsewhere, Catholic bishops and priests have done much to establish a spirit of greater respect for Jews and their religious and communal organizations, and to institute cooperation on matters of joint concern, including Catholic-Jewish dialogue groups, interfaith working groups, and, on appropriate civic occasions, joint services. In fact, such cooperation and goodwill are extensive enough that they can dominate our field of vision, obscuring the deeper problems that many—choosing to privilege the reigning spirit of genuine progress that they rightly want to further—would prefer to ignore or to pretend do not exist.

Goodwill and conviviality are not enough. The goodwill here is based on the dogmatic and imperious assumptions that the Catholic Church has done and can do no wrong, and that the Jews are fundamentally in error and eventually must come to see that they should embrace both Jesus, in whose name they have been persecuted for millennia, and the very Church that has been the progenitor of much of that persecution. This goodwill, good as it is and as positive as its consequences have been, rests on a partly flawed foundation. Moreover, it has been greatly circumscribed. The Church undertakes measures to address its principal tasks on its own terms, in its own limited way. The Church's failure in its first task of its needed moral reckoning, to confront its offenses during the Nazi period, has left it and its members with an inadequate understanding of the Church's moral culpability, and therefore with an inadequate grounding for thinking through what it must do to make amends with the victims and to right itself.

The three tasks that the Church has yet to accomplish, its partial and sometimes substantial measures notwithstanding, are the principal components of the moral reckoning that the Church must necessarily undertake if it is to discharge its duty to humanity and to God. The first task, of confronting its own and its clergy's offenses and their degree of culpability, was discussed in part two, which showed how such a reckoning would proceed and what conclusions it produces. The second and third tasks, of making amends with the victims and of reforming itself, are taken up here. As in part two, the discussion here is not meant to be comprehensive but merely to indicate some of the central issues and problems, and some ways that the Church might deal with them. Because these two distinct tasks do have many points of intersection, the discussion here moves freely between them.

RESTITUTION: MATERIAL, POLITICAL, AND MORAL

These two tasks can be properly called restitution. The Church committed numerous moral offenses against Jews—crimes and political offenses are also moral offenses—and bears great moral culpability. The way of goodness requires that for an offense, the offender make restitution to the victim. How should we conceive of restitution? What might its components be, in general and in this case?

Restitution is the perpetrator's duty to compensate his victim for an unjust injury. The perpetrator cannot undo such an injury fully or sometimes even at all, such as when the injury is murder. The burden of the restitutor then is to do whatever else he can, in order to redress the injury that he caused the victim. (This means that the victim's own sense of justice, although not necessarily determinative, must be generously incorporated into the deliberations about the restitutor's duties.) When the moral fog has cleared and the wrong is recognized, those bearing culpability for it must endeavor to right that wrong. And just as we saw in part two that it is our obligation to judge, it is also our obligation to encourage the culpable to do what they must. The Catholic Church agrees. It expresses its agreement in even stronger language: "It is praiseworthy to *impose* restitution [on someone, in order] 'to correct vices and maintain justice'" [my emphasis].[64]

This principle, of the obligation to perform restitution for inflicting unjust injury, applies not just to the Catholic Church but also to every institution and every person. The Church agrees with this. It holds that for every sin a person must do penance, which explicitly includes "works of reparation."[65] The obligation to undertake and complete restitution, or in the Church's terms, penance, applies to the Catholic Church and clergy for their offenses toward Jews and, for that matter, toward all other people against whom they committed offenses. It applies to Germany and Germans, not only for their offenses against Jews, which are well known, but also for their full ledger of offenses against non-Jews: among others, homosexuals, Gypsies, the victims of the so-called Euthanasia program, slave laborers (most of whom were not Jews), "asocials," the forcibly sterilized, persecuted German Communists and Socialists, and the many murdered and suffering people in all of the countries that Germany occupied and bludgeoned. None of them has received anything close to adequate restitution. It also applies to the German corporations that participated in mass murder, used slave labor, and committed other offenses.

It applies to all countries, institutions, and people who have committed or supported mass murder or other grievous offenses. It applies to the United States, states of the American South, and Americans, most particularly southerners, for the crimes and other offenses of slavery, discrimination against African-Americans, and segregation. African-Americans have also received only a pittance of what their country, my country, morally owes them. It applies to the United States and Americans for their country's many offenses, including for mass murder, against Native Americans, for the unjust internment of Japanese-Americans during World War II, and for a catalogue of other offenses. It applies to Serbia and Serbs for their wide-ranging crimes, including mass murder, against Croats, Bosnian Muslims, and Kosovars during the breakup of Yugoslavia. It applies to Croats for their crimes, including mass murder, against Serbs during the Nazi period and during their ethnic cleansing of Serbs during the breakup of Yugoslavia. It applies to Israel and Jewish Israelis on the one hand for their crimes and other offenses against Palestinians and other Arabs, and, on the other hand, to Palestine and Palestinians and to Arab countries and their peoples for their crimes and offenses against Israel and Jews.

This listing does not mean to imply that any or all of these offenses and the culpability attached to them are the same or equivalent, in kind or in scope. They actually vary enormously in quality and degree. The distinctions among them, which would be made using consistently applied impartial criteria, however, are best left for another discussion. Here I mean to say that in each case, institutions (this includes countries) and at least some of their members have committed grievous offenses for which they owe substantial restitution. The principle of making restitution for offenses applies to everyone. If and how it is performed is always a political issue, which does not mean that the principle does not apply, only that we recognize that in the world of politics principle may not always be, or at all be, the actual guide for conduct.

The duty of restitution is incurred by individuals and by institutional entities. This is not collective guilt or blame. Guilt and blame is never collective, never incurred for a person's identity but only for his individual choices to act (and not to act) and for the consequences of those choices. Only individuals are guilty or blameworthy, and they are so only for their individual offenses. After the offenses have occurred, a moral responsibility called restitution exists to redress the unjust harm. This responsibility is borne by two different classes of people. Individuals who are culpable for the crimes or other offenses owe restitution. Other people, who themselves are not guilty or blameworthy—nor could they be—for stances and acts that were not their own, can also owe restitution. A person, by choosing to be a member of an institution that owes restitution, obliges himself to accept the institution's duty as his own, and then must discharge that obligation as best he can.

It is accepted that a country's government, and therefore its political community and its people, bear the responsibility to discharge the treaty and other legal obligations incurred by their country, including by previous governments. Similarly, a religious institution such as the Catholic Church has ongoing duties and obligations, incurred by its and its officials' own past deeds. Conceptually and legally, political and other institutions, including the Catholic Church, have the status of persons. The Church itself recognizes itself as a person (its personhood deriving from God) and has codified it as part of its Canon Law: "The Catholic Church and the Apostolic See have the status of a moral person . . . "[66] The obligations incurred by such "moral persons" in principle are attached not to the religion of Christianity or to its Catholic variant, but to the Christian institutions that incurred the duties, especially to the Catholic Church, which is an institution with enormous physical, organizational, and doctrinal continuity.[67] It may be the oldest continuous political and social institution in the world. When a country has such obligations, it does not mean that all of its people are guilty (when guilt is at issue) or responsible for creating those obligations—many of the people often have nothing to do with them. The same holds for the duty to provide restitution. As I have repeatedly stressed, all Germans, for example, who were children during World War II or who were born after the war cannot possibly bear guilt or responsibility of any kind whatsoever for the commission of the crimes and offenses that their country and their country-men perpetrated during the Nazi period, or for creating the country's ongo-ing duty of restitution that is the consequence of these crimes and offenses. Germans who were adults during the Nazi period who did not commit offenses also bear no culpability for them. Still many people who never themselves committed offenses—though they are not in any way, collec-tively or individually, guilty or responsible for the commission of the offenses—are nonetheless, *after the offenses are committed,* by dint of their membership in the culpable institution, in some measure responsible for discharging the institution's duty to provide restitution.

Precisely because this obligation is derived not from a person's identity but from his membership choices, an individual who himself did not com-mit an offense is able to relieve himself of this obligation to provide restitu-tion. He can terminate his membership in the country or institution. A German can emigrate from Germany and renounce his citizenship. A Catholic can leave the Catholic Church. But as long as a person continues to choose to retain membership in a country or an institution, he cannot selec-tively accrue for himself the benefits of that membership without its atten-dant responsibilities and obligations, even if they are burdensome. If a German is to accept his country's political heritage of Bismarck or Weimar or even of the Federal Republic, then he must also accept Nazism as part of it, even if he—like most Germans today—abhors Nazism. If he is to accept the benefits that being a member of the Federal Republic brings him, then he must also accept the burdens that the Federal Republic bears by being the political system of the political community of Germany that succeeded the Nazi political system. But a German citizen who decides to stop being a German citizen by renouncing his citizenship is no longer obliged to dis-charge the obligations of a German citizen, including the duty of restitu-tion, because those obligations were attached to his now abandoned political membership and are not attached to his new political membership. Simi-larly, a Catholic who leaves the Church is relieved of the duty of restitution. This is true even if she remains a Christian, because it is by her institutional membership, not by her identity as a Christian or by her beliefs about God, that she incurs for herself institutionally grounded duties and burdens. Obviously, a person can be a Christian without antisemitism being a part of her beliefs or practices. And there are *many* such Christians today who are not antisemitic and who have utterly rejected the antisemitism that contin-ues to exist in Christian scripture and teachings as false and pernicious. If a person chooses to be such a Christian, without being a member of a Church that institutionally bears the duty of restitution toward Jews, then that person's duties and obligations to Jews are no different from, or greater than, her general duties and obligations to human beings.

It cannot be emphasized enough that a collective entity based on identity, such as the German *people,* can never be guilty or responsible. In addition to the individual Germans who themselves bear culpability for their own unjust offenses against Jews during the Nazi period, it is the political community, the Federal Republic of Germany, which includes its members, that bears the responsibility to discharge the duty of restitution, even if it is the case, as it is today, that the overwhelming majority of its members are themselves not guilty of anything. (The distinction here is substantive, not semantic. A member of the German political community, namely a citizen of the Federal Republic of Germany, who is of exclusively non-German ancestry, say Italian, and whom most Germans would therefore not consider to be a member of the German *people* [das deutsche Volk] has the same responsibilities regarding restitution that other German citizens have. However, an ethnic German, who is considered a member of the German people but who is not a citizen of Germany does not have any such responsibility unless he as an individual committed an offense.) Similarly, it is not the Catholic people but the religious, social, and political community of the Catholic Church, with its members, that have the responsibility to discharge the Church's duty of restitution, even if few individual Catholics alive today bear guilt, responsibility, or blame for the commission of the deeds. This assertion is hardly radical. Indeed, it is the commonly accepted convention for political and social institutions and their members. The Catholic Church itself agrees with this view of its and its faithful's responsibility to provide restitution. The American Catholic bishops explain in their booklet *Catholic Teaching on the Shoah,* that "*We Remember*'s call for the Church's ongoing repentance for these sins [against Jews], will involve for most Christians an assumption of responsibility for our collective Christian past, not personal guilt. . . . those born after the war have no reason to feel personally guilty; but members of the one Body of Christ, the Church, have every reason to assume responsibility to ensure that nothing like it can ever happen again."[68]

A *people*—Germans, Christians, Jews, Americans, French—*can never bear guilt or even the subsequent responsibility to provide restitution for offenses.* Those who assert otherwise are spreading the moral abomination of collective guilt, which includes the collective inheritance of such guilt. Collective guilt and inherited collective guilt are a moral abomination whether they are attributed to the Jewish people, as was the case for millennia, to the German people, as was popularly done after World War II, to Catholics, or to any other people. It cannot be emphasized enough that it is only culpable individuals and culpable institutions, and then, after the commission of the offenses, the institutions' free and willing members, that bear responsibility for making amends with the victims and for restitution.

As a moral and practical matter, it is the institution itself and its leaders that are most responsible for taking the measures necessary to discharge the institution's duty of restitution. Precisely because they govern and run the institution, the leaders of an institution that is in need of providing restitution are the ones who must fashion, set in motion, and implement restitutive measures, who must mobilize the institution's members, its rank and file, behind them, and who must ensure that the restitution is successfully completed. Even though an institution's members—whether they are the citizens of the Federal Republic of Germany, the citizens of the United States, or the members of the Catholic Church—also bear the responsibility of providing the restitution owed by the membership of an institution, individual members as a practical matter discharge their responsibility easily. They must urge their leaders to accomplish what they must. They must support such initiatives when their leaders and others put them forward. And they must themselves contribute, in whatever manner each person reasonably believes that he or she can, to the fulfillment of the outstanding duty. Where prejudice has been an issue, this includes individuals educating themselves, and helping to educate their families, friends, and acquaintances, about the falseness of the prejudice and the real substantial injuries that it causes. The practical burden of providing restitution that ordinary lay Catholics bear is therefore not onerous.

In the case of the Catholic Church, the leadership responsible for providing the necessary restitution is the clergy, starting with its leader, the Pope, and moving on down the hierarchy to national Catholic Church leaderships, to individual bishops, to parish priests. Given that a core duty of the clergy at all levels is pastoral care and instruction, substantial features of the restitution owed to Jews, as we shall see, can easily and naturally be incorporated into what the clergy already does.

Although institutions routinely fail to discharge their duty of restitution fully and often fail to do so at all, this no more reduces the outstanding duty of any given institution to provide restitution than it makes the moral shirkers right or virtuous. That one institution cannot disembarrass itself of its duties by pointing to others that have committed great evil yet that have not provided restitution is that much more obvious in the case of an institution, such as the Catholic Church, that claims to be not only a moral institution but *the* moral institution of the world. This is also true for people, such as Popes, bishops, and priests, who present themselves, foremost, as spiritual and moral leaders and who, certainly most of them, are genuine in their desire to conduct moral lives.

All restitution is moral because it is the word used to name the duty to right moral wrongs. Restitution has not typically been understood in this way. Discussions about restitution usually focus on material restitution (money and lost property), for which the word "restitution" has, unfortunately, become almost a synonym.[69] The need to provide material restitution is real, but material restitution is only one of three components of restitution. The other two components are political and more exclusively moral. When I say that the Catholic Church needs to perform restitution, I mean it in the broadest sense of the term, including material, political, and moral kinds. We need to investigate what the various components of the Church's restitution might be, with reference to the Holocaust, though the components would, in principle, apply and be binding upon those needing to provide restitution for any crimes against any victims in any era.

The operational principle adopted here is that restitution should, as much as possible, be given in kind for the type and character of the transgression. Providing restitution of the most similar in type and quantity to the harm done has the advantages of being, as a rule, the easiest to specify, the fairest, and the most likely to be satisfactory to the victims. This, it should be clear, is not a moral principle but a practical procedure, which seems to me to be the best but which is certainly subject to discussion or revision, either in general or in specific circumstances.

MATERIAL RESTITUTION is the most conventional and straightforward type. For the material benefits that institutions or people accrued owing to the eliminationist persecution of the Jews or for material losses they inflicted on the Jews, they owe material restitution. A person who steals from others or enriches himself through the criminal misuse of others or who through unjust acts causes others to suffer material losses needs to make good for the victims' losses. This is so obvious and well established in law and in our conventional moral notions that it need not be elaborated upon. So it is disheartening that this principle is contested when it comes to the victims of the Holocaust, and that the just claims of these victims have been denounced as outrageous and extortionist by many Germans, Swiss, and their apologists, including neo-Nazis and other antisemites.[70]

Material restitution, for all its necessity, has several shortcomings. For large-scale crimes it is difficult to bring about in any but token sums. The larger the scope of the crime, the more politically unfeasible it is to transfer the massive sums owed the victims. Even if an amount equivalent to the real material losses of the victims would somehow be offered, it would still be inadequate as restitution because when mass murder is the issue, the victims lose incalculably more. In the case of the Holocaust, six million of the Jewish victims lost their lives. Virtually all survivors, and many other Jews from countries not conquered by Germany, lost family members. And the survivors suffered injuries, indignities, and trauma of incomprehensible magnitude. Material restitution is incommensurate with the crimes of the Holocaust. Neal Sher, the former head of United States government's Office of Strategic Investigation, which brings legal proceedings against the mass murderers of the Nazi period, has said, that if we use contemporary jurisprudential standards of monetary compensation for injuries, there would not be enough money in the world to compensate Jews for what they lost.[71] Even if adequate material restitution were somehow possible, it would still address only one aspect of the outstanding obligations. For the other aspects of those obligations different kinds of restitution are needed.

The Church did engage in this kind of criminality, but unlike in the cases of certain European countries, corporations, and individuals, it was probably the least of its violations. Material restitution is critical when discussing what Germany, Switzerland, and other countries, and what many profiteering, once criminal corporations, including German firms, such as Allianz, Daimler-Benz (now DaimlerChrysler), Siemens, and Volkswagen, Swiss banks, such as UBS, Italian insurance companies, such as Generali, need to do. The German Catholic Church has acknowledged that it also used several thousand people who were not Jews as slave labor from which it benefited materially. It has agreed to contribute individual compensation directly to surviving victims and 5 million deutsche marks (about 2.5 million dollars) to the German Foundation for former slave laborers set up as part of the recent slave-labor settlement that the German government and industry concluded with Jewish groups and other interested parties (of the foundation's 10 billion deutsche marks, or about 5 billion dollars, roughly 80 percent is expected to go to non-Jews).[72] So the Church, at least here, though only under public pressure from the German government and other German politicians, has conceded that it committed a great crime (not just an offense of omission), for which it must pay monetary restitution. Yet even for just this one crime, the Church has yet to confront the other kinds of restitution, especially moral restitution, that it owes.

It appears all but certain that the Catholic Church profited from the gold that Croatian mass murderers stole from their Jewish and Serbian victims and brought with them to the Vatican when the Church gave them refuge there. The Vatican however, unlike the Swiss, refuses to make its bank records accessible to independent auditors, so the actual size of the sums that it may have received are unknown. It is likely that the figure is considerably less than eight million dollars in today's money.[73] As we will see, compared with the other aspects of restitution for which the Church bears responsibility, the material restitution that it appears to owe, though substantial, is small. (I, for one, so as not to muddy the discussion of the more critical issues of political and moral restitution, would deem it advisable not to press for the sums, except for the necessary payments to former slave laborers and an additional symbolic payment for outstanding debts that would sustain the principle of material restitution. Others might reasonably differ.)

Political restitution, the second kind of restitution, is owed explicitly for the political harm that countries, institutions, and individuals inflicted upon Jews. It is also owed more generally as part of the broader moral obligation to give political aid to politically vulnerable Jews. Countries and institutions that undermined, indeed, often destroyed the political capacities and standing of Jews are obliged to help restore them. As a moral and political debt and principle, this seems obvious and incontestable, even though restitution is not ordinarily discussed in this way. What this moral obligation of political restitution means in practice is more complicated and subject to different interpretations, especially because the Jews of many countries no longer exist or exist only as a tiny fraction of their former number. To whom, then, is this obligation owed? To the Jews' descendants, wherever they may be? To Jews everywhere, because Jews everywhere were under assault, at least by the Germans (and in its own enormously less but still substantial way by the Catholic Church)? Or to Israel?

Israel is a most difficult topic. (I endeavor to write now, as much as possible, from the viewpoint of a neutral analyst, my own political views about the Arab-Israeli conflict aside.) In principle, those who perpetrated grievous political injury upon Jews, including by destroying their communities, do have an obligation to provide restitution in kind, namely, to give substantial political help to Jews so that they could reconstitute their communities in safety. This includes a country for Jews. In this world of nation-states, it is only peoples with nation-states who have full political protection, especially when their state is democratic, as Israel is. Anyone who would deny this right to Jews today without similarly denying it to all other peoples—

which is the typical prejudiced view of those who hide behind the smoke-screen of anti-Zionism—is an antisemite. This becomes that much clearer when one realizes that Israel is actually older than the majority of countries in the world, and that it is one of the very few countries that existed in 1948 and that have had unbroken democracy and an enduring constitutional system since then.[74] This cannot be said, for example, about the Federal Republic of Germany (founded a year after Israel) or about France, which had its Fourth Republic destroyed in 1958 by a quasi coup d'état that led to the Fifth Republic.

Of course, institutions and people that owe political restitution do not have the obligation to extend unconditional, blind political support to Jews in their efforts to establish secure political communities for themselves. If Jews, as part of founding or governing their political communities, are committing disqualifying unjust harm that is fairly adjudicated according to defensible general principles impartially applied to all countries of the world, then the restituter's political obligation of this kind would be lifted or reduced appropriately.

As everyone knows, Israel has been embroiled in conflict that has had many aspects, including multiple wars, over the last fifty years. People of good faith can have different opinions about how to apportion responsibility and blame for the conflict between Israel and Jewish Israelis on the one hand, and the various Arab states and their peoples, and the Palestinian Authority (formerly the PLO) and Palestinians on the other. Whatever the range of reasonable conclusions may be—and Israel and Israelis have certainly committed their fair share of criminal, political, and moral offenses— I do not see how any such conclusion would mean that an institution or people that owes Jews political restitution (for that matter how any democratic country) could legitimately act to weaken the foundation of Israel, or could support or take any measure that might imperil its existence or the lives of many of its citizens. Indeed, those owing political restitution to Jews would have the obligation to work against any such developments or measures, even if they wish to be critical and nonsupportive of aspects of Israeli politics and society that they, in good faith, find unjust. (To support the creation of a Palestinian state in no way conflicts with this obligation. Palestinians, like Jews, deserve a secure and democratic country of their own.) Certainly anyone who believes that Germans deserve a country—and this does not appear to be contested by virtually anyone—even after the crimes of mass murder, expulsions, enslavement, systematic torture, and wholesale theft that Germany and many Germans during the 1930s and 1940s committed against people both outside and within their country—cannot, without being an unabashed antisemite, maintain that the Jews have less right to a country and that their country, Israel, more than half a century since it was founded, should cease to exist or be put in peril. Seen in this light, it becomes clear that anti-Zionism, namely, the belief that today's Israel has no right to exist, is a thoroughgoing and extreme kind of political antisemitism, calling into question the legitimacy, and even calling for the liquidation of, only one country in the world, the one that is principally a home to Jews.

Eventually this obligation of political restitution should be lifted. But when? After all the victims (survivors of the Holocaust) are dead? After a set length of time, say one hundred years? Until certain objective conditions of safety for Jews are met? Or according to some other criterion? This is a difficult issue. However long it is to be, political restitution is certainly owed, in addition to Israel, to the Jewish communities of Europe, especially those that find themselves under antisemitic pressure, threats, or attacks including in former Communist countries, France, and Germany. And those institutions and people who, until now, have not adequately discharged their responsibilities of restitution in this regard certainly continue to bear this obligation.

Political restitution is owed to Jews by the Catholic Church. As we discussed in part two, the Church inflicted enormous political harm upon Jews, which included its contributions to the destruction of Jewish communities throughout Europe (though the nature of the Church's contribution and therefore its culpability varied greatly from country to country). In addition to this, Jews still suffer significantly from the Church's political transgressions, in particular the legacy of its antisemitism. This includes the by now well-understood phenomenon of anti-Zionism as the contemporary political form for antisemitism, or put differently, as the only remaining acceptable way in most of the West to couch and publicly express antisemitism; the almost garrisonlike existence of Jewish communal and cultural institutions in Germany and elsewhere in Europe, where the very real threat of attack by neo-Nazis and others necessitates elaborate security measures and permanent police protection; the antisemitic atmospheres that Jews have lived in and continue to live in in the 1970s and 1980s in South America and today in Russia and other countries of Eastern Europe and, with the resurgence of its intense and widespread open and public expression, also in Western Europe; the wholesale adoption of Christian antisemitic demonology in many non-Christian antisemitic movements and publications, especially in much of the Arab and Islamic world, in order to further sustain and legitimize an ideology that mobilizes their peoples for

Cover of the Madrid, 1963, Spanish edition of the Protocols of the Elders of Zion. *The cover reads: "Plan: Destruction of Christianity/Enslavement of Humanity." The three heads of the snake represent the Jewish religion, the State of Israel, and Communism.*

their own political conflict with Israel—indeed, once-standard Christian antisemitic motifs and penchant to fantastical notions about Jewish power and malevolence have for a few decades pervaded the political cultures of many Arab and Islamic countries almost as uniformly as they once did medieval Europe.[75] The Catholic Church, at least as much as any country except perhaps Germany, needs to extend political restitution to Jews.

Moral restitution, the third kind of restitution, is owed for moral transgressions. It has several major components:

1. A public mea culpa: to admit fully in public the nature of the transgressions and culpability.
2. Repentance: to genuinely feel sorrow, regret, and contrition for the offenses, to really ask the victims for forgiveness—which means that it might not be given—to want to hear the anguish of the victims and

their views, to make an effort to heed them, when they are construc-
tive and insightful, and for a person to dedicate himself to the necessary amendment of his life or institution.

3. The undoing of moral wrongs to the Jews: to work to reduce the lasting effects of the moral offenses as much as possible, with the hope of
effacing altogether those that can be made to disappear.

4. Institutional self-reformation: to change the institution in a manner
that removes from it, whether organizationally, culturally, doctrinally,
or in other ways, the unwholesome elements, especially the structures
that made its offenses possible so that the institution will no longer be
a potential source for their recurrence.

The justification for moral restitution and its various components is
straightforward. For a person to admit culpability, to genuinely ask the victims for forgiveness, and to dedicate himself to self-improvement, to work
to reduce the harm he has created, and to try to ensure that it will not happen again, are basic prescriptions, or follow on basic prescriptions, of many
moral and religious systems, including Catholicism. The Catholic Church's
name for this is "moral reparation."[76] No less a personage than Konrad
Adenauer, the first Chancellor of Germany after World War II, explicitly
agreed that the need for restitution extends beyond the material to include
the moral. After the war he volunteered that "unspeakable crimes were
committed in the name of the German people, crimes which oblige us to
moral and material restitution."[77] Note that even if, in Adenauer's faulty,
conventionally exculpatory formulation, the offenses were committed only
"in the name of the German people," rather than also by a large number of
Germans, Adenauer still acknowledges that the duty of restitution, including moral restitution, incurs to "us," namely, to the members of the German political community, Germany's citizens.

Moral restitution is the most multifaceted kind of restitution. It is at least
as important as the other kinds of restitution, in no small part because the
others, explicitly or implicitly, partly rest upon it. It is also the kind most
likely to be genuine. Material restitution is typically given reluctantly, owing
to political or economic calculation by the restitutor, which is typically
brought about by political or economic pressure from others. This has been
true of Germany and more recently of the Swiss banks. Political restitution
is by definition political, which is, if ever, seldom given purely out of the
kindness of the restitutor's heart or out of a sense of moral duty. Political
calculations have certainly influenced Germany in this respect. The many
aspects of moral restitution, particularly the pose of a true repentant, are
much harder to fake, and less likely to be faked.

MORAL RESTITUTION

Let us begin considering moral restitution with a simple maxim. It can be an unremarkable maxim cast in the Church's religious terms rather than in secular ones:

> All the members of the Church who have sinned during the genocide must have the courage to bear the consequences of the deeds that they have committed against God and against their future.

Two immediately notable things would be that the statement assumes the moral agency and responsibility of Church members, and asserts that they have a duty: Catholics have to act. It is not conditional. It is a moral "must." It is an unavoidable obligation. If such a statement would issue from a source legitimately bearing the requisite authority—an institution, a person, a moral imperative—then the "must" would be a command that the sinners are duty-bound by their chosen faith to enact.

In order to know how this maxim should be implemented for actual instances of mass murder, we need concrete information: Who are the "all"? What are the sins? Will they find the courage? What are the consequences? Which future? If we were to pause to consider a recent example of large-scale mass murder—1994 in Rwanda, when during just three months the government, Hutu militias, and ordinary Hutu systematically slaughtered at least half a million Tutsi—we would say the members of the Church and the sins would include the recently convicted Hutu nuns who were among as many as one hundred priests and nuns, who directly participated in the slaughter of Tutsi, the other Church officials who lent support to the mass murder, and of course, ordinary Hutu who—though they might have been Catholics were not acting as Catholics—killed Tutsi and committed other grievous unjust harms against them. However many Catholics, clergy or lay, committed offenses in Rwanda, we speak there not of the Catholic Church "as such," as an institution or of its doctrines, for the offenders acted in clear and open defiance of each. (No doctrinal or theological source in Catholicism even remotely suggests that Tutsi are guilty of crimes and should be punished.) It appears likely that we would be justified, however, in speaking of the culpability of the Rwandan Catholic Church as an institution. "Senior members of the clergy" were enmeshed in Rwandan politics. The Church did promote, including through its twisted presentation of Christianity, widespread prejudice, fear of, and hatred of Tutsi. Many Catholic clergy who were Hutu had been aware of or attended political meetings of Hutu extremists before they began killing. And the

"Church hierarchy" was characterized by "near passivity" during the mass murder itself.[78]

If, after the fact, the perpetrators choose to listen to the Church, then it would be right to invoke the Church's good religious and moral principles to get them to face up to their culpability. In the case of Rwanda, no less than the Holocaust, who the "all" is and what the "sins" are are either known or certainly, in principle, knowable. What is less clear is where the sinners' "courage" would come from and what the "consequences" and a "future" might be. And, of course, the question would remain, who or what is the authority that commands these moral agents known as Catholics to act?

John Paul II. The Pope. The maxim that we have just been examining is not some hypothetical, heuristic starting point that I conjured up but an existing papal command. The underlying authority for his command is not his office—as much force as the papacy has with Catholics—but a moral imperative, whether one believes, as the Pope does, that it comes from God, or that it has nondivine origins. John Paul II's is a powerful statement, a forceful command. "All the members of the Church who have sinned during the genocide must have the courage to bear the consequences of the deeds that they have committed against God and against their future." We might quibble with aspects of it—for example, it might have included other human beings, not just God and their futures, against whom the perpetrators committed offenses. Yet in its essence, it is incontestably right.

But it brings sadness with it and makes certain questions unavoidable: neither John Paul II nor any other Pope has seen fit to make such a direct and forceful public statement about Catholics' culpability and the need for "all the members of the Church who have sinned" during the Holocaust to repent for their many different kinds of offenses and sins against Jews. Yet John Paul II did make such a command to Rwandans in his letter to them of 1996.[79]

Among the questions that we should ask about the Pope's statement is: Which genocide? Only Rwanda? But the Pope has clearly chosen to cast his command in general terms. So why not the Holocaust? Or is it the only "genocide" to which it does not apply? The question might seem mischievous, because it is hard to imagine John Paul II or any responsible Catholic maintaining that the only Catholic perpetrators of crimes or other injuries during mass murder who need not heed the Pope's seemingly unambiguously, universally applicable command are those who harmed or killed Jews. But the question must be asked, at least rhetorically. Why? Because, in contrast to John Paul II's issuing of this statement about Rwanda two years after the mass murder ended (which itself was tardy), for fifty-seven years after the Holocaust, and for twenty-four years of his own papacy, and for six years after issuing the letter to Rwandans neither he nor any other Pope ever wrote such a letter to Germans, Poles, French, Slovaks, Italians, or the Catholic people of any other country regarding offenses against Jews during the Nazi period. With regard to the Jews, the Catholic Church and its clergy have also decidedly not acted upon this maxim, this moral command. The best that the Vatican could do is issue its mainly self-exculpatory "We Remember," waiting to do even this until after most of the victims who survived the Holocaust and most of the perpetrators were dead.

John Paul II, with this letter to Rwandans, has enunciated as a Catholic principle the same principle proposed here: that the Catholic Church and Catholics (clergy and lay) owe moral restitution for the moral transgressions that they commit, including during campaigns of mass murder that are initiated by others. By the Pope's own command, then, the Church, or at least its representatives and culpable Catholics owe moral restitution to the Jews for their offenses against the Jews as part of the Germans' and their helpers' eliminationist onslaught.

John Paul II does not elaborate upon the specifics of this admittedly large and complex task that he commands Catholics to undertake. Of what exactly should this moral restitution consist? We might not all agree upon its every detail. Still, it seems to me that in thinking about "consequences" and a "future," any minimal moral restitution on the part of the Church and its clergy for their offenses against Jews would begin with the obvious.

Tell the truth. Become genuinely repentant. Eliminate antisemitism. And, especially in light of the magnitude of the Church's crimes and other offenses, work to ensure that the Church will never again inspire the persecution of Jews.

TELLING THE TRUTH

The Church has yet to own up to its extensive contributions to, and direct part in, the eliminationist persecution of the Jews. It must stop its denials, obfuscations, prevarications, and self-exculpations—to itself and its faithful, to Jews and to the world. It should finally admit, publicly, its offenses and culpability in full. It should state clearly, to use the Pope's categories for Rwanda, who the "all" are, what the sins are, what the consequences should be, and what "future" the Church and its clergy should build.

Should anyone still doubt that a reckoning with the Church's and Pius XII's responsibility for the Holocaust must begin by confronting the

Church's antisemitism, or that it is simply those outside the Church who are making this call, the following statement should be taken to heart:

> It is a well-proven fact that for centuries, up until Vatican Council II, an anti-Jewish tradition stamped its mark in differing ways on Christian doctrine and teaching, in theology, apologetics, preaching and in the liturgy. It was on such ground that the venomous plant of hatred for the Jews was able to flourish. Hence, the heavy inheritance we still bear in our century, with all its consequences which are so difficult to wipe out. Hence our still open wounds.
>
> To the extent that the pastors and those in authority in the Church let such a teaching of disdain develop for so long, along with an underlying basic religious culture among Christian communities which shaped and deformed people's attitudes, they bear a grave responsibility. Even if they condemned antisemitic theories as being pagan in origin, they did not enlighten people's minds as they ought because they failed to call into question these centuries-old ideas and attitudes. This had a soporific effect on people's consciences, reducing their capacity to resist when the full violence of National Socialist antisemitism rose up, the diabolical and ultimate expression of hatred of the Jews, based on the categories of race and blood, and which was explicitly directed to the physical annihilation of the Jewish people.

The authors should know of what they speak. They are the French bishops in their 1997 "Declaration of Repentance." They forthrightly reject many of the current Pope's and the Church's defenders' prevarications about the past. Their apology is obviously heartfelt in a way that still eludes the Vatican: "For this failing of the Church of France and of her responsibility toward the Jewish people are part of our history: We confess this sin. We beg God's pardon, and we call upon the Jewish people to hear our words of repentance."[80]

The Catholic Bishop Christopher Budd of England is even more explicit about the direct link between the Church's deicide charge and the persecution of the Jews over the centuries, including during the Nazi period. In a pastoral letter of November 1994 that was read in every Catholic Church in his diocese, he told his faithful:

> We need to ponder with true regret that the one we accept as the Messiah, truly God and truly man, we have often used to bring not peace and justice, but pain, injustice and destruction on many of our fellow human beings, particularly the Jewish people. . . .
>
> The death of Jesus and the death of millions of Jews this century are tragically and inextricably linked. For centuries Jews have been pilloried, perse-

cuted and blamed for the death of Jesus. The charge of deicide or killing God was leveled against them—this was the fertile soil in which the evil of Nazism took root with such catastrophic effect.[81]

After the first step of acknowledging the truth about the contribution of the Church's antisemitism to the eliminationist persecution of the Jews, a moral reckoning with the Church and its clergy for the character and degree of their responsibility for the Holocaust must undertake, as its next step, a confrontation with the actions and inactions of the Church, its national churches, and its clergy during the Nazi period. This has been recognized not just by those outside the Church. A private letter written in 1946 by Adenauer, the longtime revered German Chancellor and leader of Germany's Christian Democratic Party—himself imprisoned by the Nazis—to a priest should be taken to heart by anyone who still doubts the necessity of such a searching confrontation:

> In my opinion the German people as well as the bishops and clergy bear a great guilt for the events in the concentration camps. It is perhaps true that afterwards not a lot could be done. The guilt lies earlier. The German people, including a great part of the bishops and clergy, accepted the National Socialist agitation. It allowed itself to be brought into line (*gleichgeschaltet*) [with Nazism] almost without resistance, indeed in part with enthusiasm. Therein lies its guilt. Moreover, even if one did not know the full extent of the events in the camps, one knew that personal freedom and all the principles of justice were being trampled underfoot, that in the concentration camps great atrocities were being perpetrated, and that the Gestapo and our SS and in part also our troops in Poland and Russia treated the civilian population with unexampled cruelty. The pogroms against the Jews in 1933 and in 1938 took place in full public view. The murders of the hostages in France were officially announced by us. One cannot therefore truly assert that the public did not know that the National Socialist government and army command constantly and as a matter of principle violated natural law, the Hague Convention, and the most simple laws of humanity. I believe that much could have been prevented if all the bishops together on a certain day from their pulpits had publicly protested against all this. This did not occur and for this there is no excuse. If for this the bishops had been sent to prison or concentration camp, then this would not have been a loss, on the contrary. All this did not occur, therefore it is best to be silent.[82]

Just as Adenauer was not being anti-German or condemning every last German when he said that Germans owe moral restitution to Jews, he is not here, by speaking these truths, condemning every member of the Catholic clergy or being anti-Catholic.

Anyone who, unwilling to acknowledge the incontrovertible facts and plain truths contained in this book, attacks this book or me as anti-Catholic must also attack Adenauer, the champion of German Christian democracy, and the French Catholic bishops, and Bishop Budd of England, and Cardinal Edward Cassidy for his willingness to acknowledge in 1998, as he put it, that the Church's ghetto became "in Nazi Germany the antechamber of the extermination." Adenauer places blame squarely on the German Catholic clergy for their failure to resist the crimes against humanity occurring before their eyes, and for their undeniable enthusiasm for Nazism. He condemns them so harshly, because he believed that their resistance would have been effective. The French Catholic bishops, in assigning broader responsibility, place blame squarely on the Church's teachings, on "the Church as such." They do not palm off the blame onto misguided "sons and daughters of the Church," as the Vatican's "We Remember" does. Bishop Budd in pointing to the Church's conception and construction of Jews historically could not be clearer that it was aspects of the Church's core doctrine about Jesus that produced such enormous suffering of Jews, and that the Church also has much to answer for regarding the Holocaust: "The death of Jesus and the death of millions of Jews this century are tragically and inextricably linked." Adenauer, the French bishops, Bishop Budd and others, show us that the true Catholic Church and true sons and daughters of the Church will confront Catholicism's past as a way to ponder the path needed for a truthful and moral future.

But within the Catholic hierarchy, the French bishops and Bishop Budd are exceptions. An examination of the central Catholic texts regarding the Church's role in the Holocaust reveals how far the Church has to go. "We Remember," with its fallacious, utter dissociation of Nazi antisemitism from the Church's own, seeks to remove all responsibility from the Church for the antisemitism of Germans during the Nazi period. It fails to give even a minimal sense of the broad extent and often intensive character of the Church's persecutions or inspired persecutions of the Jews historically, with all their lethal consequences. It does not explain the unambiguous Catholic scriptural, doctrinal, and theological sources of the Church's past offenses. It fabricates history by having only a few Catholics helping the Germans (as if the many German perpetrators who were Catholics were not) and many more Catholics resisting them. It does not specify the varied offenses of the Church, and of its Popes, bishops, and priests (not to mention of those lay Catholics inspired by Catholic teachings, whom we have generally excluded from this discussion) or the kinds of weighty culpability they incurred. It implies a wholly fictive equivalency between Catholics and Jews in their attitudes and deeds to one another. All this in a document that is supposed to offer repentance for the Church's role in the Holocaust.

In 1995, three years before "We Remember," the Polish bishops marked the fiftieth anniversary of the liberation of Auschwitz with an official statement about the Holocaust. Their statement, "The Victims of Nazi Ideology," makes "We Remember" look like a full, even fulsome confession. The Polish bishops do the minimum in expressing regret at the persecution and killing of the Jews and in decrying antisemitism and racism. Overwhelmingly and essentially, the statement is an apologia for Poles and for the Polish Church. The document leads away from the most basic facts, including that the Church was the progenitor of substantial anti-Jewish sentiment or that there was much antisemitism in Poland. It would have people believe the historical fairy tale that, with the exception of a few bad apples, the Polish people stood arm in arm with their Jewish compatriots, imperiling themselves by doing an enormous amount to aid the Jews.[83]

The German Catholic bishops also issued a statement on the fiftieth anniversary of the liberation of Auschwitz. It is essentially a whitewash. They criticize their Church and its members during the Nazi period, but only for having failed to come to the aid of the persecuted Jews. They employ the time-tested strategy of seeming to come clean by confessing to the lesser offense (the acts of omission), all the while passing over the greater offense, its Church's and its members' willful crimes and other transgressions. The German bishops rightly reiterate that the Catholic Church is a "sinful Church and in need of conversion," but they cover up their own Church's and their clerical predecessors' responsibility for spreading antisemitism by saying nothing more about it than the wan statement that after medieval times, "an anti-Jewish attitude remained, also within the Church."[84]

These and other official national Catholic Church statements never disclose who the "all" is. They never fully or clearly enunciate the sins. They address, at best tangentially, the consequences and the future.[85] Their perfunctory calls to action are insufficient, faulty in their assumptions and meager in their recommendations (such as making an apology and wishing for a better future without antisemitism). They provide no real recognition of the character of the substantial existing problems, let alone maxims for dealing with them adequately. Even the statement from the French bishops of 1997, containing many points that are clear-eyed, direct, and worthy of wide dissemination, is deeply inadequate. Though longer than the others, it is brief, just a few pages. Its treatment of the history and the Church's actions is superficial and fleeting. The moral accounting is general and vague, even when what it says is correct and important. It provides little by way of a road map to a better future.

The best of these Catholic Church documents is the American Catholic bishops' instructional manual, *Catholic Teaching on the* Shoah: *Implementing the Holy See's* We Remember. It does suffer from many of the same defects as the others—brevity, superficiality, and, on many important issues, evasiveness. But in critical aspects it is a good document, worthy of wide dissemination. It is better than the others in several ways: framing the Church's historical role in spreading antisemitism and in inflicting injuries upon Jews; making clear the Church's responsibility for laying the groundwork for Nazi antisemitism to flourish; providing guidelines for teaching Catholics truthfully about the past and for reducing the further spread of antisemitism and of discredited Church notions about Jews and Judaism; and calling clearly on Catholic educators and clergy to carry out its guidelines. It does not, however, address the many other aspects of restitution that the Church has not undertaken.

The Catholic Church and its many national churches have yet to tell the truth. They have yet to tell the truth about the nature and full extent of their contributions to the eliminationist persecution of the Jews. Among other things, this would require the kinds of concerted historical investigations, as yet unexecuted, into the internal workings of the Vatican and into the attitudes and actions of national Catholic churches and their clergy during the Nazi period that I call for in part one. It would also require the Church to conduct serious moral thinking, to a greater degree than it appears to have done, about the variety of offenses that it and its clergy committed. In part two I propose a moral road map, which is not to say that it is the only possible, legitimate one. But something along its lines—an emphasis on moral agency and individual responsibility, and general and principled evaluative categories of types of offenses and types of culpability, impartially applied—is necessary so that the analytical confusion that besets moral discussions of the Holocaust does not encumber or derail the Church's needed moral self-scrutiny. This is not to say that, coming from the Church, there would not be a greater doctrinal component to such an evaluation. Of course, there would be—and it would be welcome. Basic Catholic moral principles are worthy of emulation. I refer to them repeatedly, showing how they powerfully support the foundation and reasoning of this moral reckoning. But the Church must recognize that when confronting its offenses against Jews—the political transgressions among them by definition being a public, nonexclusively Catholic matter—Catholic doctrine and theology are neither necessary nor sufficient to draw the conclusions that a well-considered moral reckoning produces. It is precisely because the Church has been and continues to be a political institution that it is subject to the general principles that ought to govern any public institution and public actors. Catholic doctrine and theology also do not trump the principles and views of other involved peoples, especially of Jews. In the end, the Catholic Church would have to say, without equivocation and not just for one or another of its many offenses, but for all of them: mea culpa.

The Catholic Church's failure to be truthful is that much more glaring in light of the statements by many Protestant churches, which sometimes with minor changes would apply also to the Catholic Church. In 1987 the Presbyterian Church (USA) described how the church's teachings of antisemitism directly and indirectly led to mass murder:

> In subsequent centuries . . . the church misused portions of the New Testament as proof texts to justify a heightened animosity toward Jews. For many centuries, it was the church's teaching to label Jews as "Christ-killers" and a "deicide race". This is known as the "teaching of contempt". Persecution of Jews was at times officially sanctioned, and at other times indirectly encouraged or at least tolerated. Holy Week became a time of terror for Jews. . . .
>
> It is painful to realize how the teaching of the church has led individuals and groups to behaviour that has tragic consequences. It is agonizing to discover that the church's "teaching of contempt" was a major ingredient that made possible the monstrous policy of annihilation of Jews by Nazi Germany.[86]

Seven years later in 1994 the Evangelical Lutheran Church in America explained how inescapable its church's antisemitism was and how catastrophic were its consequences:

> In the long history of Christianity there exists no more tragic development than the treatment accorded the Jewish people on the part of Christian believers. Very few Christian communities of faith were able to escape the contagion of anti-Judaism and its modern successor, anti-Semitism. Lutherans . . . feel a special burden in this regard because of certain elements in the legacy of the reformer Martin Luther and the catastrophes, including the Holocaust of the twentieth century, suffered by Jews in places where the Lutheran Churches were strongly represented. . . .
>
> In the spirit of truth-telling, we who bear his name and heritage must with pain acknowledge also Luther's anti-Judaic diatribes and the violent recommendations of his later writings against the Jews. As did many of Luther's

own companions in the sixteenth century, we reject this violent invective, and yet more do we express our deep and abiding sorrow over its tragic effects on subsequent generations. . . .

Grieving the complicity of our own tradition within this history of hatred, moreover, we express our urgent desire to live out our faith in Jesus Christ with love and respect for the Jewish people.[87]

Let us be plain. Is it so hard to speak the truth? Is the Catholic Church so insecure in its self-understanding and so frightened for its hold on its believers that it must persist with its cover-up, including the transparent falsehood in "We Remember" that the Nazis' "antisemitism had its roots outside of Christianity"? The Presbyterian Church (USA) and the Evangelical Lutheran Church in America have not ceased to exist or lost their faithful because they uttered the truth about their tradition. What is wrong with the Catholic Church, an institution that claims to, and obviously in many ways does, serve God and goodness, that it treats its long and sinful history of antisemitic invective and practice, institutionalized at its core, as incidental to itself, as "errors and failures of those sons and daughters of the Church" but never of the Church itself?

The American Presbyterian and Evangelical Lutheran churches were obviously not involved in the eliminationist persecution of European Jewry, so they did not need to repent for direct complicity in the Holocaust. But churches in Germany and Austria did. The Austrian Evangelical Church has publicly confessed in a declaration in 1998 that "not only individual Christians but also our churches share in the guilt of the Holocaust/Shoah."[88]

In 1980 the Synod of the Evangelical Church in the Rhineland (West Germany) drew a direct line between the eliminationist theology that was its and the Catholic Church's common property and the exterminationist variant that the Nazis decided upon:

Throughout centuries the word "new" has been used in biblical exegesis against the Jewish people: the new covenant was understood in contrast to the old covenant, the new people of God as replacement of the old people of God. This disrespect to the permanent election of the Jewish people and its condemnation to non-existence marked Christian theology, the preaching and work of the church again and again right to the present day. Thereby we have made ourselves guilty also of the physical elimination of the Jewish people.[89]

The Northern Protestant State Church of Germany (*die nordelbische Landeskirche*), which includes Hamburg, Germany's second-largest city, has gone the furthest. It is telling the German public across northern Germany in graphic detail the unvarnished truth about its past.

This regional Protestant church has organized an exhibition of documents, publications, photos, and other materials that reveals the great extent of its involvement in the eliminationist assault on the Jews. The exhibition "Church, Christians, Jews in Nordelbien, 1933–1945," which opened in 2001, is scheduled to travel from city to city around northern Germany for three years, so that the truth can become widely known throughout the church's region.

The exhibition shows how intensely antisemitic the Protestant clergy of this region were during the Nazi period. It brings to light their extensive participation with the Hitlerian regime in defaming, repressing, and expelling the Jews. With the exhibition, the church acknowledges its culpability for its and its clergy's crimes and offenses.

A German newspaper reporting on the exhibition emphasizes that "by no means" can it be said that its member churches acted "under compulsion." The churches were willing persecutors of Jews. Churchmen, the exhibition recounts, "eagerly emulated" the antisemitic measures of the regime. The church of the state of Schleswig-Holstein announced that it would "joyfully" serve the regime in the pursuit of racial purity.

According to this regional Protestant church, the vast majority of its parishioners did not differ from the clergy in their phobic hostility toward the Jews. When all Jews in Germany, including converts to Christianity, were required to wear a yellow star, parishioners objected to receiving communion side by side with these racially tainted Christians who displayed the stigmatic badge. The racist antisemitism of the members of this church was so great that they eventually decided to expel eight thousand members who had Jewish ancestry.

The exhibition, which the German newspaper calls "path-breaking," shows the "unbelievable extent to which the churches of the region had participated in the Holocaust. [It] declares courageously 'the majority of the church supported the persecution of the Jews.' " The exhibition is a "venture from which all other churches of the Federal Republic had for more than fifty-five years recoiled in horror."[90]

An exhibition about the views and actions of the German Catholic Church and its membership during the Nazi period would not look very different, with the notable exception of the expulsion of converts from the Church. But neither the German Catholic Church nor the Vatican, nor any other national Catholic church, has ever done anything like it. Instead the Catholic Church insists on not telling the truth about itself, its clergy, its flock, on not telling the truth about its and its clergy's deeds and the resulting culpability, and on not seeking to genuinely educate its members about its past and about the catastrophes that its antisemitism helped to produce.

More broadly virtually everything that these many Protestant churches have declared about their pasts is also true of the Catholic Church's past. Yet Pope John Paul II and almost all the national Catholic churches have either denied or not seen fit to acknowledge and make known these aspects of their history.

Let us ask again: Is it so hard to speak the truth? What is wrong with the Catholic Church that it cannot?

REPENTANCE

If truth telling is the first task of moral restitution—the Jewish survivors, like the survivors of all mass slaughters, want the truth to be told as much as they want anything else—then repentance is the second. Moral restitution requires that the Church and its leaders—as the bearers of the Church's obligations and continuing doctrines and practices—become penitents. If the Church, the Pope, and its bishops lived by the Church's own doctrines when responding to the Church's past culpability regarding the suffering and deaths of Jews, then they would recognize the need for this. According to the Catholic Church, "repentance is a radical reorientation of our whole life, a return, a conversion to God with all our heart, an end of sin, a turning away from evil, with repugnance toward the evil actions we have committed."[91] This conversion to God must also be expressed in one's relations with human beings: "Conversion is accomplished in daily life by gestures of reconciliation . . . the exercise and defense of justice and right, by the admission of faults to one's brethren, fraternal correction, revision of life, examination of conscience."[92]

The kinds of searching confrontation with the past and self-renovation of the Church in its stance toward Jews that a genuinely repentant Church would undertake have been missing from the Church's public conduct regarding the Holocaust and toward Jews. The Church, several Popes, and its bishops have not approached its relations with Jews by "practice[ing] complete humility" as its own teaching about "penance requires."[93] When has the Church or the Pope officially and with "complete humility" asked Jews, survivors and others, what they would have the Church do to make amends with them and to prevent the Church and Catholics from perpetrating future harms? At minimum, Jews would surely answer that they want a full public accounting of the Church's past offenses. Surely, they would want the Church to admit culpability and apologize for the Church's and its clergy's past offenses without equivocation or qualification. Surely, they would ask for the Church to stop all teaching of all falsehoods about Jews and all notions that breed suspicion, ill will, and hatred of them. Surely, they would tell the Church that all Catholic claims or intimations that Christianity has replaced Judaism must cease. The half-truths and prevarications of "We Remember," and the half-steps of Vatican II and since, have not been enough.

In the Church's attempts to confront the Holocaust, tardy and inadequate as they have been, what is most striking, even when the attempts contain praiseworthy elements and genuine sorrow for the horrors of the Holocaust, is the decided lack of empathy for the Jews. Where is the evidence that the Church's leaders, not to mention lower clergy, have pondered the agonizing historical condition of Jews surrounded, often hounded, by the Christian majority in their society that was animated by the multiple libels that the Church had placed on Jews' heads? This is not to say that the Church's and its officials' statements regarding the Holocaust or Jews fail to say appropriate things about condemning antisemitism and the need to build a future with greater understanding of Jews and Judaism. In this respect, they are typically fine. But their statements fail to dig below the surface gloss of their own moral rectitude to explore and convey how deeply their Church has hurt Jews and, because of the legacy of its teachings, continues to do so. They fail to make vivid and therefore real to their parishioners the extent and character of the Church's offense and the Jews' suffering. As the Central Committee of German Catholics has pointed out with incredulity, the Church's official instructional manual for all Catholics, the new *Catechism of the Catholic Church*, fails to discuss the Church's antisemitism "at all."

Why has the Church shown so little empathy for the suffering of the Jews, for what it must have been like to have been Jews listening to the Church's antisemitic charges and fearing their consequences, including the annual "terror" of "Holy Week," for centuries across Europe? To live in fear for their lives and then during the Holocaust to know that they, their loved ones, their people, were slated for total annihilation? The Church and its leaders know how to speak insistently and with feeling about suffering, yet genuine emotion is strikingly absent from its rare and formal statements regarding the suffering of Jews. Why has the Church not grieved for the Jews who have fallen by the hands of Church-inspired antisemites? Why has the Church not regularly mourned what it has wrought? Why is the Church's discussion of the anguish of the Jews, and of the Church's transgressions in causing that anguish, often perfunctory compared with its attempts at self-exculpation? Why, the exceptions of certain churchmen notwithstanding, is the Church's show of penitence not recognizably that of a genuine penitent?

Anyone who mistakenly believes that the Church has done these things should read James Carroll's seven-hundred-page book to see what one devout Catholic's heartfelt confrontation with this past really looks like.[94] *Constantine's Sword* is an unsparing, deeply affecting investigation of the character and extent of the Church's responsibility for antisemitism, for the persecution of Jews over the centuries, and for the Holocaust. It is a searching, profound attempt to prescribe for the Church how it must renovate itself in light of the false paths it has taken and its centuries of sinful conduct toward the Jews. Carroll, who as much as any Catholic, has struggled with and against the antisemitism of his religious tradition and Church, accepts his ongoing responsibility for working to repair the evil that others of his faith have wrought. On such a note, he ends his magisterial work:

> This has been the story of the worst thing about my Church, which is the worst thing about myself. I offer it as my personal penance to God, to the Jewish dead, and to my children, whom I led, by accident, to the threshold of Hitler's pit [his bunker complex in Berlin]. Nietzsche warned that if we stare into the abyss, it may stare back, and this book proves Nietzsche right. My faith is forever shaken, and I will always tremble. The Christian conscience—mine—can never be at peace. But that does not say it all. This tragic story offers a confirmation of faith, too. God sees us as we are, and loves us nevertheless. When the Lord now turns to me to ask, "Will you also go away?" I answer this too with Simon Peter, "Lord, to whom shall I go?"[95]

To get a sense, from a different perspective, of the lack of empathy on the part of the Church, its clergy, and many Catholics (and other Christians) for the situation of Jews living in a Christian world, imagine that some other institution had had for millennia, at its core, these fictitious notions: Christians are children of the Devil, responsible for killing the Son of God, and cursed for all time. What would Catholics and other Christians say about an institution that defamed and spread hatred of Christians by propagating such beliefs to hundreds of millions of people over many centuries? Imagine that such an institution had also harmed Christians historically as the Catholic Church and its faithful, informed by the Church's teachings, have harmed Jews. Can Catholics or other Christians honestly say that they would not see that institution as having spread hatred, as having been deeply prejudiced at its core? Would they not call for the institution to renounce and denounce completely these libelous and hate-filled views and to stop disseminating them completely? Imagine how much more irate Catholics would be if this institution's principal text, which spread the prejudice and produced enmity, was deemed sacred and authoritative and was the best-selling, most read and reread, and most influential book in the world, as the Christian Bible is.

If Catholics, whether in St. Peter's or in a provincial parish, would agree that such an institution is bigoted and would have to stop teaching its prejudice and hatred, then they must agree that the Catholic Church, which is not above moral law, must do the same. Perhaps this hypothetical example will fail to make Catholics (or other Christians) more genuinely empathetic with what Jews have suffered and to a lesser degree continue to suffer, even if Catholics would ponder what it might be like to live in a society where the majority of people are taught or are exposed to these views of them. But at least it will get all Catholics (and other Christians) who are intellectually honest to see the inescapable moral logic of what their Church must do, and that it is their duty to call upon it to do what it must.

In the United States and other countries, people realize how pernicious public prejudice is, particularly when it is articulated by political or moral leaders and made part of important institutions. They guard against it vigilantly, descending with a fury upon public people who give even a hint of prejudice against African-Americans, Asian-Americans, Jewish-Americans, and others. Admittedly, this protection against prejudice does not extend to all groups, like gays, against whom it is still possible, with relative impunity, to say publicly the most hateful things. Nevertheless, the source of people's denunciatory fury against prejudice is their by now visceral understanding of how hurtful and how dangerous public prejudice is.

Once prejudice is in the public sphere, it becomes a more likely basis for political mobilization and for a political program of spreading hatred and of persecuting the hated and feared people. This happened throughout Europe regarding Jews—most catastrophically in Germany—and happens in many countries around the world today against many groups, including in predominantly Hindu India and many Arab countries, which are largely Islamic. Why, then, does one institution and its leadership remain immune from such censure, even though that institution still spreads an enormous quantity of hurtful and dangerous prejudice in the United States, Europe, and around the world? How can anyone not believe that it is high time that this institution remedy itself?

We have seen that the Church approaches its relations with Jews on its own terms. On one level the Church, John Paul II, many bishops and clergy

genuinely want to end Catholic hostility to Jews. They recognize that the
Church's doctrinal statements, theology, and liturgy should not and simply
cannot any longer contain explicitly hate-filled antisemitism. The public
preaching of such prejudice would no longer be tolerated by the peoples,
including Catholics, of many countries. Moreover, it is clear that the ecumenical spirit of our more pluralistic world has, if not doctrinally, then at
least socially and morally affected the Church for the better. John Paul II, in
"Novo Millennio Ineunte," his apostolic letter to end the jubilee of the year
2000, has acknowledged "the climate of increased cultural and religious
pluralism" as one reason to welcome and further "a relationship of open-
ness and dialogue with the followers of other religions."[96]

But the Church's intentions toward Jews, as it made clear in 2000 in its
definitive declaration *"Dominus Iesus": On the Unicity and Salvific Universality of Jesus Christ and the Church,* remain unchanged: the Jews, while they
are to be tolerated and not subjected to coercion, need to recant and accept
Jesus. On this point the Church is adamant. *"Equality,* which is a presuppo-
sition of inter-religious dialogue, refers to the equal personal dignity of the
parties in dialogue, not to doctrinal content . . . the Church," it continues,
is "guided by charity and respect for freedom." What does the Church
understand this to mean? Not what we might suppose. It means that when
the Church is in dialogue with other religions, it *"must* be primarily committed to . . . announcing the *necessity* of conversion to Jesus Christ and
adherence to the Church through Baptism, and the other Sacraments . . ."
[my emphasis].[97] While respecting the "equal personal dignity" of Jews,
this Church, which has inflicted so much harm on Jews in the past, decidedly does not approach—as it never has—Judaism and Jews with genuine
respect, and still insists that they ought to renounce who they are and
embrace that Church.

Since the Holocaust the Church has been willing to be beneficent to Jews
in some measure, a substantial measure, as long as it is done on the Church's
terms as an act of charity bestowed upon the Jews, not as a meeting of equals.

In 1948 the Catholic Church refused to recognize the founding of the
state of Israel. Given the primacy that the Church had always given to its
supersessionist claim against Judaism over the physical security and well-
being of Jews, it followed that the Church would be hostile to Jews'
attempts to secure themselves politically in the land that was to become
Israel. Theodor Herzl, the founder of the political movement for Jewish
national re-creation, known as Zionism, appealed to the Church in 1904 for
support in his project to protect Jews. The Vatican Secretary of State, Cardinal Merry del Val, cited the Church's "highest principles" in rebuffing

him, and explicitly denied the right of Jews to remain Jews: "I do not quite see how we can take any initiative in this matter. As long as the Jews deny the divinity of Christ, we certainly cannot make a declaration in their favor. Not that we have any ill will toward them. . . . The history of Israel is our own heritage, it is our foundation. But in order for us to come out for the Jewish people in the way you desire, they would first have to be converted."

Herzl learned in his subsequent meeting with Pope Pius X that this Pope also did not recognize the Jews' right to exist as Jews. "The Jews have not recognized our Lord, therefore we cannot recognize the Jewish people. . . . The Jewish religion was the foundation of our own; but it was superseded by the teachings of Christ, and we cannot concede it any further validity."[98] Frustrated with the Pope's insistence that the Jews' religion is invalid, Herzl let the Pope know that "terror and persecution may not have been the right means for enlightening the Jews." Pius X did not repudiate the use of such means but instead implicitly justified them, given, from the Church's perspective, the obstinacy of the Jews: "The Jews," he imperiously told Herzl, "therefore had time to acknowledge his [Jesus'] divinity without any pressure. But they haven't done so to this day."

When the State of Israel was declared in May 1948, *L'Osservatore Romano*, the Vatican's newspaper, reflecting the Church's unabated eliminationist spirit, imperiously announced to the world, including to the remnants of the slaughtered Jewish communities of Europe seeking a safe home: "Modern Israel is not the true heir of Biblical Israel, but a secular state. . . . Therefore the Holy Land and its sacred sites belong to Christianity, the True Israel."[99] For decades the Vatican would not even utter the country's name. In 1964 Pope Paul VI spent a day in Jerusalem refusing to let the word "Israel" pass his lips. During the decades after Israel's founding, the Church did recognize virtually every other country in the world, one tyranny after another, including atheistic Communist states and many mass-murdering regimes, for example, in Central and South America during the 1970s and 1980s.[100] But not the political state of the Jews. The same Church that signed the Concordat with Hitler, granting Nazi Germany international legitimacy, withheld international legitimacy from the country that became the home of the survivors of Europe's broken Jewish communities. With every passing year of its nonrecognition, the Church again singled out the Jews as pariahs—this time as a political community.

All the Church's justifications for its injurious stance toward the political home of the Jews cannot hide the simple fact that the Church's politics of its own supremacy over Judaism, its supersessionism, its antisemitism, and its theology derived from Augustine—that Jews were exiled from their land

and condemned to wander the world forever because of their rejection of the divinity of Jesus—trumped the most basic needs of the Jews, and the moral necessity of treating them with the same respect, and of according to them the same political rights that the Church does to other peoples. The Church's multifarious offenses leading up to the Holocaust and during the mass murder itself did not in 1948 and for decades thereafter temper the Church's supersessionist hostility to Jews. Instead of being at the forefront of protecting the political rights of Jews, as its obligation of political restitution requires, the laggard Church, was still, almost fifty years after the Holocaust, denying the Jews their right to political security.

By the early 1990s the Church's continuing denial of the legitimacy of Israel, of the right of Jews, alone among the nations, to have a country of their own, became too embarrassing and too great a political liability for the Church, as the former Communist countries resumed diplomatic relations, and India, China, Arab countries, and others recognized Israel. This left the Vatican "in a tiny minority of the most irreconcilable enemies of Israel—the lone Christian voice in a Muslim chorus." So the Church agreed at the end of 1993 to recognize Israel, which was not formalized until late 1994 when ambassadors were exchanged.[101]

With regard to the Holocaust there remains a deeper issue. Whatever the contemporary Church's obvious condemnation of the Germans' and others' persecution and extermination of the Jews—and who can believe that contemporary bishops and priests look upon the mass murder as anything other than one of the greatest crimes in human history—when dealing with the Holocaust the Church continues to practice its age-old undermining of Jews. The Church's attempt, at least in part, to Christianize the Holocaust, to incorporate the Holocaust into its own Christology, takes several forms: the invention of false Christian martyrs, false Christian heroes, and false Christian victims, and the appropriation of Jewish suffering as its own.

In 1998 the Church canonized Edith Stein, a convert to Christianity. The Germans killed her not because she was Catholic or a nun, which they deemed irrelevant, but because she had been born a Jew. So the Church has sent her on the path to sainthood under the false pretext that she was a Holocaust martyr to her Christian faith. In 1982 the Church canonized Father Maximilian Kolbe, who in Auschwitz did nobly volunteer to give his life to save another inmate (a non-Jew), but who was not in the camp because of his Christianity and did not die for his faith, a condition for his canonization as a martyr; and Kolbe was the expressly antisemitic editor of an antisemitic Catholic journal. The Church fictitiously transforms Pius XII himself into a hero of the Holocaust, and its representatives, such as Father Gumpel and Fisher, try to shield this man, culpable for so much, from criticism by transubstantiating him into a victim with the claim that those who speak disturbing truths about him are really libeling him.

"We Remember," the Church's public reckoning with its role in the Holocaust, alongside its long-awaited and much anticipated admission of some Catholic wrongdoing, turns the Church into a co-victim of the Nazis, along with the Jews. It falsely celebrates Catholics more as helpers than as persecutors of Jews. It calls equally for Jews to stop being "anti-Christian" just as Christians should stop being anti-Judaic, as if the catastrophic anti-semitism of the Church and anti-Jewish violence of Catholics has been but the flip side of an equivalent anti-Christian persecution by Jews.

Since these measures and declarations are deeply offensive to many Jews, survivors and nonsurvivors, and since it is clear that several of these cases for sanctification are dubious even according to Catholic doctrine, why does the Church insist upon them? The Church practices a politics of turning itself into a victim of Nazism of the sort that it was not. The Nazis were ideologically anti-Catholic and, had they defeated the Allies, would have turned on the Church and destroyed it. But the Church did not understand this aspect of Nazism, so in much of Europe, before and during the war, the Church was more a collaborator than a victim of Nazism and its allied states. The Church's attempt to transform itself into a kind of equal of the Jews, therefore, contributes to its politics of whitewashing its past, which necessitates not only the fallacious defense of Pius XII but also transubstantiating him from culpable offender into a saint.

Symbolically, the Church's most egregious act has been the Carmelite nuns' establishment of a convent at Auschwitz in 1984, where they planted a twenty-foot-high cross. Their actions have been insistently defended by Poland's Catholic primate, Cardinal Jozef Glemp, as recently as 1998, despite all the obvious pain it was causing Jewish survivors including survivors of Auschwitz. The conflict over the Carmelite convent and the crosses at Auschwitz is both another example of the Church's political misappropriation of victim status for itself—making Auschwitz into a Christian holy site—and of its unwillingness to heed legitimate concerns of Jews when the concerns conflict with its own politics of victimization. With its handling of this incident, the Church, with all its culpability for the persecution of Jews, committed a moral travesty: At the grave of a million Jews, it insisted on erecting the symbol, whatever else it is to Catholics, that for centuries had been used to vilify and persecute Jews as "Christ-killers." Carroll is certainly correct that " 'Christianizing' the Holocaust, using Christian categories to 'redeem' the genocide, using the cross to deny the role of ancient Christian Jew-hatred in preparing the soil for the Holocaust . . . all this could have no other effect than the demeaning of the overwhelmingly Jewish presence at Auschwitz."[102] With such actions the Church has sought to appropriate this great European catastrophe suffered by the people that it had persecuted, as an assault on itself.[103]

When an outcry erupted from Jews around the world, the Church responded not with an apology and the immediate removal of the offending Catholic institution and symbol, but with foot dragging, dissimulation, broken promises, and even sometimes vehement attacks, including antisemitic ones. Cardinal Glemp, the Church's principal representative in this matter, is an antisemite. In a homily pronouncement to all of Poland and the world, Glemp invoked the Church's antisemitic tropes and fabrications of centuries past by implying falsely that some Jews had tried to murder the Carmelite nuns, and by imperiously warning Jews that they should not "talk with us from the position of a nation above all others and don't lay down conditions which are impossible to fulfill,"[104] the conditions being nothing more than that the structures that would serve to Christianize Auschwitz be removed. Cardinal Glemp seems to have learned little from the Holocaust or from the post–Vatican II, formally anti-antisemitic dispensation of the Church. And if the leading cardinal of the Polish Catholic Church has not fully absorbed Vatican II's message, how can we expect that the lay Catholics of Poland have done better?

Why did John Paul II not discipline Cardinal Glemp? If the Pope is serious about fighting antisemitism, how can he tolerate, how can he with his silence approve, a national church leader publicly spreading antisemitism in his religious pronouncements, particularly when dealing with the most pressing of issues relating to the Holocaust and to Jews in general? John Paul II's inaction becomes that much more significant and troublesome in light of the regularity with which he disciplines and tries to silence liberal and progressive members of the Church, precisely because they have made pronouncements of which he disapproves. Such targets of his have included the prominent Swiss Catholic theologian Hans Küng and the American Catholic theologian Roger Haight.[105]

It should therefore have come as no surprise that Cardinal Glemp's Polish Catholic Church reacted badly to the recent revelation about Jedwabne, where during the Holocaust the Polish townspeople, now unleashed by German occupation to act upon their preexisting hatred, committed wholesale mass murder against their sixteen hundred Jewish neighbors, including by burning many of them alive in a barn.[106] Jan Gross's book on the mass murder shocked Poles into confronting how, during the Nazi period, ordinary members of their society willingly persecuted and slaughtered Jews. The Polish Church did hold a ceremony at which it decried Poles' persecution of their Jewish neighbors, but it chose to do so on the Jewish holiday of Sukkot, effectively precluding the attendance of Jewish community leaders. Later, while President Aleksander Kwasniewski of Poland, in a national ceremony, was asking Jews for forgiveness for the "particularly cruel crime" of the ordinary Poles who slaughtered their Jewish neighbors, the Catholic Church once again led the fight to forfend the truth. The parish priest of Jedwabne boycotted the national ceremony, defiantly asserting that "these are all lies." Cardinal Glemp, in contradiction to the spirit of the Church's earlier ceremony, absented the Polish Catholic Church from the ceremony, claiming that it was the Jews who are guilty. For what? Glemp trotted out the old antisemitic lie that the Jews—as if the Jews of Poland were not also Poles—had collaborated with the Soviets against the interests of the Polish people.[107]

As recently as May 2001 the Church chose to pursue its political interests at the expense of its need to provide restitution. This occurred when John Paul II was visiting Syria. John Paul II allowed himself to be portrayed by the dictator of Syria, Bashar Assad, an acknowledged sponsor of international terrorism, as Assad's ally against Israel and Jews in general. With the Pope by his side, Assad let loose an antisemitic diatribe that was broadcast by television to the entire Christian world. Assad was, in Carroll's view, openly trying "to recruit the Pope and all Christians into nothing less than a holy war not only against Israel, but against all Jews."[108] He presented Jews as ontological enemies of God, who oppose the "heavenly tenets" and "try to kill all the principles of divine faiths." He invoked the Christian blood libel of Jews as Christ-killers and, in order to persuade Christians that they share with him a common anti-Jewish heritage and cause, Assad fabricated an Islamic analogue that "in the same way" as the Jews "betrayed" and "tortured" Jesus, the Jews also "tried to commit treachery against Prophet Mohammad."[109]

The Catholic Church, in its Vatican II declaration on the Jews, had promised to eschew political considerations when confronting "hatred, persecutions and displays of antisemitism directed against Jews at any time and in any form and from any source." "We Remember" quoted this promise in 1998, affirming that "we make [it] our own." John Paul II reiterated this solemn pledge in his speech at Yad Vashem in March 2000, adding that it is motivated by the "Gospel law of truth and love," which means that this pledge is binding upon him and the Church.[110] But when John Paul II listened to Assad's antisemitic libels and hatred, he acted as if the Church's and his own words of promise had no meaning. Although he undoubtedly disagreed with Assad, John Paul II did not repudiate the antisemitism and the call to violence against Jews. He did not denounce the incendiary lies. He did not utter a single word of protest. He remained silent, even as the charge that Jews are deicides was being beamed anew, in his presence, to the Christian world. But John Paul II did more than nothing. He chose, by continuing his visit, to lend himself still more to the Syrians' propaganda bonanza against Jews and Israel.

In all these instances the Church decided that its political interests overrode its moral obligations to Jews. It was more important to the Church to turn itself into a victim of Nazism, to whitewash its own past, to maintain its supersessionist claims, and to extend its influence into other countries. The Church's choices, when its political interests and its moral obligations conflict, suggest that the Church is nice to Jews when it suits the Church, not when and because morality and duty dictate. If it means that the Church will tolerate, indeed tacitly lend support to, antisemitism, then that appears also to be acceptable, at least to this Pope. In these several instances we see also old attitudes reemerging, sparked by anger, breaking through what can begin to look like but a patina of change.

The Church's sometimes pious words are welcome. Again, I am sure that they are often meant genuinely, including when spoken by John Paul II. There can be no doubt that substantial progress has been made by the Church, beginning with Vatican II, in reducing its overt anti-Jewish teachings and in acknowledging, at least in some measure, the truth of its antisemitic past. Its forward strides since the death of the antisemitic Pius XII have, in many ways, been more than anyone during his reign could have reasonably predicted. Recognizing and applauding all of this does not, however, mean that we should not remain critical of today's Church for its substantial failings in these matters. Upon Pius XII's death, the Church faced such an immense task of dismantling and transforming the structures of antisemitism that were embedded at its core that it should not surprise anyone that it has much left to do. Over the years John Paul II has continued this needed work. When he has met with Jews or visited important Jewish sites, he has personally borne himself as a mensch, with evident good feeling and humility. Upon visiting the synagogue in Rome in 1986, becoming (as hard as it may be to believe) the first Pope ever to do so, he referred to Jews as "our elder brothers."[111] John Paul II obviously believes that the Church must make some kind of amends for the past. He obviously wants his Church and Catholics to have better relations with Jews.

But until the Church stops insisting that this happens on its terms, and until it lives by its words even when its pronouncements mean that it must sacrifice other interests or bear new burdens, the words also remind us of how much remains for the Church to do. The Vatican's dealings with the historical commission and John Paul II's complicity with Assad are two cautionary tales that suggest that the Church's expressions of remorse and goodwill may be superficial. When something is at stake for the Church—the image of one of its Popes or its political relations with Syria—the Church violates its promise to eschew politics, in one case condemning the Jews, in another allowing an antisemitism-spouting dictator to use it to incite millions of people against Jews. No matter that Jews are merely seeking the truth that the Church promised them, and which they are owed. No matter that Jews are once again being lied about and threatened by a hostile power.

That this Pope would stand in silence by a dictator of a highly repressive regime, who would annihilate the Jews' political community, as he spews libelous hatred of Jews is proof that not enough about the Church has changed. What more evidence could anyone want? After more than fifty years since the end of the Holocaust, the Catholic Church, to serve its politics, still abandons Jews. What more evidence would anyone want that the Church and its leadership have not developed genuine empathy with what Jews have suffered and some continue to suffer? What more proof would anyone want that the Church and its leadership have not become penitents who are "contrite of heart, confess with the lips, and practice complete humility and fruitful satisfaction"?[112]

A repentant Church would energetically seek to develop the requisite empathy and to practice sincere humility, expressing it in word and in deed, until it produces the fruitful satisfaction. It would ask explicitly, without historical or moral equivocation, for forgiveness. It would seek to do whatever it could to remove the structures and practices of, in its terms, sin against the Jews. Given the injustices and injuries that this Church has over the centuries perpetrated against Jews, it would not be too much to expect some demonstrable actions. One such step has already been discussed, that the Church should commission teams of independent scholars, with full access to all Church materials and archives in the Vatican and around the world, to write comprehensive histories of every national Catholic Church's attitude toward and treatment of Jews before, during, and after the Holocaust.

Four other obvious remedial measures that the Catholic Church should undertake come to mind.

The Church should publicly name and repudiate the criminal or other grave offenses against the Jews that clergy committed. It should name the perpetrators and, when warranted, repudiate them as well. This would include all relevant Popes, bishops, and priests. If the Evangelical Lutheran Church in America can explicitly and publicly repudiate the antisemitism of its founder, Luther, correctly blaming his antisemitism and its legacy for the enormous harm that it produced, then the Catholic Church can certainly publicly repudiate the mass-murdering clergy, as well as those clergy who publicly supported the eliminationist persecution of the Jews, such as the Slovakian bishops.

The Church should not canonize, and should rescind the canonization of, anyone who helped to persecute Jews, certainly those who did so most injuriously or from the most visible ecclesiastical positions.

The Church should erect memorials, especially in Europe, to the Jews who have suffered because of its antisemitism, memorials adequate in form and content, and in prominence to the extent of that suffering, which includes all the Jews who were felled by Church-inspired hands, and not just during the Holocaust. Such memorials, which would become part of urban fabrics and therefore of people's daily lives, would produce the additional good of teaching Catholics and others who came upon them of the evil of antisemitism, of bigotry of all kinds, of the Church's commitment to eradicating such evil, and of the obligation of all people to be vigilant against antisemitism and other prejudices and hatreds.[113]

John Paul II, or if he does not, then a successor, should issue an encyclical on the Church's relations to Judaism and to Jews, or as John Paul II calls the Jews, to Christians' "elder brothers." Such a declaration would not be the slight Vatican II statement, which at fewer than 650 words is shorter than the standard op-ed piece in *The New York Times*, or even the glancing and relatively brief statement of "We Remember" at fewer than 4,000 words but a full, lengthy encyclical, at least as long and weighty as other encyclicals, such as *Ut Unum Sint* of May 25, 1995, on Christian ecumenism, at over 24,000 words or *Redemptoris Missio* of December 7, 1990, on the permanent validity of the Church's missionary mandate, at over 30,000 words.[114] In the early 1960s John XXIII had intended that Vatican II would produce a substantial statement devoted exclusively to refashioning Catholicism's stance toward Judaism and Jews, but with his premature death and the assumption of the papacy by the reactionary Paul VI, its meager and problematic statement, which eventually emerged after the politicking, was embedded in a declaration about all non-Christian religions.[115] The long-overdue papal encyclical would recount, without mincing words, the Church's history of antisemitism and of persecuting the Jews. It would plainly explicate the Christian sources of antisemitism, would explain why antisemitism of any kind—including so-called anti-Judaism—is a sin against God and an affront against humanity, and would enjoin Catholics to combat antisemitism wherever they find it. It would call for a fundamentally new basis for understanding Catholicism's relationship to Judaism, one of unqualified respect and of equality in every aspect.

ERADICATING ANTISEMITISM

Moral restitution has a third component, which parallels the Church's concept of repentance. It requires that the offender works to undo ongoing harm to the victims. There is much antisemitism in the world. Most of it, save for much of the antisemitism in Islamic countries, has its ultimate origins in the Catholic Church's teachings. As with the antisemitism of Lutheran and other Protestant churches, such Catholic origins are sometimes to be found in the distant past. But much of the harmful effects of the Church's antisemitism is recent. If the Catholic Church is to undo the harm it has produced, then it must work assiduously to combat, to reduce, to teach people the falseness and, in its terms, the sinfulness of antisemitism.

This aspect of moral restitution is not discharged with a few paragraphs from Vatican II's *Nostra Aetate*, and with the subsequent alteration in doctrine, theology, liturgy, and teaching that stops the Church and its clergy from promoting some of the antisemitism that it would have otherwise continued to spread. It is not discharged with occasional statements from the Pope, the Vatican, national churches, and clergy that antisemitism violates the teachings of the Church and Christian principles. The effort required of the Church to rid the Catholic world of antisemitism is much greater. Simply put, because the Church is responsible in full or in part for the existence today of a great deal of antisemitism among Catholics, particularly in Europe, and less directly among non-Catholics as well, it is the Church's duty to undo this unjust harm, this grievous moral offense.

This duty has been recognized by the Catholic bishops of the Netherlands, who accept the Church's continuing responsibility for antisemitism today, which they attest "arise[s] repeatedly in our society." They insist that for the Church "there is still much to do." "This," they exhort, "demands vigilance and decisiveness."[116] Our conclusion that the Church has such a duty also exactly accords with the Church's own doctrine. It is the Church's unequivocal position that penance requires that "one must do what is possible in order to repair the harm" of the sin. In stating this principle in its official teachings, the Church explicitly mentions the duty to "restore the reputation of someone slandered" and that "the duty of reparation also concerns offenses against another's reputation."[117] Antisemitism—the assertion that the Jews killed or are guilty for killing Jesus included—is slander. Directly and indirectly, the Church has committed an offense against, injured, and sometimes destroyed the reputation of Jews around the world. It is a moral imperative that the Church restore it. In the Church's own words, it is a "duty," a "must."

This would require the Church to mobilize its vast institutional and clerical resources in a vigorous educational campaign that would work to reeducate all Catholics who are still antisemitic (many Catholics today are not) and to educate Catholics about the history of the Church's propagation of antisemitism and the additional horrors to which the antisemitism led. It could certainly start by creating formal curricula to this end for its parochial schools, Sunday schools, and seminaries, and by mandating that they be taught in its educational institutions worldwide. It would have to make this effort into a core mission of the Church. The Church would have to explain that it was the institution, and its doctrine and theology were the ideas, that were the principal sources of these hate-filled libels about Jews, and it would have to do so because most Catholics do not know this. Father Edward Flannery, one of the principal Catholics officially involved in Catholic-Jewish relations, writes:

> The vast majority of Christians, even well educated, are all but totally ignorant of what happened to Jews in history and of the culpable involvement of the Church. They are ignorant of this because, excepting a few recent inclusions, the antisemitic record does not appear in Christian history books or social studies, and because Christians are not inclined to read histories of antisemitism. . . . It is little exaggeration to state that those pages of history Jews have committed to memory are the very ones that have been torn from Christian (and secular) history books.[118]

The Church would also have to teach in its publications, sermons, and schools that prejudice against and hatred of Jews has been the Church's great sin and is a moral offense. It would need to have no illusions that imparting the message of this anti-antisemitic mission to its faithful just once or a few times would serve to erase what is in many people a deep-rooted prejudice. It would have to assign this mission the highest priority, devoting the enormous amount of time and effort required for bringing about its successful completion.

The evidence for the necessity of such a mission is everywhere. To be sure, since 1945 antisemitism has declined markedly among Catholics and other Christians. The horrors of Auschwitz helped to dispel this old and lethal hatred and imposed a powerful taboo against its recrudescence. A critical development during the postwar period was the relative taming of antisemitism: the antisemitism that exists today in the Western world is far less ferocious and demonological, less violent in content—overwhelmingly, it is not eliminationist.

Nevertheless, the virtual disappearance of antisemitism from the public sphere of the West, lasting for decades after the Holocaust, proved to be partly an illusion. A substantial amount of antisemitism was hibernating. Today it flourishes around Europe, even in countries from which Jewish communities have virtually disappeared. In Catholic Poland it persists with enormous tenacity. In predominantly Catholic Hungary and Slovakia, after having been prohibited by Communist regimes, it has reemerged into the public domain. In Germany it has, in the last few years, seen a substantial resurgence of expression. In other European countries, such as France, it is also widespread. In the United States the evidence for the Church's ongoing and direct responsibility for producing antisemitism is clear. Among Catholics (and other Christians), the greater their religiosity, the more likely they are to be antisemitic. In other words, the many exceptions notwithstanding, the more that Catholics (and Christians more broadly with Christianity), orient themselves to Catholicism, and the more that Catholicism informs their worldviews, then the more that they tend to be suspicious of, hostile toward, or feel threatened by Jews.[119]

Europe has experienced the return of the antisemitic demons that it had repressed. They have not reappeared in all their traditional, unashamed, often exhibitionist nakedness but often cloaked in the guise of anti-Zionism, as condemnation of Israel's policies toward the Palestinians. It is no doubt true that very many of those who criticize the conduct of the Israeli government and Israelis for participating in or supporting the government's policies bear no ill will toward Jews qua Jews. But many others betray by the tone and content of their condemnations and denunciations an antipathy to Jews that, though veiled and unacknowledged, bears the visible marks of the ancient hatred.

We should have no illusions that even if a miracle were to occur and the Church, its national churches, and all its clergy should immediately resolve to undertake full moral restitution to Jews, that this Herculean task of dispelling antisemitism would be completed anytime soon. As a core element in the substructure of prejudicial belief and hatred in the modern world, antisemitism today has a life, and institutional foundations, that are substantially independent of the Church that originally spawned the hatred. This makes it only more pressing that this mission of moral education and emotional repair be institutionalized at the center of the Catholic Church. Aside from this being a moral necessity, it might serve other goods, such as being an ongoing needed reminder and warning of the Church's capacity to be unjust and do harm (in its terms, to sin) and of the need of Catholics (and others) to be vigilant against all kinds of prejudice and intolerance.[120]

Until the Church could bring about the dissipation of antisemitism, it would also have to enjoin its faithful to do good works specifically toward Jews, as a way to compensate concurrently for the injuries of antisemitism that Jews continue to suffer. Such works could take many forms, including giving aid to elderly Jews, particularly Holocaust survivors; volunteering in Jewish communal institutions; helping to support and sustain Jewish communities in parts of the world where they are threatened or are trying still to rebuild themselves.[121]

In embarking on such a program, the Church would still better learn what it knows well: how easy it is to spread prejudice, hatred, and fear and how hard it is to undo it. The passion that the bearers of prejudice and hatred have for teaching others to share in their hatreds is almost always greater than the commitment of those who dissent from or decry the same hatreds. Learning to hate is much easier than learning to undo hatred, let alone learning to love and respect others. Even the well-meaning people who would wish to repair the moral caesura in the fabric of goodness that antisemitism is, when faced by the multifarious needs of all of humanity and of all human societies, might understandably balk at directing so much of their energy toward undoing prejudice and animosity against one group.

Given that so much antisemitism still exists, including the Glempian complaint that Jews want the Church to bow before them, it would be likely that any such Church attempt would backfire at least with some people, who would interpret this through their antisemitic prisms as evidence of the Jews capturing the Church itself, and therefore further seeming confirmation of their own fears and hatred. But with proper guidance from the Pope and the clergy this would likely be true of only a small minority. Many practical matters would have to be worked out, including how to teach people to relinquish their prejudice, no longer to think ill of, hate, or fear the people that they do. Notwithstanding the many substantial problems of getting the Church to act upon its duty and then to successfully complete such an enormous and difficult task, it is incumbent upon us to recognize the moral consequences of what the Church has wrought and to lay out the lineaments of the changes for the future that it is duty-bound to bring about. If we do not work to figure out what the world should look like, we will not make it in

hat image or even more resembling that image, whether we believe the
mage is one generated by the right thinking of beneficent humans or
derived from God.

BREAKING WITH THE PAST

Such measures point the way to a fourth component of moral restitution,
which bears an affinity with a central element of the Church's own concept
of repentance: a break with the past. Moral restitution necessitates, and the
Church's own doctrine requires, that the Catholic Church reform itself.
The reforms should achieve two related aims: altering the structures that
have repeatedly led the Church and its clergy to harm Jews unjustly, and
ensuring that the Church will not again play a part in the persecution of
Jews, or even be an indirect source of such persecution. This would require
the Church to change its institutional nature, its structure and culture of
authority, and several of its core doctrines.[122]

It is a truism of American politics, democratic thinking, and of principles
of pluralism that religion wedded to politics undermines democracy, universalism, and pluralism. A person does not have to be a foe of religion or an
obsessively tolerant pluralist to recognize this. The separation of church
and state was enshrined in the American Constitution by deeply religious
men who understood the corrosive and explosive admixture that is religion
and politics. This politics of separation continues to be supported by religious authorities.[123]

Two principal arguments and intended safeguards underlie the wisdom
of maintaining separate spheres. The state and therefore society must be
protected from religion. When a state becomes wedded to a religion, religion may capture the state, which is bad for society because such a state has
a tendency to lead to intolerance of many kinds including of other religions.
Many Islamic countries today—Afghanistan as it was under the Taliban
and Iran—are clear if extreme examples of this. The politicization of religion may produce also religious conflicts in the political sphere, which is
inherently dangerous. This is true in many parts of South Asia, including
India, where Hindus, Muslims, and Sikhs have bitter political conflicts that
are religiously based and are at least partly a consequence of religious political mobilization.

If the state must be protected from religion, religion must also be protected from the state. If there is legal separation of the two spheres, then
freedom of religion is ensured because the state has no right, is legally forbidden, to interfere with the doctrines and practices of religion, or with

people's right to exercise the religion of their free choosing. The absence o
any such separation in the former Soviet Union and in other Communis
countries, including China today, has spelled catastrophic consequences fo
various religions and their adherents, including Christianity and Christian

There is a third, equally important but little-understood reason to sup
port the separation of church and state. Religion must be protected fron
itself. Religion wedded to politics is bad for religion. A religion mixing i
politics is not a religion but a political organization. Political entanglement
all but inevitably lead religious leaders to compromise religious and mora
principles, essentially to betray their faithful. The medieval and early mod
ern Catholic Church—which was to its core a political institution, involve
in political intrigue throughout Europe, seeking its earthly power through
variety of means—is perhaps the best example; its offenses against huma
beings, Jews included, and its betrayal of its own religious and moral princi
ples were legion.[124] More than a few Popes committed grievous crimes an
other offenses in the pursuit of power.

Politics and morality, though bedfellows, are strange and typicall
estranged ones. The basic unit of politics, which is public power, and th
basic unit of morality, which is goodness or virtue, are not the same. Ofte
they are in tension with each other, and frequently they are diametricall
opposed. Although politics can and should serve the public good, it
rhythms in practice are often those of extending influence, seeking advan
tage, and overcoming worldly opposition. The rhythms of morality ar
those of deliberating about what is good, seeking to act well, and trying t
help others. Politics is a universe, frequently, of us against others. Moralit
is a universe of us with others. Much of politics is a zero-sum game. Moral
ity is, and seeks to create, a positive-sum game. By definition, then, a politi
cal institution cannot, in its essence, be a moral institution. And the mor
politically engaged an institution and its officials are, the less able they are t
be governed, and to live, by moral considerations.

For the Catholic Church to become a moral institution, an institutio
governed principally by considerations for the moral well-being of i
members, it must cease to be a political institution. This does not mean tha
the Church should not teach and speak out about matters that inevitabl
have a political dimension, such as the need for societies to provide soci
and political justice for all of their members. Teaching its adherents or, fo
that matter, those outside of the Church who would want to listen to its cor
values and the implications of those values for living in complex societies i
to impart to them moral values and to urge them to live morally. This is th
mission of a moral institution and is decidedly different from what th
political Church does when it pursues its own political institutional agend

Aside from the inherent tension if not contradiction between the universes of politics and morality, as a practical matter, the catastrophic failures of the Catholic Church both before the Nazi period and then during the Germans' eliminationist onslaught against the Jews, sprang in large measure from the Church's political nature. For millennia the Church's political aspirations to extend its earthly domain and power, including over Jews, have led its leaders to forget repeatedly, indeed to violate repeatedly, its basic doctrines and moral principles of goodness.

This leads to a few inevitable reforms. The Church needs to give up its state and cease having formal diplomatic relations with other states (which does not mean that it cannot have its representatives meet with other states). It must stop calculating its place in the world politically. Considerations of politics, namely, of extending its power and influence, must no longer trump considerations of what is good. The Pope's recent moral fiasco of politically supporting Assad's antisemitic incitement (by politely lending his august papal presence to it instead of denouncing it) is just a reminder of this moral inversion. The needs of politics must stop overriding the moral duty of speaking truth to power. For many Catholics the most powerful argument for the Church to shed its political nature and praxis may be that it is bad for the Church and bad for Catholics.

This would also mean that the Church would have to give up its imperialist ambitions. It could, of course, continue to tell people that it has a godly message of love, goodness, and salvation, which it believes worthy of their attention and adherence. But this is distinct from the Church's two-thousand-year core mission of actively seeking to create a world in which the Church—to the exclusion of all rival ways, secular or religious, to goodness, salvation, or God—reigns supreme and uncontested, and in which all people are under its doctrinal and institutional authority.

The Church continues to treat what it calls religious "indifferentism," the belief that other religions may also lead to salvation, as heresy. It continues to deprecate "religious pluralism." The continuity and centrality of the Church's universal imperialism is almost impossible to miss when looking at central Church texts. The title of the Church's declaration "*Dominus Iesus": On the Unicity and Salvific Universality of Jesus Christ and the Church* from August 2000 already indicates the imperialist nature and purpose of the document. It declares:

In treating the question of the true religion, the Fathers of the Second Vatican Council taught: "We believe that this one true religion continues to exist in the Catholic and Apostolic Church, to which the Lord Jesus entrusted the task of spreading it among all people. Thus, he said to the Apostles: 'Go therefore and make disciples of all nations baptizing them in the name of the Father and of the Son and of the Holy Spirit, teaching them to observe all that I have commanded you' (*Mt* 28:19–20)."[125]

From the time of the Christian Bible's writing to the progressive Second Vatican Council to the beginning of the third millennium, the Church's imperialistic ambition has been a constant. Such an ambition all but requires a political institution to effectuate it and a political strategy to succeed. In a sense, a prerequisite for the Church to give up politics is that the Church renounces its claim to being the single way to eternal salvation. As long as the Church seeks to acquire religious sovereignty over humanity, it will be hard for it to resist the temptation of politics and its power.

Integrated political and religious movements that claim to know the path to salvation, whether this-worldly or otherworldly, and insist that they should become sovereign over others, in many cases the entire world, are dangerous. Some such movements are honest about their merged political and religious natures. Political Islam as it exists in several countries today is an example. Other such movements are partly closeted, presenting themselves as political movements without acknowledging their quasi-religious character. Communism, a secular religion par excellence, did this.[126] Still other movements hold up a religious face to the world without acknowledging their fundamental political nature. For a long time this has been the way of the Catholic Church. Why do these last kinds of religious-political movements not receive our censure or at least more of it? They have shown that they are dangerous and that their menace generally increases with their political sway.

Religions tend toward intolerance of others; this has been true of Catholicism, Hinduism, Islam, Judaism, many forms of Protestantism, and the list goes on; the most dangerously intolerant religion today, in general and for Jews in particular, is certainly not Catholicism but Islam as it is practiced in many, though by no means all, countries. The Catholic Church today is, in relative terms, far weaker than Islamic states or than Communist states once were (and China still is). In world-historical terms, today's Catholic Church is relatively benign politically. But it has not always been so. The medieval Catholic Church was politically powerful and perpetrated great crimes. The much weaker Catholic Church during the Nazi period exercised its still considerable political influence in many countries, often to catastrophic ends. The Catholic Church may not always remain as politically weak as it now is.

The doctrine of the Pope's and the Church's infallibility is one of the pillars of the Church's politics. Although, like other aspects of the Church, the infallibility doctrine has a religious face and justification, it is in its essence a political doctrine that calls for political obedience and supports an authoritarian governing structure and culture. This is clear because it was promulgated in historical terms, only recently, in 1870, as an explicit response to the Church's political crisis, which included the cultural challenge of modernity and the political challenge to its worldly authority by Italian nationalism, which led Italian troops to wrest Rome from the Pope's suzerainty in 1870 and, not incidentally, to liberate the Jews of Rome from hundreds of years of the Church's oppression and cruelty. This newly enunciated infallibility doctrine was to maintain the Pope's ironclad social and cultural control over the Church's faithful, and to present a united political front to the other political entities in a world of waning Church power and the Church's growing defensiveness.[127]

The problems of the doctrine of infallibility have been written about extensively. It has been discussed as being the buttress to the Church's many systematic dishonesties about itself and its past, about matters such as its exclusion of women from the priesthood, its doctrine of priestly celibacy, and its past regarding the Jews. The doctrine of infallibility is now so entrenched in the Church's stance toward the world that Garry Wills has analyzed it as a "structure of deceit."[128] The Church and the Pope's problem is that to acknowledge the wrongness of certain fundamental Church doctrines, aspects of their justifications, or papal pronouncements would be to admit that the Church and the Pope have been in error, and in error over fundamental matters. But from the perspective of the Church, this is dangerous to do. The doctrine of infallibility might be shaken and perhaps begin to crumble. This bind, that the Church must continue to dissemble about its past and propagate indefensible anachronisms, is in no area more evident than regarding its past persecution of the Jews.[129]

It is here that the structure of deceit is perhaps most deeply entrenched and certainly the most transparent. According to the Church, a "structure of sin," deceit being one kind of sin, is a sin that leads people to commit other sins.[130] To deny that the Church itself (as opposed to misguided children of the Church) ever spread antisemitism or ever persecuted Jews is a historical falsehood on the order of the denial that the Holocaust ever occurred. To maintain that Pius XII, supposedly harboring no antisemitism, did everything he could to help Jews is an affront to all those Jews whom he might have easily helped, yet whom he chose to forsake knowing what their fates would be. Such churchly denials and prevarications are seen to be necessary if the doctrine and aura of Church and papal infallibility are to be maintained, if the self-injurious authoritarian structure and culture of the Church is to be sustained (and if the Church is to continue to retain general immunity from scrutiny regarding its continuing antisemitic elements). Insisting that such transparent falsehoods are true digs the Church into a moral hole down into which ever more people, including Catholics, look with disbelief and condemnation. The structure of sin, namely, the doctrine of infallibility, prevents an honest accounting of the past. In the Church's terms, it precludes repentance. From the Church's perspective, this is a serious matter because it holds that "to die in mortal sin without repenting . . . means remaining separated from [God] forever by our own free choice," in other words, it means being in "hell."[131]

The doctrine of the Church's and the Pope's infallibility prevents the Church from doing what many Protestant churches have done: tell the truth about its past. The Catholic Church (the partial exception of some of its national churches notwithstanding) cannot even speak the simplest truths about its culpability for producing antisemitism, for its antisemitic doctrines and teachings being the direct source of enormous anti-Jewish violence over the centuries, for its own antisemitism feeding modern European antisemitism, and for its role in producing the unsurpassed catastrophe and crime of the Holocaust. Instead, the Catholic Church continues with its silences, evasions, and dissimulations, which are made ever more glaring as Protestant church after Protestant church admits the difficult truths about their pasts. This is where the Church's claim to its own infallibility and its own incapacity to do wrong has left it: looking the peoples of the world in the eyes and telling them that what just about everyone knows to be true is not true, and that it could not possibly be true.

That the Catholic Church cannot admit that it and the Pope, not to mention many of its national churches and clergy, committed offenses and, in its own terms, sin with regard to the Jews before, during, and after the Holocaust has led some, perhaps many Catholics to struggle with and call into question the moral standing of the Church. For many Catholic (and Protestant) clergy and theologians, the Holocaust produced a crisis in theology, which, starting in 1945, led to substantial self-critical reflection and investigation, and then to some of the important reforms of Vatican II and since then.[132] It would be no small irony if the Church's greatest and most constant complex of offenses—its treatment of the people it fantasized as its greatest enemies, the Jews—and then its incapacity to confront its own offenses fully and honestly, were in any measure a catalyst that also led to the end of the Church's imperialistic and authoritarian ways, that compelled the Church finally to embrace modernity.

The Church should replace its intolerance with genuine tolerance, and replace its exclusivism, tempered since Vatican II by a grudging tolerance of other religions, with religious pluralism. This would pertain to Judaism and Jews and to other religions and their adherents alike. The Church's greatest political mistake of the nineteenth and twentieth centuries was to reject modernity, to fight a rearguard action against democracy by supporting tyranny—which eventually in the twentieth century included Nazism and its allied regimes in Italy, Vichy, Slovakia, Croatia, and elsewhere—and to fight liberalism by promoting illiberalism and antisemitism. Although the Church has, if perhaps only by default, finally accepted political democracy, though not its liberal political culture, by doing so it has embraced this long-established critical aspect of modernity.

If modernity has different normative and substantive stages, then the first part of the twenty-first century is the time to reduce the intensity and detrimental consequences of national and ethnic allegiances and for all peoples to embrace, even celebrate, peoples other than themselves. Tolerance, pluralism, multiculturalism—values that are entirely distinct from the philosophical and moral nihilism of various forms of relativism—are central to the project of contemporary modernity. If the Church is to avoid a repetition of its nineteenth-century mistake in the twenty-first century, it needs to eschew fighting a rearguard, destructive action to defend its anachronistic, exclusivist intolerance. It should embrace modernity in its multifarious possibilities, accepting and celebrating that there are many ways to God, none obviously better than many others. If Catholicism has demonstrated anything with its intolerance and contempt, it is that the road to earthly hell has been paved by a claimed monopoly on the road to heaven.

THE CHURCH'S MANY predicaments are enmeshed in its being a political institution, with imperialistic and authoritarian politics. Its greatest offenses of helping, even if unintentionally, to cause the mass murder of millions of Jews, was substantially owing to the Church's political nature. During the Nazi period, it legitimized and gave support to the Nazi regime. It consistently refused to speak truth to murderous power. If the Church wants finally to become the genuine moral institution that it professes to be, which is probably a practical necessity if it is to perform the necessary work of restitution, including moral restitution to Jews, then it must begin a campaign of self-examination and soul searching that is pointed toward righting itself in this way.

Such an investigation would necessarily include a reexamination of core Church doctrine and theology. Any discussion of this issue would profitably begin with Carroll's call for a Third Vatican Council, to complete and greatly extend the work begun at the Second Vatican Council. Carroll, a former Catholic priest, has grappled with the Church's doctrine and theology, especially with the place of Jews in Catholicism. He sees the Church's false and injurious attitudes and practices toward Jews not merely as *a* major problem but as *the* principal problem of the Church, having been throughout its history and being still today the root of its intolerance and of many of its unworthy stands and practices, toward other religions, women, gays, and many other matters: "The Church's attitude toward Jews is at the dead center of each of [its] problems" of power, intolerance, democracy, and repentance.[133] The early Church's need to differentiate itself from Jews, triumph over them, and sustain, doctrinally and psychologically, its claims to be the true bearer of the Jewish tradition and the only path to salvation produced its well-known antisemitism and, over the ages, inspired intensive persecutions and mass murders of the Jews. It also helped to produce the Church's by-now foundational structures of intolerance and authoritarianism, as the insecure and threatened Church sought to sustain itself by enforcing, theologically and politically, ironclad control over its world.

In Carroll's view, the Church righting itself with regard to Jews is a prerequisite, an indispensable first step, for it righting itself in many other important ways. The Church has been correct that the Jews are a critical concern. But, in Carroll's inverted view of the Church's self-understanding, the Jews are also critical, even the key, to the Church's own salvation. "It seems clear," Carroll writes, "that authentic Church reform, defined as shaping something according to its own essential being, is tied to the Jews, if only because the perversion of that essential being, the perversion, that is, of the message of love preached and lived by Jesus—has so clearly been tied to the Jews from the beginning."[134] The Catholic Church can become a moral institution only when it unambiguously and with finality supersedes its own supersessionist stance toward the Jews, not just by what it says but also by what it believes, teaches, and practices day by day.

All aspects of Catholicism (and other forms of Christianity) that might promote antisemitism—an offense in our terms, a sin according to the Church—must be changed. Even though various Church pronouncements, including John Paul II's, have declared antisemitism to be a sin, and even though the Church, especially under him, has worked hard and effectively to cease teaching most of its former antisemitic doctrine, theology, and liturgy, these measures remain an incomplete formula, so long as the

Church fails to expunge all antisemitism from its teachings, practices, and utterances.

Again, let me emphasize that theologically, the Church has made substantial and impressive progress. Since Vatican II the Catholic Church and many of its clergy and theologians have struggled with the problem of Catholicism's relationship to Judaism and to Jews. The Church has made enormous strides in moving away from its pre–Vatican II hate-filled, accusatory, and loudly supersessionist bearing toward Jews. Today the Church as a whole and certainly many clergy, from the Pope on down, approach Jews, Judaism, and the Church's problematic relationship to them historically and today, with good feeling, in the spirit of wanting to right wrongs, and in the hope of developing a theology that will give less offense to Jews and provoke as few antipathies to them as possible.

Still, whatever some Church theologians say, whatever statements or hints to the contrary are to be found in Church pronouncements, whatever hair-splitting formulations clergy and theologians think up in order to try to soften the Church's positions regarding the Jews, the Church still has its doctrine, its official positions contained in its *Catechism* and elsewhere. If the Pope and the other leaders of the Catholic Church accept as true the most positive and respectful developments in Catholic thinking regarding Jews, which are enunciated in that small part of the Catholic world that participates in the Jewish-Christian dialogue groups or hinted at by Church officials in their pronouncements, then let the Church qua Church declare them to be officially true. Let the Pope, every national Catholic Church, the Church's official *Catechism,* and every doctrinal and theological statement and teaching medium that deals with these matters declare in the plainest and most direct language: The Roman authorities of Palestine killed Jesus. The Jews are not responsible for the death of Jesus. Christianity has not superseded Judaism. The Jews' way to God is as legitimate as the Christians' way. The Catholic Church and Christianity are irrelevant to the salvation of Jews, which remains the concern solely of Jews, their religion, and their God. The ultimate salvation of Christians is in no way dependent upon the actions of Jews; any claim that Jews need to be converted, or that the Jews' actions in any way impede or hasten salvation for Christians, is wrong. And let the Church also state, so there can be no misconceptions, that all past positions or statements, doctrinal or theological, that contradict any of these just enunciated, whether they have emanated from the Church, any of its institutions or organs, or its clergy, are wrong, null and void.

Take, for example, the Catholic Church's denial that Jews can be saved without embracing Jesus. This critical view encompasses and fuels many of the Church's deprecating views of Jews and of Judaism as inferior, false, and wayward. Some have argued that it is a root cause, if not the root cause, of Christian antisemitism. A prominent Christian participant in Christian-Jewish dialogue, Helen Fry, who has edited a wide-ranging and searching volume with many of the dialogue's most important contributions from Catholics, Protestants, and Jews, reflects on the unfinished tasks ahead in the volume's concluding essay, "Challenges for the Future." She observes that "until the churches make theological space for Judaism by accepting it as a legitimate path of salvation, then much anti-Judaism will remain. As long as Judaism is not granted a salvific status in its own right, Christians will continue to see it as an inferior and inadequate faith. This soteriological reappraisal is, I suggest, vital for future relations between Jews and Christians."[135]

Although some progressive Catholics assert that the Jews can find salvation through Judaism, and although Church representatives occasionally drop hints that this is possible, the Christian Bible is unambiguous in stating that "there is no salvation through anyone else [but Jesus], nor is there any other name under heaven given to the human race by which we are to be saved."[136] The Church's official doctrine, faithful to Christian Scripture and now in existence for almost two millennia, is unbending and unequivocal: Jews cannot attain salvation through Judaism. It declares "Outside the Church there is no salvation." It admits possible exceptions only for those "who, through no fault of their own, do not know the Gospel of Christ or his Church." If this exception and other exclusionary Church doctrinal statements exclude anyone from salvation, which they are clearly intended to do, then surely it is Jews living in Christian countries. So the Church declares, "Baptism is necessary for salvation for those to whom the Gospel has been proclaimed and who have had the possibility of asking for this sacrament." How would this not pertain to Jews? The Church's doctrinal account of who will descend into the "eternity" of hell "where they suffer the punishments of . . . 'eternal fire,' " announces that hell, or as Jesus calls it, "Gehenna," is "reserved for those who to the end of their lives *refuse to believe and be converted*" (my emphasis)—as Jews do today and as they did during the time of Jesus and when the Gospels were written and for whom the Gospel authors seemed to have specifically inserted such damning statements.[137]

John Paul II and other Vatican leaders are aware that some progressive Catholics are adopting pluralist positions on salvation, and that there is grumbling within the Church among those who would loosen Catholicism's claimed stranglehold on salvation even ever so slightly. In an explicit and pointed rebuke to them and their religious "relativistic mentality"—

including to those in the Christian-Jewish dialogue who are particularly concerned with countermanding Catholicism's supersessionist teachings about Jews, with Catholicism's antisemitic tradition, and with its explicit denial that Judaism is a path to salvation—the Pontifical Congregation for the Doctrine of the Faith, led by Cardinal Joseph Ratzinger, defiantly ushered in the new millennium by reaffirming in *Dominus Iesus* of 2000, a document which John Paul II "with sure knowledge and by his apostolic authority, ratified and confirmed" that it is "contrary to the faith to consider the Church as *one way* of salvation alongside those constituted by the other religions." Why? Because "the prayers and the rituals of the other religions" are lacking in "a divine origin or an *ex opere operato* salvific efficacy." So that there can be no misunderstanding, *Dominus Iesus* declared that "those solutions that propose a salvific action of God beyond the unique mediation of Christ would be contrary to Christian and Catholic faith."[138]

Until the Catholic Church inscribes in its official doctrine reformed statements of the sort that I have just discussed, and until the Church announces them loudly, emphatically, and repeatedly, so that there is no doubt and no possibility of misunderstanding about them, we should not mistake the theological reflections of some Catholics or hints by the Church, no matter how encouraging they may sound, as anything but what they are: laudable personal reflections and intimations.[139] Given the damage that the Church's antisemitic, anti-Jewish, anti-Judaic—call them what you will—doctrinal and theological positions have caused is it really too much to expect the Catholic Church to announce their nullification and replacement of such still existing injurious and demeaning doctrine and theology as unambiguously and forcefully as it possibly can?

The distressing heart of the matter is the Christian Bible, most critically the Gospels, with its libelous account of Jews during Jesus' time and its pronouncements and implications about their abominable nature and unending accursedness. It is a thorny problem, even or especially for the Catholics, including Carroll, who are the most committed to excising antisemitism from the Church. What is to be done with the libelous and hate-inducing passages about Jews that are in a book that is the basis for a religion, a book that is supposed to be of divine origin? The Church's current, only partly articulated position is to deemphasize the antisemitic content of the Christian Bible when discussing or commenting upon it, by skirting the subject, trying to put the best face on the pointedly offending portions, and instructing its clergy to discuss Jews in a manner that is not entirely in keeping with—in other words, far more positive than, or simply denying—what the Christian Bible say about Jews.[140]

Praiseworthy as this strategy is in that it reduces the teaching of falsehoods and of suspicion, hatred, and contempt, it is neither honest nor entirely effective—or even effective enough. It is not honest because the Christian Bible continues to impart its injurious libels about Jews. It is not effective, in part because the Church, in its teachings, is determinedly unwilling to go all the way. It still insists on a fictional antisemitic account of Jesus' trial and crucifixion. It still maintains that everything in the Christian Bible is true, which, though it does not explicitly say so, includes its many demeaning, dehumanizing, and incendiary statements about Jews. So even if the Church's own teachings today—which are not even known to many of its faithful—do not explicitly endorse and sometimes take issue with these aspects of the Christian Bible, the Catholic Church, by teaching Catholics that its Bible's contents are true, are God's word, is de facto encouraging them to accept the many libels about Jews of Jesus' time as truths, and their extension—sometimes explicit, sometimes implicit in the text—to Jews of all time also as truths. The Christian Bible holds that Christianity has superseded Judaism. It holds that Jews qua Jews cannot attain salvation. It holds that they killed the son of God and are forever accursed.

The antisemitism of the Christian Bible is not incidental to it but constitutive of its story of Jesus' life and death and of its messages about God and humanity. It is not just that the Christian Bible contains a few unfortunate antisemitic remarks. It is not just that the antisemitism is liberally spread throughout the text. And it is not just that the antisemitism is not casual in character but ferocious. The Christian Bible presents its Christian faithful with a relentless and withering assault on Jews and Judaism. The structure of the Gospels in particular is antisemitic. The Jews are presented as the ontological enemy of Jesus and therefore of goodness. They are *the* impediment in the books' story of Jesus. The story's narrative structure, its force, its many warnings and inducements depend upon the castigation of the Jews as the essential and dramatic villains who oppose, reject, and assault Jesus and whom he must overcome but does so only through the tragedy of his end. For Christians to understand evil in this world, a Satan opposes God. For the authors of the Christian Bible to understand Jesus on earth as they want, they needed a terrestrial Satan, and so they invent and present a Satan in the person of the Jews.

Even if we confine ourselves to just an inventory of the explicitly antisemitic passages contained in just five of the Christian Bible's twenty-seven books, without delving into the deeper narrative and ontological structure of these books, we can still see how central and acute the problem is. Biblical scholar Norman Beck provides such an inventory of these books' "defamatory anti-Jewish polemic."[141]

The Gospel According to Mark has approximately forty explicitly antisemitic verses. They include the fictitious theatrical scene of Pontius Pilate, who was the real killer of Jesus, innocently wondering what Jesus had done to deserve the wrath of the Jewish priests and crowd, while the Jews shout to Pilate more than once to "crucify him."[142]

The Gospel According to Luke has approximately sixty explicitly antisemitic verses. He has John the Baptist calling Jews who would believe that being Jews is a way to God a "brood of vipers" who will suffer "from the coming wrath."[143] In some verses it tells of the Jews of Nazareth, upon hearing unwelcome truths from Jesus in their synagogue, being "filled with fury," driving Jesus from their town, and leading "him to the brow of the hill on which their town had been built, to hurl him down headlong." But Jesus escaped their attempt to murder him.[144]

The Gospel According to Matthew has approximately eighty explicitly antisemitic verses. Among them, Matthew tells of John the Baptist dubbing the Jews, called Pharisees and Sadducees, "you brood of vipers," which Matthew has Jesus himself expanding upon when he addresses the Jews who were Pharisees as "You brood of vipers, how can you say good things when you are evil?"[145] It should come as no surprise that according to Matthew such a people and their religion have been superseded, replaced as null and void. Jesus declares: "I say to you, the kingdom of God will be taken away from you [Jews] and given to a people that will produce its fruit [the Christians]."[146] Later, Matthew's Jesus addresses the Jews (Pharisees):

Thus you bear witness against yourselves that you are the children of those who murdered the prophets; now fill up what your ancestors measured out! You serpents, you brood of vipers, how can you flee from the judgment of Gehenna [hell]? Therefore, behold, I send to you prophets and wise men and scribes; some of them you will kill and crucify, some of them you will scourge in your synagogues, and pursue from town to town, so that there may come upon you all the righteous blood of Abel to the blood of Zechariah, the son of Barachiah, whom you murdered between the sanctuary and the altar.

Matthew has Jesus continuing by describing the Jews as "Jerusalem, Jerusalem, you who kill the prophets and stone those sent to you," and telling them that for rejecting him, "your house will be abandoned, desolate."[147] This account of the Jews, coming from the mouth of the man presented as the Son of God, is soon followed by Matthew's infamous and fictitious crucifixion scene, in which the entire Jewish people willingly pronounce the guilt for Jesus' death upon themselves and upon their descen-

dants, in other words, upon Jews for all time. Was "the *whole* [Jewish] people," numbering several million, there? Did they all miraculously "reply" in
unison with the infamous line attributed to them: " 'His blood be upon us
and upon our children' "?[148] How can anyone take such a scene, concocted
fifty to seventy years after the death of Jesus by an enemy of the Jews, who
declares Jews to be a "brood of vipers," as a true account of historical facts?

Certainly, dispassionate modern historical scholarship does not. Geza
Vermes, recognized as perhaps the preeminent authority on Jesus and his
times, writes that "the large majority of Jewish contemporaries of Jesus—
those who lived outside Palestine—had never heard of him."[149] The bla-
tantly contradictory and mutually exclusive accounts of the Gospels on
critical facts, the known historical falsehoods that they contain about Jews
and Judaism, and the historical implausibility, even impossibility of crucial
events in the narratives putatively implicating Jews make clear that the
Christian biblical accounts are not a truthful guide to what really happened,
not a reliable rendition of facts and events, but legend.[150]

Even the Catholic Church, undoubtedly influenced by contemporary
scholarship, in its more candid and less guarded moments acknowledges the
fictionalized nature of the Christian Bible's account of Jews and their putative deeds. The American Catholic bishops write that "after the Church had
distanced itself from Judaism, it tended to telescope the long historical
process whereby the gospels were set down some generations after Jesus'
death. Thus, certain controversies that may actually have taken place
between church leaders and rabbis *toward the end of the first century were
'read back' into the life of Jesus*" [my emphasis].

In plain language, which because of its directness the bishops would
likely reject, they, echoing eminent biblical scholars, are saying that the
authors of the Gospels, writing many decades after Jesus' death, made it up.
This does not mean that everything the Gospels' authors say is not true, but
it does mean that not everything they say is true. Given the total absence of
reliable and contemporaneous historical sources on Jews' relations with
Jesus, and given the blatant anti-Jewish biases and agendas of the Gospel
writers, which the Church itself concedes to have existed, we have no way
of knowing that any of the Gospels' authors specific accounts about Jews'
character and conduct and particularly about Jews' relations with Jesus,
including his death, are true. Instead we have very good reason to suspect
that these accounts are part of what the Gospels' authors fictionalized, for it
was precisely their contemporaneous conflict with Jews decades after Jesus'
death and the need for the early Church to triumph over Judaism and to
make its supersessionist claim convincing that led them to demonize Jews
and saddle them for all time with the most heinous accusations.

The American bishops quote the Vatican's own statement from its 1985 guidelines on how to present Jews and Judaism as affirmation of the fictionalized character of the Gospels' accounts of Jews. It explains that "some [New Testament] references hostile or less than favorable to Jews have their historical context in conflicts between the nascent Church and the Jewish community. Certain controversies reflect Christian-Jewish relations *long after the time of Jesus*" [my emphasis].

The American bishops also refer in this way explicitly to the Christian biblical account of Jesus' death and crucifixion as being tenuous. They explain that "it is necessary to remember that the passion narratives do not offer eyewitness accounts or a modern transcript of historical events," which they say have been rendered through (it would not be unfair were they to say, distorted by) each individual Gospel author's "theological 'lenses,' " which include "the perceived needs and emphases of the author's particular community *at the end of the first century, after the split between Jews and Christians was well underway*" [my emphasis].

Again, the American bishops appear to be saying that the Gospel authors are unreliable, specifically regarding those portions of their accounts that show Jews in a bad light, which, of course, specifically includes the death and crucifixion of Jesus. The Vatican, in *Nostra Aetate* and many subsequent statements, the American Catholic bishops in their statements, and many other national Catholic churches (following *Nostra Aetate* and the Vatican's guidelines) have indicated that the Gospel According to Matthew's charge that "the whole [Jewish] people" accepted the guilt for Jesus's death for themselves and for their children is a fabrication.[151] So why should we believe that any of the Christian Bible's injurious accounts of Jews and especially of Jews' role in Jesus' crucifixion are true?

Put simply, how can anyone see this immoral and hate-inducing charge against the entire Jewish people of *collective* and *intergenerational* guilt for what was indisputably the Roman authorities' crucifixion of Jesus as being anything but antisemitism and a blood libel?

The Acts of the Apostles has approximately 140 explicitly antisemitic verses. Only eight of its twenty-eight chapters are free of antisemitism. The Acts tell of Peter repeatedly asserting the guilt of the Jews for the death of Jesus, including with the formulation, similar to Matthew, that it was "the whole house of Israel" that crucified him. Paul proclaims that through the Jewish Bible Jews cannot gain forgiveness. He condemns the Jews for never understanding God.[152]

The Gospel According to John contains approximately 130 antisemitic verses. John has Jesus telling the Jews that they do not know God, the "one who sent me," and that they "do not belong to God." John's Jesus accuses the Jews of trying to kill him. He reasons that those who are the children of God would "love me, for I came from God and am here." Therefore, John's Jesus concludes that those who reject him, the Jews, "belong to [their] father the devil."[153] Vermes writes that "one of the most dismaying features of the Fourth Gospel [of John] is its determined claim that *the* Jews, or at least the inhabitants of Judaea—the Greek Ioudaioi can designate either—were profoundly and universally inimical to Jesus. Indeed, to all intents and purposes the Jesus of John was almost from the start of his career the target of repeated Jewish murder plots." Vermes continues, "According to John, this bloodthirstiness revealed the true color of the Jews: they behaved like their father, the devil, who was a 'murderer from the beginning' (8:44). Though they claimed to be 'the sons of Abraham' (8:37, 40), they descended from the prince of darkness. John's hatred of the Jews was fierce."[154]

Just these five books contain enough explicitly antisemitic verses, totaling approximately 450, to average more than two per page in the Christian Bible's official Catholic edition. Antisemitic scenes (such as of the events leading up to the Crucifixion), speeches from Jesus deprecating the unbelieving Jews, images (such as Jews being a brood of vipers), and libelous assertions (such as that all Jews are guilty for Jesus' death) are repeated again and again. Through repetition their lessons are reinforced, driven home, made unforgettable. Through repetition these lessons come to constitute the Christian Bible's conception of Jews. Those who read this Bible as God's word or even as a reliable historical guide to the events—which, written many decades after the events and with *no* contemporaneous substantiation, it is anything but—take away from it this image of Jews. Because the structure of the Gospels is to present Jews as the ontological enemy of God, the damaging individual statements about Jews qua Jews get subsumed into the nature and essence of Jews. The cumulative damage of the Christian Bible's defamatory account of Jews to their image and reputation among its credulous readers would be hard to exaggerate.

I expect that some will protest that my account here ignores the progressive reforms of Vatican II and since then, and the contemporary Catholic Church's doctrinal and theological claims, or especially its intimations, that are far more respectful and positive about Jews and Judaism. Or that it ignores the more progressive views of Jews and Judaism that exist within certain national churches, among progressive theologians, and even among many lay Catholics who are more liberal, tolerant, pluralistic, and positive toward Jews and Judaism. Or that it ignores certain statements in the Christian Bible that can be interpreted to mean that Christians should look more favorably on Jews and Judaism. None of these objections would be true. As I have explained several times, the reforms initiated with Vatican II and subsequently taken much further, and the contemporary Church's desire to create a respectful and even positive stance toward Jews are important and welcomed.[155] The goodwill behind these developments and their far-reaching, positive significance for the Church should be emphasized and appreciated. Everyone interested in the themes under discussion should therefore read *Nostra Aetate* and several official Church publications from the last thirty years that instruct the clergy on how to present Jews and Judaism to their parishioners, that lay down guidelines for teaching about the Holocaust, and that in many ways present a more positive view of Jews and Judaism, and a more expansive view of Catholics' need for repentance. Some of these publications even diverge in a welcome way from the less accommodating Church doctrine on these topics.[156] There *are* more open and pluralistic views of Jews and Judaism in certain national Catholic churches, such as the American and German churches. And the Christian Bible does not only and always disparage all Jews.[157]

But none of this changes, effaces, or undoes the harm of the systematic and enormously damaging antisemitic content of many portions of the Christian Bible—which Catholics are taught by their Church is the unerring and infallible word of God—and of its underlying structure that Jews are the ontological enemy of Jesus and God. The Christian Bible's message has remained the same since its text was codified. And its message is unmistakable: The Jews killed the son of God who is God. All Jews are guilty for this crime. Because Jews do not hear Jesus, they do not hear God. For their rejection of Jesus, they are to be punished. Jews, the willful spurners of Jesus, cannot gain salvation, cannot go to heaven. And their religion, which cannot bring them to salvation, has been made invalid, superseded, replaced by Christianity. Granted, there are many parts of many religious traditions, including Judaism, that disparage different groups, that create or have been the basis for prejudice against them, that produce demonstrable harm. Many religions are ethnocentric, self-celebratory, intolerant of others. But the Christian Bible's assault on Jews is qualitatively different. This assault is greater in its defamatory content, in its frequency, and in its emotional intensity. Its deprecation of Jews is not in any sense incidental to the Christian Bible's account of its own religious claims and truths. It is a constitutive feature of biblical Christianity. And the injustices and injuries that this concerted scriptural assault on Jews has led Christians to inflict on real, living Jews—a brief outline of which is to be found at the beginning of part one—is also without historical parallel from any other major religion.

One billion Catholics have the Christian Bible as their guide to God's infallible word. That Bible asserts something as defamatory and as injurious to the reputation of a people as anything could be: that that people, the Jews, killed God and that Jews continue to be guilty and accursed for this imputed deed.[158]

THE CATHOLIC CHURCH has a bible problem. The Catholic Church owes it not only to Jews, but also to Catholics, to deal with it forthrightly and morally. It owes it to Catholics not to lead them astray, not to teach them antisemitism. It owes it to itself, if it is to successfully claim the place that it wants and deserves as a moral institution, and if it and its members are to repent. The degree of moral irresponsibility, the moral offense, of continuing to spread such injurious things about another people and to say that these things are divinely inspired and ordained would be hard to overstate. Yet the Church spreads such things every day as Catholics read its Bible. This state of affairs is that much more saddening because so many of the people who continue to turn a blind eye to, and even defend, such injurious teachings are men and women of goodwill, who have devoted their lives to goodness by giving themselves to their Church and to God.

But the Christian Bible is held to be a sacred text, divinely revealed, God's word. It has been in existence for almost two thousand years. For many Catholics, for many Christians, it is not just a fixed part of their spiritual and moral landscape, it *is* that landscape. It is not just a book that offers contingent truth, wisdom, and guidance, it is the bedrock in which their outlook on the world, their very essence, is grounded.

Here we have the most difficult conundrum. The requirements of moral restitution, of moral repair and simple justice, which can also be derived from the Church's own doctrine, are that the evil of antisemitism, which necessarily includes the antisemitism contained in and that animates the Christian Bible, cannot be allowed to take root in another person's heart. Yet the Christian Bible is a sacred text that, as the word of God, Catholics and other Christians believe must remain as it is. What should be done? What can be done?

Any solution must remain fully cognizant of these two conflicting absolutes: the Church's obligation of restitution, and our obligation to respect Christians' beliefs about the divinity of their sacred text. In this respect, this aspect of moral restitution is different from all others. For the other matters we discuss here, the Church can obviously undertake the necessary measures. They touch on aspects of the Church, its doctrine, theology, or policies, that are all in principle easily changeable if the Church would decide to do so. Altering even contemporary, central Church doctrines, such as the doctrine of papal infallibility, is not in principle at odds with the fundamentals of Christianity. After all, the doctrine is, in the long history of the Church, but a recent political creation of a nineteenth-century reactionary Pope in his attempt to defend so many things that the Church has long since repudiated.

We must pause here to consider the clash of seeming irreconcilable necessities. The necessity of not exempting the Christian Bible's anti-semitism from the ineluctable conclusions of moral restitution is self-evident. The necessity of respecting Christians' deepest beliefs about their God's divine word is also self-evident. It is worth clarifying what this respect is not, so as to clarify what it is. It is not deference to the Catholic Church, which by its actions has forfeited its claim to deference that it would otherwise have. I have maintained repeatedly that the Church, this political institution, should not be granted immunity because it claims for itself divine authority. Just as it was and continues to be wrong for the Church to legitimize itself during the Nazi period as a religious, namely, a moral, institution and then to defend its conduct in the terms of a political institution, it is wrong for the Church today to forestall the restitution, including the internal changes, that necessarily follows from its political conduct by cloaking itself in religious garb. Instead, respect is owed to the beliefs of Catholics and other Christians and of their nonpolitical clergy about the integrity of their sacred texts.

So what is to be done? The Church's own solution is deeply inadequate. It is actually no solution because it does not address the problem. It does maintain the integrity of the sacred text but by pretending that the Christian Bible is not a profoundly antisemitic text, it ignores the obligation of restitution. As a solution, the Church's position therefore renders itself moot by privileging one of the imperatives completely as if the other imperative did not exist.

James Carroll, by contrast, proposes a powerful solution. The Catholic Church, which according to Catholicism mediates between God and Catholics by interpreting his words for them, should teach the antisemitic passages of the Christian Bible as falsehoods that constitute the Church's own sin, its own, metaphorical, original sin: "The anti-Jewish texts of the New Testament show that the Church, even in its first generation, was capable of betraying the message of Jesus, establishing once and for all that 'the Church as such' can sin. The Church as such stands in need of forgiveness. The Church must therefore preach the anti-Jewish texts of the Gospels—not against the Jews, but against itself."[159] Carroll wants to invert these texts' meaning, so that they would be a source not of continuing ill will and animosity for Jews but of Catholic self-knowledge and humility. As Carroll emphasizes, that "the first followers of Jesus violated his message by slandering their rivals [the Jews], even demonizing them, establishes better than anything else that the Church, at its core, is as sinful as any other institution."[160] Carroll's proposition contains a powerful logic and appeal. It is a radical solution that would use the text's antisemitism to undermine the text itself. If the Church would live by this maxim, it would be an extremely welcome development.

Still, it would likely be inadequate. Obviously we could not count on this message getting through to everyone. The message of Vatican II, which is official Church policy, certainly has not. Charlotte Klein, for example, reported ten years after Vatican II of her experiences teaching in the theology department of a German university about Judaism during the time of Jesus: "The anti-Judaism which could not but be noticed in all the [students'] essays arose wholly and entirely from the works of reference which were read and extensively quoted by the students. Vatican II had exercised no influence here; on the whole the students had scarcely read the Declaration on Judaism, nor—despite the efforts of the lecturer—had they understood its background." These works of reference from the most esteemed Catholic biblical scholars and theologians were poisoned by the belief in "the guilt of the Jews for the death of Christ and the [intergenerational] consequences of this guilt."[161]

People who have lectured in the United States, Europe, and around the world on the Holocaust, Jewish history, and Judaism learn from their audiences that Vatican II has failed to penetrate not only to many theologians and theology students but also to ordinary Catholics. The recent response around the Philippines to a Jewish American professor's talks in Catholic churches on Judaism is symptomatic. He was "assailed by a host of hostile questions headed by 'Why did you Jews kill Jesus Christ?' "[162] In the United States as well the Church's prescribed post–Vatican II instruction about Jews may be more on the books than in the books, the classroom, and the pulpit, not having sufficiently percolated down to lay Catholics. One scholar of the subject recounts: "When I have inquired of Catholic clergy (i.e., those who have been consistently involved in Catholic-Jewish dialogue and are therefore most knowledgeable and progressive) how many have actually sponsored any programs in their specific churches designed to convey the subjects explored in Catholic-Jewish symposia to their lay constituents, the response has been disappointing, indeed disconcertingly so."[163] Twenty-five years after *Nostra Aetate*, Father Reinhard Neudecker, in an assessment of the state of the Catholic Church and the Jews, had to begin his essay with an explication of the most basic facts. Why? He wrote: "The text of *Nostra aetate* and of the two later documents of the Commission for Religious Relations with the Jews [from 1974 and 1985] must be explained here in some detail, since surveys have shown that many of the readers to whom these writings are addressed have little, if any, knowledge of them."[164] Here he appears to be referring to the clergy of the Catholic Church, in Europe, North America, and the rest of the world, because the two later writings, on implementing *Nostra Aetate* and on the proper way to preach and teach about Jews, are addressed specifically to the clergy. If the Church's own clergy are ignorant of the Church's disavowals contained in these documents, how can we expect lay Catholics to be better informed? Micha Brumlik writes similarly, specifically about Germany, which he characterizes as a country whose churches have been at the forefront of reassessing Christian attitudes toward Jews and Judaism:

> Appreciation for the altered Christian perspective toward Judaism must not be naïve. Changes in academic theology and in attitudes found among the more educated, activist laity are not the same as widespread changes in thinking among churchgoers. There is no proof that these changes—as expressed in revised Protestant church regulations and Catholic bishops' declarations—have become an accepted part of the beliefs held by the majority.

Brumlik adds something that is ignored by those who like to put the best face on the Church, as if its most progressive elements were representative of the Church as a whole. "In addition," he observes, "it should be noted that the [progressive] theologians whose work is outlined here remain a minority, still outnumbered by their conventionally minded colleagues."[165]

Vatican II has had an undeniably and substantial positive effect on Catholics' views and attitudes toward Jews. Of particular note is the American Jewish Committee's Catholic-Jewish Educational Enrichment Program, which it carries out in high schools in cooperation with archdioceses in major cities around the United States, including New York, Chicago, and Los Angeles. According to the American Jewish Committee, "On a weekly basis, rabbis and Jewish teachers visit Catholic schools to teach about Judaism, and priests and sisters visit Jewish schools to teach about Catholicism." Since 1993 ten thousand students have benefited by learning about the history, teachings, and traditions of the other religion.[166] We can only hope that this and other educational initiatives become much more widespread, and not just in the United States.

Notwithstanding the many positive developments of Catholic-Jewish intercommunal discussion and cooperation, the good effects of Vatican II have been partial; Vatican II initiated only limited changes, and even those changes have reached and been accepted by only a limited number of Catholics. It is the failures of Vatican II's reforms that are relevant to the consideration of the limitations of Carroll's proposal and related issues. In today's Europe not to mention in the rest of the world tens of millions of people still deem Jews guilty or accursed for killing Jesus.

All Catholics who would not receive Carroll's prescribed message about the falseness of the Christian Bible's account of the Jews would still innocently be reading its antisemitic passages, passages that induce suspicion, animosity, and even enmity. Many of them would come to believe, or maintain their existing beliefs, in its many falsehoods and libels about Jews, including that the Jews crucified Jesus, that they are children of the devil, that they are part of the assembly of Satan, that they are accursed for all time. They would still read the Gospel According to John's presentation of the Jews as the ontological enemy of Jesus (and, by implication, of Christianity and goodness), with Jesus saying to the Jews, "You belong to what is below, I belong to what is above. . . . But now you are trying to kill me, a man who has told you the truth that I heard from God."[167] They would still learn in so many ways that Judaism is delegitimized because Christianity has replaced it and that the Jews no longer hear God because they do not hear Jesus.

Even for those Catholics who would receive the prescribed teaching about the sinfulness of these passages, the problem would not so evidently be solved. To tell the Catholic faithful that the Christian Bible is not divine, even though Jesus is, even though it tells his story, and even though it is the scriptural basis of Christianity, is a complex message that would likely often not be interpreted in a manner to Carroll's liking and commensurate with what the Church owes Jews. It is likely that many believers, in confronting such a paradoxical message, would decide to accept the literalness of the Christian Bible's libels as the word of God, concluding that they are correct. Carroll's appealing and thoughtfully constructed solution to the Church's Bible problem is too tenuous. Bold and promising as it is, it does not go far enough.

Carroll is trying to square two circles in an ingenuous and commendable way. Unlike the Church, he fully acknowledges and confronts the Christian Bible's antisemitism and takes seriously the necessity of moral restitution, but his proposal for that restitution is ultimately a half measure. Like the Church, he respects the integrity of the text ("there is no question of simply eliminating [the 'troubling texts']," he writes, "nor of rewriting them") but proposes that the Church not treat the Christian Bible as a divine and sacred text.[168] As a devout Catholic, it is Carroll's privilege to contest his

Church over matters of the divine. But if Carroll is willing to declare that the Christian Bible is not divine, if he is willing to say that Jesus' early followers, the authors of the Christian Bible, betrayed Jesus' message and "slander[ed] their rivals," the Jews, then why does he not go all the way and say that the falsehoods, the antisemitism must be removed?

If, for a moment, we leave aside Catholics' belief in the divinity and sacredness of the text, as Carroll and some other progressive Christians are willing to do, the Christian Bible would still be a central historical text or document of Western and much of world civilization. For a person to argue that because of this canonical status the Catholic Church may not or ought not to change its Bible, he would have to be able to assert that the harm that its text produces, owing to the antisemitism it spreads, is not sufficiently great to warrant removing the textual source of that harm. This assertion would be hard to defend given the great extent of that harm and the violation of the moral principle (and Christian religious imperative) not to commit unjust harm (or sin) against others. (Our question is worth repeating: Would all those who would defend maintaining the content of the Christian Bible even if we agree that the text is not the word of God also approve of handing a book to a billion people that asserted that blacks, Mexicans, Turks, Italians, or Baptists, Lutherans, Muslims killed God and are forever guilty?) If a person concedes what appears obvious—that the principle of not doing unjust harm is violated in too great a measure by leaving the Christian Bible just as it is—then to find Carroll's proposal (or something like it) adequate, he would have to be able to assert that it would be effective enough in reducing the text's harm so that resultant injuries would be diminished enough as to no longer warrant removing the textual source of that harm. It is hard to see, for all the good that Carroll's solution would bring about, how it could meet this standard of sufficiency.

If Pope John Paul II and if the Church were to act upon his commissioned and approved moral imperative from "We Remember"—"the spoiled seeds of anti-Judaism must never again be allowed to take root in any human heart"—then he would ask how the biblical anti-Jewish libels and imprecations can remain, for surely they will take antisemitic root in some, and probably very many, human hearts. Since the Pope was obviously genuine in his support for "We Remember," then he must confront the consequences for the Catholic Church and its Bible of the maxim that antisemitism "*must* never again be allowed to take root in *any* human heart" (my emphasis).

Christianity has consecrated a heinous set of charges against Jews in its foundational text. It continues its almost two-millennia-long offense of violating the Eighth Commandment by "bearing false witness" against Jews. Would the Pope or other Catholics countenance for a moment, let alone passionately defend, the unceasing repetition of such charges, if some religion or political institution insisted in its foundational religious text or constitution that blacks or Italians were children of the devil, the ontological enemy of God, the slayers of God's son—in other words, of God—and intergenerationally cursed for these fictitious things? Would the Pope or other Catholics countenance it if Judaism declared such things in its sacred texts explicitly about Christians? So why is it acceptable to bear false witness in such a way about Jews?

It would be reasonable to conclude that the only measures adequate to the problem are ones that would be obvious in other contexts: Declare the falsehoods false and sinful, and remove them from the text. The logic of moral restitution would require the Catholic Church—and other Christian churches—to declare that such hate-filled lies are not the word of God because neither God nor Jesus would tell such lies and spread such injurious, unjust hatreds. The Catholic Church, it might be thought, owes it to Jews to perform this "duty of reparation." The Church itself suggests as much when discussing how someone who violates the Eighth Commandment by bearing false witness must act: "Every offense committed against justice and truth entails the *duty of reparation*. . . . This reparation, moral and sometimes material, must be evaluated in terms of the extent of the damage inflicted."[169] How many offenses against truth have in human history inflicted greater damage than the Church's offense against the Jews? What debt of "moral" reparation could be greater? What acts, short of setting the record straight, exposing the falsehoods, and removing them so as not to spread further libels, could be ultimately adequate to the "extent" of this task and could fulfill what the Church holds to be a "duty of reparation"?

Many Catholics, other Christians, and non-Christians might recoil at this idea. It is a radical step for a religion to alter a sacred text or even just a foundational historical document, especially one that has been around for almost two millennia. Let me be clear: I am not saying that the Catholic Church must alter the Christian Bible. To assert that it must do so, is to heed one of the imperatives, the obligation of restitution, but it is, at least for a non-Christian, to ignore the second imperative, to respect the beliefs about the sacred that Catholics and other Christians share. This is the one instance where the powerful logic of moral inquiry, which I have laid out here, butts up against a moral obstacle of equivalent force. It is here that the problem of moral restitution and repair becomes most intractable, the course for proceeding with it most shrouded in moral and practical ambiguity and uncertainty. Also, that I devote considerably more space to explicating why the dictates of moral restitution require that the antisemitism of the Christian Bible be excised than I do to explaining the need to respect Catholics' notion of the sacred should not be understood to mean that I secretly support the first over the second. The disproportionate space given to the two positions reflects only the obvious: that convincing people of an unfamiliar, surprising, even discomforting notion, to which there will undoubtedly be much reflexive resistance, in this case that the Christian Bible might need to be changed, is a far more difficult task than is confirming a widespread, probably axiomatic, and virtually unquestioned view of Christian culture and of the peoples of many countries, namely, that the Christian Bible should not, and may not be changed.

The Catholic Church itself could change its Christian Bible. If, heeding its understanding of its own doctrinal imperatives, the Church would decide to excise from its Bible all antisemitism, then it would surely find a way and mechanism for doing so. And as the Church of its faithful, the accepted interpreter of God's word for Catholics who freely give it their ongoing allegiance, the Church, in taking such a step, would not only not be violating the imperative to respect people's beliefs about God but it would be carrying out its self-conceived duty to help Catholics better understand God and goodness.

The problem posed by the antisemitism of the Christian Bible remains. The Church's current way ignores the duty of restitution. Carroll's way, appealing as it is and great progress though it would be, is regarding each of the two imperatives, a half measure. The third possibility, of fulfilling the duty of restitution by excising the antisemitism, unless it comes directly from the Church, fails to respect the sacred. So what is to be done with this most vexing and morally troubling of problems?

In thinking about this, three things, in addition to the two imperatives, must be kept in mind: (1) there is no obvious and easy solution to this problem; (2) addressing the problematic aspects of the Christian Bible is not even subject to the exclusive control of the Catholic Church because its text is shared by other Christian churches and Christians who also deem it sacred; and (3) the solution, at least for Catholics, must come, in the end, from within the Church itself.

All of this suggests that the way to proceed is by initiating an open-ended process with the purpose of finding a way for the Church to carry out its obligation of restitution regarding its Bible. The Catholic Church should call for a public convocation of all Christian churches in a collective effort to resolve the problem of the Christian Bible's antisemitism. Jewish religious and communal leaders ought to be full members of the congress for purposes of the deliberations, though the Jews would not have a formal say in the outcome. Put differently, Jews would have a full voice during discussion but no vote. The starting basis of the congress must be a full recognition on the part of the Catholic Church, and this would also hold for other Christian churches, of the duty of moral restitution, of the need to prevent the Christian Bible from spreading antisemitism, from inciting suspicion, hatred, and enmity of Jews, from teaching more Christians to sin in antisemitism. The Congress' task would be to devise a means to carry out this duty.

Perhaps in the end the Catholic Church and other Christian churches would adopt something like Carroll's proposal. Perhaps they would go further. While keeping the text intact, they could include in every Christian Bible a detailed, corrective account alongside the text about its many antisemitic passages, and a clear disclaimer explaining that even though these passages were once presented as fact, they are actually false or dubious and have been the source of much unjust injury. They could include essays on the various failings of the Christian Bible, and a detailed running commentary on each page that would correct the texts' erroneous and libelous assertions. In doing this, the Church would do only what conservative Judaism has already tried to do to correct the historical inaccuracies and temper the injurious content of the Jewish Bible's Torah, the five books of Moses, in its translation and commentary published in 2001, called *Etz Hayim*.[170] But if the congress's participants were willing to recognize both the sinfulness of the text and that it is not divine, or even to tell the readers of the text that important parts of it are not true, and would cause more harm if they were believed and spread further, have caused great harm, then why would they not also recognize the need to change that Bible, given the various imperatives—of moral restitution, of not sinning, of not inducing others to sin—that the antisemitism of the Christian Bible contravenes?

At the very least, such a congress would initiate a process to carry out a moral imperative, a duty of restitution, which is different from what Vatican II was. John XXIII convened Vatican II because he wanted to move the antimodern Church of Pius XII forward organizationally, doctrinally, and in its practices, including with regard to Jews; what Vatican II did promulgate about Jews was from the Church's point of view—however theologically necessary it seemed to many because of the Holocaust—an act of charity toward the Jews. Not surprisingly, in the end it was deeply inadequate.[171] Initiating a new congress with this fundamentally different mission of moral restitution, understanding its terms, which include a duty that the Church has to Jews that it must discharge by bringing moral restitution to a successful end, the congress would be far more likely to result in something reasonably adequate. It would also, perhaps, be the beginning of a long process, of an ongoing congress or a series of congresses, of a real Christian-Jewish dialogue in which the Jews are seated as equals—not just with low-level church representatives ill-equipped for the task or with specialists in the Church's relations with Jews, but with the leaders of the Catholic Church.[172] The initial measures would likely be half measures, fine ones like Carroll's, but they might be followed by another half measure and then another, until the gap between what the Catholic Church and other Christian churches are doing to prevent their Bible from producing further injury might approach an adequate solution.

That the Catholic Church and other Christian churches would have to confront, in a discourse of public reason, the explicit and implicit antisemitism of the Christian Bible; all the libelous, hurtful, and hate-filled statements in it, and its very structure that treats the Jews as the ontological enemy of God, would in itself be salutary because men and women of good conscience, when forced publicly to defend the indefensible, find it difficult to do so. They would find it far more difficult than simply maintaining the current state of affairs, where they can take the easy path of ignoring or when necessary side-stepping the problem, some of them likely with uneasy consciences, but ignoring it nonetheless. If bishops and other Christian leaders would choose to defend the Christian biblical antisemitism against the historical facts that belie the biblical claims undergirding it, and in the face of all the harm their Bible has wrought, and if they would also be willing to do so to the faces of their inevitably many disapproving coreligionists, their Jewish interlocutors, and to a world of Christians and non-Christians ever less tolerant of such prejudice and hatreds, then at least transparency would be achieved and everyone would be able to draw the conclusions that he or she deems appropriate. The Christian leaders would now be honest and open about what they are doing, including about the further harm that they are choosing to inflict willfully on Jews, and also on Christians who are misled into prejudice and sin by their churches. The rest of the world, including many Christians, would see them for the defenders of bigotry that, in such a scenario, they would essentially be declaring themselves to be.[173]

It seems likely that a congress of Christian churches convened in public explicitly for the task of confronting the antisemitism of their Bible would find it hard to resist going a long way toward doing the right thing. Such an

CONCLUSION

MUSTERING
the Will

Progress in virtue, knowledge of the good, and ascesis enhance the mastery of the will over its acts.
>   *Catechism of the Catholic Church,* parag. 1734

T HE TASKS OF RESTITUTION are clear. Material restitution requires that the Catholic Church acknowledge, in principle, the monetary debts it owes to the Jewish victims and devise, in consultation with them or their heirs, a fair settlement. Political restitution requires that the Church vigorously supports, sustain, and protect Jewish political communities. Moral restitution requires that the Church eliminates antisemitism from the Church and Catholicism. This means not just certain cosmetic changes but a purging of explicit or implied antisemitism from the Church and its teachings, including by finding some adequate good-faith solution to what can be called its Bible problem. It also means a systematic, diligent educational effort—a mission that might last generations before it has fulfilled its own maxim to "restore the reputation of [the people] slandered"—to inform Catholics and non-Catholics that antisemitism is falsehood, an offense, and in Catholicism's terms a sin. The Church must also reform those aspects of its nature, organization, and doctrine, including its political core, that made its part in the Holocaust possible, in order to ensure that it and its clergy will not contribute to any crimes, political transgressions, or moral transgressions against Jews again. And it must adopt the pose, before the people it harmed—Jews for their injuries and Catholics for its moral betrayal of them—of a true penitent. If the Catholic Church and Catholics had been the victims of all that the Church, its Popes, bishops, and priests have perpetrated against Jews, it, its clergy and its faithful would expect no less of the people who had victimized it.[1]

Two questions remain. Is it realistic to expect an institution, indeed a powerful institution, to provide restitution, including moral restitution? Is it likely that this specific institution, the Catholic Church, will?

A POWERFUL INSTITUTION REPENTING?

A far more powerful institution than even the Catholic Church has already done so. The Federal Republic of Germany, for all its shortcomings in this area, has gone a long way to providing restitution, including moral restitution to Jews for Germans' crimes and other offenses against them. It has certainly taken many of the steps discussed here, which the Catholic Church has not. Of course, however great the Church's substantial culpability is for its anti-Jewish offenses, including for those contributing to the Holocaust, Germany's, because of the Holocaust, is enormously greater.

It is well known that Germany has provided, in absolute measures, substantial sums in monetary restitution, with the running total now of 115 billion deutschmarks (more than sixty billion dollars).[2] Even if the material losses of Jews and non-Jews dwarf the payments they have received, which renders the monetary restitution more symbolic than actual, Germany has given a large sum of money. Much less well known are Germany's trials of Germans (and some non-Germans) who murdered Jews and non-Jews during the Nazi period. After the Nuremberg trials, conducted by the Allies, the Federal Republic of Germany began in the late 1950s to investigate the perpetrators of the Holocaust and of other mass murders systematically, putting several thousand of them on trial. Although the German justice authorities, influenced by politics, unconscionably restricted the prosecutions generally to men who were in command positions, and the sentences given by judges were often ludicrously light, Germany at least convicted many criminals and established and acted with some energy on the principle that offenders had to be punished.[3]

If we move from the material and legal components of restitution, which, although not as widely known as they should be are at least recognized and conceptualized for what they are, we see that Germany has also substantially engaged in political and various forms of moral restitution, of the kinds called for here, even if these acts have not been conceptualized or intended explicitly as restitution—and even though they remain unrecognized as restitution. Politically, Germany, which destroyed Jewish communal and political life across Europe, has given considerable political restitution: political support to Jews, both to Israel and in Germany itself, helping them to build new communal institutions and to sustain and increase their shrunken communities.

Germany, its leaders, and many of its people have said mea culpa again and again, and asked genuinely for forgiveness. Germany, reflecting democratic thinking in many European countries that is less absolutist on free speech, made it illegal to express antisemitism either orally or in writing, a prohibition that was enforced for decades. It thereby created a public sphere almost completely devoid of antisemitism. This included the banning of Nazi books and literature, such as Hitler's *Mein Kampf,* the foundational texts of Nazism, and the immediate ideational inspiration for Germany's eliminationist assault on the Jews during this period.

More than just this legal prohibition of public antisemitism, the political elites, academics, and the media have, by now, educated Germans about the horrors of Nazism, the Holocaust, and antisemitism. This is not to say that the education has been first-rate in every respect or that there is no antisemitism among Germans today. Far from it. Antisemitism's recent resurgence, and the unwillingness until now to fight it seriously within both the government and broad reaches of civil society is a disturbing turn of events. But even still, the German elites have, since the war, by and large succeeded in two undertakings: de-demonizing Jews and delegitimizing the politics that produced the Holocaust. Most Germans today no longer consider Jews, as most Germans once did, to be a powerful race, genetically malevolent, responsible for much of the world's evil. It is all but an axiom of contemporary German society that during the Nazi period their countrymen committed one of the greatest crimes in human history, for which there is no justification whatsoever.[4]

This reeducation of Germans would never have been accomplished had the German elites modeled themselves on the Catholic Church, doing little more than issue a few brief public condemnations of the Holocaust—and waiting fifty years to do so. It would never have taken place had the world let Germany completely off the hook, denying its crimes and other offenses and the centrality of the country's dominant beliefs for producing them, the way it has the Catholic Church for its different, though still reprehensible, deeds and beliefs regarding Jews. For decades now there has been, by and large, good public education in Germany about the Nazi period, especially outside of the classroom, in newspapers and magazines (which provide extensive coverage of new findings, new books, and the meaning of historical events and anniversaries), and on television (where documentaries about the period and its horrors have long been regular fare). It would not be an exaggeration to say that Germans who wished to remain ignorant of the true character of this past and to bask undisturbed in its prejudices and hatreds would have had to walk around their country with their eyes closed and ears stopped up in order to avoid exposure to the truth.

Germany has also remade itself substantially, altering its fundamental structures, practices, and doctrines. The Germans have replaced a murderous tyranny of totalitarian, imperialist, and apocalyptic ambitions, indeed arguably the most volcanically destructive and antihuman regime in modern history, with genuine democratic institutions and laws. They have replaced inhuman practices domestically and internationally, with the rule of law at home, including broad legal protections of the rights of individuals, and a pattern of cooperation abroad. In these respects, Germany is a European and world leader. Germans have replaced core doctrines of racism, antisemitism, and hatred and the celebratory use of violence with the Enlightenment doctrines of universalism, tolerance, and the desire for peace, even if, as they are in greater or lesser measure everywhere, these doctrines are only imperfectly adhered to and practiced.

Essentially, what Germans have done is reconceptualize and reconstitute their society politically, socially, and culturally, making Germany a better place for Germans and a less threatening place for non-Germans, at home and abroad. Germans have provided substantial restitution—material, legal, political, and moral—to Jews, always keeping in mind that they could never make good on even a small fraction of the crimes and other offenses that their country and so many of its people perpetrated against Jews. The most important part of the Germans' moral restitution is, perhaps, that they have changed the structures, political and ideational, that produced the Holocaust, and thereby removed as best as they reasonably could the foundation for Germans to produce another Holocaust or even a lesser, violent persecution of the Jews (or of another people).

To be sure, the duty of providing restitution to the Jews was not what motivated Germans to do all of this. The replacement of the political and legal structures that produced the Holocaust was initiated by the Allies and then done by Germans in pursuit of their own interests and without reference to Jews at all. Germany performed many aspects of restitution because Germans, at least its elites, realized that it was necessary for the health and soul of Germany, and to improve Germany's fortunes and standing in the world. At times the country's elites had to drag many of their citizens along with them. Many of these measures, including a public display of contrition, served as a ticket for reentry into the community of nations.

This praise of what the Germans have accomplished could be accompanied by another discussion of how they have not done enough, how the often acted reluctantly and without moral conviction, and how they initially and for a long time acted primarily owing to pressure from other countries and other peoples, and out of considerations for their own interests and well-being.[5] It would include a consideration of why Germany awarded pensions to the mass murderers among its citizens that far exceeded the payments to Jewish victims.[6] It would include a somber assessment of the current situation of Jews in Germany, and of the unjustified belief among a substantial percentage of Germans that, in continuing to provide material and certain aspects of moral restitution to the victims, Germans are now being victimized.

The German writer Martin Walser gave prominent expression to this resentment in a speech he delivered upon receiving the Peace Prize of the German Booksellers Association in Frankfurt in 1998. At a solemn ceremony, before an audience consisting of a good part of the German political and cultural elite, Walser delivered a blistering denunciation of the public dwelling on the horrors of the Holocaust and of the concomitant use of Auschwitz as a "moral cudgel" to browbeat Germany. No matter that this last assertion was fatuous—Germany has hardly been beaten down by those who putatively wield this nonexistent moral cudgel—for when Walser finished, the illustrious audience rose virtually in unison and applauded enthusiastically.

The concerted attack by those who wish to suppress further dissemination of the truth about the Holocaust and about the continuing moral duties of Germany and Germans is part of a broader trend. During the past few years antisemitism has reappeared in the public sphere of Germany. With the passage of time and with the resurgence of German power, the taboo of five decades' duration has been losing its potency. Verbal and physical attacks on Jews or their institutions, property, or symbols are no longer, as they had hitherto been, extremely rare occurrences that are promptly and universally condemned. Nor are the verbal attacks confined to fringe groups. Antisemitism has manifested itself in respectable quarters of society, among political leaders, intellectuals, and the business elite. This trend has gained considerably in scope and intensity since the latest Palestinian intifada began in 2000. The renewal of the Israeli-Palestinian armed conflict has allowed those Germans who are antisemitic to exhibit their hitherto circumspect antipathies openly in public, cloaked in the, for some, seemingly respectable guise of anti-Zionism. Whether moved by good-faith criticism of Israeli policy—as no doubt many of them are—or by antisemitic sentiments, Germans could now condemn the actions of Israel, denouncing them as heinous offenses. The singular passion and aggressiveness of these protests have led many analysts to conclude that this anti-Zionism is, in the words of one German scholar of antisemitism, "ersatz antisemitism; it says Israel but means the Jews."[7] As if to confirm this view, there have been instances when this antisemitism shed its disguise, parading itself in its hideous nakedness. According to a signed editorial in a leading German liberal newspaper, "It has been a long time since Jew hatred now disguised as anti-Zionism has been as respectable as it is today. During the demonstration in favor of Palestine last weekend it was permissible to bellow the slogans for which neo-Nazi marches are prohibited and for which the NPD [the radical right party] is to be outlawed: 'Jewish swine' and [the Nazi] 'Sieg Heil' and so on."[8] This recent activation and emergence in Germany of the antisemitism that had not dissipated during the postwar period but which had nevertheless become latent and gone mainly underground, reminds us of this prejudice's tenaciousness in Western and Christian culture which leads it, as the Dutch bishops attest to "arise repeatedly in our society." These recent developments remind us also of the immense effort that is needed for us to eradicate antisemitism.[9]

Still, however disquieting recent developments are in Germany, the state of Germans' attitudes and conduct toward Jews is enormously better than in 1945. Even if many Germans would like to put an end to the post-Holocaust era, it is broadly acknowledged in Germany that it *was* morally necessary for Germans, and good for Germany, to have undertaken restitution toward Jews in the broad sense in which I have used it here. Germans today are committed to democracy. Jews have been de-demonized in Germany. Except among fringe elements, Nazism is dead. It will not be resurrected.

When the attitudes and conduct of an institution or people are only partly praiseworthy, even the most precise of complex evaluations tends to get misrepresented. The problem with praise and criticism, when they are simultaneously necessary, is that the message that both are deserved is difficult for people to digest, in part because such a message often gets distorted by partisans of one side or the other; such complex messages, particularly when each of its aspects is forcefully delivered, are displeasing to just about all partisans—to an institution's defenders and to its critics, neither of whom likes to have their often politically informed positions powerfully undercut. To say that Germany has done a good deal toward providing restitution, including moral restitution, to Jews, is not to mean that it has not also fallen short in substantial ways or that it has nothing left to do. Similarly, to say that the Church has a long way to go before it has discharged its moral duties of restitution is not to say that it has not taken important steps forward. Many within the Church have, in good faith, genuinely grappled with its offenses and its attendant moral needs, wanting to reform the

Church's injurious doctrines and ways. And the Church's official positions on a range of issues regarding Jews, Judaism, and the Holocaust have become markedly better with every decade since Vatican II.

I focus here on the positive steps that Germany has taken to provide a heuristic, to show that more than the Church's meager steps is not only possible but also has already been done—and done by a more powerful and just as prideful an institution. I focus here more on the Church's shortcomings than on its positive steps because they are more glaring, unacknowledged, and in need of recognition. If moral and contextual conditions are to improve for Catholics and for Jews, it is not the relatively easy progress already made by the Church—difficult as it has been, the progress has been *relatively* easy—but the many, much larger untended tasks that must be placed squarely before the lenses of the Church's moral senses and faculties of action, and before those outside the Church who should encourage it and help it move progressively forward.

Of all the measures Germany has adopted that the Catholic Church has not, the most critical is the destruction and replacement of the political, legal, and ideational structures that were necessary components for it, and for the Germans who participated, to have perpetrated their offenses. Barring unforeseeable and, indeed, difficult-to-imagine radical reversals in Germany, the features that made the Germans' eliminationist persecution of the Jews possible—political structures and eliminationist antisemitism—have been destroyed, if not by the Germans alone, then certainly with their substantial help. The features that made the Church's offenses against the Jews—its political nature and structures and its foundational anti-semitism—are, by contrast, still in place. This, the most critical element of the Church's needed moral restitution, structural transformation to prevent the offenses of everyday antisemitism and the horrors of its worst manifestations from recurring, the Church has yet to do. As was the case with Germany and Germans after the defeat of Nazism, the Catholic Church and its clergy still seem to need an enormous amount of outside help, including pressure, to do what they must. The Church's doctrine suggests that in the eyes of the Church, those who helped, indeed, pressured Germans in this way are "praiseworthy." Why should those who would apply the Church's doctrine to itself and its clergy, and help, urge, even pressure the Church to do what it must—heeding the Church's powerful call to "impose restitution" on those who owe it in order "to correct vices and maintain justice"—be any less "praiseworthy"?[10]

It should be abundantly obvious by now, but just to be sure, let me make it absolutely explicit: I am not equating the Catholic Church, as it is now or as it was during the Nazi period, with Nazi Germany. Among their many fundamental differences in kind, whatever their once overlapping though not entirely congruent ideas and projects regarding the Jews, is that while after World War II the country that was Nazi Germany needed to have itself remade from top to bottom because, at its core, its moral culture and politics had become reprehensible, racist, violent, and murderous, the Catholic Church and its moral creed, as I have said repeatedly, is, at its core, good and admirable. Nazism could be subjected only to external critiques to condemn it. It had to be destroyed for Germany's renewal. By contrast, the Church has already drawn upon its own creed to alter itself substantially and positively since the war. While in need of external critiques to spur it to act further, the Church can be and ought to continue to be criticized using its own good moral principles, which, when worked out, support and suggest the conclusions presented here. The Church and Catholicism contain the ideational and moral resources for their own renovation, for the removal of structures of authority and antisemitic ideas that violate their otherwise admirable principles of being a moral guide to Catholics and teaching them to seek goodness, to love others, and to act well.

MORAL REPAIR AND THE CATHOLIC CHURCH

Moral restitution is difficult. Material and political restitution, even if they seem taxing, are comparatively easy. That is one reason that they are the principal currency of restitution efforts. Moral restitution, on the face of it, may seem the easiest, but in critical ways it is the hardest of all. It requires among many other things a change in self-conception and in fundamental doctrines and practices. It brings about the most fundamental and necessary changes, but such changes are often the most difficult to accept and to successfully institute. It is easier, not that it is easy, to spend money and extend diplomatic support than to admit that deeply ingrained and previously cherished habits and ways are pernicious, and then to change them—and to change not just the habits and ways of acting but also the habits and ways of thinking, feeling, and conceiving of oneself.

Moral restitution for crimes and other offenses against Jews in the years before, during, and after the Holocaust is yet to be done by many countries, by Protestant churches, especially German Protestant churches, by private institutions, including financial institutions and industrial concerns, by public institutions, such as universities, and by their individual members. This book's mode of investigation; its insistence on the need to recognize the conceptual and moral centrality of human agency and moral responsibility, and its continuous emphasis on them throughout; its proposal of a framework for assessing the nature of offenses and culpability according to generally applicable and impartial categories; and its conclusions about the need for restitution and moral repair and what their various components are; all may be applied, as warranted, to all the other actors, institutions and individual persons, that were involved in some way in the Holocaust, or for that matter in any other crime or offenses by any people against any other people, historically or in the contemporary world. As I have said all along, it is not just the Catholic Church that owes restitution, including moral restitution, and it is not just Jews who are owed it. It is not just the Catholic Church that needs to be subjected to and to subject itself to a moral reckoning regarding its role in the persecution of the Jews, it is just that here we have focused on the Catholic Church as an exemplary investigation.

The Church's provision of moral restitution, kindred to its doctrine of repentance, is important for its victims and necessary for the Church itself. Without it the Church cannot regain its moral wholeness, in its terms, to convert itself back to God's ways: "The movement of return to God, called conversion and repentance, entails sorrow for and abhorrence of sins committed, and the firm purpose of sinning no more in the future. Conversion touches the past and the future and is nourished by hope in God's mercy."[11] With every day that the Church does not act upon its moral imperatives, it injures itself, its standing in the world, and its faithful.

This investigation's conclusions about the Catholic Church's need to undertake restitution—comprising all facets of a moral reckoning with its past, which include altering Church structures, practices, and doctrine and theology—follow inevitably from seemingly incontestable basic principles, principles that the Church in its own terms explicitly shares as doctrinal imperatives.[12] Some of the conclusions also find considerable support in the works of some of the most prominent progressive Catholic theologians today and devout Catholics who write about the Church, such as Hans Küng, Johann-Baptist Metz, and Roger Haight, and James Carroll, John Cornwell, and Garry Wills among others. Most of them begin with a set of concerns about the Church that do not focus on the Church's need to provide restitution for its wrongs against Jews, yet they argue for many of the same structural and doctrinal remedies. They come to their conclusions for internal Catholic theological reasons and out of concern mainly for the well-being of Catholics. However persuasive their conclusions are, their prescriptions do not necessarily have the same binding force that our investigation shows the universal and unavoidable moral duty of restitution does have. Notwithstanding the congruence of our conclusions with those that flow from Catholic doctrinal principles and with those put forward by prominent Catholic theologians and thinkers, it is likely that our conclusions will be received as a surprise and as an affront to the Church and to many Catholics, and to those, Jews and non-Jews alike, who curry the powerful Church's favor. Why? Our discussion has already suggested two different kinds of reasons.

In the secular public realm, the Church and its leadership have historically enjoyed relative immunity from the kind of dispassionate scrutiny given other political institutions and leaders who have committed analogous crimes and offenses, mainly because of the deference that the Church has commanded, which its religious nature, its vast political resources, and its hundreds of millions of adherents have produced. That is not to say that the Church has escaped all criticism. But those who have criticized it for its stances and actions during the Nazi period have confined themselves mainly to an enumeration of the Church's historical transgressions—often restricting their focus even more narrowly to Pius XII—without drawing the obvious and unavoidable conclusions that flow from an extended moral reckoning about those transgressions.[13]

The character of the judgments about the Church's and its clergy's culpability, and of the restitution that such grave culpability requires, is also completely at odds with the Church's self-understanding and practices. The Church approaches its relations with Jews not as a meeting of equals, but on its terms, granting what it does to Jews not out of self-understood duty but out of political necessity or as an act of charity. The Church is an institution that has never conceded that it has wronged others or that its Pope can even be wrong about core matters because it claims that, given their nature, neither is possible. Now it is being asked to admit enormous culpability, moral ugliness, and, in its own terms, sin. The logical conclusion of this moral reckoning—that the Church must remake itself in fundamental ways—is not a message that the self-appointed embodiment of God hears readily from human beings, particularly ones who are not even Catholic.

I ASKED EARLIER what the likelihood is that the Catholic Church and its leaders would do what their moral duty says that they must. Where will the courage, which John Paul II commanded to Rwandans, come from for the Church and its leadership, especially its European leadership, to face the consequences of the Church's and its clergy's past actions? Will the Church build a better, a restituted future? It is easy to say that the likelihood is not great, at least in the foreseeable future, and it would probably be right to say this.[14] After all, the Church still has so much internal resistance to overcome, and it appears to be difficult for many within the Church including many of its leaders to genuinely empathize with Jews. These considerable obstacles aside, it is asking a great deal of any institution to make such confessions, as the Church must, and to transform itself as thoroughly as its own good and its moral duty requires.[15] Even with the best of intent and will, it would be hard to do.

Still, if the Northern State Protestant Church of Germany can undertake an important part of moral restitution, telling the truth and seeking to educate its members about the horrors that the antisemitism of its own Christian tradition helped to produce, then obviously the Catholic Church can do the same. If Germany could remake itself then the Catholic Church can also do so. Aside from these existing examples of a Christian Church on its own initiative implementing this foundational element of moral restitution and of a great power, defeated and under enormous pressure, going still further, there are other reasons for thinking that the Catholic Church might find its way, or at least make substantial progress, in these matters. They are:

The Church's political trajectory: During the last four decades the Church has already moved itself a good deal forward, with Vatican II and other initiatives and changes, from where it was in 1945 and for almost two millennia before.

The Church's progressive voices: There are powerful, if still a small minority of, theological and thoughtful lay voices within the Church that are insisting on the truth, on drawing the necessary consequences from it, and on acting upon them.

The Church's heart: The Church is made up of people with good hearts who, if presented with the truth about the Church's history and bearing toward the Jews, would find it difficult to bear inflicting still more harm upon the members of this people whom it so victimized in the past.

The Church's principles: The Church's core moral doctrines are powerful. Love your neighbor. Do good to others. Repent of your sins. Such dictums always contain the potential to undermine and sweep away the false and injurious structures and doctrines that have been faultily and shakily built upon them or in disregard of them.

The Church's habit of mind: The Church is a resilient institution, having remade itself many times in many ways because of its formidable and admirable internal intellectual culture, which (its historical blind spots regarding Jews notwithstanding) nurtures a thirst for, and a drive to seek, enlightenment, truth, and goodness.

The Church's own potentially paradoxical structure of authority: If a man becomes Pope who sees the necessity of completing the journey of the Church's postwar trajectory, listens to the progressive voices, takes into his own heart the immense goodness of the faithful's hearts, applies the Church's core moral doctrines, and seeks to remake the Church according to all of this, or if such a man just comes to see that the Church does have the duty to perform restitution, then he would have the authority (at least until he himself undoes it) to transform the Church into the pluralist, tolerant, publicly self-critical, anti-antisemitic institution that the twenty-first century demands.

We should admire the Catholic Church in principal aspects of its self-understanding, Christianity in its essence, Catholic priests and nuns who devote their lives to a beneficent God, and lay Catholics in their religiously inspired goodness. Respect for their goodness and for their search for truth demands an honest and blunt engagement with the past. It also demands a blunt engagement with the present. This necessarily produces a picture of the Church's construction and treatment of Jews of substantial ugliness: the past has been ugly, and to the extent that its marred features persist today or have not been adequately repaired, the present is also ugly. Who would argue, what good Christian or good Jew would argue, that the true picture should be locked away in the catacombs and be replaced by an inauthentic, relatively inoffensive, officially inspired portrait that celebrates and sustains the powerful, that makes it easier for the Church to further injure a people whom it has so injured in the past, and that gives the Church and its faithful reason to continue to commit grave offenses against other human beings and, in the Church's terms, to sin against God? Who, in good faith, could argue for the current state of affairs?

WE BEGAN THIS inquiry with a question: What must a religion of love and goodness do to confront its history of hatred and harm, to make amends with its victims, and to right itself so that it no longer is the source of a hatred and harm that it today would no longer endorse? Now that the answer has been given, the question for the Catholic Church becomes: Will it muster the will to do what it must?

NOTES

Introduction: Framing the Problem

1. Daniel Jonah Goldhagen, *Hitler's Willing Executioners: Ordinary Germans and the Holocaust* (New York: Alfred A. Knopf, 1996).

2. "Foreword to the German Edition," in the softcover edition of Goldhagen, *Hitler's Willing Executioners* (New York: Vintage, 1997), p. 479.

3. A stunning example of this was the German newsmagazine, *Der Spiegel,* which made its multiarticle, lengthy treatment of the book its cover story, telling the German public that it was a "New Controversy About Collective Guilt" (Neuer Streit um Kollektivschuld) and entitled its lead article "A People of Demons?" ("Ein Volk von Dämonen?"), *Der Spiegel* 21 (May 20, 1996), pp. 48–77. Many analysts have exposed and dissected the various fictitious positions, especially "collective guilt," that dishonest critics were attributing to my book or to me personally. Perhaps most relevant to the discussion here are Martin Kött's devastating account of such attempts in *Goldhagen in der Qualitätspresse: Eine Debatte über "Kollektivschuld" und "Nationalcharakter" der Deutschen* (Goldhagen in the Quality Press: A Debate About the "Collective Guilt" and "National Character" of the Germans) (Konstanz: UVK Medien, 1999); and the point-by-point factual refutation of many falsehoods attributed to my book, Michael Pinto-Duschinsky, "Wehler on *Hitler's Willing Executioners:* A Comment," *German History* 16, 3 (1998), pp. 397–411. For a further sampling, see also Wolfgang Wippermann, *Wessen Schuld? Vom Historikerstreit zur Goldhagen-Kontroverse* (Berlin: Elefanten Press, 1997); Jürgen Elsässer and Andrei S. Markovits, eds., *"Die Fratze der eigenen Geschichte": Von der Goldhagen-Debatte zum Jugoslawien-Krieg* (Berlin: Elefanten Press, 1998), pp. 54–55; Matthias Küntzel et al., *Goldhagen und die deutsche Linke* (Berlin: Elefanten Press, 1997); Fred Kautz, *Gold-Hagen und die "Hürnen Sewfriedte": Die Holocaust-Forschung im Sperrfeuer der Flakhelfer* (Berlin: Argument Verlag, 1998); Robert E. Herzstein, "Daniel Jonah Goldhagen's 'Ordinary Germans' A Heretic and His Critics," *The Journal of the Historical Society 2,* 1 (winter 2002); Lars Rensmann, " 'Zorn von Alttestamentarishem Atem': Reflexionen zur politischen Psychologie der 'Goldhagen-Debatte,' " in *Kritische Theorie über den Antisemitismus: Studen zu Struktur, Erklärungspotential und Aktualität* (Berlin: Argument Verlag, 1998), pp. 336–360; Michael Klundt, *Geschichtspolitik: Die Kontroversen um Goldhagen, die Wehrmachtsausstellung und das "Schwarzbuch des Kommunismus"* (Köln: Papy Rossa Verlag, 2000); and the essays in "Goldhagen und die Deutschen," special issue, *Psyche* 51, 6 (June 1997). See also Daniel Jonah Goldhagen, "The Fictions of Ruth Bettina Birn and "Der neue Vermeidungsdiskurs" (which appears in English) at <www.goldhagen.com>. For a compilation of materials from the German discus-

sion of my book, see Robert R. Shandley, ed., *Unwilling Germans? The Goldhagen Debate*, Jeremiah Riemer, trans. (Minneapolis: University of Minnesota Press, 1998). For accounts of the German public's rejection of the attacks on my book, see Robert R. Shandley "Introduction," and Volker Ullrich, "A Triumphal Procession: Goldhagen and the Germans," in Shandley, *Unwilling Germans?*, pp. 1–30 and 197–201; see also Frank Schirrmacher, "Wunderheiler Goldhagen," *Frankfurter Allemeine Zeitung* (Sept. 13, 1996); Amos Elon, "The Antagonist as Liberator," *New York Times Magazine* (Jan. 26, 1997) and my "Afterword to the Vintage Edition," in Goldhagen, softcover *Hitler's Willing Executioners*, pp. 463–466.

4. "Foreword to the German Edition," Goldhagen, softcover *Hitler's Willing Executioners*, p. 482. During the five months between the book's publication in English and its subsequent publication in German I refused to engage in an almost surrealistic debate about a book that the German public could not yet read, which meant that Germans would not be able to see for themselves who was telling the truth about what it actually contains. I did, however, publish a brief open letter to the German booksellers correcting a few of the most egregious extant misrepresentations. It included an explicit statement that my book contains no charge of collective guilt. That the critics in Germany for months, including in the *Spiegel* cover story two weeks later, continued—and that to this day some in Germany and elsewhere continue—to maintain the falsehoods that I do make such a charge is proof of their bad faith.

5. Jürgen Habermas, "Goldhagen and the Public Use of History: Why a Democracy Prize for Daniel Goldhagen?" in Shandley, *Unwilling Germans?*, p. 264.

6. See, for example, for John Paul II, <www.vatican.va/holy_father/john_paul_ii/index.htm>; for the National Conference of Catholic Bishops of the United States Catholic Conference, see <www.nccbuscc.org/chronological.htm>; for the Deutsche Bischofskonferenz, see <dbk.de>; also see James E. Dougherty, *The Bishops and Nuclear Weapons: The Catholic Pastoral Letter on War and Peace* (Hamden, Conn.: Anchor Books, 1984); and National Conference of Catholic Bishops, *Economic Justice for All: Pastoral Letter on Catholic Social Teaching and the U.S. Economy* (Washington, D.C.: United States Catholic Conference, 1986).

7. One notable early exception was Karl Jaspers, *The Question of German Guilt* (1947, New York: Fordham University Press, 2000). Another exception is the discussion within the legal and scholarly communities of the legal issues that emerged from the Nuremberg trials. See, for example Steven R. Ratner and Jason S. Abrams, *Accountability for Human Rights Atrocities in International Law: Beyond the Nuremberg Legacy*, Second Ed. (New York: Oxford University Press, 2001).

8. Most prominent perhaps is Raul Hilberg, who presents such dubious notions in *The Destruction of the European Jews* (New York: New Viewpoints, 1973, originally published in 1961). That Hilberg adopted such an essentializing view of Germans in 1961, when such views were still in vogue, though just barely, is one thing, but that he continues to insist upon them is another. Hilberg affirmed that he wishes to spread such views as recently as 1996 in *The Politics of Memory: The Journey of a Holocaust Historian* (Chicago: Ivan R. Dee, 1996), where he euphemistically calls this long-discredited, some might say quasi-racist idea, a "national

character analysis," which he laments "is not pursued in the United States as in Europe" (p. 126). Where and by whom in Europe exactly, Hilberg does not say. In Germany, a notable example is the historian Norbert Frei. On September 7, 1996, in Frankfurt during a panel discussion about *Hitler's Willing Executioners*, Frei took issue with my explicit rejection of the notion of collective guilt. He emphatically endorsed the concept of collective guilt, asserting that it applies to Germans during the Nazi period, though only for turning a blind eye. See Jurgen Dahlkamp, "Goldhagen vertiedigt sein Buch: 'Von keiner These abgerückt,' " *Frankfurter Allgemeine Zeitung,* September 8, 1996.

9. For examples of such moral neutering, see Hans Mommsen, "The Realization of the Unthinkable: The 'Final Solution of the Jewish Question' in the Third Reich," in Gerhard Hirschfeld, ed., *The Politics of Genocide: Jews and Soviet Prisoners of War in Nazi Germany* (London: Allen & Unwin, 1986); in a debate about *Hitler's Willing Executioners* in Berlin, Mommsen went so far as to assert that the killers did not understand what they were doing. It was not "fully clear in their minds." But to the Berlin audience, it was fully clear what Mommsen was up to. They booed him. See Elon, "The Antagonist as Liberator," p. 44. In Germany the exculpatory refrains of the postwar period were so widespread, insistent, and ludicrous that a parodic counterrefrain has become part of the critique of the country's central self-exculpatory tendency: "Niemand war dabei und keiner hat's gewußt." "No one was there and no one knew about it." See Jörg Wollenberg, ed., *"Niemand war dabei und keiner hat's gewußt": Die deutsche Öffentlichkeit und die Judenverfolgung 1933–1945* (München: Piper, 1989). There is reason to believe that, in private, discussion of the Nazi period was sometimes more truthful.

10. Hannah Arendt, *The Origins of Totalitarianism* (New York: Meridian Books, 1971) and *Eichmann in Jerusalem: A Report on the Banality of Evil,* rev. ed. (New York: Viking, 1965); Stanley Milgram, *Obedience to Authority: An Experimental View* (New York: Harper Colophon, 1969); Christopher R. Browning, in a classic example of this, latched on to Arendt and Milgram in order to try to lend universal significance to his faulty conclusions about the men of the one German police battalion. See his analytically confused concluding chapter in *Ordinary Men: Reserve Police Battalion 101 and the Final Solution in Poland* (New York: HarperCollins, 1992), pp. 159–189, especially pp. 171–176, p. 184, and p. 216, n. 5.

11. For a discussion of the law, see Ingo Müller, *Hitler's Justice: The Courts of the Third Reich* (Cambridge: Harvard University Press, 1991), pp. 254–256.

12. See Goldhagen, *Hitler's Willing Executioners,* especially pp. 5–14, where the need for finally recognizing the moral agency of the perpetrators is laid out, as well as the denial of such agency by the then-existing conventional views; for further discussion of these issues, see Daniel Jonah Goldhagen, "The Paradigm Challenged: Victim Testimony, Critical Evidence, and New Perspectives in the Study of the Holocaust," *Tikkun* 13, no. 3 (May/June 1998), pp. 40–47; for a few of the many recent books that have adopted this perspective of agency and choice, and that further substantiate that the German populace was not terrorized and willingly persecuted Jews, see Robert Gellately, *Backing Hitler: Consent and Coercion in Nazi Germany* (Oxford: Oxford University Press, 2001); Eric A. Johnson, *Nazi Terror:*

The Gestapo, Jews, and Ordinary Germans (New York: Basic Books, 1999); and Marion A. Kaplan, *Between Dignity and Despair: Jewish Life in Nazi Germany* (New York: Oxford University Press, 1998).

13. For examples of such fawning praise, see the unreliable Ronald J. Rychlak, the Pope's most dogged recent defender, in *Hitler, the War, and the Pope* (Columbus, Miss.: Genesis Press, 2000), pp. 239–248, which presents such praise falsely as determinative evidence of historical facts. Rychlak's denial, omission, and misconstrual of basic facts is systematic and blatant. Susan Zuccotti, "Debate with Ronald Rychlak, Trinity College," *Journal of Modern Italian Studies* (Summer 2002, in press), in a devastating point-by-point exposé of Rychlak's falsehoods and misuse of sources, writes, "The problems with Rychlak's book . . . begin when he writes about what the pope did behind the scenes to help Jews just before and during the Holocaust. But since that is the primary thrust of his book, these are major problems, literally arising on nearly every page. Here it is not a question of agreeing or disagreeing on concepts or interpretations. In his writing about what the pope did, Rychlak is simply wrong on nearly all of his facts. In the limited space allotted to me, I will only be able to discuss some of Rychlak's most glaring errors regarding the pope and Jews in Italy. He makes similar errors when he writes about Slovakia, France, Hungary, and nearly everything else." Rychlak responds to those who tell the truth, including Zuccotti, about the failings of Pius XII and the Catholic Church during the Holocaust with unprincipled attacks. See also John Cornwell, *Breaking Faith: The Pope, the People, and the Fate of Catholicism* (New York: Viking, 2000) for the exposure of Rychlak's falsehoods about Cornwell (pp. 5–10). What Susan Zuccotti, *Under His Very Windows: The Vatican and the Holocaust in Italy* (New Haven: Yale University Press, 2000), writes about the damage done by two men who in the 1960s helped to create positive myths about Pius XII also applies to so many others: "There is no need to decide here whether these writers' errors were intentional or inadvertent. Certainly, however . . . they were damaging to the task of historical truth" (pp. 303–304).

14. See Rolf Hochhuth, *The Deputy* (New York: Grove Press, 1964); Eric Bentley, ed., *The Storm Over the Deputy* (New York: Grove Press, 1964); and Pierre Blet, Robert A. Graham, Angelo Martini, and Burkhart Schneider, eds., *Actes et documents du Saint Siège relatifs à la seconde guerre mondiale*, 11 vols. (Vatican City: Libreria Editrice Vaticana, 1965–1981).

15. James Carroll, *Constantine's Sword: The Church and the Jews* (Boston: Houghton Mifflin, 2001); David I. Kertzer, *The Popes Against the Jews: The Vatican's Role in the Rise of Modern Anti-Semitism* (New York: Alfred A. Knopf, 2001); Georges Passelecq and Bernard Suchecky, *The Hidden Encyclical of Pius XI*, Steven Rendall, trans. (New York: Harcourt Brace, 1997); Michael Phayer, *The Catholic Church and the Holocaust, 1930–1965* (Bloomington: Indiana University Press, 2000); Garry Wills, *Papal Sin: Structures of Deceit* (New York: Doubleday, 2000); and Zuccotti, *Under His Very Windows*. Also of note is John F. Morley, *Vatican Diplomacy and the Jews During the Holocaust, 1939–1943* (New York: Ktav, 1980), a painstaking investigation, country by country, of the failures of the Vatican and its representatives to make genuine efforts to help the Jews. While I use the evidence

that these authors and others have uncovered and systematized, I do not always agree with their specific or more general interpretations and explanations. This means that when I employ evidence from their works, or the works of others, it implies nothing about their agreement or disagreement with the significance or meaning that I lend to that evidence or to any other point that I make in this book. Unless I explicitly invoke another author's interpretive authority on a given point, no one should infer that I am implicitly claiming such authority for my views. Similarly, because this book is not a historiographic exercise, I do not carry on a running discussion with views that these authors or others may have that differ from my own. Their books and those of other interpreters are readily available for readers who wish to deepen their knowledge of the issues.

16. So much academic and nonacademic writing about the Holocaust treats the Holocaust as an extraordinary phenomenon to which our ordinary methods, rules of analysis, and modes of interpretation do not apply. Writers insistently reject standard social scientific practices, violate the rules of inference, say that we are not allowed to describe certain facts (the perpetrators' cruelty), maintain that those who often know the actors' (the perpetrators') attitudes toward their deeds best (namely, the victims) know them least well, that the Holocaust is the only genocide where the perpetrators did not hate their victims and did not want to do what they freely chose to do. It is true that many of these bizarre and self-delegitimizing positions seem to be motivated by politics, personal or national, but there is also genuine confusion. I have argued repeatedly that we must adopt standard social scientific methods and rules of evidence, while still presenting the information and conclusions in transparent and accessible ways. The Holocaust is, in principle, describable and explainable. It is, in principle, no more or no less understandable than other crimes or other events. Similarly, the Holocaust's events and participants are not beyond our moral judgment. In principle, those who lived through it, whether as perpetrators, so-called bystanders, or victims, are no more or no less subject to our judgment than the actors are from any other contemporaneous or past event. The widespread failure to reason morally about the actors therefore is properly seen as but a particular instance of the general failure to reason properly about many aspects of the Holocaust. For a discussion of some of these issues, see Goldhagen, "The Paradigm Challenged."

17. For Germans' use of slave labor in general and for various German companies that were involved, see Ulrich Herbert, *Fremdarbeiter: Politik und Praxis des "Ausländer-Einsatzes" in der Kriegswirtschaft des Dritten Reiches* (Berlin: Dietz, 1985); and Benjamin B. Ferencz, *Less than Slaves: Jewish Forced Labor and the Quest for Compensation* (Cambridge: Harvard University Press, 1979). For Swiss banks and Switzerland more generally, see Independent Commission of Experts Switzerland—Second World War, *Switzerland, National Socialism, and the Second World War: Final Report*, and the twenty-five single volume reports <www.uek.ch/en/index.htm>, and Philippe Braillard, *Switzerland and the Crisis of Dormant Assets and Nazi Gold* (London: Kegan Paul International, 2000). For the German historians, see Götz Aly, "Rückwärtsgewandte Propheten: Willige Historiker—Bemerkung in eigener Sache," in *Macht-Geist-Wahn: Kontinuitäten deutschen*

Denkens (Berlin: Argon Verlag, 1997), pp. 153–183. The Nazi historians' faithful
and most prominent students include Hans Mommsen and Hans-Ulrich Wehler (p.
154). For an analysis of Wehler's and Mommsen's respective unprincipled writings
about the Holocaust, see Pinto-Duschinsky, "Wehler on *Hitler's Willing Executioners*" and Kautz, *Gold-Hagen und die "Hürnen Sewfriedte."*

18. The most prominent contemporary popular exponent of such attacks upon
Jews or those referred to as "Zionists" is perhaps Norman G. Finkelstein, in *The
Holocaust Industry: Reflection on the Exploitation of Jewish Suffering* (London:
Verso, 2000), and in Norman G. Finkelstein and Ruth Bettina Birn, *A Nation on
Trial: The Goldhagen Thesis and Historical Truth* (New York: Owl Books, 1998).
Christopher Browning, Raul Hilberg, and Hans Mommsen, perhaps to buttress
some of their own dubious works, have resorted to endorsing Finkelstein and
Birns, which is marred by repeated inaccuracies and inventions. Finkelstein
famously claims that "Holocaust studies" is "mainly a propaganda enterprise" and
that " 'the Holocaust' is in effect the Zionist account of the Nazi holocaust" *New
Left Review* (July/Aug. 1997), pp. 83–84, and *A Nation on Trial*, p. 94. In doing so,
Browning, Hilberg, and Mommsen have lent their respectability and legitimacy to
the work of a man who publicly spreads antisemitic conspiracy theories and other
falsehoods. Finkelstein is opposed by those in Germany who most vigorously combat and expose the neo-Nazi right. For a discussion of the neo-Nazi embrace of
Finkelstein by such opponents of the neo-Nazis, see Martin Dietzsch and Alfred
Schobert, eds., *Ein "jüdischer David Irving"? Norman G. Finkelstein im Diskurs der
Rechten-Erinnerungsabwehr und Antizionismus* (Duisburg: Duisburger Institut für
Sprach und Sozialforschung, 2001). Their thorough documentary study of the
effect of Finkelstein's *The Holocaust Industry* in Germany shows that it was a boon
to the radical right and neo-Nazis. Antisemites acclaim Finkelstein for his attacks
on Jews. The notorious Holocaust denier Ernst Zuendel in a gushing tribute to
Finkelstein calls him a "Jewish David Irving." Finkelstein does not deny that there
was a Holocaust but in attacking Jews for daring to seek compensation for their
injuries, Zuendel says that he still deals a blow to Jewry akin to that which Irving
had delivered. The study's authors conclude that Finkelstein "undermines the
remembrance of Holocaust." He "harms the still living victims" of the Holocaust.
He "provides grist for the mills of the extreme right" (pp. 6–7). For various additional articles exposing the dubiousness of Finkelstein's and Birn's work, see
<www.goldhagen.com>.

19. This should be no surprise, given that national and institutional self-
conceptions are wrapped up in notions of innocence and blame. If an investigation
of a topic, historical or contemporary, could be interpreted to suggest that a state or
an institution or a large number of a nation's or institution's members have committed heinous deeds and are therefore blameworthy, then the defenders of the
realm (some of whom toil under cover in universities) immediately, even preemptively rise to defend the good name and honor of the country, institution, or people
who might be criticized. Probably no kind of discussion is more threatening to
more people than moral discussion about large-scale crimes, in which many people
are implicated, such as the Holocaust. From the point of view of the self-styled

defenders of national or institutional honor, the imperative to nip such discussions in the bud trumps scholarly standards or any other kind of legitimate standard, honesty, and truth. It is not even a contest.

20. For a discussion of the contingent nature of common sense, see Clifford Geertz, "Common Sense as a Cultural System," in *Local Knowledge: Further Essays in Interpretive Anthropology* (New York: Basic Books, 1983).

21. That the Catholic Church has been obscured from our moral view and, to a great extent, even from our historical view can be seen in recent works addressing issues of justice and reparations. Specific ones focusing on the Nazi period and general ones that deal more broadly with these issues fail even to mention that the Church and its clergy committed offenses, let alone to consider what it must do to make amends with the victims. The Church, though, is discussed as a victim of communism after the war. See István Deák, Jan T. Gross, and Tony Judt, eds., *The Politics of Retribution in Europe: World War II and Its Aftermath* (Princeton, N.J.: Princeton University Press, 2000); and Elazar Barkan, *The Guilt of Nations: Restitution and Negotiating Historical Injustices* (New York: Norton, 2000). Barkan puts forward a different conception of restitution. He does not treat it as a moral duty. Instead he maintains that "restitution as a theory of international relations proposes a process, not a specific solution or standard" (p. 320). Barkan therefore does not provide a moral road map for thinking about what kinds of things restitution ought to provide, arguing that that would be a mistaken notion of restitution. Instead, he understands that restitution is but a "system" that characterizes "both sides enter[ing] voluntarily into negotiations and agreements" (p. 317). That negotiations are decidedly not a formula for satisfying the dictates of conventional notions of justice or for arriving at just outcomes for the victimized, especially since the victimizer is often the stronger party, is something that Barkan, of course, knows. Still, he opts for the procedural view of restitution and is therefore of little help in thinking about the moral duties of the victimizers.

22. For an analysis of such elementary failures on the part of some of the most vocal academics writing about the Holocaust, see Daniel Jonah Goldhagen, "Motives, Causes, and Alibis: A Reply to My Critics," *New Republic* (Dec. 23, 1996), and my subsequent exchange with Christopher Browning and Omer Bartov in *New Republic* (Feb. 10, 1997). A somewhat different version of this essay, focused on my German critics, "The Failure of the Critics," originally published in *Die Zeit* (Aug. 2, 1996), is reprinted in Shandley, *Unwilling Germans?*, pp. 129–159); from the viewpoint of basic social-science methodology, the positions adopted by many of these people are surrealistic. For example, they routinely declare generalization, which is one of the foundations of human thought, impermissible when discussing Germans during the Nazi period (even though they themselves also routinely smuggle in such generalizations of their own). See, for example, Browning's social-scientifically fatuous generalization in *Ordinary Men*. There, from a sample of slightly more than two hundred mass-murdering Germans during the Nazi period, Browning draws conclusions about all of humanity, irrespective of time and place. He writes: "If the men of Reserve Police Battalion 101 could become killers under such circumstances, what group of men cannot?" (pp. 188–189).

23. See George Lakoff, *Women, Fire, and Dangerous Things: What Categories Reveal about the Mind* (Chicago: University of Chicago Press, 1987); and Dorothy Holland and Naomi Quinn, eds., *Cultural Models in Language and Thought* (Cambridge: Cambridge University Press, 1987).

24. Dana R. Villa, "Conscience, the Banality of Evil, and the Idea of a Representative Perpetrator," in *Politics, Philosophy, Terror: Essays on the Thought of Hannah Arendt* (Princeton, N.J.: Princeton University Press, 1999), p. 230, n. 71; Arendt, *Eichmann in Jerusalem;* Richard Kamber, "Goldhagen and Sartre on Eliminationist Anti-Semitism: False Beliefs and Moral Culpability," *Holocaust and Genocide Studies* 13, no. 2 (Fall 1999), p. 252; and Jean-Paul Sartre, *Anti-Semite and Jew* (New York: Schocken Books, 1948), especially p. 20. It should be noted that Villa does seem to engage arguments about what moved the perpetrators (aside from Eichmann). Leaving aside his important misrepresentations of my book and of the literature and the state of our understanding of the Holocaust, Villa's "engagement" with this topic relies not on evidence, but consists of him reasoning backward from philosophical and moral predilections in order to arrive at explanations of their actions. Kamber's use of "evidence" is to misconstrue aspects of my empirical accounts of the perpetrators' actions as contradicting my explanation of those actions. Essentially, he repeatedly asserts as a fact what is not a fact, namely, that anyone doing what the perpetrators were doing should have considered that it was wrong, and concludes that my explanation is faulty because it recognizes the facts that he declares to be impermissible, namely, that in general the perpetrators did not comprehend their deeds as wrong and that they genuinely believed their actions to be necessary and just. Kamber's claims are not substantiated with evidence. In the end he is asserting that my explanation is wrong because he wants to believe that it is wrong.

25. Quoted in Jacob Robinson, *And the Crooked Shall Be Made Straight: The Eichmann Trial, the Jewish Catastrophe, and Hannah Arendt's Narrative* (Philadelphia: Jewish Publication Society of America, 1965), p. 37. Arendt's defenders typically fail even to mention this stunning, devastating admission by Eichmann, which renders as fiction the empirical foundation on which Arendt's interpretative, philosophical, and moral edifice is constructed (Arendt does not mention it but dismisses it as being inconsequential, an example of Eichmann being a braggart for his buddies.) They also typically fail to mention, among many other inculpatory statements and facts, Eichmann's explicit statement that he had concluded that killing Jews was the right thing to do: "Had I been just a recipient of orders, then I would have been a simpleton. I was thinking matters over. I was an idealist. When I reached the conclusion that it was necessary to do to the Jews what we did, I worked with the fanaticism a man can expect from himself" (quoted in Robinson, p. 34). For Arendt and her followers, whatever they might claim, many of the facts about Eichmann hold little interest because they confirm that he was a moral agent, an antisemite, and a willing executioner. Hans Safrian, *Die Eichmann-Männer* (Vienna: Europaverlag, 1993), in a detailed study of the men working closely under Eichmann, shows that they and their milieu, of which Eichmann was the leader, were also thoroughly antisemitic (pp. 17–22).

26. Jean-Paul Sartre and Benny Lévy, *Hope Now: The 1980 Interviews* (Chicago: University of Chicago Press, 1996), pp. 101–103; and Sartre, *Anti-Semite and Jew*, p. 35. When Kamber, without evidence, asserts the superiority of Sartre's analysis of antisemitism, he fails to tell the reader of Sartre's confession of utter ignorance about much of the reality that he was purportedly analyzing.

27. Robinson, *And the Crooked Shall Be Made Straight*, is a 350-page point-by-point exposure of her misuse of evidence and of her inventions.

28. Matthew 27:25. See also Acts 2:22–23, 36, which has "the whole house of Israel" crucifying Jesus. Many other passages suggest more or less clearly that either the whole Jewish people agitated for Jesus' death or are to be held account-able for it, including by punishment. See, for example, Luke 21: 20–24.

29. John 8:44. Joshua Trachtenberg in his classic study, *The Devil and the Jews: The Medieval Conception of the Jew and Its Relation to Modern Anti-Semitism* (Philadelphia: Jewish Publication Society, 1986), writes: "Little wonder, too, that Jews were accused of the foulest crimes, since Satan was their instigator. Chaucer, in his 'Prioresses Tale,' placed the ultimate blame for the alleged slaughter of a Christian child by a Jew upon '. . . our firste fo, the Serpent Sathanas, that hath in Iewes herte his wasps nest.' . . . Everyone knew that the devil and the Jews worked together. This explains why it was so easy to condemn the Jews a priori for every conceivable misdeed, even if it made no sense" (pp. 42–43).

30. Nur. Doc. 032-M, *International Military Tribunal*, vol. 38, p. 130. English translation in "Propaganda in Education," *Shoah* 3, nos. 2–3 (Fall/Winter 1982–1983), p. 31.

31. Matthew 3:7 and 12:34; and John 8:44.

32. For an in-depth discussion of the varieties of antisemitism, how to analyze them, and of antisemitism's evolution over the millennia, see *Hitler's Willing Executioners*, pp. 27–128; for a general discussion of the varieties of prejudice, see Gordon W. Allport, *The Nature of Prejudice* (New York: Anchor Books, 1958).

33. For a general discussion of such prejudicial actions, see Allport, *The Nature of Prejudice*, pp. 47–61; I have added "elimination" to the list.

34. This has been a common tactic among those who do not like the truths that Jewish scholars or survivors present about the Nazi period. They declare the Jews, based solely on their identities as Jews, to be biased or filled with hatred, to be unfit to engage in rational discussion of the issues. Typically, those employing such tactics deflect attention from their illegitimate assertions by declaring that they sympathize with the suffering and the imputed anger (which they declare to be justified) of the Jews, which only serves to reinforce the invented notion that the Jews' views are not to be taken seriously. See, for example, Martin Broszat's letter to Saul Friedländer of Sept. 28, 1987, in "A Controversy About the Historicization of National Socialism," in Peter Baldwin, ed., *Reworking the Past: Hitler, the Holocaust, and the Historians' Debate* (Boston: Beacon Press, 1990), where he asserts that Jews have a "mythical memory," which "functions to coarsen historical recollection" but which nevertheless must "be granted a place" out of "respect for the victims of Nazi crimes." But according to Broszat, only the Jews and their descendants do this. The Germans do not. The Jews' alleged mythical memory creates a

big problem for historical understanding because it impedes the work of younger German historians who are themselves supposedly completely unburdened by the past and therefore employ "rational understanding" (p. 106). With this, Broszat (who we now know was hiding his own membership in the Nazi Party!) delegitimizes members of the victim group, the Jews, and exalts those coming from the country of the perpetrators. For Hans-Ulrich Wehler's essentializing rant to delegitimize Jewish scholars and scholars sharing identities of other victim groups, but not scholars sharing identities of perpetrator groups, of which he as a German and a student of prominent Nazified historians, according to *his* essentializing thinking, would be one, see his "The Goldhagen Controversy: Agonizing Problems, Scholarly Failure and the Political Dimension," *German History* 15, no. 1 (1997), pp. 86–87, and the analysis of this and Wehler's many other scholarly transgressions and misrepresentations by Pinto-Duschinsky, "Wehler on *Hitler's Willing Executioners*," pp. 401–402. For a general treatment of such antisemitic attacks occasioned by the publication of *Hitler's Willing Executioners*, See Lars Rensmann, "Die Walserisierung der Berliner Republik: Geschichtsrevisionismus und antisemitische Projektion: Einwände gegen die These vom geläuterten Deutschland," in Elsässer and Markovits, "*Die Fratze der eigenen Geschichte*," especially pp. 54–55.

35. See Wolfgang Gerlach, *And the Witnesses Were Silent: The Confessing Church and the Persecution of the Jews* (Lincoln: University of Nebraska Press, 2000); and Richard Gutteridge, *The German Evangelical Church and the Jews, 1879–1950* (New York: Harper & Row, 1976).

36. *Catechism of the Catholic Church* (New York: Doubleday, 1995), parag. 2487.

37. I am not interested in arguing against those people, who would pretend that there are no moral duties. I am also not interested in arguing foundational philosophical issues regarding the moral assumptions of this investigation. My contention is that it is not necessary because the moral reckoning that follows is founded on principles so basic to conceptions of the moral life that it is compatible with a wide range of standard schools of moral philosophy and morality. Kantians, utilitarians, Rawlsians, Habermasians, Catholics, and the adherents of still other schools should recognize what follows as derivable from their moral precepts. If people hold moral views that seem to conflict with this book's presuppositions, then I will leave it to them, uncontested, to press their cases that, for example, one is not morally blameworthy if one tortures and kills children, or if one assents to others doing so.

38. *Catechism of the Catholic Church*, pp. 5–6. Similarly, all quotations from the Christian Bible are taken from *The New American Bible* (Wichita: Fireside Bible Publishers, 2000–2001), which is the English translation and commentary officially authorized by the National Conference of Catholic Bishops and the United States Catholic Conference.

39. "What Would Jesus Have Done? Pope Pius XII, The Catholic Church, and the Holocaust," *New Republic* (Jan. 21, 2002), pp. 21–45. The material from this review essay, in somewhat altered form, is the basis here of part one, with a smaller portion of it appearing in other parts of the book, mainly in part three. The source citations in part one reflect its origins as a review essay.

Part One: Clarifying the Conduct

1. For a partial inventory of expulsions, ghettoization, and mass murder of Jews historically, see Paul E. Grosser and Edwin G. Halperin, *Anti-Semitism: The Causes and Effects of a Prejudice* (Secaucus, N.J.: Citadel, 1979); and Martin Gilbert, *The Dent Atlas of Jewish History* 5th ed. (London: JM Dent, 1993).

2. Iwona Irwin-Zarecka, "Poland, After the Holocaust," in *Remembering for the Future: Working Papers and Addenda*, vol. 1 (Oxford: Pergamon Press, 1989), p. 143.

3. This is true even, or most noticeably, for many academics writing about the Holocaust. See, for example, the first edition of Christopher R. Browning, *Ordinary Men: Reserve Police Battalion 101 and the Final Solution in Poland* (New York: HarperCollins, 1992), where he has no concerted discussion of antisemitism, fails to plumb the extent and nature of antisemitism of German society even though he is writing about why ordinary Germans were slaughtering Jews, and consistently downplays the men's antipathies toward Jews—a position from which he has been steadily backtracking since I pointed out his book's devastating conceptual and empirical problem in Daniel Jonah Goldhagen, "The Evil of Banality," *New Republic* (July 13 and 20, 1992), pp. 49–52; and in our subsequent exchange from Dec. 1993, published in Michael Berenbaum and Abraham J. Peck, *The Holocaust and History: The Known, the Unknown, the Disputed, and the Reexamined* (Bloomington: Indiana University Press, 1998), pp. 252–265 and 301–307. Robert E. Herzstein, "Daniel Jonah Goldhagen's 'Ordinary Germans' A Heretic and His Critics," *The Journal of the Historical Society 2*, 1 (winter 2002), explains that Browning's 1998 new afterword to *Ordinary Men* contains a "Goldhagen-prompted discussion of anti-Semitism in German history and culture" (p. 109).

4. The literature demonstrating this is vast. See, for example, Joshua Trachtenberg, *The Devil and the Jews: The Medieval Conception of the Jew and Its Relation to Modern Anti-Semitism* (Philadelphia: Jewish Publication Society, 1986); David Berger, ed., *History and Hate: The Dimensions of Anti-Semitism* (Philadelphia: Jewish Publication Society, 1986); Jeremy Cohen, *The Friars and the Jews: The Evolution of Medieval Anti-Judaism* (Ithaca, N.Y.: Cornell University Press, 1982); and Bernard Glassman, *Anti-Semitic Stereotypes Without Jews: Images of Jews in England, 1290–1700* (Detroit: Wayne State University Press, 1975).

5. See Martin Luther, *Von den Jueden und Iren Luegen*, in Walther Linden, ed., *Luthers Kampfschriften gegen das Judentum* (Berlin: Klinkhardt & Biermann, 1936); for a translation of the passage cited here, see Robert S. Wistrich, *Antisemitism: The Longest Hatred* (New York: Schocken, 1991), pp. 39–41; "homiletic massacre" is James Carroll's phrase from *Constantine's Sword: The Church and the Jews* (Boston: Houghton Mifflin, 2001), p. 367.

6. Trachtenberg, *The Devil and the Jews*, p. 186.

7. Quoted in Carroll, *Constantine's Sword*, p. 371.

8. For a discussion of the various dimensions of antisemitism, of the relationship of antisemitic belief to anti-Jewish action, and of its evolution to the point where it became the principal motive for the Holocaust, see Daniel Jonah Goldhagen, *Hitler's Willing Executioners: Ordinary Germans and the Holocaust* (New York: Alfred A. Knopf, 1996), pp. 25–163 and pp. 373–454.

9. Carroll, *Constantine's Sword*, p. 218.

10. Georges Passelecq and Bernard Suchecky, *The Hidden Encyclical of Pius XI* (New York: Harcourt Brace, 1997), p. 246. It continues with a half-truth: "These persecutions have been censured by the Holy See on more than one occasion, but especially when they have worn the mantle of Christianity."

11. Passelecq and Suchecky, *The Hidden Encyclical of Pius XI*, p. 2.

12. It came into public view because of the dogged work of Georges Passelecq, a Belgian monk, and Bernard Suchecky, a Jewish historian, who managed to publish it in France in 1995.

13. John Cornwell, *Hitler's Pope: The Secret History of Pius XII* (New York: Viking, 1999); Susan Zuccotti, *Under His Very Windows: The Vatican and the Holocaust in Italy* (New Haven: Yale University Press, 2000); and Garry Wills, *Papal Sin: Structures of Deceit* (New York: Doubleday, 2000).

14. See Zuccotti, *Under His Very Windows*, pp. 167 and 310–322. Her analysis of them is on the whole incisive, though I disagree with it on certain points.

15. See, for example, Ronald J. Rychlak, the Pope's misleading and most dogged recent defender, in *Hitler, the War, and the Pope* (Columbus, Miss.: Genesis Press, 2000), especially pp. 167–181; and Pierre Blet, *Pius XII and the Second World War* (New York: Paulist Press, 1999).

16. Zuccotti, *Under His Very Windows*, pp. 300ff.

17. Quoted in Zuccotti, *Under His Very Windows*, p. 1. Half a year later, on June 2, Pius XII addressed the Sacred College of Cardinals, conveying his compassion for "those who have turned an anxiously imploring eye to Us, tormented as they are, for reasons of their nationality or descent (*stirpe*), by major misfortunes and by more acute and grave suffering, and destined sometimes, even without guilt on their part, to exterminatory measures." These two speeches were published in *L'Osservatore Romano* and *Civiltà cattolica*. See Zuccotti, *Under His Very Windows*, pp. 1–2 and 329, ns. 1 and 2.

18. Quoted in Owen Chadwick, *Britain and the Vatican During the Second World War* (Cambridge: Cambridge University Press, 1986), p. 216; and Michael Phayer, *The Catholic Church and the Holocaust, 1930–1965* (Bloomington: Indiana University Press, 2000), pp. 62–63.

19. See Rychlak, *Hitler, the War, and the Pope*, p. 177; like other defenders of Pius XII, he falsely translates the Italian word *stirpe*, which means "descent," as "race." For a corrective, see Zuccotti, *Under His Very Windows*, pp. 1–2 and 329, n. 3. For the pressure on the Pope coming from both the Americans and the British, see Chadwick, *Britain and the Vatican During the Second World War*, pp. 199 and 213; and Phayer, *The Catholic Church and the Holocaust*, p. 49.

20. Klaus Scholder, *The Churches and the Third Reich*, vol. 1 (Philadelphia: Fortress Press, 1988), pp. 242–243.

21. For a discussion of the Pope's preference for a German victory over the Soviet Union, and his privileging of this over the fate of the Jews, see Phayer, *The Catholic Church and the Holocaust*, pp. 56–61. In effect, the arguments of Andreas Hillgruber during the *Historikerstreit* in Germany were but an articulation of the policies that Pius XII actually pursued in this respect. Those in Germany and else-

where weighing in on this debate condemned Hillgruber's assertion that Germans should identify with, and be thankful to, the German soldiers who held off the Soviets on the eastern front; although Hillgruber did not say so explicitly, as the critics pointed out, the longer they kept the Soviets at bay, the longer Germans would also continue to slaughter the Jews. As a matter of consistency, all those who criticized Hillgruber must be at least equally harsh toward Pius XII, who actually practiced what Hillgruber has only since preached. See *Historikerstreit: Die Dokumentation der Kontroverse um die Einzigartigkeit der Nationalsozialistischen Judenvernichtung* (München: Piper, 1987).

22. Rychlak, *Hitler, the War, and the Pope*, p. 184.

23. Phayer, *The Catholic Church and the Holocaust*, pp. 60–61.

24. See Phayer, *The Catholic Church and the Holocaust*, p. 160.

25. For Hungary, see Randolph L. Braham, *The Politics of Genocide: The Holocaust in Hungary*, vol. 2 (New York: Columbia University Press, 1981), pp. 1,070–1,071. For his sympathetic statements, see for example, see Zuccotti, *Under His Very Windows*, pp. 295–296.

26. For a discussion of Pius XII's many reliable sources of knowledge about the unfolding mass murders, and examples of his defenders' dissimulations, see Zuccotti, *Under His Very Windows*, pp. 93–112.

27. Cornwell, *Hitler's Pope*, p. 75.

28. The use of this exclusionary terminology, with its clear antisemitic implications, cannot be brushed aside as carelessness. Few documents are composed with as much attention to linguistic nuance as papal encyclicals.

29. Against the dark hinterland of the wayward Jews, the Christian elect alone are raised to salvation. As Pacelli explains, "It is precisely in the twilight of this background that one perceives the striking perspective of the divine tutorship of salvation, as it warms, admonishes, strikes, raises and beautifies its elect."

30. Pius XI, *Mit brennender Sorge* (March 14, 1937), <www.vatican.va/holy_father/pius_xi/encyclicals/index.htm>, parags. 10–11, 15–17, and 34; see also Zuccotti's discussion of the encyclical in *Under His Very Windows*, pp. 21–23. Pierre Blet in *Pius XII and the Second World War*, which is a narrated summary of the Church's sanitized official publication of documents relating to World War II by one of the publication's editors, and Rychlak, *Hitler, the War, and the Pope*, discuss the encyclical exclusively as an anti-Nazi document without mentioning Pacelli's or Pius XI's antisemitism (Blet, pp. 51–52; and Rychlak, pp. 92–94). More surprising, the International Catholic-Jewish Historical Commission in "The Vatican and the Holocaust: A Preliminary Report" (<www.jcrelations.net>, 18 pp.) also wrongly presents it as "forceful condemnation of National Socialism" (sec. a.1.) instead of as a document that narrowly, if forcefully, condemns its religious practices and policies.

31. For an analysis of the varieties of antisemitism, see Goldhagen, *Hitler's Willing Executioners*, pp. 27–48.

32. Blet, *Pius XII and the Second World War*, pp. 42–44.

33. Blet, *Pius XII and the Second World War*, p. 75. This is a rare instance where the Pope says that Nazism is worse than communism. Blet also quotes Pius XII declaring in June 1943 that he wanted to bring special attention "to the tragic fate of

the Polish people who, surrounded by strong countries, are being tossed about by the vicissitudes and the uncertainties of a dramatic cyclone of war. Our teaching and Our declarations, so often repeated, leave no room for doubt as to the principles with which the Christian conscience should judge such actions, no matter who is responsible for them" (p. 85). Pius XII could speak for the Polish people, so why could he not add a few words here for the Jews of Poland?

34. G. B. Cardinal Montini, "Pius XII and the Jews," in Eric Bentley, ed., *The Storm Over "The Deputy"* (New York: Grove Press, 1964), p. 68.

35. Rychlak, *Hitler, the War, and the Pope;* as is characteristic of his and the Pope's defenders' general selective and misleading use of evidence, Rychlak fails to mention the deportation of the Dutch Protestants, which gives the false impression that the Catholic Church rightly believed that its silence had saved the Catholics whom he presents as Jews (pp. 171–172). Because the Germans killed a higher percentage of Dutch Jews than of the Jews of any other Western country, the Pope's defenders, like Rychlak, also contend, incredibly, that it was the Church's intervention alone that somehow was responsible for this. Unmentioned are the well-documented factors (length of occupation, geographic density of the country, concentration of the Jews, lack of safe refuge either within the country, say, in forests, or across borders, etc.) that produced this high death rate. Had Dutch churches not intervened, the Germans and their Dutch helpers would have killed at least as many Jews.

36. Leni Yahil, *The Rescue of Danish Jewry: Test of a Democracy* (Philadelphia: Jewish Publication Society of America, 1969), pp. 233–234.

37. Quoted in Carol Rittner, Stephen D. Smith, and Irena Steinfeldt, eds., *The Holocaust and the Christian World: Reflections of the Past, Challenges for the Future* (New York: Continuum, 2000), pp. 244–245. For an account of the events surrounding Bishop Fuglsang-Damgaard's appeal, see Yahil, *The Rescue of Danish Jewry,* pp. 234–237.

38. Zuccotti, *Under His Very Windows,* pp. 166–167.

39. For Bulgaria, see Michael Bar-Zohar, *Beyond Hitler's Grasp: The Heroic Rescue of Bulgaria's Jews* (Holbrook, Mass.: Adams Media, 1998), pp. 170–177, 195, and 268; for Greece, see Mark Mazower, *Inside Hitler's Greece: The Experience of Occupation, 1941–1944* (New Haven: Yale University Press, 1993), pp. 257–261.

40. Quoted in Rittner, Smith, and Steinfeldt, *The Holocaust and the Christian World,* p. 242. See also Samuel Abrahamsen, "The Role of the Norwegian Lutheran Church During World War II," in *Remembering for the Future,* vol. 1, pp. 9–11; and Leni Yahil, *The Holocaust: The Fate of European Jewry* (New York: Oxford University Press, 1991), pp. 394–396.

41. The inventive imputation to Pius XII of exculpatory states of mind and laudable motives characterizes much of the writing about him regarding the Holocaust. It is even accepted in defense of Pius XII (this time by Zuccotti, who in her interpretations of motives is less reliable than in her meticulous research), that though Pius XII knew that the Germans were systematically exterminating the Jews of one European country after the next, he was nevertheless certain that they would not harm the Jews of Rome, whom they were deporting. Why? Because the Germans had told him so. See Zuccotti, *Under His Very Windows,* p. 159.

42. For Bishop Santin's intervention, see Zuccotti, *Under His Very Windows*, pp. 281–290 and 292.

43. Zuccotti, *Under His Very Windows*, pp. 294–295.

44. The Vatican concocted this line of argument to stave off the Allies, who were pressuring the Pope to speak out. This was part of the Vatican's extensive strategic effort of disinformation about the mass murder and its own activities, which had three components: concealing or minimizing the extent of the Germans' and their helpers' (including within the Church itself) mass murdering of Jews; pretending that the Church was strenuously taking initiatives to help the Jews that it was not; providing fictitious reasons as to why the Church and its officials could not do more. For some examples of the duplicity of the Vatican and of Pius XII himself, see Zuccotti, *Under His Very Windows*, pp. 294–296; and Phayer, *The Catholic Church and the Holocaust*, pp. 48–49.

45. Zuccotti, *Under His Very Windows*, p. 304.

46. Similarly, we do not say that the Allies should have done less to help Jews than they did or that they were right not to have tried to do more. David Wyman, the foremost expert on the conduct of the United States during the Holocaust, argues that the Allies should have done much more. In "What Might Have Been Done," he discussed twelve programs for helping and rescuing Jews that "could have been tried," that were proposed at the time, and that Wyman maintains ought to have been attempted. See David Wyman, *The Abandonment of the Jews: America and the Holocaust 1941–1945* (New York: Pantheon, 1984), pp. 331–340.

47. Le Chambon, France, is another example of the effectiveness of religious leadership in mobilizing ordinary people to save Jews. The Protestant minister of this small French town got virtually the entire town to participate in an all-out rescue effort for the Jews in the region, hiding them in barns, attics, and wherever they could. This small effort in one tiny corner of Europe preserved the lives of more than three thousand Jews. How many more Jews would have been saved if every Catholic priest, or even just a handful, in overwhelmingly Catholic France had led a similar rescue effort? See Philip P. Hallie, *Lest Innocent Blood Be Shed: The Story of the Village of Le Chambon and How Goodness Happened There* (New York: Harper & Row, 1979).

48. Pius XII, *Mystici Corporis Christi*, June 29, 1943, <www.vatican.va/holy_father/pius_xii/encyclicals/index.htm>. See also Carroll, *Constantine's Sword*, p. 603. Pius XII seems to have been drawing on some of the most antisemitic passages of the Christian Bible, which explain that the Jewish law had always produced sin and death, and that for life, a person must free himself of "the law of sin and death" by accepting Jesus. See Romans 7:7–10 and 8:1–13; and 2 Corinthians 3:6–7.

49. Wills, *Papal Sin*, p. 1.

50. Carroll, *Constantine's Sword*, p. 532.

51. Two more strategies are inversion and relativizing. With the first, the Church's defenders falsely present the Church as the victim so as to deflect attention from its cooperation with the victimizers. This I discuss in part three. With the second, the defenders seek to excuse the Church by saying that it was no worse, or less bad, than others. Contrary to what the defenders would have us believe, the crimes and offenses that the Church or its clergy committed and the

culpability that they bear for their deeds are not diminished in magnitude by the existence of others who did similar or worse things. For a discussion of the Church's culpability that does not succumb to this sort of relativism and nihilism, see part two.

52. Daniel Carpi, *Between Mussolini and Hitler: The Jews and the Italian Author-ities in France and Tunisia* (Hanover, N.H.: Brandeis University Press, 1994), writes that the French bishops "found themselves standing alone in the field (insofar as they had in fact entered it), with no support whatsoever, either diplomatic or theo-logical, on the part of the Holy See" (p. 75). On the failure of the Vatican in France, see John F. Morley, *Vatican Diplomacy and the Jews During the Holocaust, 1939–1943* (New York: Ktav, 1980), pp. 68–70.

53. See Maxime Steinberg, "Faced with the Final Solution in Occupied Bel-gium: The Church's Silence and Christian Action," in *Remembering for the Future*, vol. 3, pp. 2,745–2,752 and 2,758.

54. A maxim that would do away with such misleading bias would be that the proportion of space devoted to those who helped Jews and to those who failed to help Jews or who persecuted them should reflect the number of people in each group.

55. On Benoît, see Zuccotti, *Under His Very Windows*, pp. 144–148. In 1943, Father Benoît went to Rome where he organized rescue efforts of Jews. For an account of such diocesan efforts and, more generally, of Catholics who rescued Jews, see Phayer, *The Catholic Church and the Holocaust*, pp. 111–132.

56. "Volksgenealogie," *Klerusblatt*, Sept. 12, 1934, p. 501.

57. "Die Regelung des Rasseproblems durch die Nürnberger Gesetze," *Klerus-blatt*, Jan. 22, 1936, p. 47.

58. For an account of the role of the German Church, see Guenther Lewy, *The Catholic Church and Nazi Germany* (New York: McGraw-Hill, 1964), especially pp. 268–308.

59. Ernst Christian Helmreich, *The German Churches under Hitler: Background, Struggle, and Epilogue* (Detroit: Wayne State University Press, 1979), p. 360.

60. Lewy, *The Catholic Church and Nazi Germany*, pp. 264–265.

61. Office of United States Chief of Counsel for Prosecution of Axis Criminal-ity, *Nazi Conspiracy and Aggression*, vol. 6 (Washington, D.C.: United States Gov-ernment Printing Office, 1946), 3701-PS, p. 408.

62. Lewy, *The Catholic Church and Nazi Germany*, pp. 265–266. Periodically, in sermons and pastoral letters, German bishops and priests would remind their parishioners of the criminality of killing such people, and in Lewy's view, "these pronouncements probably helped stave off a renewal of the program" (p. 266). Yet they continued to remain silent about the mass murder of the Jews.

63. Friedrich Heer, *God's First Love: Christians and Jews Over Two Thousand Years* (New York: Weybright and Talley, 1967), p. 324.

64. See Ian Kershaw, *Popular Opinion and Political Dissent in the Third Reich. Bavaria 1933–1945* (Oxford: Oxford University Press, 1983), pp. 205–208 and 340–357; and Jeremy Noakes, "The Oldenburg Crucifix Struggle of November 1936: A Case Study of Opposition in the Third Reich," in Peter D. Stachura, ed., *The Shaping of the Nazi State* (London: Croom Helm, 1978), pp. 210–233.

65. Lewy, *The Catholic Church and Nazi Germany,* p. 293.

66. See Doris L. Bergen, "Between God and Hitler: German Military Chaplains and the Crimes of the Third Reich," in Omer Bartov and Phyllis Mack, eds., *In God's Name: Genocide and Religion in the Twentieth Century* (New York: Berghahn Books, 2001), pp. 128–132.

67. Gordian Landwehr, "So sah ich sie sterben," in Katholischen Militärbischofsamt und Hans Jürgen Brandt, eds., *Priester in Uniform: Seelsorger, Ordensleute und Theologen als Soldaten im Zweiten Weltkrieg* (Augsburg: Patloch, 1994), pp. 349–350.

68. Quoted in Bergen, "Between God and Hitler," p. 128.

69. Bergen, "Between God and Hitler," p. 134.

70. Livia Rothkirchen (transliterated as Rotkirkchen in this publication), *The Destruction of Slovak Jewry: A Documentary History* (Jerusalem: Yad Vashem, 1961) pp. xx–xxi.

71. Livia Rothkirchen, "The Churches and the Deportation and Persecution of Jews in Slovakia," in Rittner, Smith, and Steinfeldt, *The Holocaust and the Christian World,* p. 106.

72. See Morley, *Vatican Diplomacy and the Jews During the Holocaust,* pp. 76, 84, and 86; and Rothkirchen, "The Churches and the Deportation and Persecution of Jews in Slovakia," pp. 105–106.

73. Quoted in Rothkirchen, *The Destruction of Slovak Jewry,* p. 146.

74. Rothkirchen, "The Churches and the Deportation and Persecution of Jews in Slovakia," p. 107.

75. See Morley, *Vatican Diplomacy and the Jews During the Holocaust,* pp. 98–101, for the analysis that demonstrates this.

76. Phayer, *The Catholic Church and the Holocaust,* p. 87.

77. Rothkirchen, "The Churches and the Deportation and Persecution of Jews in Slovakia," pp. 104–107; see also Morley, *Vatican Diplomacy and the Jews During the Holocaust,* pp. 92–93, for Monsignor Domenico Tardini's cynical high-level internal Vatican memo of April 7, 1943, in which he counsels that the Vatican, out of fear that the Church will be blamed for Father Tiso's actions, should protest to Tiso, so that the Vatican could leak the protest's contents, in order "to make known to the world that the Holy See fulfills its duty of charity." He then muses that in the event that "the Jews . . . are among the victors," such a protest will not help the Church with them because they "will never be too friendly to the Holy See and to the Catholic Church." Aside from this cynicism (which is not tempered by the memo's opening paragraph decrying the persecutions and stating that "the Jewish question is a question of humanity" giving the Church "full reason to intervene"), we might ask what he meant by the Jews as "victors." They were being slaughtered en masse, were powerless, and were without an army. How was he conceiving of Jews' power that he could conceptualize them as victors?

78. See part two for a discussion of such late and tepid interventions.

79. Rothkirchen, "The Churches and the Deportation and Persecution of Jews in Slovakia," p. 107.

80. Menachem Shelah, "The Catholic Church in Croatia, the Vatican and the Murder of the Croatian Jews," in *Remembering for the Future,* vol. 1, p. 269.

81. Yahil, *The Holocaust,* p. 431.

82. Phayer, *The Catholic Church and the Holocaust*, pp. 37–40 and 169.

83. See Helen Fein, *Accounting for Genocide: National Responses and Jewish Victimization During the Holocaust* (New York: Free Press, 1979), pp. 71–75. For the American Catholic Church, see Gerald P. Fogarty, *The Vatican and the American Hierarchy from 1870 to 1965* (Stuttgart: Anton Hiersemann, 1982), pp. 177–194. Within the Catholic Church the liberal character of the American Church was understood to be precisely a consequence of the influence of American civilization and democracy upon it.

84. Sarah Neshamit, "Rescue in Lithuania During the Nazi Occupation (June 1941–August 1944)," in *Rescue Attempts During the Holocaust: Proceedings of the Second Yad Vashem International Historical Conference, Jerusalem, April 8–11, 1974* (Jerusalem: Yad Vashem, 1977), pp. 312–316.

85. Holy See's Commission for Religious Relations with Jews, "We Remember: A Reflection on the Shoah," in Rittner, Smith, and Steinfeldt, *The Holocaust and the Christian World*, p. 260. The American Catholic bishops provide a much more forthcoming account of the relationship between the Church's antisemitism and modern racial antisemitism and the Holocaust, which, without them saying so, contradicts "We Remember." See *Catholic Teaching on the Shoah: Implementing the Holy See's* We Remember (Washington, D. C.: United States Catholic Conference, 2001), pp. 9–11.

86. Carroll, *Constantine's Sword*, p. 29.

87. Examples include Blet, *Pius XII and the Second World War;* Cornwell, *Hitler's Pope;* Phayer, *The Catholic Church and the Holocaust;* and Rychlak, *Hitler, the War, and the Pope.*

88. For a discussion of the problems besetting the works of many historians of the Holocaust, including that they write about it in a stridently ahistorical manner, as if German political culture, including its antisemitism, prior to the Nazi period was of little relevance, see Daniel Jonah Goldhagen, "The Paradigm Challenged: Victim Testimony, Critical Evidence, and New Perspectives in the Study of the Holocaust," *Tikkun* 13 no. 3 (May/June 1998), pp. 40–42. For classic examples of such ahistoricism, see Browning, *Ordinary Men;* and Mommsen, "The Realization of the Unthinkable."

89. See Goldhagen, *Hitler's Willing Executioners*, pp. 27–79, for a more extensive treatment of these issues. For a masterful and original account of the development of Christian antisemitism, and then after the Reformation of its continuation as Catholic antisemitism, see Carroll, *Constantine's Sword.*

90. John 8:47.

91. John 8:44–46.

92. Carroll, *Constantine's Sword*, p. 59.

93. Carroll, *Constantine's Sword*, p. 250.

94. See Goldhagen, "Foreword to the German Edition," *Hitler's Willing Executioners* (New York: Vintage, 1997), pp. 479–481.

95. See Amnon Linder, *The Jews in the Legal Sources of the Middle Ages* (Detroit and Jerusalem: Wayne State University Press and the Israel Academy of Sciences and Humanities, 1997), pp. 417–443. Gregory I argued prudentially that forced

conversions are not real conversions, so the Jews should be won over with justice and reason.

96. Carroll, *Constantine's Sword,* pp. 219 and 248; see also Trachtenberg, *The Devil and the Jews,* p. 7.

97. Carroll, *Constantine's Sword,* p. 250.

98. Quoted in Robert Chazan, *European Jewry and the First Crusade* (Berkeley: University of California Press, 1987), p. 225; see also Carroll, *Constantine's Sword,* p. 237.

99. Carroll, *Constantine's Sword,* p. 277; see also pp. 191, 196, and 202.

100. For Matthew's account of Jesus' sentence of death, see Matthew 27:15–26.

101. Carroll, *Constantine's Sword,* relates it with narrative flow, telling insights, apposite personal reflections, and unyielding rectitude and directness; for other examples, see Malcolm Hay, *Europe and the Jews: The Pressure of Christendom Over 1900 Years* (Chicago: Academy Chicago Publishers, 1992); William Nicholls, *Christian Antisemitism: A History of Hate* (Northvale, N.J.: Jason Aronson, 1995); and James Parkes, *Antisemitism: A Concise World History* (Chicago: Quadrangle, 1963).

102. Trachtenberg, *The Devil and the Jews,* p. 12.

103. For the text of the Concordat with contemporaneous commentary, see *Church and State in Germany: The Concordat of 1933 Between the Holy See and the German State* (New York: Friends of Germany, 1933).

104. Helmreich, *The German Churches Under Hitler,* p. 249.

105. *Documents on German Foreign Policy, 1918–1945,* ser. C, vol. 1, no. 188 (Washington, D.C.: United States Government Printing Office, 1957), p. 347.

106. *Documents on German Foreign Policy, 1918–1945, ser. C. vol. 1,* no. 425, pp. 793–794; for a broader discussion of this issue, see Helmreich, *The German Churches Under Hitler,* pp. 253–255.

107. See Goldhagen, *Hitler's Willing Executioners,* pp. 27–79, especially pp. 66–67. Walter Zwi Bacharach, *Anti-Jewish Prejudices in German Catholic-Sermons* (Lewiston, New York: The Edwin Mellen Press, 1993), concludes: "The anti-Jewish pronouncements in Catholic churches, and the inflammatory statements in catechistic literature, were dogmatic and emphatic, and were presented to churchgoers as divine edicts. And since they were accepted as absolute statements stemming from the divine will, they were perceived by the public at large as unquestionable truths. When the Nazis came to power, they allocated hatred of Jews a central role in their ideology. Nazi antisemitism activated Christian hostility and addressed Catholics (and Protestants) in familiar and common language." Bacharach's study shows that, "the Catholic-Christian prejudice . . . set the Jew apart from the rest of mankind and poisoned the hearts of millions of Germans." This, he says, "facilitated Hitler's scheme for winning support, since his language was familiar" (pp. 138–139).

108. David I. Kertzer, *The Popes Against the Jews: The Vatican's Role in the Rise of Modern Anti-Semitism* (New York: Alfred A. Knopf, 2001), p. 10. Kertzer presents a wealth of evidence to demonstrate the "modern" character of the Church's antisemitism.

109. Kertzer, *The Popes Against the Jews,* p. 137.

110. Kertzer, *The Popes Against the Jews,* p. 7.

111. Kertzer, *The Popes Against the Jews*, p. 145.

112. Kertzer observes, "Much of the Church's anti-Jewish campaign involved denunciations of Jews not only as enemies of the Church but as enemies of the nation, not only as threats to the Christian religion but to Christian people. Yet with the addition of this new category, the whole carefully constructed anti-Semitic/anti-Jewish distinction evaporates" (*The Popes Against the Jews*, p. 9). Kertzer's work should put to rest any notion that the Church can dissociate itself from all responsibility for modern European antisemitism by asserting this fallacious distinction between "anti-Judaism" and antisemitism.

113. Kertzer, *The Popes Against the Jews*, pp. 249 and 250–251.

114. Kertzer, *The Popes Against the Jews*, p. 260.

115. Kertzer, *The Popes Against the Jews*, p. 263.

116. Wills, *Papal Sin*, p. 19.

117. For an account of the commissioning and fate of the encyclical, see Passelecq and Suchecky, *The Hidden Encyclical of Pius XI*, pp. 24–92.

118. Passelecq and Suchecky, *The Hidden Encyclical of Pius XI*, p. 123. For the passages from *Civiltà cattolica* contained in the next four paragraphs, see Passelecq and Suchecky, *The Hidden Encyclical of Pius XI*, pp. 123–136.

119. Kertzer, *The Popes Against the Jews*, p. 135.

120. Henry Picker, ed., *Hitlers Tischgespräche im Führerhauptquartier, 1941–42* (Bonn: Athenäum, 1951), p. 346.

121. Kertzer, *The Popes Against the Jews*, p. 270.

122. Passelecq and Suchecky, *The Hidden Encyclical of Pius XI*, pp. 247–253.

123. Quoted in Bernd Nellessen, "Die schweigende Kirche: Katholiken und Judenverfolgung," in Ursula Büttner, ed., *Die Deutschen und die Judenverfolgung im Dritten Reich* (Hamburg: Christians, 1992), p. 265.

124. Lewy, *The Catholic Church and Nazi Germany*, p. 294.

125. *Catechism of the Catholic Church* (New York: Doubleday, 1995), parags. 830–831.

126. *Catechism of the Catholic Church*, parags. 823–824 and 830–831, and 224, 253–255, 262, and 689. The *Catechism* explains, "The Incarnation of God's Son reveals that God is the eternal Father and that the Son is consubstantial with the Father, which means that, in the Father and with the Father, the Son is one and the same God" (parag. 262).

127. *Hitler: Sämtliche Aufzeichnungen 1905–1924*, ed. Eberhard Jäckel (Stuttgart: Deutsche Verlags-Anstalt, 1980), pp. 119–120.

128. Pius XI, *Divini Redemptoris* (March 19, 1937), <www.vatican.va/holy_father/pius_xi/encyclicals/index.htm>, parags. 4, 7, 8, and 9; see also Zuccotti, *Under His Very Windows*, p. 23.

129. See, for example, Passelecq and Suchecky, *The Hidden Encyclical of Pius XI*, pp. 101–102.

130. *Catechism of the Catholic Church*, parags. 1852–1861.

131. See Rychlak, *Hitler, the War, and the Pope;* and Blet, *Pius XII and the Second World War*. Even some who are critics of the Church do this. See Zuccotti, *Under His Very Windows*, pp. 167–168 and 313–316.

132. Quoted in Kertzer, *The Popes Against the Jews*, p. 126.

133. Kertzer, *The Popes Against the Jews*, pp. 126–127. The contemporary Catholic Bible has altered the translation that was used historically so that it now reads in the Revelation to John as the "assembly of Satan" (2:9 and 3:9).

134. Zuccotti, *Under His Very Windows*, p. 24.

135. See part two for a discussion of the German bishops' ardor for Nazi Germany's military victory.

136. See Eli Tzur, "Collaboration," in Walter Laqueur, ed., *The Holocaust Encyclopedia* (New Haven: Yale University Press, 2001), pp. 127–133; and Gerhard Hirschfeld, "Collaboration in Nazi-Occupied France: Some Introductory Remarks," in Gerhard Hirschfeld and Patrick Marsh, eds., *Collaboration in France: Politics and Culture during the Nazi Occupation, 1940–1944* (Oxford: Berg, 1989), p. 3.

137. Philippe Burrin, *France Under the Germans: Collaboration and Compromise* (New York: New Press, 1996), p. 221.

138. Phayer, *The Catholic Church and the Holocaust*, p. 94.

139. *Catechism of the Catholic Church*, parag. 2269.

140. Luke 10:29–37.

141. *Catechism of the Catholic Church*, parag. 1756.

142. Wills, *Papal Sin*, p. 5. He writes this about the historical dishonesty of attempts to whitewash the Church's past attitudes toward Jews.

Part Two: Judging the Culpability

1. See Daniel Jonah Goldhagen, *Hitler's Willing Executioners: Ordinary Germans and the Holocaust* (New York: Alfred A. Knopf, 1996); by now there has been abundant confirmation of my various conclusions (even among those who attack the book, by pointing to exceptions, or by falsely claiming that they already said as much); see Marion A. Kaplan, *Between Dignity and Despair: Jewish Life in Nazi Germany* (New York: Oxford University Press, 1998); here the two central analytical concepts, "social death" and that the Germans wanted the Jews to "disappear," directly follow my introduction of these notions (I called the latter "eliminate") into the study of the Holocaust; for a few of many other examples, see Christiane Kohl, *Der Jude und das Mädchen: Eine verbotene Freundschaft in Nazideutschland* (Hamburg: Spiegel Buchverlag, 1997); and Thomas Sandkühler, *"Endlösung" in Galizien: Der Judenmord in Ostpolen und die Rettungsinitiativen von Berthold Beitz, 1941–1944* (Bonn: Dietz, 1996); see also part three for the discussion of the current traveling exhibition by the Northern Protestant State Church of Germany, which confesses that "the majority of the church supported the persecution of the Jews." Those who lived through the events themselves, the eyewitnesses, have also, in droves, communicated their agreement, orally and in writing. For some examples, see *Briefe an Goldhagen*, introduced and answered by Daniel Jonah Goldhagen (Berlin: Siedler Verlag, 1997).

2. Matthew 27:25. See part three for a further discussion of this issue.

3. For Cardinal Bertram, see Ludwig Volk, ed., *Akten deutscher Bischöfe über die Lage der Kirche 1933–1945*, vol. 5, (Mainz: Matthias-Grünewald-Verlag, 1983), p. 944. For Bishop Gföllner, see David I. Kertzer, *The Popes Against the Jews*, pp. 274–275.

4. Ronald Modras, *The Catholic Church and Antisemitism: Poland, 1933–1939* (Chur: Harwood Academic, 1994), pp. 284–285, 315–316, and 345–347; see also Kertzer, *The Popes Against the Jews*, pp. 275–276; and Celia S. Heller, *On the Edge of Destruction: Jews of Poland Between the Two World Wars* (Detroit: Wayne State University Press, 1994), pp. 109–114.

5. Quoted in Menachem Shelah, "The Catholic Church in Croatia, the Vatican and the Murder of the Croatian Jews," in *Remembering for the Future: Working Papers and Addenda*, vol. 1 (Oxford: Pergamon Press, 1989), pp. 270 and 276.

6. Quoted in Shelah, "The Catholic Church in Croatia, the Vatican and the Murder of the Croatian Jews," p. 269.

7. Michael R. Marrus and Robert O. Paxton, *Vichy France and the Jews* (New York: Schocken, 1983), p. 272.

8. For a discussion of the circumstances of the epistle—including its tepid and elliptical protest against the deportation without even mentioning the word "Jew" in this context, and its eventual failure to be delivered—see Moshe Y. Herczl, *Christianity and the Holocaust of Hungarian Jewry* (New York: New York University Press, 1993), pp. 205–216. In contrast to the Catholic bishops, the bishops of two Protestant churches prepared their own Shepherds' Epistle, which, whatever its problems and the otherwise deplorable record of the Protestant leadership, did explicitly call for the complete cessation of the violence against and deportation of the Jews. Cardinal Serédi had refused several requests by the Protestants that they present a united front regarding the fate of the Jews (p. 210).

9. See Mark Aarons and John Loftus, *Unholy Trinity: How the Vatican's Nazi Networks Betrayed Western Intelligence to the Soviets* (New York: St. Martin's, 1991), pp. 128–129.

10. See, for example, Susan Zuccotti, *Under His Very Windows*, pp. 54–55.

11. Quoted in Kertzer, *The Popes Against the Jews*, p. 285.

12. Guenter Lewy, *The Catholic Church and Nazi Germany* (New York: McGraw-Hill, 1964), p. 294; on Poland, see Jan T. Gross, "A Tangled Web: Confronting Stereotypes Concerning Relations Between Poles, Germans, Jews, and Communists," in István Deák, Jan T. Gross, and Tony Judt, eds., *The Politics of Retribution in Europe: World War II and Its Aftermath* (Princeton, N.J.: Princeton University Press, 2000), pp. 80–84.

13. Herczl, *Christianity and the Holocaust of Hungarian Jewry*, pp. 214–215.

14. For an account of the German Catholic Church's use of antisemitism to discredit Corvin, see Lewy, *The Catholic Church and Nazi Germany*, pp. 278–279.

15. Such a breakdown looks different for different national groups (Germans, French, Lithuanians, Poles, Danes, etc.) and for the members of different religious and nonreligious institutions, including national churches.

16. See Zuccotti, *Under His Very Windows*, pp. 45–46.

17. Marrus and Paxton, *Vichy France and the Jews*, p. 272.

18. Quoted in Modras, *The Catholic Church and Antisemitism*, p. 346. Cardinal Hlond violated his own maxim in the pastoral letter by slandering the Jews, as quoted above. For Bishop Gföllner's rejection of anti-Jewish violence and also of racism, see Kertzer, *The Popes Against the Jews*, p. 274. For Bishop Cazzani's opposition to "excessive punitive measures," see Zuccotti, *Under His Very Windows*, p. 55.

19. Quoted in Shelah, "The Catholic Church in Croatia," pp. 272–273.

20. For Monsignor Duca's heartfelt intervention of March 1943, on the order of Monsignor Giovanni Battista Montini, the future Pope Paul VI, see Daniel Carpi, *Between Mussolini and Hitler: The Jews and the Italian Authorities in France and Tunisia* (Hanover, N.H.: Brandeis University Press, 1994), pp. 101–135, especially pp. 131–132; and Zuccotti, *Under His Very Windows*, pp. 129–130. It turned out that the intervention was unnecessary, because Mussolini was not intending to deport these Jews in any case. The mass murder led the German bishops to consider proposals at their annual meeting of 1942 and 1943 that they speak out against the most lethal aspects of their country's eliminationist program. The bishops rejected the proposals. For a discussion of this, see Michael Phayer, *The Catholic Church and the Holocaust, 1930–1965* (Bloomington: Indiana University Press, 2000), pp. 74–75, though his explanations for the bishops' inaction are not credible.

21. Pius XII's Christmas message and his address to the Sacred College of Cardinals on June 2, 1943, were also published in *L'Osservatore Romano* and *Civiltà cattolica*. See Zuccotti, *Under His Very Windows*, pp. 1–2 and 329, ns. 1 and 2. For the pressure on the Pope coming from both the American and the British, see Owen Chadwick, *Britain and the Vatican During the Second World War* (Cambridge: Cambridge University Press, 1986), pp. 199 and 213; and Phayer, *The Catholic Church and the Holocaust*, p. 49.

22. Lewy, *The Catholic Church and Nazi Germany*, p. 294.

23. Obviously, those clergy who thought that the death penalty was a just punishment for the Jews did not protest on the Jews' behalf for that reason.

24. Marrus and Paxton, *Vichy France and the Jews*, p. 273.

25. Quoted in Carol Rittner, Stephen D. Smith, and Irena Steinfeldt, eds., *The Holocaust and the Christian World: Reflections of the Past, Challenges for the Future* (New York: Continuum, 2000), p. 242. Living in a far more pluralistic and less antisemitic society, the Catholic bishops of the United States saw the assault on the Jews as the crime that it was. In a pastoral letter in November 1942, the American bishops told American Catholics: "Since the murderous assault on Poland, utterly devoid of every semblance of humanity, there has been a premeditated and systematic extermination of the people of this nation. The same satanic technique is being applied to many other peoples. We feel a deep sense of revulsion against the cruel indignities heaped upon the Jews in conquered countries and upon defenseless peoples not of our faith." They continued by quoting the earlier French bishops' statement, " 'Deeply moved by the mass arrests and maltreatment of Jews, we cannot stifle the cry of our conscience. In the name of humanity and Christian principles, our voice is raised.' " Quoted in Archbishop Oscar Lipscomb, "Commemorating the Liberation of Auschwitz," Jan. 1995, in *Catholics Remember the Holocaust* (Washington, D.C.: Secretariat for Ecumenical and Interreligious Affairs, National Conference of Catholic Bishops, 1998), p. 17. Unlike the Vatican, the American Catholic bishops recognized Nazism as irredeemably evil and were therefore critical of the Vatican's neutrality, which included its accommodation and cooperation with Nazism. In the same pastoral letter, they characterized Nazism and its allies as "united in waging war to bring about a slave world . . ." In what was all but an explicit rebuke of the

Vatican, they explained that the "conflict of Principles" with Nazism made "compromise impossible." See Gerald P. Fogarty, *The Vatican and the American Hierarchy from 1870 to 1965* (Stuttgart: Anton Hiersemann, 1982), pp. 286–287.

26. See, for example, Phayer, *The Catholic Church and the Holocaust,* pp 120–121. For the small percentage of Catholic religious institutions in Rome that sheltered Jews, see Zuccotti, *Under His Very Windows,* p. 201.

27. For an account of the rescue of Jews by Catholics, both clerical and lay, see Phayer, *The Catholic Church and the Holocaust,* pp. 111–132, especially pp. 124–126. For the Italian Catholic Church, see Susan Zuccotti, *The Italians and the Holocaust. Persecution, Rescue, Survival* (New York: Basic Books, 1987), pp. 207–217. Zuccotti points out that during the German occupation the Germans and their Italian helpers killed more than 170 priests for their resistance activities of helping anti-Fascists and Jews (p. 208). The number helping Jews is unspecified, perhaps unknown. Phayer presents the figure of 170 to suggest that all the priests died for helping Jews, even though his source is Zuccotti (p. 125). For a discussion of the Vatican expulsion order, see Zuccotti, *Under His Very Windows,* pp. 224–232.

28. Similarly, the relatively low level of antisemitism in Italy led many Italian clergy and ordinary Italians to resist the annihilation of the Jews as an obvious course of action. See Zuccotti, *The Italians and the Holocaust,* pp. 278–282.

29. *Catechism of the Catholic Church* (New York: Doubleday, 1995), "Man's Freedom," parags. 1730–1748.

30. If today we are going to judge, legally or morally, those who commit single offenses against one individual, then why should those people who committed offenses during the Nazi period be immune from our judgments just because the number of transgressors, the number and type of offenses, and the number of victims were all immense? It is a perversion of justice and morality to treat a person who willfully commits a crime or another harmful act more leniently if many others did the same and if the act was the worst imaginable, such as the mass annihilation of Jews, than some lone individual is treated who does something far less bad, such as stealing a car. To maintain that we should not inquire morally about people during the Nazi period is to imply that we should never do so, or that Germans and others who killed and harmed Jews are a special case deserving of moral immunity. It is unlikely that many would admit to either view.

31. Quoted in James Carroll, *Constantine's Sword: The Church and the Jews* (Boston: Houghton Mifflin, 2001), p. 436.

32. See the discussion of many such documents in John F. Morley, *Vatican Diplomacy and the Jews During the Holocaust, 1939–1943* (New York, Ktav, 1980) and Zuccotti, *Under His Very Windows.*

33. *Catechism of the Catholic Church,* parags. 846–848 and 1257–1261 on salvation, and parags. 1033–1037 on hell. See part three for a discussion of the Church's position on salvation and hell.

34. *Catechism of the Catholic Church,* parags. 823–829 and 891.

35. For an account of such deeds of the perpetrators, see Goldhagen, *Hitler's Willing Executioners,* especially pp. 376–378, 385–389, and 396–399. For examples of the misconstruing of the perpetrators' cruelty as owing to the logistical pressures of killing operations, see Christopher R. Browning, *Ordinary Men: Reserve*

Police Battalion 101 and the Final Solution in Poland (New York: HarperCollins, 1992), p. 95; and Raul Hilberg, *Perpetrators, Victims, Bystanders: The Jewish Catastrophe, 1933–1945* (New York: Asher Books, 1992), p. 54; for a further discussion of this issue see Daniel Jonah Goldhagen, "The Paradigm Challenged: Victim Testimony, Critical Evidence, and New Perspectives in the Study of the Holocaust," *Tikkun* 13, no. 3 (May/June 1998), pp. 43–44.

36. The actors' moral agency, our obligation to judge them, to judge them fairly, and to judge them in a noncasual way that is worthy of a genuine moral reckoning seems so obvious that one might be astonished that this all must be asserted, and asserted against so much resistance.

37. This question assumes and implies that the Pope and others in the Church disapproved of the persecution of the Jews, and thereby immediately excludes the most dangerous and unwelcome question (for the Pope's and the Church's defenders) of what the Pope's and the clergy's views were of the many aspects of the eliminationist persecution.

38. For a different and problematic treatment of culpability, see Karl Jaspers, *The Question of German Guilt* (1947; New York: Fordham University Press, 2000). Aside from Jaspers' endorsement of the notion of collective guilt, his categorization is unsystematic and woolly, often diffusing different kinds of guilt over the entire population, including, for example, what he calls metaphysical guilt. See especially pp. 25–30 and 65–75.

39. "Noncriminal" is preferable to "civil" because the category is more expansive than what ordinarily falls under civil law (in the United States and elsewhere). The category includes many blameworthy things that are not considered to be torts and that are explained below.

40. Bernard Williams, "How Free Does the Will Need to Be?" in *Making Sense of Humanity and Other Philosophical Papers, 1982–1993* (Cambridge: Cambridge University Press, 1995), explains that blame "is conceived of as the rough analogy in the moral realm to legal penalties and denunciations" (p. 14).

41. *Catechism of the Catholic Church*, parag. 1853; on the nature of freedom and free will, see parags. 1730–1748.

42. *Catechism of the Catholic Church*, parags. 1849–1850 and 1868.

43. *Catechism of the Catholic Church*, parags. 1868 and 2477.

44. *Catechism of the Catholic Church*, "The Gravity of Sin: Mortal and Venial Sin," parags. 1854–1864. The Jewish Bible actually says: "Do not murder," but "murder" has consistently been rendered in Christian texts as "kill."

45. *Catechism of the Catholic Church*, parag. 1868.

46. *Catechism of the Catholic Church*, parags. 2464 and 1858.

47. *Catechism of the Catholic Church*, "Sin," parags. 1846–1876, especially parags. 1852–1864; "Charity," parags. 1822–1829; and "Offenses Against Truth," parags. 2475–2487.

48. International Law Commission, "Principles of International Law Recognized in the Charter of the Nürnberg Tribunal and in the Judgment of the Tribunal," *Yearbook of the International Law Commission, 1950*, vol. 2, reproduced at International Law Commission, <www.un.org/law/ilc/texts/nurnberg.htm>.

49. International Law Commission, "Draft Code of Offenses Against the Peace

and Security of Mankind, 1954," *Yearbook of the International Law Commission 1954,* vol. 2, reproduced at International Law Commission, <www.un.org/law/ilc/texts/offfra.htm>.

50. "Statute of the International Tribunal," for Yugoslavia, Nov. 30, 2000 <www.un.org/icty/basic/statut/stat2000.htm>.

51. This was the principle underlying the Nuremberg trials: "Any person who commits an act which constitutes a crime under international law is responsible therefore and liable to punishment. . . . The fact that internal law does not impose a penalty for an act which constitutes a crime under international law does not relieve the person who committed the act from responsibility under international law." See International Law Commission, "Principles of International Law Recognized in the Charter of the Nürnberg Tribunal and in the Judgment of the Tribunal." For additional international norms that are relevant to assessing the offenses of Catholic clergy during the Nazi period, see United Nations General Assembly, "Universal Declaration of Human Rights," Dec. 10, 1948, <www.un.org/Overview/rights.html>, especially articles 2, 3, 5, 7, 8, 9, 10, 12, 15, 16, 17, 21, 22, 23, and 27.

52. Even according to the laws of Germany during the Nazi period, the killing of Jews was formally illegal. Prosecutions of Germans for the murder of Jews in the Federal Republic of Germany have relied on such statutes. See Ingo Müller *Hitler's Justice: The Courts of the Third Reich* (Cambridge: Harvard University Press, 1991), pp. 254–255.

53. "Charter of the International Military Tribunal" in Office of United States Chief of Council for Prosecution of Axis Criminality, *Nazi Conspiracy and Aggression,* vol. 1 (Washington, D.C.: United States Government Printing Office, 1946) pp. 4–12; see also "Statement of Criminality of Groups and Organizations," in "Indictment Number 1," pp. 68–73.

54. *Catechism of the Catholic Church,* parag. 2477.

55. Donald J. Dietrich, *Catholic Citizens in the Third Reich: Psycho-Social Principles and Moral Reasoning* (New Brunswick, N.J.: Transaction Books, 1988) writes: "The structure and ideology of the Church, however, abetted the consolidation of Nazi rule. There existed a congruence between Catholic attitudes and those of the Nazi regime, whose popularity was basically due to its endorsing the policies favored by the conservative elites—national revival, territorial expansion, the abolition of democratic pluralism, and ethnocentrism" (p. 207). For the Vatican and Italy, see Klaus Scholder, *The Churches and the Third Reich,* vol. 1 (Philadelphia Fortress Press, 1988), pp. 242–243; for Croatia, see Shelah, "The Catholic Church in Croatia, the Vatican and the Murder of the Croatian Jews," p. 268; for France see Phillipe Burrin, *France under the Germans: Collaboration and Compromise* (New York: New Press, 1996), pp. 217–218; in Slovakia, as we have seen, the Catholic Church and the new regime were intimately intertwined.

56. Quoted in Lewy, *The Catholic Church and Nazi Germany,* p. 226. For a discussion of the German church's positive attitudes toward the war, see pp. 224–242 Lewy writes of the German "bishops' often-asserted beliefs that Germany was fighting a just war for the attainment of *Lebensraum* and for the defense against plutocracy and Bolshevism" (p. 233).

57. See Lewy, *The Catholic Church and Nazi Germany*, pp. 226 and 232 for the statements of these bishops, and Gordon C. Zahn, *German Catholics and Hitler's Wars: A Study in Social Control* (New York: Sheed and Ward, 1962), p. 17.

58. *Catechism of the Catholic Church*, parags. 2477 and 2479; and Exodus 20:26. In Judaism the prohibition against bearing false witness is the ninth commandment. For someone to commit calumny in the eyes of the Church requires only that his statement injurious to the reputation of another be untrue, not that he knows that it is untrue. The Church distinguishes a calumny from a lie, which is "the most direct offense against the truth. To lie is to speak or act against the truth in order to lead someone into error," in other words, an untruth that its speaker knows to be untrue. See *Catechism of the Catholic Church*, parag. 2483.

59. Quoted in Lewy, *The Catholic Church and Nazi Germany*, p. 90.

60. Modras, *The Catholic Church and Antisemitism*, p. 396; see also Heller, *On the Edge of Destruction*, pp. 109–114.

61. The most famous and theatrical such instance has been the Oberammergau Passion Play. For an account of its continuing antisemitism, see Leonard Swidler, "The Passion of the Jew Jesus: Recommended Changes in the Oberammergau Passion Play after 1984" (Anti-Defamation League of B'naï B'rith, 1999), <http://ecumene.org/SHOAH/oberammer.htm>.

62. *Trials of the Major War Criminals Before the International Military Tribunal*, vol. 5, p. 111.

63. John 8:44.

64. Quoted in Carroll, *Constantine's Sword*, p. 376. It is noteworthy that in an address to Jewish leaders, Cardinal Cassidy said this, but in an official Church document, such as "We Remember," of which he was the principal author, this truth is not only not mentioned but essentially denied. For an analysis of the pernicious content and consequences of Church teachings, see Walter Zwi Bacharach, *Anti-Jewish Prejudices in German Catholic-Sermons* (Lewiston, New York: The Edwin Mellen Press, 1993), esp. pp. 138–139.

65. Sebastian Haffner, *Geschichte eines Deutschen: Die Erinnerungen, 1914–1933* (Stuttgart: Deutsche Verlagsanstalt, 2001), p. 139.

66. See "Bolshevism" and "Rasse," in Archbishop Conrad Gröber, ed., published with the "Recommendation of the Whole German Episcopate, *Handbuch der religiösen Gegenwartsfragen* (Freiburg im Breisgau: Herder and Co., 1940), pp. 83–88 and 532–537; and Lewy, *The Catholic Church and Nazi Germany*, pp. 275–277. For a discussion of the Nazis' view of a hierarchy of races, see Goldhagen, *Hitler's Willing Executioners*, pp. 409–412.

67. For the law, see <www.de/Library/stgb/130.htm>.

68. For a discussion of the Jews' social death, see Goldhagen, *Hitler's Willing Executioners*, pp. 135–136 and 168–170; for the concept of social death, see Orlando Patterson, *Slavery and Social Death: A Comparative Study* (Cambridge: Harvard University Press, 1982), esp. pp. 1–14. For an extensive adoption of my application of Patterson's concept of social death to Germans' treatment of Jews during the Nazi period, see Marion A. Kaplan, *Between Dignity and Despair: Jewish Life in Nazi Germany* (New York: Oxford University Press, 1998), especially pp. 5, 9, 150–200, and 229.

69. Quoted in Georg Denzler and Volker Fabricius, *Die Kirchen im Dritten Reich: Christen und Nazis Hand in Hand?* (Frankfurt/M: Fischer Taschenbuch Verlag, 1984), p. 160. The bishops also acknowledged that antisemitism was extremely widespread in Germany: "An antisemitic tradition existed in broad segments of the German people, which included also Catholics."

70. For a further discussion of these themes, see Goldhagen, *Hitler's Willing Executioners*, pp. 37–38, a small portion of which is reproduced in this paragraph.

71. Bérard's report is reproduced in "Pope Pius XII and the Jews," *Jewish Spectator* (Feb. 1964), pp. 13–17. See Zuccotti, *Under His Very Windows*, p. 55.

72. See Kertzer, *The Popes Against the Jews*, p. 289.

73. Zuccotti, *The Italians and the Holocaust*, pp. 36–40.

74. Quoted in Zuccotti, *Under His Very Windows*, pp. 109–110. It should be noted that the report had some details wrong: among others, Majdanek was actually in Lublin and Treblinka was near Warsaw.

75. See Zuccotti, *Under His Very Windows*, pp. 27–41, for a discussion of the Church's positive attitude toward the possibility of anti-Jewish laws. The Church was happy to have such laws but did not want them to define the Jews as a race and create disabilities for them on that basis.

76. Why do Father Rosa and the Church not delimit clearly who is not to be persecuted? Was it because for the Church it was virtually no Jew and that its position that exceptions exist is only a theoretical position that the Church doctrinally must propound?

77. See Zuccotti, *Under His Very Windows*, p. 25.

78. Zuccotti, *Under His Very Windows*, pp. 48–49.

79. Kertzer, *The Popes Against the Jews*, p. 9. For an illustration of Nazi anti-Jewish Law's relationship to its earlier canon-law precedents, see Raul Hilberg, *The Destruction of the European Jews* (New York: New Viewpoints, 1973), pp. 4–7.

80. Quoted in Lewy, *The Catholic Church and Nazi Germany*, p. 281. On Bishop Hudal's friendship with Pius XII, see Gitta Sereny, *Into That Darkness: An Examination of Conscience* (London: Picador, 1977), pp. 305–306.

81. Zuccotti, *Under His Very Windows*, p. 54.

82. Quoted in Zuccotti, *Under His Very Windows*, pp. 54–55. As was the Church's custom, along with an impassioned antisemitic plea and, here, a program calculated to whip up anti-Jewish passion and action, the Church provided the proforma disclaimer against excesses.

83. Less than four weeks after Pius XII took office, his representative, Father Tacchi Venturi, essentially confirmed to Mussolini the Church's continuing support for the antisemitic legislation. Father Tacchi Venturi asked Mussolini personally for small alterations in the laws as they affected Christians who had converted from Judaism or who were in mixed marriages. But he did not contest the laws themselves or seek to ameliorate their affect on Jews. See Zuccotti, *Under His Very Windows*, p. 64.

84. "Die Regelung des Rasseproblems durch die Nürnberger Gesetze," *Klerusblatt*, Jan. 22, 1936, p. 47.

85. "Rasse," in Gröber, *Handbuch der religiösen Gegenwartsfragen*, p. 536.

86. Jean Lacouture, *Jesuits: A Multibiography* (Washington, D.C.: Counterpoint, 1995), pp. 173–175. My understanding is that in the wake of the Holocaust the Jesuits abolished their blood purity requirement in 1946.

87. Konrad Repgen, ed., *Staatliche Akten über die Reichskonkordatsverhandlungen, 1933* (Mainz: Matthias-Grünwald Verlag, 1969), p. 419. In 1923, the Jesuits decided to lift the absolute prohibition on Catholics whose Jewish blood was no fresher than five generations back.

88. For an account of the evolution of the Nazis' eliminationist assault, see Goldhagen, *Hitler's Willing Executioners*, pp. 131–163.

89. Quoted in Lewy, *The Catholic Church and Nazi Germany*, p. 281. For an account of the violence against Jews prior to the Nuremberg Laws, see Goldhagen, *Hitler's Willing Executioners*, pp. 93–96.

90. Lewy, *The Catholic Church and Nazi Germany*, p. 107.

91. See Dietrich, *Catholic Citizens in the Third Reich*, pp. 184–187 and 66–67; and Carroll, *Constantine's Sword*, pp. 517–520.

92. Quoted in Lewy, *The Catholic Church and Nazi Germany*, p. 279; and Dietrich, *Catholic Citizens in the Third Reich*, p. 116.

93. Dietrich, *Catholic Citizens in the Third Reich*, p. 185.

94. See Lewy, *The Catholic Church and Nazi Germany*, p. 279; Dietrich, *Catholic Citizens in the Third Reich*, pp. 113–118; Michael Lukens, "Joseph Lortz and a Catholic Accommodation with National Socialism," in Robert P. Ericksen and Susannah Heschel, eds., *Betrayal: German Churches and the Holocaust* (Minneapolis: Fortress Press, 1999), pp. 149–168, especially pp. 153–155.

95. Pius XII, *Summi Pontificatus* (Oct. 20, 1939). <www.vatican.va/holy_father/pius_xii/encyclicals/index.htm>, parag. 19.

96. The Church could not but know that many Germans and the Europeans would understand silence to mean a lack of disapproval, to mean approval. The Church leaders willingly let this happen. See the discussion below on the blame a person accrues for allowing things to occur.

97. When people believe that they are facing great evil or injustice, or are just unhappy with a political or social system, they find ways to express their disapproval. They have many ways to do so. Even people who lack resources and are illiterate, and are facing punishing violence, routinely manage to do so. Examples abound from slaves, serfs, members of oppressed castes, and exploited peasants. There is no reason to believe that the highly literate, barely threatened possessors of great resources, the bishops and priests of the Catholic Church, would not be able to express their opposition to their countrymen's crimes. But the record of such principled disapproval of the general eliminationist persecution barely exists. If it did, those people within the Church and those outside of it who have devoted so much energy to defending the Church would have certainly, with fanfare, brought it all to our attention. See James C. Scott, *Domination and the Arts of Resistance: Hidden Transcripts* (New Haven: Yale University Press, 1985).

98. Quoted in International Catholic-Jewish Historical Commission, "The Vatican and the Holocaust: A Preliminary Report," <www.jcrelations.net/vatican_holocaust.htm> (Oct. 2000), n. 58.

99. International Law Commission, "Draft Code of Crimes Against the Peace and Security of Mankind, 1996," *Yearbook of the Internatinal Law Commission, 1996*, vol. 2, reproduced at www.un.org/law/ilc/texts/dcodefra.htm.

100. See Monsignor Burzio's letter, reproduced in Morley, *Vatican Diplomacy and the Jews During the Holocaust, 1939–1943*, pp. 239–243. The Vatican at the same time initiated a meeting with Slovakia's representative to the Holy See and a few days later sent a formal note that reaffirmed the Church's formal opposition to the further deportations of Jews and of Catholics who had converted from Judaism, indicating that the Church "deplore[d] these regulations and measures which strike so gravely at the natural rights of men, for the simple fact of belonging to a particular race" (p. 95).

101. See Morley, *Vatican Diplomacy and the Jews During the Holocaust, 1939–1943*, pp. 92–101, especially pp. 92 and 100. Sorting out the fine points of the Vatican's concerns and its approaches to the Slovaks regarding the country's eliminationist policies would require a long discussion. In essence, though, the Vatican was focused overwhelmingly on Christians who had converted from Judaism, and aside from the Church's obligatory acknowledgment of the inhumanity of what the Germans and Slovaks were doing to Jews ("an offense against justice, charity, humanity"), it did virtually nothing for the Jews. Morley concludes his analysis of the Vatican's dealings with Slovakia with the condemnation that "Vatican diplomacy, however, was content to limit itself to the narrow confines of strictly Catholic interests" (p. 101). Zuccotti similarly concludes that "the Vatican's record in Slovakia is indeed dismal," and that "there is little truth to the claims of papal apologists that diplomatic interventions of the Holy See saved Slovakians who were Jewish by religion or culture" (p. 101).

102. For an account of the camp system and what Germany was becoming, see Goldhagen, *Hitler's Willing Executioners*, pp. 170–178 and 455–461; for a treatment of the regime's broader criminality, see Michael Burleigh and Wolfgang Wippermann, *The Racial State: Germany 1933–1945* (Cambridge: Cambridge University Press, 1991). It is clear, however, that when the German bishops believed that a policy of the regime violated their deepest values, such as the so-called Euthanasia program, they stridently ignored the Concordat and spoke out.

103. Lewy, *The Catholic Church and Nazi Germany*, p. 93.

104. The power of such ideas is illustrated in the famous church scene from Claude Lanzmann's film *Shoah*, where a man, speaking for his fellow Catholic congregants, explains why the Jews were killed with a story that, even if it obviously never happened, conveyed the prevailing folk wisdom: A rabbi was said to have informed the Jews of his town, whom the Germans had assembled for deportation, of the cause of their impending deaths by quoting the Christian Bible: " 'Let his blood fall on our heads and on our sons' heads.' The rabbi then told them: 'Perhaps the time has come for that, so let us do nothing, let us go, let us do as we're asked.' " The man who related this as the representative of his community deemed the mass murder "God's will," his punishment of the Jews for their alleged Christ-killing. For the text, see Claude Lanzmann, *Shoah: An Oral History of the Holocaust* (New York: Pantheon Books, 1985), pp. 99–100.

105. *Trials of the Major War Criminals Before the International Military Tribunal,* vol. 5, p. 118.

106. See Judgment Against Julius Streicher, *Trials of the Major War Criminals Before the International Military Tribunal,* vol. 1, pp. 301–304.

107. Quoted in Lewy, *The Catholic Church and Nazi Germany,* p. 277.

108. This paragraph reproduces, with minor changes, a passage in Goldhagen, *Hitler's Willing Executioners,* p. 112. The proclamation is in *Kirchliches Jahrbuch für die Evangelische Kirche in Deutschland, 1933–1944* (Gütersloh: C. Bertelsmann Verlag, 1948), p. 481.

109. Pius XII's representatives' confirmation of Italy's antisemitic laws is far more persuasive evidence of his attitudes toward Jews than his or the Vatican's occasional self-serving and obviously untruthful remarks that the Vatican was doing as much as it could to help the Jews or that he disapproved of the Nazis' treatment of the Jews, which he made to foreign diplomats whose countries were arrayed against Nazism. See Meir Michaelis, *Mussolini and the Jews: German-Italian Relations and the Jewish Question in Italy, 1922–1945* (Oxford: Clarendon, 1978), for another such example, this time of Pacelli's protestations in 1933 (as Secretary of State) to a British diplomat whom Pacelli was trying to convince that, his signing of the Concordat with Hitler notwithstanding, the Church thoroughly abhorred and rejected Nazism (pp. 424–425). Pacelli, the chief diplomat of the Church, was with his dissimulations doing all he could to maintain Britain's goodwill.

110. For a discussion of this, see part one, note 77; and Morley, *Vatican Diplomacy and the Jews,* pp. 92–93.

111. Phayer, *The Catholic Church and the Holocaust,* pp. 75–76; and Saul Friedländer, *Pius XII and the Third Reich: A Documentation* (New York: Alfred A. Knopf, 1966), p. 138.

112. Zuccotti, *Under His Very Windows,* p. 167.

113. See Zuccotti, *Under His Very Windows,* pp. 217–219.

114. Livia Rothkirchen, "The Churches and the Deportation and Persecution of Jews in Slovakia," in Rittner, Smith, and Steinfeldt, *The Holocaust and the Christian World,* p. 107.

115. *Catechism of the Catholic Church,* parag. 1868.

116. Bernard Williams, "Acts and Omissions: Doing and Not Doing," in *Making Sense of Humanity and Other Philosophical Papers, 1982–1993* (Cambridge: Cambridge University Press, 1995), p. 59. Williams adds that "the much discussed distinction between doing and allowing seems not to be a distinction at all."

117. See Williams, "Acts and Omissions," p. 62.

118. Quoted in Rittner, Smith, and Steinfeldt, *The Holocaust and the Christian World,* p. 242.

119. Lewy, *The Catholic Church and Nazi Germany,* p. 275.

120. Among those who have plumbed the relationship of Christian antisemitism to the Holocaust, including many Christian theologians, it is a truism that the former was a necessary cause, though not a sufficient cause, of the latter. Donald J. Dietrich, *God and Humanity in Auschwitz: Jewish-Christian Relations and Sanc-*

tioned Murder (New Brunswick, N.J.: Transaction, 1995), expresses this consensus: "What now seems clear is that the Christian anti-Jewish polemic was a necessary, even though not complete, cause for the Nazi assault" (p. 107). For a representative sampling of such views, see Helen P. Fry, ed., *Christian-Jewish Dialogue: A Reader* (Exeter: University of Exeter Press, 1996), pp. 18, 22, 23–25, 30–32, 36–37, and 153. Also, many Christian churches have admitted as much. See part three for the discussion of the churches' statements of their own culpability regarding the Holocaust.

121. Phayer, *The Catholic Church and the Holocaust*, p. 175. The German Catholic bishops also sided with the perpetrators over the Jewish victims, denying Germans' responsibility for the Holocaust, protesting the Nuremberg trials as unjust, and agitating on behalf of the mass murderers (pp. 133–148). For an in-depth discussion of these issues, see Vera Bücker, *Die Schulddiskussion im deutschen Katholizismus nach 1945* (Bochum: Studienverlag Dr. N. Brockmeyer, 1989).

122. Alois C. Hudal, *Römische Tagebücher: Lebensbeichte eines alten Bischofs* (Graz: Leopold Stocker, 1976), p. 21.

123. Ernst Klee, *Persilscheine und falsche Pässe: wie die kirchen den Nazis halfen* (Frankfurt/M.: Fischer Taschenbuch Verlag, 1991), p. 25.

124. Quoted in Klee, *Persilscheine und falsche Pässe*, p. 25.

125. Phayer, *The Catholic Church and the Holocaust*, p. 173.

126. *Catechism of the Catholic Church*, parag. 1868.

127. Pius XI, *Mit brennender Sorge* (March 14, 1937), <www.vatican.va/holy_father/pius_xi/encyclicals/index.htm>, parag. 3.

128. Lewy, *The Catholic Church and Nazi Germany*, pp. 264–265.

129. Pius XII, *Summi Pontificatus*, parag. 19.

130. Karl Barth, *Eine Schweizer Stimme 1938–1945*, third ed. (Zürich: Theologischer Verlag, 1985), pp. 90 and 318; "Eingeständnis führte zur Absage an den Antisemitismus," *Neue Osnabruecker Zeitung*, April 23, 2002; and French bishops, "Declaration of Repentance," Sept. 1997, in Rittner, Smith, and Steinfeldt, *The Holocaust and the Christian World*, p. 255.

Part Three: Repairing the Harm

1. Thomas Hobbes, *Leviathan*, Parts I and II (Indianapolis: Liberal Arts Press, 1958), p. 41. From our perspective, Hobbes did not practice what he preached.

2. The Jewish Bible actually prohibits "murder," not "killing." The Church has itself not been opposed to all killing (self-defense, death penalty, just war), so its choice to render this commandment as "You shall not kill" is curious. See Exodus 20:13 in Everett Fox's translation of and commentary on *The Five Books of Moses: Genesis, Exodus, Leviticus, Numbers, and Deuteronomy* (New York: Schocken, 1995).

3. Owen Chadwick, "Weizsäcker, the Vatican, and the Jews of Rome," *Journal of Ecclesiastical History* 28, no. 2 (April 1977), p. 182.

4. See, for example, Samuel P. Huntington, *The Third Wave: Democratization in*

the Late Twentieth Century (Norman: University of Oklahoma Press, 1991) for a discussion of the Church as a political institution, which Huntington evaluates positively, at least for its role in bringing about transitions to democracy in Latin America and elsewhere in the 1980s (pp. 77–87). He writes, "This repositioning of the Catholic Church [in the mid-1960s] from a bulwark of the status quo, usually authoritarian, to a force for change, usually democratic, was a major political phenomenon" (p. 77).

5. Philip Pullella, " 'Shadow Synod' Wants Reform in Catholic Church," Reuters (Oct. 4, 2001). For other calls from Catholics for an end to the authoritarian structure of the Church, see Hans Küng, "Church from Above—Church from Below," *Reforming the Church Today: Keeping Hope Alive* (New York: Crossroad, 1990); and James Carroll, *Constantine's Sword: The Church and the Jews* (Boston: Houghton Mifflin, 2001), pp. 588–598; John Cornwell, *Breaking Faith: The Pope, the People, and the Fate of Catholicism* (New York: Viking, 2000); and the Catholic progressive organization Call to Action, <www.cta-usa.org>.

6. *Catechism of the Catholic Church* (New York: Doubleday, 1995), parag. 882.

7. *Catechism of the Catholic Church*, parags. 890–891 and 2035.

8. Garry Wills, *Papal Sin: Structures of Deceit* (New York: Doubleday, 2000), p. 7.

9. Even if the Pope is only supposed to be infallible when he is speaking in certain circumstances and about certain things, it casts an aura of infallibility around him in all things and, most important, makes the defenders of Popes and the Church extraordinarily reluctant to admit his fallibility about anything because that would seem, and would indeed weaken, his divine claims. In the defense of the infallibility doctrine, its champions split hairs about when he is infallible. In practice, they do not split hairs, letting the Pope and the Church bask generally, for all matters, in the authoritative glow of infallibility.

10. For an extensive discussion of these issues, see Wills, *Papal Sin.*

11. *Catechism of the Catholic Church*, parags. 830–856. Some people may not like the application of standard political terms to the Church's features, but these are undeniably what the Church is and seeks. Especially given the political nature of the Church, it would be irresponsible not to use the standard applicable terminology.

12. *Catechism of the Catholic Church*, parags. 864–848 and 1257 on exclusion from salvation, and parags. 1033–1037 on hell.

13. *Catechism of the Catholic Church*, parag. 674. This is one of the many features of Catholicism, and much of Christianity, that renders the status of Judaism and Jews fundamentally different from that of other non-Christian religions and peoples.

14. *Catechism of the Catholic Church*, parags. 846 and 848.

15. Eugene J. Fisher, "Jewish-Catholic Dialogue," Letter to the Editor, *New York Times*, May 11, 2001.

16. Quoted in Clyde Haberman, "When Silence Can Seem Like Consent," *New York Times*, April 23, 2002, p. A26. See also William Donohue, "The *New Republic* Publishes Goldhagen's Assault on Catholicism," <www.catholicleague.org/

catalyst/2002_catalyst/3-02.htm>. Nonpolitical aspects of Catholicism—how to conceive of the Trinity, the role of confession, when communion is taken, what the length of a mass should be—are, to be sure, properly the sole province of the Church and its members.

17. This account of what constitutes being anti-Catholic is a summary of the discussion of antisemitism in the introduction. For the fuller discussion, which also applies here, see pp. 21–23.

18. For a strong view of the agency of Catholics as a source for the Church's renewal, see Küng, *Reforming the Church Today,* especially "Church from Above—Church from Below," pp. 52–63; see also many of the essays in David Tracy, Hans Küng, and Johann B. Metz, eds., *Toward Vatican III: The Work That Needs to Be Done* (New York: Concilium and the Seabury Press, 1977). Why, we might ask, should we be any less truthful with Catholics about their Church's past than we have been with Germans about their country's past? For accounts of the pluralism within the Catholic Church, including Catholics' dissent from the Church's doctrine or official positions, see Richard P. McBrien, *Catholicism,* new ed. (San Francisco: Harper San Francisco, 1994); and Cornwell, *Breaking Faith;* for American Catholics, Alan Wolfe, "Liberalism and Catholicism," *American Prospect* 11, no. 6 (Jan. 31, 2000). See also the Call to Action website, <www.cta-usa.org>.

19. John Rawls, *A Theory of Justice* (Cambridge, Mass.: Harvard University Press, 1971), writes:

> The idea of the original position is to set up a fair procedure so that any principles agreed to will be just. The aim is to use the notion of pure procedural justice as a basis of theory. Somehow we must nullify the effects of specific contingencies which put men at odds and tempt them to exploit social and natural circumstances to their own advantage. Now in order to do this I assume that the parties are situated behind a veil of ignorance. They do not know how the various alternatives will affect their own particular case and they are obliged to evaluate principles solely on the basis of general considerations.[11]
>
> It is assumed, then, that the parties do not know certain kinds of particular facts. First of all, no one knows his place in society, his class position or social status; nor does he know his fortune in the distribution of natural assets and abilities, his intelligence and strength, and the like. . . . They must choose principles the consequences of which they are prepared to live with.

20. Today people react with fury to prejudiced statements, particularly in public, particularly by public figures. Think of the widespread outcry in the United States that greeted Jesse Jackson's "Hymietown" characterization of New York City after the 1984 Democratic primary there, Jimmy "the Greek" Snyder's comments about the physiques of black athletes on *Nightline,* or Alfonse D'Amato's parody of Judge Lance Ito on Don Imus's morning radio show. People react with such fury because they know how hurtful and dangerous prejudice is, particularly when uttered by influential public figures. As offensive as these men's remarks were, their comments were tame compared with the extensive, extraordinarily damaging antisemitic demonology that the Catholic Church regularly spread prior to

Vatican II. Yet many scholars of the Holocaust, not to mention the Church's defenders and apologists, deny or radically minimize the enormously pernicious effects of the Church's antisemitism.

21. For a discussion of the importance, specifically, of external critiques of institutions and of people as a corrective to biased self-perceptions, see Daniel Jonah Goldhagen, "*Modell Bundesrepublik:* National History, Democracy, and Internationalization in Germany," in Robert R. Shandley, ed., *Unwilling Germans? The Goldhagen Debate,* Jeremiah Riemer, trans. (Minneapolis: University of Minnesota Press, 1998), pp. 275–285.

22. Even if the will exists to bring criminals to justice, there remains the seemingly insurmountable practical problem of dispensing justice when so many people are criminals.

23. See Bradley Abrams, "The Politics of Retribution: The Trial of Jozef Tiso in the Czechoslovak Environment," in István Deák, Jan T. Gross, and Tony Judt, eds., *The Politics of Retribution in Europe: World War II and Its Aftermath* (Princeton, N.J.: Princeton University Press, 2000), pp. 252–289. The president-priest Tiso was convicted of many crimes, in addition to the deportation of Slovak Jews. It is noteworthy that every Slovak Catholic bishop was opposed to the sentence. The Vatican's position was equivocal (pp. 273 and 285–286).

24. In some countries the opposite is happening. In Slovakia, the president-priest Tiso is experiencing, if contested, a resurgence of popularity; see Abrams, "The Politics of Retribution," p. 279.

25. Alexander G. Higgens, "Study Finds Swiss Aided Holocaust," Associated Press, March 22, 2002. Compare its conclusion, "Large numbers of persons whose lives were in danger were turned away—needlessly," with the Swiss Bishops' Conference's exculpatory explanation for the same actions—that "the totalitarian demands of her neighbors . . . forced [Switzerland] to make some compromises." For the Swiss report, see Independent Commission of Experts Switzerland—Second World War, *Switzerland, National Socialism, and the Second World War: Final Report;* and the twenty-five single-volume reports, <www.uek.ch/en/index.htm>; for the Swiss bishops, see Swiss Bishops Conference, "Confronting the Debate About the Role of Switzerland During the Second World War," March 1997, in *Catholics Remember the Holocaust* (Washington, D.C.: Secretariat for Ecumenical and Interreligious Affairs, National Conference for Catholic Bishops, 1998), p. 25.

26. Wills, *Papal Sin,* p. 45.

27. This is the title of Ernst Nolte's essay that provoked Jürgen Habermas to publish an essay that launched the *Historikerstreit* of the mid-1980s in Germany. See Ernst Nolte, "Vergangenheit, die nicht vergehen will: Eine Rede, die geschrieben, aber nicht gehalten werden konnte," in *Historikerstreit: Die Dokumentation der Kontroverse um die Einzigartigkeit der nationalsozialistischen Judenvernichtung* (München: Piper, 1987), pp. 39–47.

28. <www.jcrelations.net/stmnts/vatican12-99.htm>; and Carroll, *Constantine's Sword,* p. 27.

29. It is possible that there have been more adequate internal Church deliberations. That would be good. But since the whole Church needs to learn about the

Church's past, explorations that are private or restricted to small groups within the Church remain inadequate to the task.

30. See David I. Kertzer, *The Popes Against the Jews: The Vatican's Role in the Rise of Modern Anti-Semitism* (New York: Alfred A. Knopf, 2001), pp. 106–130. The Pope's quotation is on p. 130. See also David I. Kertzer, *The Kidnapping of Edgardo Mortara* (New York: Alfred A. Knopf, 1997).

31. Amazing as it may sound, the Commission—composed of Jewish members Michael Marrus, Bernard Suchecky, and Robert Wistrich, and Catholic members Eva Fleischner, Gerald Fogerty, and John Morley—skirted the issue of the Pope's antisemitism entirely, not asking explicitly for any archival information that might shed light on it, which they could have requested in a neutral way: "We would like to see any material that pertains to the views of Jews held by Pius XII and by other relevant Vatican diplomats and advisors, and to how such views influenced their conduct toward the persecution of the Jews." See International Catholic-Jewish Historical Commission, "The Vatican and the Holocaust: A Preliminary Report," <www.jcrelations.net>.

32. See John L. Allen, Jr., "Vatican Official Criticizes Jews," *National Catholic Reporter,* Dec. 11, 1998, <www.natcath.com>; and Carroll, *Constantine's Sword,* pp. 436 and 530–531. Father Gumpel, whose official position is "relator," asserts in a flight of antisemitic fantasy, that "eighty percent of the initial Soviet regime was Jewish."

33. "Vatican Advisor Offends Jews," interview by Mark Phillips of Father Peter Gumpel, <http://cbsnews.com> (March 22, 2000).

34. Carroll, *Constantine's Sword,* p. 437.

35. For the classical challenge to the Church about other aspects of its teachings, see Jules Isaac, *The Teachings of Contempt: Christian Roots of Anti-Semitism* (New York: Holt, Rinehart and Winston, 1964). Some might say that we should show patience with the Church because it is a slow-moving institution. But this is manifestly untrue. The Church has no trouble moving quickly when it wants to. The Church managed to condemn communism already in an encyclical of 1864 as "that infamous doctrine" which would "utterly destroy . . . even society itself." It then consistently and fervently condemned and fought communism and the Soviet Union for decades. But we are asked to believe that two millennia are not time enough to renounce antisemitism. Even after the Holocaust, it took the Church twenty years to institute the reforms of Vatican II. It took the Church more than fifty years to issue the wan "We Remember." If the explanation for the Church being so slow-moving on the one particular issue of addressing its wrongs against the Jews is that it is hard to rally Church leaders for the cause, then those arguing this position would have much to back them, including statements from prominent Catholics. Karl Rahner, a leading progressive Catholic theologian, wrote, around the time of Vatican II, regarding the Jews: "We could almost say that a supernatural demonism is exercising its power in the hatred of this people against the true kingdom of God." Pierre Benoit, the priest who edited *Ruvue biblique,* after reiterating the deicide charge, declared that "to this very day . . . every Jew suffers from the ruin undergone by his people when it refused Him at the decisive moment of its history" (Wills, *Papal Sin,* p. 21). This in 1968, after Vatican II. The Church's

defenders, if they did prove their point about the difficulty of moving the Church forward to renounce such a deep-seated enmity, would be giving up the game. And if in the mid-1960s, twenty years after the Holocaust, when antisemitism as a political ideology had been repudiated in the Western world, prominent Catholics could not restrain themselves from expressing their animosity toward Jews, and the Vatican did not see fit to repudiate them, what does that suggest about how bad antisemitism likely was before and during the Nazi period?

36. *Catechism of the Catholic Church,* parag. 674.

37. Central Committee of German Catholics, "Jews and Judaism in the New Catechism of the Catholic Church," extracts (Jan. 29, 1996), <www.jcrelations.net/stmnts/cccc.htm>.

38. John Paul II, *Crossing the Threshold of Hope* (New York: Alfred A. Knopf, 1994), pp. 99–100.

39. *Catechism of the Catholic Church,* parags. 121–123 and 128–130.

40. *Catechism of the Catholic Church,* "The Sacrament of Penance and Reconciliation," parags. 1422–1498, especially parags. 1435 and 1455–1458. Some apologists for Pius XII and the Church think that the Church ought not to offer an apology to the victims of the Holocaust. "The case for saying nothing about the Holocaust is strong," writes Owen Chadwick in "Pius XII: the legends and the truth," *The Tablet* (March 28, 1998), <www.thetablet.co.uk>. In order to justify this position of denial, this view that the Church does something wrong by apologizing for all the harm that it inflicted on Jews and led others to do to them, Chadwick caricatures what it is the Church would be repenting for (only for "the failure [of Church members] to resist crime as bravely as they should"); denies that the Church ought to "repent" because those who would be repenting did not commit the "crime"; ignores or denies the Church's and its clergy's long record of actual crimes and noncriminal transgressions for which apology is due; ignores or denies what has even come to be accepted broadly within the Catholic Church that its treatment of and teachings about Jews are cause for an apology and reform; and asserts falsely that the victims and their relatives are in any case bound to resent anything that the Church says, so what is important for the Church is to avoid such resentment. Chadwick concludes that "the notion of such a speech [of apology by today's Church] is preposterous."

41. Pius XII, address to the delegates of the Supreme Council of the Arab People of Palestine, *Acta Apostolicae Sedis: Commentarium Officiale,* Vol. 38 (1946), p. 322. Susan Zuccotti discusses another area where the Church and its defenders have fabricated good deeds to the Church's credit. She writes: "Equally disturbing is the fundamental dishonesty of claims from ostensibly reputable sources that the Vatican helped refugees far more than in fact it did." See *Under His Very Windows: The Vatican and the Holocaust* (New Haven: Yale University Press, 2000), pp. 80–81.

42. This partly reproduces sections from Goldhagen, *Hitler's Willing Executioners,* pp. 453–454 and 597, n. 86; for the original treatment, see Klaus Scholder, "A Requiem for Hitler: Cardinal Bertram, Hitler and the German Episcopate in the Third Reich," in *A Requiem for Hitler and Other New Perspectives on the German Church Struggle* (London: SCM Press, 1989), pp. 157–167.

43. Michael Phayer, *The Catholic Church and the Holocaust, 1930–1965* (Bloomington: Indiana University Press, 2000), pp. 177–183.

44. "The Christian Approach to the Jews," First Assembly of the World Council of Churches, Amsterdam, Holland, 1948, in Helga Croner, ed., *Stepping Stones to Further Jewish-Christian Relations: An Unabridged Collection of Christian Documents* (London: Stimulus, 1977), p. 70.

45. Phayer, *The Catholic Church and the Holocaust*, p. 161.

46. Phayer, *The Catholic Church and the Holocaust*, pp. 176–177 and 114–117.

47. Carroll writes: "One might say, indeed, that the first Blood Libel appears in the foundational Christian story of the death of Jesus. Thus the Church-absolving wall between anti-Judaism and antisemitism teeters at its base, just as the wall moves unsteadily between the sadism of Christian mobs and the nonviolent but contemptuous teaching of the Church establishment" (*Constantine's Sword*, p. 274).

48. Judith Hershcopf Banki, "Religious Education Before and After Vatican II," in Eugene J. Fisher, A. James Rudin, and Marc H. Tanenbaum, eds., *Twenty Years of Jewish-Catholic Relations* (Mahwah, N.J.: Paulist Press, 1986), pp. 126–127.

49. See Carroll, *Constantine's Sword;* and Wills, *Papal Sin.*

50. Wills, *Papal Sin*, pp. 19–26. The quotation from Paul VI is from Phayer, *The Catholic Church and the Holocaust*, p. 213.

51. John Paul II, *Crossing the Threshold of Hope*, p. 99.

52. The Church's removal of the phrase "perfidious Jews" from the Good Friday liturgy is frequently acknowledged and praised as a totem of the Church's progress in its presentation of Jews, yet the more damaging false accusation, that the Jews killed Jesus, remains, and is by and large ignored by commentators. This is an illustrative example of the Church's half measures and of the insufficiently critical responses to them.

53. See John L. Allen Jr., "Good Friday's Can of Worms," *National Catholic Reporter* (March 17, 2000), <www.natcath.com>.

54. These themes are discussed more fully in part three. On hell and the devil, see *Catechism of the Catholic Church*, parags. 1033–1037, and John 8:39–47.

55. For an inventory of the large number of antisemitic sections in the Christian Bible and in the *Roman Catholic Lectionary for Mass* (and in other Christian lectionaries), see Norman A. Beck, "Removing Anti-Jewish Polemic from our Christian Lectionaries: A Proposal," <www.jcrelations.net/articl1/beck.htm>, see also Lisa Palmieri-Billig, "Recognising Our Brothers and Sisters," *Common Ground* 1 (1996), reproduced at <www.jcrelations.net/artic11/brothers.htm>.

56. See Matthew 27:25 and commentary in *The New American Bible* (Wichita, Kans.: Fireside Bible, 2000–2001), p. 1059. This is the English translation and commentary officially authorized by the National Conference of Catholic Bishops and the United States Catholic Conference.

57. 1 Thessalonians 2:14–16. The Catholic biblical commentary asserts, astonishingly, that Paul's "remarks give no grounds for anti-Semitism to those willing to understand him."

58. For a discussion of some survey data from 1987 on the relationship between religious affiliation and antisemitism in Germany, see Werner Bergmann and

Rainer Erb, *Anti-Semitism in Germany: The Post-Nazi Epoch Since 1945* (New Brunswick, N.J.: Transaction, 1997), pp. 82–88 and 342. Asking people whether they have "heard" something is a technique survey researchers use to tap people's attitudes when they believe that people are unlikely to answer direct questions truthfully. The 24.3 percent figure is arrived at by adding together all those who do not disagree with the question about the Jews as Christ-killers. Eight percent explicitly agreed, and 16.3 percent said that they were undecided. To be undecided about the link between Jews' problems today and the idea that "God is punishing them for crucifying Jesus Christ" means that one does not reject the libel that the Jews are responsible for killing Jesus. If one did not believe this libel, if one believed that they are not responsible for killing Jesus, then one would automatically reject the notion that their problems are owing to God's punishment for allegedly murdering his son.

59. Godwin Lämmermann, "Christliche Motivierung des modernen Anti-semitismus? Religionssoziologische und -pädagogische Überlegungen zu einem sozialen Phänomen," *Zeitschrift für evangelische Ethik* 28, 1 (1984), p. 68.

60. Anton Pelinka, "Dismantling Taboos: Antisemitism in the Austrian Political Culture of the 1980s," *Patterns of Prejudice* 27, no. 2 (1993), p. 47.

61. *Antisemitism World Report 1995* (London and New York: Institute for Jewish Policy Research and American Jewish Committee, 1995), p. 160.

62. Survey research in the last two decades has rarely focused on the relationship between Christianity, whether Protestant or Catholic, and antisemitism. The data that we do have show the link to be strong and Christian-informed antisemitism to exist among an enormous number of people, at least in the tens of millions.

63. For a discussion of this phenomenon, see the classic study of Charles Y. Glock and Rodney Stark, *Christian Belief and Anti-Semitism* (New York: Harper Torchbooks, 1969), pp. 130–161.

64. *Catechism of the Catholic Church*, parag. 2302.

65. *Catechism of the Catholic Church*, parag. 1491; see also parags. 1459 and 2487.

66. *The Code of Canon Law* (1983), 113§1, reproduced at <www.ourladyswarriors.org/canon/>.

67. To the extent that contemporary Catholicism or other contemporary forms of Christianity have elements within their doctrine or practice that today produce unjust injuries, members of such Christian movements have the duty to work to remove such elements and to try to repair their harm, but that is a duty that arises from a person's individual choice to be a member of such contemporary Christian movements, not from a Christian institution's past deeds. There is no inherent reason that being a Christian means that one is doing harm to Jews or to anyone else.

68. Secretariat for Ecumenical and Interreligious Affairs, National Conference of Catholic Bishops, *Catholic Teaching on the Shoah: Implementing the Holy See's We Remember* (Washington, D.C.: United States Catholic Conference, 2001), p. 11. Obviously, a culpable individual bears the full responsibility for discharging his duty of restitution.

69. For a discussion of the conventional understanding of restitution and of a

view that goes somewhat beyond it, see Elazar Barkan, *The Guilt of Nations: Restitution and Negotiating Historical Injustices* (New York: Norton, 2000), pp. xviii–xix.

70. For the standard argumentation of this type, see Norman G. Finkelstein, *The Holocaust Industry: Reflection on the Exploitation of Jewish Suffering* (London: Verso, 2000); for a documentation of the applause for Finkelstein by his fulsome neo-Nazi spiritual supporters, see their critics' Martin Dietzsch and Alfred Schobert, eds., *Ein "jüdischer David Irving"? Norman G. Finkelstein im Diskurs der Rechten-Erinnerungsabwehr und Antizionismus* (Duisburg: Duisburger Institut für Sprach und Sozialforschung, 2001); they analyze the enormous harm his falsehoods have done against the truth and politically by being a boon to the neo-Nazis and the antisemitic cause, comparing his pernicious effects to those of convicted Holocaust denier David Irving.

71. "Holocaust Restitution: Reconciling Moral Imperatives with Legal Initiatives and Diplomacy," *Fordham International Law Journal*, 25 (2001), pp. 5–268–269.

72. Karl Lehmann, "Unrecht der Geschichte—Perspektiven der Versöhnung," in The German Foundation, "Remembrance, Responsibility and Future," in Klaus Barwig, Dieter R. Bauer, Karl-Joseph Hummel, eds., *Zwangsarbeit in der Kirche: Entschädigung, Versöhnung und historische Aufarbeitung* (Stuttgart: Hohenheimer Protokolle Band, 2001); "The German Foundation: 'Remembrance, Responsibility and Future,'" <www.stategov/www/regions/eur/holocaust/germanfound.html>; Joan Oleck, "A Guide to Settling Holocaust Claims," <www.businessweek.com/1998/39/b3597133.htm>; and Burt Herman, "Breakthrough: 5.2 Billion Settlement Reached in Nazi Slave Labor Case," *The Associated Press*, December 15, 1999.

73. Phayer, *The Catholic Church and the Holocaust*, pp. 170–172. The Church may owe additional compensation for the funds it received during the war from Jewish organizations to aid Jews, which it may not have used for such purposes. See International Catholic-Jewish Historical Commission, "The Vatican and the Holocaust," parag. 30.

74. Paul Charles Merkley, *Christian Attitudes Towards the State of Israel* (Montreal: McGill-Queen's University Press, 2001), pp. 216–217. Bernard Lewis, *Semites* and *Anti-Semites: An Inquiry into Conflict and Prejudice* (New York: Norton, 1986), explains that such selective criticism is an indication of antisemitism:

> One of the characteristics of the anti-Jew as distinct from the pro-Arab is that he shows no other sign of interest in the Arabs or sympathy for them, apart from their conflict with the Jews. He is completely unmoved by wrongs suffered by the Arabs, even Palestinians, under any but Jewish auspices, whether their own rulers or third parties. For him, the hundreds killed at Sabra and Shatila are of far greater concern than the thousands of Arabs slaughtered in Amman, at Tell Zaatir, in Hama, and in the many wars, in Yemen, Lebanon, the Gulf and elsewhere, that have tormented the long-suffering Arab people (p. 249).

75. See Lewis, *Semites* and *Anti-Semites*, especially pp. 132–134, 137, 172–173, 198–200, and 208–211.

76. *Catechism of the Catholic Church*, parag. 2487.

77. Quoted in Frank Stern, *The Whitewashing of the Yellow Badge: Antisemitism and Philosemitism in Postwar Germany* (Oxford: Pergamon Press, 1992), p. 367.

78. See Timothy Longman, "Christian Churches and Genocide in Rwanda," and Charles de Lespinay, "The Churches and the Genocide in the East African Great Lakes Region," both in Omer Bartov and Phyllis Mack, eds., *In God's Name: Genocide and Religion in the Twentieth Century* (New York: Berghahn Books, 2001), pp. 139–179; and Marlise Simons, "Trials Test the Faith of Rwandans," *New York Times*, May 12, 2000, p. 11.

79. Quoted in Associated Press story, June 9, 2001. See also Elizabeth Neuffer, "Evil Christians," *Boston Globe*, Dec. 12, 1996. It appears, though, that he did not follow through, at least initially, by actively pushing the Rwandan church to act upon his maxim. Until recently, the Rwandan church has been protecting priests and nuns accused of crimes, but according to the Rwandan Tribunals prosecution office, "In the last few months they have done everything to facilitate our work. It's a major change." See Marlise Simons, "Trials Test the Faith of Rwandans."

80. French Bishops, "Declaration of Repentance," Sept. 1997, in Carol Rittner, Stephen D. Smith, and Irena Steinfeldt, eds., *The Holocaust and the Christian World: Reflections of the Past, Challenges for the Future* (New York: Continuum, 2000), pp. 255–256.

81. Christopher Budd, "Pastoral Letter for 1st Sunday of Advent 1994 About Our Links with the Jewish People," in Helen P. Fry, ed., *Christian-Jewish Dialogue: A Reader* (Exeter: University of Exeter Press, 1996), p. 153.

82. Hans Peter Mensing, ed., *Konrad Adenauer Briefe Über Deutschland, 1945–1951* (Berlin: Corso, 1983), pp. 32–33.

83. Polish Bishops, "The Victims of Nazi Ideology," Jan. 1995, in Rittner, Smith, and Steinfeldt, *The Holocaust and the Christian World*, pp. 251–253; for a corrective, see Emanuel Ringelblum, *Polish-Jewish Relations during the Second World War*, eds. Joseph Kermish and Shmuel Krakowski (New York: Fertig, 1976).

84. German Bishops, "Opportunity to Re-examine Relationships with the Jews," Jan. 23, 1995, in Rittner, Smith, and Steinfeldt, *The Holocaust and the Christian World*, pp. 249–251.

85. See Hungarian Bishops and the Ecumenical Council of Churches in Hungary, "Joint Statement," Nov. 1994, in Rittner, Smith, and Steinfeldt, *The Holocaust and the Christian World*, p. 429. See also Catholic Bishops of Italy, "Letter to the Jewish Community of Italy," March 1998, <www.jcrelations.net/stmnts/italianbish1998.htm>. The Catholic Bishops of the Netherlands, "Supported by One Root: Our Relationship with Judaism," Oct. 1995, which though not so explicitly self-exculpatory, is still evasive and perfunctory in length. It is, however, more forthright at least in acknowledging the Catholic Church's role in spreading anti-semitism and in the Church's continuing responsibility for the existence of anti-semitism and for combating it (<www.jcrelations.net/stmnts/dutchbish1995.htm>).

86. General Assembly of the Presbyterian Church (USA), "A Theological Understanding of the Relationship Between Christians and Jews," June 1987, in

The Theology of the Churches and the Jewish People: Statements by the World Council of Churches and Its Member Churches (Geneva: WCC Publications, 1988), p. 115.

87. Evangelical Lutheran Church in America, "Statement on Lutheran-Jewish Relations Church Council of the Adopted," April 18, 1994, in Rittner, Smith, and Steinfeldt, *The Holocaust and the Christian World,* pp. 248–249.

88. "Declaration of the General Synod of the Evangelical Church A.B. and H.B. [Augsburg and Helvetian Confessions] in Austria," Oct. 28, 1998, <www.jcrelations.net/stmnts/evkircheoestengl.htm>.

89. Synod of the Evangelical Church of the Rhineland (FRG), "Towards Renovation of the Relationship of Christians and Jews," Jan. 1980, in *The Theology of the Churches and the Jewish People,* p. 93.

90. Philipp Gessler, "So blond wie der arische Galiläer Jesus," *die tageszeitung,* Jan. 19–20, 2002; for the exhibition itself, <www.kirche-christen-juden.org>.

91. *Catechism of the Catholic Church,* parag. 1431.

92. *Catechism of the Catholic Church,* parag. 1435.

93. *Catechism of the Catholic Church,* parag. 1450.

94. For a devout Catholic, a former priest, to confront his own tradition in this unsparing manner is remarkable. It should be an inspiration to people of all traditions and all countries, who more often than not flinch from looking at the ugly features of their spiritual or national homes. It should also be made explicit that Carroll's authority derives not from his identity as a former priest or a Catholic but from the power of his ideas. One of the most pernicious aspects of the discussion of the Nazi period is the explicit or implicit claim that a person's identity—Jew, German, Catholic, etc.—lends his ideas either more or less legitimacy, as it suits the politics of the claimant. This kind of essentialism, holding that identity determines a person's views, and the legitimacy or illegitimacy of those views, betrays a great deal about the people who employ it. It is also often used as a strategy to prevent a calm and measured discussion of the veracity of a person's views by turning his identity into the object of inquiry.

95. Carroll, *Constantine's Sword,* pp. 615–616.

96. John Paul II, *Novo Millennio Ineunte,* (Jan. 6, 2001), <www.vatican.va/holy_father/john_paul_ii/apost_letters/index.htm>, parag. 55.

97. Congregation for the doctrine of the Faith, "*Dominus Iesus*": *On the Unicity and Salvific Universality of Jesus Christ and the Church* (Aug. 6, 2000), <www.va.vatican/roman_curia/congregations/>, parag. 22.

98. Raphael Patai, ed., *The Complete Diaries of Theodor Herzl,* vol. 4, (New York: Herzl Press, 1960), pp. 1,593–1,594 and 1,602–1,604.

99. Quoted in Merkley, *Christian Attitudes Towards the State of Israel,* p. 140.

100. Pius XII himself even made an initiative in 1956 to normalize relations with the Soviet Union, which, unlike the Jews, had really conducted a war of suppression against the Church. The terms that he suggested the Soviet Union, the country of the gulag, must meet for relations to be normalized—essentially religious freedom for Catholics and respect for the integrity of the institution of the Catholic Church within the country's borders—Israel already granted. But Pius XII insisted on maintaining the Jewish state as a pariah. For Pius XII's initiative toward the Soviet Union, see Robert A. Graham, *Vatican Diplomacy: A Study of*

Church and State on the International Plane (Princeton, N.J.: Princeton University Press, 1959), pp. 383–384.

101. Merkley, *Christian Attitudes Towards the State of Israel*, p. 153. It took John Paul II almost fifteen years of his papacy before he could bring himself to have his Church recognize the legitimacy of the Jewish state.

102. Carroll, *Constantine's Sword*, p. 230.

103. The Catholic Church's artificially inflated gallery of Catholics who were heroes against Nazism, and of Catholic victims of Nazism, diverts attention from the genuinely huge rogue gallery of Catholic clergy and lay Catholics who were victimizers (only those lay Catholics who were moved to persecute Jews by Catholic teachings should be included in this gallery), and it diverts attention from the Church that had nurtured them into adulthood and then did not seek to stay their hands.

104. Cardinal Jozef Glemp, "We Trust in the Capital of Wisdom," Aug. 26, 1989, in Carol Rittner and John K. Roth, eds., *Memory Offended: The Auschwitz Convent Controversy* (New York: Praeger, 1991), p. 224.

105. See Hans Küng, "Why I Remain a Catholic," *Reforming the Church Today: Keeping Hope Alive* (New York: Crossroad, 1990), pp. 13–20; Margot Patterson, "Haight Silencing Feeds Theologians' Fears," *National Catholic Reporter*, May 4, 2001, <www.natcath.com/NCR_Online/archives/050401/050401f.htm>; and Gerald Renner, "Rome Targets Another Jesuit," *National Catholic Reporter*, Aug. 11, 2000, <www.natcath.com/NCR_Online/archives/081100/081100e.htm>; Renner reports that "several American Jesuits have been targeted by Vatican crackdowns in recent years." For a discussion of this topic with additional examples, see John Cornwell, *Breaking Faith: The Pope, the People, and the Fate of Catholicism* (New York: Viking Compass, 2001), pp. 56–57 and 196–224.

106. Jan T. Gross, *Neighbors: The Destruction of the Jewish Community in Jedwabne, Poland* (Princeton, N.J.: Princeton University Press, 2001). This is a clear case of latent eliminationist hatreds being activated and channeled in a murderous direction with a changed, now encouraging political dispensation. For a discussion of this phenomenon, see Goldhagen, *Hitler's Willing Executioners*, pp. 43–45.

107. Ian Fisher, "At Site of Massacre, Polish Leader Asks Jews for Forgiveness," *New York Times*, July 11, 2001, A1, A4.

108. James Carroll, "A Teaching Moment Missed," *Boston Globe*, May 15, 2001, A15.

109. "Speech of President Bashar Al-Assad Welcoming His Holiness Pope John Paul II on His Arrival in Damascus, Syria, May 5, 2001," <www.adl.org>. Bashar Assad was elevated to his position by his father, Haffaz el Assad, the mass murderer of at least twenty thousand Syrians when he ordered his troops to annihilate the civilian population of an entire city in 1971. Instead of inciting his people against the Jews, Bashar Assad should repudiate his father's mass slaughter of part of the people of his country and perform restitution of the kind discussed here.

110. Holy See's Commission for Religious Relations with Jews, "We Remember: A Reflection on the Shoah," in Rittner, Smith, and Steinfeldt, *The Holocaust and the Christian World*, p. 261; quoted in *The Visit of Pope John Paul II to Yad Vashem, Jerusalem, March 23, 2000* (Jerusalem: Yad Vashem, 2000), p. 16.

111. See John Paul II, "Address" in Synagogue of Rome, April 13, 1986, in *On Jews and Judaism, 1979–1986* (Washington, D.C.: United States Catholic Conference, 1987), p. 82.

112. *Catechism of the Catholic Church*, parag. 1450.

113. Germans have placed memorials in a large number of their cities and towns, including a monumental one that is planned for an area adjacent to the country's parliament, the Reichstag. For a discussion of Holocaust memorials, see James E. Young, *The Texture of Memory: Holocaust Memorials and Meaning* (New Haven: Yale University Press, 1993).

114. John Paul II, *Ut Unum Sint* (May 25, 1995) and *Redemptoris Missio* (December 7, 1990), <www.vatican.va/holy_father/john_paul_ii/encyclicals/index.htm>.

115. Carroll, *Constantine's Sword*, pp. 552–553.

116. But their prescriptions for what such steps should be are insufficient in kind and scope. See the Catholic Bishops in the Netherlands, "Supported by One Root."

117. *Catechism of the Catholic Church*, parags. 1459 and 2487.

118. Edward H. Flannery, *The Anguish of the Jews: Twenty-Three Centuries of Antisemitism*, rev. ed. (New York: Stimulus Books, 1985), p. 1. There is no reason to believe that the state of knowledge among the vast majority of Christians has, in the interim, substantially improved. To the extent that educational initiatives have been pursued, such as those by the American Catholic Church alone and in conjunction with the American Jewish Committee, which are recent, they are to be applauded. See *Catholic Teaching on the Shoah;* and "AJC's Catholic-Jewish High School Education Program Expands to Pittsburgh, San Diego, Washington, D.C." (November 12, 2001), <www.ajc.org/press>.

119. This well-known relationship was definitively established by Glock and Stark in their classic study, *Christian Belief and Anti-Semitism*, see especially pp. 130–138.

120. See Carroll, *Constantine's Sword*, pp. 566–569, for a discussion of the necessity of such a reminder.

121. This kind of aid is distinct from political support for Jews. These good works are on the social and personal level.

122. When governments must perform restitution, they also must change those aspects of the legal structure that were instrumental in producing the unjust harm.

123. In the United States, even religious organizations and leaders who disagree about how the principle is to be applied in every case generally accept the principle.

124. The Church's brutal Inquisition, a tool of political and social control, was used for hundreds of years to persecute Jews and Christians across the Catholic world for not accepting Church orthodoxy and thereby challenging its political control.

125. Congregation for the Doctrine of the Faith, *"Dominus Iesus,"* parag. 23.

126. For an analysis of communism as a secular religion, see Gustav A. Wetter, *Dialectical Materialism: A Historical and Systematic Survey of Philosophy in the Soviet Union* (London: Routledge and Kegan Paul, 1958).

127. Congregation for the Doctrine of the Faith, *The Popes Against the Jews*, pp. 128–130.

128. Wills, *Papal Sin*.

129. Wills, at the beginning of his discussion of "We Remember," conveys the Church's bind well: "The debilitating effect of intellectual dishonesty can be touching. Even when papal authority sincerely wants to perform a virtuous act, when it spends years screwing up its nerve to do it, when it actually thinks it has done it, when it releases a notice of its having done it, when it expects to be congratulated on doing it—it has not done it. Not because it did not want to do it, or did not believe it did it. It was simply unable to do it, because that would have involved coming clean about the record of the papal institution. And that is all but unthinkable" (*Papal Sin*, p. 13).

130. *Catechism of the Catholic Church*, parag. 1869.

131. *Catechism of the Catholic Church*, parag. 1033.

132. Donald J. Dietrich, *God and Humanity in Auschwitz: Jewish-Christian Relations and Sanctioned Murder* (New Brunswick, N.J.: Transaction, 1995): "The Jewish-Christian dialogue is currently reshaping Christian identity because it has demanded that theologians go back to the basics. In all likelihood, however, there probably would have been precious little interaction if the horrors of 1933–1945 had not elevated the issue to a theologically imperative plateau" (p. 145). For a survey of Christian theological initiatives prompted by the Holocaust, see Alan Davies, "The Holocaust and Christian Thought," in Marvin Perry and Fredrick M. Schweitzer, eds., *Jewish-Christian Encounters Over the Centuries: Symbiosis, Prejudice, Holocaust Dialogue* (New York: Peter Lang, 1994), pp. 341–367. For Germany, see Micha Brumlik, "Post-Holocaust Theology: German Theological Responses Since 1945," in Robert P. Erickson and Susannah Heschel, eds., *Betrayal: German Churches and the Holocaust* (Minneapolis: Fortress Press, 1999), pp. 169–188.

133. Carroll, *Constantine's Sword*, p. 560. He includes "Christology" as one of the Church's core problems. For his account of what a Third Vatican Council should do, see pp. 547–604. For earlier calls for a Third Vatican Council, see Tracy, Küng, and Metz, *Toward Vatican III*.

134. Carroll, *Constantine's Sword*, p. 560.

135. Helen P. Fry, "Challenges for the Future," in Fry, *Christian-Jewish Dialogue*, p. 288.

136. Acts 4:12.

137. *Catechism of the Catholic Church*, parags. 846–848 and 1257 on salvation and parags. 1033–1037 on hell.

138. It continues by demeaning other religions, claiming that "other rituals insofar as they depend on superstitions or other errors constitute an obstacle to salvation." See Ratzinger, *"Dominus Iesus,"* parags. 21, 22, and 14. The point of *Dominus Iesus* is to reassert emphatically, which it repeatedly does, that it is only through Jesus and his Church that salvation is attainable and to delegitimize every other path to God and salvation.

139. The Church and its defenders, when dealing with these difficult issues, like to treat the slightest positive hints from the Church, or from Catholics engaged in

Catholic-Jewish relations, with great fanfare and as if they are the Church's official positions or are of such great significance, when the hints are in fact flatly contradicted by the Church's unchanged official positions. A recent example of this are the reports about Cardinal Joseph Ratzinger's new book, where he reportedly says that Jews may also wait for the Messiah. This has been presented as an important change in Catholic doctrine. But if that is all that his book says on this issue, then it is neither a change in the Church's doctrine nor of any real significance. The *Catechism of the Catholic Church* has for years already stated that the Jews may wait for the Messiah, but the Jews do so not realizing that their wait is "accompanied by the drama of not knowing or misunderstanding Christ Jesus" (parag. 840). In other words, the Jews are wrong, but it is fine if they wait; when the Messiah arrives, they will discover that the Christians have been right all along. Clearly, that the Church grants that Jews can wait in error has no bearing on the Church's continued delegitimizing of Judaism. In the *Catechism* just two pages later, the Church restates its long-standing position that "outside the Church there is no salvation" (parag. 846). See also A. James Rudin, "While the Messiah Tarries . . ." *Forward,* Feb. 22, 2002.

A few days before this book was being sent to the printer, the liberal American Catholic Church again moved ahead of the Church as a whole by stating its view that Jews may attain salvation and should not officially be targeted for conversion. See Consultation of the National Council of Synagogues and the Bishops Committee for Ecumenical and Interreligious Affairs, "Reflections on Covenant and Mission," August 12, 2002, <www.nccbuscc.org/comm/archives/2002/02-154.htm>. On these issues, this is significant and welcome local progress. Let us hope that the American Catholic Church will now take up the Church's many other outstanding tasks, and that the Catholic Church will follow the American Catholics' lead by publicly renouncing its continuing claimed monopoly on salvation, by declaring that all portions of its hitherto exclusionist doctrine, theology, and teachings to be null and void, and by officially replacing them with appropriate pluralistic ones.

140. See, for example, 1 Thessalonians 2:14–16, where the Catholic biblical commentary asserts that Paul's antisemitic inventions about the Jews killing of Jesus and the prophets "give no grounds for anti-Semitism to those willing to understand him"; see Dietrich, *God and Humanity in Auschwitz,* for a discussion of the measures taken by the Church to the incidence of the Christian Bible giving needless offense against Jews (pp. 99–103). For central documents of the Catholic Church providing guidance on these matters and on how to improve the image of Jews among Catholics and also relations with Jews, see Croner, *Stepping Stones to Further Jewish-Christian Relations,* pp. 1–68; and Helga Croner, ed., *More Stepping Stones to Further Jewish-Christian Relations: An Unabridged Collection of Christian Documents, 1975–1983* (Mahwah, N.J.: Stimulus, 1985), pp. 37–153.

141. Norman A. Beck, "Removing Anti-Jewish Polemic from Our Christian Lectionaries: A Proposal," <www.jcrelations.net/articl1/beck.htm>, 15 pp. He includes a list of the verses in each of the books. See also Norman A. Beck, "The New Testament and the Teaching of Contempt: Reconsiderations," in Perry and Schweitzer, *Jewish-Christian Encounters Over the Centuries,* pp. 83–99; Norman A. Beck, *Mature Christianity in the 21st Century: The Recognition and Repudiation of the Anti-Jewish Polemic of the New Testament,* exp. and rev. ed. (New York: Cross-

road, 1994); and Robert Michael, "Antisemitism and the Church Fathers," in Perry and Schweitzer, *Jewish-Christian Encounters Over the Centuries*, pp. 101–130.

142. Mark 15:6–15.

143. Luke 3:7–9.

144. Luke 4:28–30.

145. Matthew 3:7 and 12:34.

146. Matthew 22:43.

147. Matthew 23:31–38.

148. Matthew 27:25.

149. Geza Vermes, *The Changing Face of Jesus* (London: Penguin Compass, 2002), p. 232.

150. The literature detailing the historical falsehoods and inaccuracies in the Christian Bible is vast. For a classic exposé of such critical matters, see Jules Isaac, *The Teaching of Contempt: Christian Roots of Anti-Semitism;* for a recent, more comprehensive treatment, see Lillian C. Freudmann, *Antisemitism in the New Testament* (Lanham, Md.: University Press of America, 1994), who concludes after a detailed analysis of the Gospels, "To fill in the picture of Jesus as deity, Jews as his enemies, and Romans as innocents abroad, facts had to be manipulated and history rewritten. The roles and functions of various institutions and leaders in Judea at the time of Jesus had to be scrambled and reconstituted so that they fit the mold created by the authors. The end which was served by the evangelists and which justified their means, was to prove that Christianity offered no threat or challenge to the Roman establishment. The longer lasting result was continuous enmity for the Jews" (p. 284).

151. Bishops Committee on the Liturgy, National Conference of Catholic Bishops, *God's Mercy Endures Forever: Guidelines on the Presentation of Jews and Judaism in Catholic Preaching* (Washington, D.C.: United States Catholic Conference, 1989), pp. 10–12.

152. Acts 2:22–23, 36, 3:13–15, 4:10, and 5:30; 13:38; and 28:25–28.

153. John 7:28 and 8:37–47.

154. Vermes, *The Changing Faces of Jesus*, pp. 19–21.

155. For positive Catholic documents, see Croner, *Stepping Stones to Further Jewish-Christian Relations*, pp. 1–68; and Croner, *More Stepping Stones to Further Jewish-Christian Relations*, pp. 37–153. For various and wide-ranging discussions of such progress, see Fisher, Rudin, and Tanenbaum, *Twenty Years of Jewish-Catholic Relations;* and Fry, *Christian-Jewish Dialogue.*

156. See, for example, Vatican Commission for Religious Relations with the Jews, "Guidelines and Suggestions for Implementing the Conciliar Declaration Nostra Aetate (no. 4) (Dec. 1, 1974)," and "Notes on the Correct Way to Present the Jews and Judaism in Preaching and Catechesis in the Roman Catholic Church (June 24, 1985), in *Catholic Jewish Relations: Documents from the Holy See* (London: Catholic Truth Society, 1999), pp. 22–30 and 31–49; Bishops Committee on the Liturgy, National Conference of Catholic Bishops, *God's Mercy Endures Forever: Guidelines on the Presentation of Jews and Judaism in Catholic Preaching*, 19 pp.; and Secretariat for Ecumenical and Interreligious Affairs, National Conference of Catholic Bishops, *Catholic Teaching on the Shoah*, 27 pp. Also see the various state-

ments and addresses given by John Paul II, collected in Eugene J. Fisher and Leon Klenicki, eds., *On Jews and Judaism, 1979–1986,* (Washington, D.C.: NCCB Committee for Ecumenical and Interreligious Affairs and the Anti-Defamation League of B'nai B'rith, 1987). It should be emphasized that while these publications contain many important positive aspects, they still suffer from serious limitations and defects, which include their brevity and superficiality.

157. For a discussion of this, see Dietrich, *God and Humanity in Auschwitz,* p. 107; and Bishops' Committee on the Liturgy, National Conference of Catholic Bishops, *God's Mercy Endures Forever,* pp. 9–10. The more positive statements about Jews and Judaism compose a few chords that can barely be heard against the din of the Christian Bible's condemnation of Jews and Judaism.

158. Catholic doctrine holds Jesus to be the Son of God and also God: "The incarnation of God's Son reveals that God is the eternal Father and that the Son is consubstantial with the Father, which means that, in the Father and with the Father, the Son is one and the same God" (*Catechism of the Catholic Church,* parag. 262; see also parags. 240, 242, and 663).

159. Carroll, *Constantine's Sword,* p. 566.

160. Carroll, *Constantine's Sword,* pp. 566–567.

161. Charlotte Klein, *Anti-Judaism in Christian Theology* (Philadelphia: Fortress Press, 1978), pp. 127–142, especially p. 129, and pp. 92–126, especially p. 126.

162. See Palmieri-Billig, "Recognizing Our Brothers and Sisters."

163. Michael J. Cook, "The Bible and Catholic-Jewish Relations," in Fisher, Rudin, and Tanenbaum, *Twenty Years of Jewish-Catholic Relations,* p. 112. Presumably things are somewhat better today.

164. Reinhard Neudecker, "The Catholic Church and the Jewish People," in René Latourelle, ed., *Vatican II: Assessment and Perspectives: Twenty-five Years After (1962–1987),* vol. 3 (New York: Paulist Press, 1989), p. 285.

165. Brumlik, "Post-Holocaust Theology," p. 169. Brumlik continues: "Furthermore, a distinct new form of anti-Judaism has developed within progressive church circles and on the margins of the political left."

166. "AJC's Catholic-Jewish High School Education Program Expands to Pittsburgh, San Diego, Washington, D.C."

167. John 8:23 and 8:40.

168. For a discussion of these issues, see Carroll, *Constantine's Sword,* pp. 563–565. Carroll rules out altering the Christian Bible: "There is no question of simply eliminating them [the troubling texts], nor of rewriting them to purge the Epistles and Gospels of what the contemporary ear finds offensive" (p. 566). But he does not explain why he says this.

169. *Catechism of the Catholic Church,* parag. 2487.

170. *Etz Hayim: Torah and Commentary* (New York: Rabbinical Assembly, 2001).

171. Although the congress proposed here would share some aspects with Carroll's proposed Third Vatican Council—which would have as its task a broad agenda of Church reform, with putting an end to the Church's antisemitism as a central part—it would also differ.

172. For a discussion of the unsuitability of some of the Church's representatives, see Neudecker, "The Catholic Church and the Jewish People," p. 311.

173. For a succinct discussion of "a discourse-centered approach to ethics" taking place in the public sphere, see Jürgen Habermas, "Further Reflections on the Public Sphere," in Craig Calhoun, ed., *Habermas and the Public Sphere* (Cambridge, Mass.: MIT Press, 1992), pp. 421–461, especially 446ff.

Conclusion: Mustering the Will

1. We know this because for centuries the Catholic Church believed that it was such a victim of its fantasized Jewish satanic menace. The Church, its Popes, bishops, and priests were not content to ask from the putatively guilty Jews only the humane reforms of restitution. Instead, they reacted by inflicting on Jews all the real, epochal injustices and harm, for which the Church today and its officials now owe restitution.

2. Ronald W. Zweig, *German Reparations and the Jewish World: A History of the Claims Conference* (London: Frank Cass, 2001), p. 186.

3. See Ingo Müller, *Hitler's Justice: The Courts of the Third Reich* (Cambridge: Harvard University Press, 1991), pp. 240–260. Fritz Bauer, the former prosecutor general of the state of Hesse, said that the brevity of the sentences came "close to making a mockery of the victims' suffering" (pp. 256–257). For some statistics on such trials as of 1970, see Adalbert Rückerl, ed., *NS-Prozesse: Nach 25 Jahren Strafverfolgung* (Karlsruhe: C. F. Müller, 1971), pp. 197–198.

4. See Werner Bergman and Rainer Erb, *Anti-Semitism in Germany: The Post-Nazi Epoch Since 1945* (New Brunswick, N.J.: Transaction, 1997) for an account of the changes in postwar German antisemitism.

5. I do not mean to suggest that Germany has been a paragon of virtue. Far from it. There is no reason to believe that Germany and Germans did all of this with the express purpose of fulfilling their duty to perform restitution. For a discussion of these issues, see Daniel Jonah Goldhagen, "*Modell Bundesrepublik:* National History, Democracy, and Internationalization in Germany," in Robert R. Shandley, ed., *Unwilling Germans? The Goldhagen Debate,* Jeremiah Riemer, trans. (Minneapolis: University of Minnesota Press, 1998), pp. 275–285; Frank Stern, *The Whitewashing of the Yellow Badge: Antisemitism and Philosemitism in Postwar Germany* (Oxford: Pergamon Press, 1992), pp. 365–385; and Lily Gardner Feldman, *The Special Relationship between West Germany and Israel* (Boston: George Allen & Unwin, 1984), pp. 51–65.

6. Müller, *Hitler's Justice,* pp. 261–269.

7. Quoted in Steffi Kammerer, " 'Da kommt die ganze Jauche hoch,' " *Süddeutsche Zeitung* (April 12, 2002), p. 11.

8. Heribert Prantl "Und wieder sind die Juden schuld: Wie mit der Eskalation des Nahost-Konflikts der Antisemitismus auch in Deutschland erstarkt," *Süddeutsche Zeitung* (April 15, 2002), p. 4.

9. See Lars Rensmann, "Die Walserisierung der Berliner Republik: Geschichts-

revisionismus und antisemitische Projektion: Einwände gegen die These vom geläuterten Deutschland," in Jürgen Elsässer and Andrei S. Markovits, eds., *"Die Fratze der eigenen Geschichte": Von der Goldhagen-Debatte zum Jugoslawien-Krieg* (Berlin: Elefanten Press, 1998), pp. 44–63; and interview with Paul Spiegel, the leader of the Jewish community in Germany, *Der Stern* (Jan. 17, 2002). For the resurgence of Christian, including Catholic, antisemitic supersessionist notions that are then used as the basis for denying that Jews may have a state in Israel, and for hostile attacks upon Jews, see Melanie Phillips, "Christians Who Hate the Jews," *Spectator,* Feb. 16, 2002.

10. *Catechism of the Catholic Church*, parag. 2302.

11. *Catechism of the Catholic Church* (New York: Doubleday, 1995), parag. 1490.

12. If we asked survivors of the Holocaust whether justice demands that the Church tells the truth about the past, fights antisemitism, and reforms itself, organizationally, culturally, theologically, and doctrinally, so that it erases the sources of past and future persecution of the Jews, they would certainly support this.

13. James Carroll and Garry Wills are two exceptions.

14. The conventional wisdom is that the Church will probably remain doctrinally and institutionally conservative in the foreseeable future. John Paul II, a theological conservative, some would say reactionary, is increasingly frail. He has appointed 125 of the 135 cardinal electors (those who may choose a new pope) and they are of a demonstrably conservative cast. They are likely to elect a conservative Pope. Conservatives in the Church have not been the most progressive regarding Jews. See John Cornwell, *Breaking Faith: The Pope, the People, and the Fate of Catholicism* (New York: Viking Compass, 2001), p. 278.

15. The greatest mistake was, after World War II, sparing the Church what Germany was not spared: the severe censure it had earned for its and its clergy's crimes and other offenses, and concerted pressure that it transform itself by replacing the doctrines and practices that led it and its clergy to perpetrate the harm that they did.

ACKNOWLEDGMENTS

In spare moments since the publication of my first book, I have thought about many possible projects on a range of topics that I might undertake. Some are more contemporary than others, some are more concrete in formulation than others, some are more likely to be done than others, some are lighter in tone than others. But among them there was no hint of a project of any kind that would touch on the Catholic Church and the Holocaust, let alone a moral reckoning with the Church. It had never entered my mind, until Martin Peretz prodded me to focus on it. To my surprise, the article that was to emerge from his suggestion grew further, in size and intellectual scope, into a far more substantial project, this book, than I had initially envisioned. The gratitude I owe Marty for getting me started, I also owe Leon Wieseltier for his patience, support, and suggestions, especially considering how long it took me to deliver the promised *New Republic* article, most of which has made it into this book.

I am thankful to friends for reading the manuscript with critical eyes during its preparation. Mustafa Emirbayer, Dagmar Herzog, Stanley Hoffmann, Andrei Markovits, and Paul Pierson each made important suggestions that improved the book in crucial ways. My thanks are also due to Robin Schuldenfrei, my research assistant, for her invaluable help when I was preparing the manuscript and to the people at the many photo archives, especially the United States Holocaust Memorial Museum Photo Archives, for their assistance. I am particularly thankful to Esther Newberg, my literary agent, for her passionate support for the project and the benefits of her ever-focused and perspicacious mind.

To Carol Brown Janeway, my editor at Knopf, I am once again indebted and grateful, for her sharp intellect, good eye, and judicious sense, and also for her passion that a book gets published correctly, in the form and manner that its subject and author need. Many other people at Knopf are also deserving of my thanks, personally and professionally, for ensuring that the book's spirit was given corporeal form. Stephanie Katz has again made every stage of producing a book easy and cheerful, also wanting only that it be done correctly. Margaret Wimberger ensured that every little piece is right. Lydia Buechler that they all fit together. Peter Andersen that those constructing it would know what to do and to do it with interior grace. Tracy Cabanis that they would produce it with quality. Chuck Antony and Judy Eda that the inevitable errors that creep in during the complex process of making a book were then excised. Max Franke that the book would be navigable for those in search of specific items. And Abby Weintraub that it has several handsome faces (front, back, and profile). If a book's first life is created privately at the nexus of the author's mind and computer, and those producing its physical instantiation give it its public second life, then when this book was taking shape Paul Bogaards and Gabrielle Brooks let me have confidence that upon entering the world it would be shepherded in my native land with care. Carol, with the help of Stephanie and Suzanne Smith, have ensured that the same would be true in other countries.

Again I turn most thankfully to my family. My mother, Norma Goldhagen, again offered improvements to the manuscript and aided in other tangible and intangible ways. My father, Erich Goldhagen, to whom my general intellectual debt would be hard to overstate, and who was immensely helpful during my preparation of this book, has again shown why I am as fortunate a father's son as a son could be. My wife, Sarah Williams Goldhagen, with her creative, deft, sober intellect, made countless improvements to this book. With this intellect of hers and with her many other unsurpassably fine qualities, she has done the same also to my life. To her I am grateful and delighted to have been able to dedicate both.

INDEX

Italicized page numbers indicate illustrations

ILLUSTRATION CREDITS